China's Geography

China's Geography

Globalization and the Dynamics of Political, Economic, and Social Change

GREGORY VEECK, CLIFTON W. PANNELL,
CHRISTOPHER J. SMITH, AND YOUQIN HUANG

ROWMAN & LITTLEFIELD PUBLISHERS, INC.
Lanham • Boulder • New York • Toronto • Plymouth, UK

ROWMAN & LITTLEFIELD PUBLISHERS, INC.

Published in the United States of America
by Rowman & Littlefield Publishers, Inc.
A wholly owned subsidiary of The Rowman & Littlefield Publishing Group, Inc.
4501 Forbes Boulevard, Suite 200, Lanham, Maryland 20706
www.rowmanlittlefield.com

Estover Road
Plymouth PL6 7PY
United Kingdom

British Library Cataloguing in Publication Information Available

Library of Congress Cataloging-in-Publication Data

China's geography : globalization and the dynamics of political, economic, and social
change / Gregory Veeck . . . [et. al].
        p. cm. – (Changing regions in a global context.)
    Includes bibliographical references and index.
    ISBN-13: 978-0-7425-5402-3 (cloth : alk. paper)
    ISBN-10: 0-7425-5402-3 (cloth : alk. paper)
    1. China.   I. Veeck, Gregory, 1956–   II. Title.   III. Series.
    DS706.C51138 2006
    915.1–dc22
                                                                    2006013517

Printed in the United States of America

♾™ The paper used in this publication meets the minimum requirements of American
National Standard for Information Sciences—Permanence of Paper for Printed Library
Materials, ANSI/NISO Z39.48-1992.

Contents

Images and Tables

Figures

Maps

Photographs

Tables

Acknowledgments

Acknowledgments tend to be either very short or very long. Those that know me should hardly be surprised that I have opted for the latter. There are many people who have my respect and gratitude for help with this book and the career on which it is partly based. The book is the product of true collaboration among four scholars with markedly different areas of expertise and perspective. But, we are joined through our enduring respect for China's great history, culture, and peoples, as well as through our shared belief in the importance of presenting the complexities of China as clearly as we possibly can at this particular time. Working collectively on a manuscript of this length is never easy, and I will always be grateful for my collaborators' willingness to meet deadlines, review each other's chapters, and share their opinions and data. It has been a privilege to work with my coauthors, especially my friend and mentor Clifton W. Pannell.

Many people have reviewed the manuscript during its longish journey. From an early discussion at the Billy Goat in Chicago, Susan McEachern of Rowman & Littlefield has displayed patience and enthusiastic support for the project. Many others at Rowman & Littlefield have helped and guided us, including Sarah Wood, Jessica Gribble, Alden Perkins (*feichang xiexie*), John Shanabrook, and David Luljak. I know they go home at night and wonder how we get fed and dressed each day. We gratefully recognize the important contributions of several anonymous reviewers, our series editors Alexander Murphy and David Keeling, and Jason Glatz—a converted English teacher recently graduated from the MA program in geography at Western Michigan University who attacked our passive tense with active fury. Mary Lee Eggart, friend and cartographer divine, designed most of the graphics in my chapters, turning my crummy diagrams into publishable maps and figures. The librarians at Western Michigan University were always able to find what I needed, no matter how obscure, and it is safe to say this holds true for the librarians at the University of Georgia and the State University of New York, Albany, as well. I also recognize the many hundreds of students who have participated in our class discussions, and who often raise the most challenging questions, while exhibiting the least tolerance for artifice. The great group of scholars who participate in the China Specialty Group of the Association of American Geographers, now more than two hundred strong, has annually provided stimulating lectures and articles related to where China has been, where the nation is going, and what has happened along the way. While all errors are our own, this vibrant scholarship is vital in a book that tries to do as much as this one does.

One measure of globalization is the ever-increasing ease of communication and collaboration between Western scholars and those living and working in China. Simply put, this book could not have been written without the help of our Chinese friends and colleagues in universities, research institutes, nongovernmental institutions, and government agencies. In my own case, researchers at the Rural Development Institute of the Chinese Academy of Social Sciences; Nanjing Agricultural University; Nanjing Institute of Geography; Nanjing Forestry University; Northeast Agricultural University; Qingdao Academy of Social Sciences, and Jilin University have all been important in my education. My coauthors would add another dozen or so institutions that have been equally important to them. Further, Chinese friends far from the academy that I so love also play a role—sharing their opinions and concerns about contemporary issues and problems. I am not the most traveled of people, but never have I felt as at home as when I am in China, largely because of the gracious way my friends in China give of their time and talents, and their enthusiasm for an adventure no matter how large or small.

None of the research projects that provide the foundation for this book would have been possible without funding from agencies such as the National Science Foundation; National Geographic; the Fulbright Program; and the American Council of Learned Societies, including the Committee on Scholarly Communication with the People's Republic of China (CSCPRC). The Lucia Harrison Fund of the Geography Department of Western Michigan University has also proven an important source of support for my own work. We are all grateful for this support. I also wish to underscore the importance of such funding at the present time. Never was there more a time to understand China than the present.

I wish especially to thank my wife Annie and my children Sarah and Robin. I dedicate this book to Annie with gratitude for our collaborative projects, the pleasure of our many trips to China for more than two decades, and her love and friendship. I am grateful for my children's enthusiasm. My children enjoy China, and it is an important part of their lives, but let's face it, they have endured hearing about this book for years, and those of you with a writer in the household will know what this is like. Fred and Kay Krehbiel's infectious enthusiasm for travel started us down this road lo' these many years ago, and I want to thank them for their support when support was more difficult to locate. And finally, everyone should know of my gratitude and admiration for my parents, Mary-Frances and Bill Veeck, and all their fine children.

—Gregory Veeck

This book had its origins and evolution over a long period, and I wish to thank Greg Veeck for his enduring commitment and patience and for pushing to advance this work to its conclusion. Colleagues in Hong Kong, China, the United States, Canada, and Britain have offered much wisdom and knowledge that has contributed to my work and for which I am grateful. Any errors of fact or interpretation are mine. I also want to thank Wyatt W. Anderson, former dean of the Franklin College of Arts and Sciences at the

University of Georgia, for his support of my scholarly work on China, which included allowing time and support for a faculty administrator to do research and writing in Hong Kong and China. Let me add great thanks to my wife Sylvia for sharing in this writing, work, and travel; she has been a great and most supportive partner in our China adventure.

—Clifton Pannell

CHAPTER 1

China's Path and Progress

The current pace of economic, sociocultural, and political change in China is stunning. No matter where you go, every city, town, and village seems to be under construction. The highway network has more than doubled from 1978 to 2003, expressways have gone from nothing to almost 30,000 km, rail freight has more than tripled in the same time period, and air passengers have increased from 2.3 million to 87.6 million (National Bureau of Statistics 2004, 626, 628). On the back of increased industrial output (especially in manufacturing and trade), the economy has grown at 8–10 percent a year for more than two decades, outpacing all other nations during this time (Jefferson and Rawski 1999; World Bank 2004). Foreign trade has increased more than twelvefold since 1985 (National Bureau of Statistics 2004, 714). Contemporary China is booming—a speedy and potent work in progress! Her 1.3 billion citizens must continue to adjust to fast-changing economic, political, and social conditions while seeking to maintain connections to the threatened traditional values that many of them feel lie at the core of being Chinese (Croll 1994).

How does this happen and what is its significance? In this book we seek to explore and explain the truly extraordinary changes underway in China and their impact on China's people as well as their implications for those outside China. Geographic approaches that focus on people and places by employing various scales of analysis are used to examine and determine the many features of this change. In this way we present a fresh and different view and perspective of rapidly changing China.

Global Forces and China's Development

Part of what is driving this rapid change is the force of globalization (Dicken 2003). Powerful new economic, political, and technological pulses are at work, and China has been quick to adapt and adjust to them. This adaptation in turn is linked to a much more open economic system, what the Chinese call "socialism with Chinese characteristics." The result is an astounding growth in trade with and exports to major economic powers such as Japan and the United States. Based on low labor costs and related land, environmental, and distribution costs, China's ability to attract investment in manufacturing is supported by a carefully crafted state policy that emphasizes innovation and high technology, and has led to rapid development of a broad manufacturing base. Beginning with low-end consumer products, China has rapidly expanded this base to include a vast array of consumer and producer goods as well as electronics and transport equipment.

1

China's manufacturing capacity is paralleled by its rapidly increasing trade and investment linkage with other Asian economic tigers such as South Korea and Taiwan. These new trade and investment trends have led in turn to new spatial arrangements as economic regions that reflect new global economies and technologies emerge in China. The arrangements include not only key trading patterns, but also equally important new technologies in transportation and logistics that undergird China's ability to move and distribute goods now that it has become so skilled at manufacturing. A whole array of new transport systems is under construction, as China strives to integrate its disparate regions and provinces into a greater whole that will fulfill its destiny as a functioning modern economic and political system. Yet the cost of building this new infrastructure of highways, railways, pipelines, and electrical and communications grids is enormous, and the country must continue to expand this basic structure in support of national development over the coming decades.

The spatial redeployment associated with the rapid economic growth of the last twenty-five years has been felt mainly in China's coastal regions, the areas most closely tied to the global trading system (see maps 1.1 and 1.2). Consider three key emerging regions. The foremost example among these is the booming Pearl River Delta region on China's southeast coast, focused within the triangle of Hong Kong/Shenzhen,

Map 1.1. China and Its Asian Neighbors

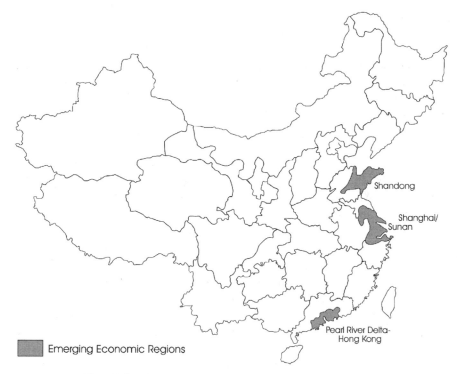

Map 1.2.   China's Three Emerging Economic Regions

Guangzhou/Dongguan, and Macao/Zhuhai, with its long-standing shipping, commercial, and capital links to Southeast Asia and the world economy. Hong Kong remains the world's largest container port and a major banking center, and it serves as China's linchpin in a long-term tradition of doing business based on a legal and commercial system that has the confidence of the global business community. A second emerging region is the Lower Chang Jiang or Shanghai/Sunan region with its powerful manufacturing and trade economy and strong links to Taiwan and the global trading system. Shanghai has attracted substantial Taiwan and foreign investment and has emerged as a great manufacturing center, but it has not yet recaptured the banking and commercial functions that made it so famous as a Chinese business center early in the twentieth century.

The Shandong economic region, though smaller and less active than the above two, nevertheless offers a third example of China's vibrant economy and shifting foreign policy in its strong and growing trade and commercial ties to South Korea. While the primary motivation behind these ties appears to be economic, there are clearly significant political and security ramifications in such new relationships and evolving spatial patterns.

There are numerous other large and small regions that reflect a dynamic pace of spatial rearrangement on various scales and the remarkable processes of economic growth at local, provincial, and subnational levels that are underway in China today. Many of these will be explored as we examine China in greater detail. While it is important to recognize the powerful impulse of the shifting global system and its opportunities for and effects on China, we must remember that China's socialist revolution was in part about reasserting the primacy of China's integrity as a sovereign and independent state. Consequently, in assessing the significance and role of global forces, we must remember China's remarkable historical record as a central state and empire and its confidence in continuing to play that role while it also assumes a place as a responsible and rising player in the global economic, political, and security systems of the twenty-first century. It is the interplay among China's central government, the provincial governments, local officials, local enterprises, and multinational firms and players that comprises the framework and context in which the new economic and political geography of today's rapidly rising China appears. We must search here for an explanation and understanding of the extraordinary and far-reaching changes underway in China today.

The now famous 1978 reforms championed by then paramount leader Deng Xiaoping that opened up the nation and radically altered its entire socioeconomic system are now twenty-five years old, and yet there is little indication of any slowdown. It seems that the entire nation, that all of China's people can hardly catch their breath, can hardly keep up with the myriad changes to their everyday lives. Maintaining values and perspective is not easy in these unpredictable if sometimes gilded times when fortunes are so often influenced by social connections, access to college, socioeconomic status, ethnicity, gender, and certainly where one lives (on social stresses, see Huang 1998). As we would expect, in any place, at any time, and because social and economic systems shift rapidly, new conditions provide opportunities for some to succeed beyond their wildest dreams, but cause others to slip from their already precarious places in society. Many people feel lost. Imagine your thoughts if you were over forty, had not gone to college, and had worked loyally for a state-owned factory that then closed three years ago and reported a bankrupt pension fund just before the doors were locked. Remember that many people in China today grew up in the propagandized "Worker's Paradise" where everyone supped from Mao's "iron rice bowl"—where each person was provided for "according to their needs," and where everyone was equal, even if only equally poor. In reality, the sort of life implied by the "iron rice bowl," always full and never broken, was seldom so easy, but it certainly was more predictable than that of the present.

For most Chinese people, urban or rural, current politics, economic opportunities, and social norms and views are startlingly different from what passed for convention in their lives only twenty years ago. Many have benefited from China's changes, others have lost considerably more than income (Mok 2000, 57–64), but all have had to change their attitudes and ideals as the reforms roll on. The past quarter century has witnessed greater changes of all types on more people and at a faster pace than perhaps any time in China's long history. In fact, it may be the pace of this change, the startling rapidity of China's newest "revolution," that has fostered so much interest in the country in recent years.

Manifestations of these changes are apparent at all levels of Chinese society, from the individual to the corporate, the urban to the rural, or from the provincial to the national. As might be expected, these social, economic, cultural, and political changes have not evolved in homogeneous fashion throughout China's many regions and provinces. Most studies indicate growing disparities in income and per capita gross domestic product (GDP) between wealthy and poorer places (Fan 1995, 1997; Gipouloux 2000; Lyons 2000; Wei 1999). Beyond income or productivity, however, there are also important differences across regions and provinces with respect to hospitals and healthcare professionals per capita, social services, dedicated education funds, and transportation infrastructure (National Bureau of Statistics 2004). The changes have resulted in an increasingly uneven landscape—socially, culturally, and economically.

Readers are probably aware of China's growing impact on the world economy. Originally stimulated by the landmark economic reforms promulgated by Deng Xiaoping and boosted by subsequent and arguably greater adjustments, the change is transforming a once-backward economy into one of the world's largest. In 2005, China's reported gross national income of US$1.981 trillion ranked sixth in the world (Xinhua News Service 2005). Very soon China's high annual economic growth will likely propel its economy past those of France, the United Kingdom, and Germany to rank third after the economies of the United States and Japan. Ongoing reforms have also transformed the fundamental structure of China's economy from one based on agriculture and heavy industry to one that is much more balanced—now including considerable light manufacturing and a fast-growing service sector (Lardy 2002; Chow 2002). Most economists believe that despite some significant domestic economic problems, China's global economic role will continue to grow (Chow 2002; Lardy 1992, 2002; Perkins 2001). American homes and those of the people of virtually every industrial nation in the world are full of Chinese products—testimony to the benefits of low-cost labor, flexible production, and increased global trade. China's entry into international markets for consumer durables, electronics, household items, sporting goods, clothing, and even some agricultural products such as crayfish, fruit juice, honey, and essential oils, has already radically altered global trade in these items (Moore 2002; Studwell 2002; Walcott 2002; Veeck 2005).

Manufacturing and exports continue to burgeon. In 2005 for the fifth year in a row, the United States' largest trade deficit ($201.6 billion on $285.3 billion total trade with China) was recorded with the People's Republic of China (PRC; U.S. Census Bureau 2006). Most EU nations are also running large trade deficits with China, attesting to the massive impact of China's reforms on the global economy. With such favorable terms of trade and trade balances, it was no surprise that China had accumulated more than US$800 billion in foreign reserves by 2006. China then invests some of these foreign reserves in the treasury bonds of countries like the United States and in that way increases its influence and power in global capital markets.

China's role in global politics has also expanded, not only with its vital participation in the resolution of regional issues such as North Korean instability and nuclear proliferation, but also more broadly as China takes a more active role in global politics via international organizations such as the UN and the UN Security Council, the World Health Organization (WHO), and the World Trade Organization (WTO; Zhao 2000a, 2000b). There is a new world order emerging, and while it is most difficult to anticipate the China of fifty years hence, it is certain that China will play an increasingly important role in global affairs in the coming decades.

Internal Forces of Change and Spatial Rearrangement

Less observable from afar, and less reported in the popular press of Western nations, are the continuous changes and challenges that have emerged in Chinese society, culture, domestic politics, and environment. In tandem with economic and international political change, Chinese society and cultural values are also being reformed and redefined at an astounding pace. Most would argue that there is a trend toward growing differences across China, or in other words, China is becoming more heterogeneous. The pace of change and the impacts of this change now vary considerably from place to place, sector to sector, and even household to household (Fan 1995; Wei 1999). These growing differences throughout the nation currently influence some of China's most significant and confounding development policy debates. Beyond the income disparities mentioned above and discussed in several of the chapters to follow, unequal economic growth and development has created many other new social, cultural, and political problems that vary significantly by location and socioeconomic status. And there are many clear winners (especially in coastal areas), those whose lives are appreciably better in many ways than they were prior to reform (Croll 1994; Dwyer 1994; Fan 1995). In short, it is increasingly inappropriate to make broad generalizations about China or the Chinese people.

Generation gaps, economic gaps between rich and poor, regional gaps in economy and opportunity, new environmental challenges, and tensions between modernity and tradition abound in this large, ancient, and great nation. There are spatial patterns associated with all of these issues. In the chapters that follow, many of these issues will be explored with the goal of making sense of contemporary China. There is what might be called a spatial "geography" to China's economic and social changes, challenges, and outcomes (Veeck 1991). Of course, different places in China have different resources, variable infrastructures, and different social problems, and they also have developed different resolutions to these problems over time. In the reform era, more of these solutions, and unfortunately problems, are of local character and/or origin. Exploring these locational differences in issues, resources, and solutions allows us to move beyond national generalizations to gain a more comprehensive and accurate understanding of contemporary China's true complexity as well as of the diversity of issues confronting China's people and leaders today.

Goals and Conceptual Approaches

A major goal of this volume is to elucidate and analyze the changes and challenges facing China in the present and those that it has faced in the past. At the same time, we want to summarize and explain China from a geographic perspective. It is certainly true that there have been many books, originating from many disciplines, that have presented summaries of modern China. Many of these are cited in our own chapters. The impetus for this specific volume, however, is to explore modern China in terms of two geographic themes: (1) China's spatial organization, including its rapidly growing links to the changing global system, and (2) the human occupancy and use of the many types of environments (physical and cultural) found within the country's current borders.

These themes are common in geographic research, but are sometimes overlooked in studies originating in less-synthetic disciplines. Geography, unlike most social-science disciplines, might best be distinguished by its approach—the ideal of a genuine synthesis of information and explanation from many disciplines dedicated to the exploration of change across space and time—rather than by any claim to a unique subject matter. In this book we apply this holistic approach, weaving research from many disciplines beyond geography into a tapestry or framework that allows useful generalization while at the same time representing the diversity that is modern China. As geographers, we believe an effective assessment of China can best be made through simultaneous appreciation of the complex forces caught up in what might be viewed as the interactions between axes of time and space. The geographer's art is to explore the nuances and implications of location, not just in terms of changing environmental and cultural landscapes, but also as these landscapes and their uses (in this case, by the people of China) change over time (Hart 1982; Williams 2002, 223). Like those of any country, the history and geography of China are always interconnected, with contemporary society, culture, economy, and politics emerging as distillations of both past and present conditions in any specific location.

Our challenge is to present this mosaic in a manageable volume free from jargon and excessive over-simplifications. The challenge for our readers is to constantly recall that the chapters that follow provide, at best, a series of insightful explanations, and snapshot summaries, of a nation that is reinventing itself in all aspects at astonishing speed. At the outset it is of paramount importance that readers recognize the vast implications not only of the changes that have come to China during the past several decades of reform, but also of the very pace of these changes and their implications for the world. Rapid change makes policy development and implementation more difficult because the major issues associated with seminal problems change constantly, just as the facets of a gemstone variably refract light and color throughout the course of a day. Recognition of the pace of change as an almost independent factor is vital to any understanding of contemporary China.

It could be argued that during the Maoist era (1949–1976) strong Chinese Communist Party (CCP) control of China's economic, political, and social infrastructure and ideology resulted, at least briefly and somewhat superficially, in the homogenization of not only national goals and aspirations, but to some extent of many aspects of Chinese culture and society as well (Blecher 2000; Lippit 2000; *Rural Cadre Handbook* 1981). Under Mao, central planning directed not only the use of resources and capital, but the spatial organization of the nation and its ideological views as well. This resulted in relatively uniform strategies for the nation as a whole as well as a strong inward orientation and self-imposed isolation—a plan and policy direction that were not altogether successful. Admittedly, the impact and implications of policy formed at the national level were buffered by regional and local conditions, but prior to the 1978 reforms, there was far greater consensus, at least among those making decisions, regarding how best to proceed.

This is not to imply that after 1978, market forces were given free rein. Indeed, while the future role of the state with respect to directing the economy is not clear, its control over many important aspects of everyday life in China remains a general feature of "socialism with Chinese characteristics" (Liu and Wu 1986; Xue 1986). Yet in economic matters and in many sectors, the central government continues to play a critical role in guiding and buffering the economy (Duckett 1998; Hinton 2000; Garnaut 2001, 15–17). As we will discuss at length in many of the following chapters, the consensus viewpoint of the Mao years has to some extent been lost in contemporary China—local conditions matter more now than at any time in the last fifty years. Research from many places in China reflects the growing importance of varying levels of regionalism by which provinces, prefectures, counties, and cities increasingly manage their own affairs, resolve disputes, and plan their future in parallel with increasing ties to and interactions with the global system (Chu and Yeung 2000; Lin 1997; Ma and Cui 2002; Shieh 2000).

The fundamental American debate represented by the contrasting views of Thomas Jefferson and Alexander Hamilton regarding the role of the central government is as important in contemporary China as in most industrial nations. What is the role of the central government in promoting economic growth and social equity? How should revenues be raised and distributed? What should be taught in the schools, and how should schools be supported? How should health care and social services be provided and how should they be paid for? In the reform era in China, it is clear that many more decisions, once determined by central government fiat, will now be made by local governments (Lin 1997). The periphery is growing in power on the back of variable economic growth, differential revenue streams, and changing political realities and government policies. Yes, the CCP is still in charge, but as the party is slowly separated from the day-to-day functions of local government, the possibility of multiple political parties, for at least local elections, does not seem so preposterous as it did even a decade ago. There are multiple candidates in local elections, and sometimes non-CCP candidates win.

An explosion of scholarship, in and out of China, coupled with the rapid pace of change noted above, makes any summation of contemporary China both easier and more difficult. China is so large, and the many histories of the people and places now found within its national borders are so complex and different, that generalizations will always be problematic. Still, without any generalization, there can be no comprehension of the whole. We hope to achieve balance while presenting this remarkable nation from a variety of perspectives.

The remaining sections of this chapter provide additional background information and introduce our geographic approach to the material in the topical chapters that follow.

China's Land and People: Implication for State Organization and Control

As will be discussed in considerable detail in chapter 2, an understanding of the vastness and grand scale of China, and of the implications of this scale with respect to China's varied environments and human activities, is essential. Consider the size of several

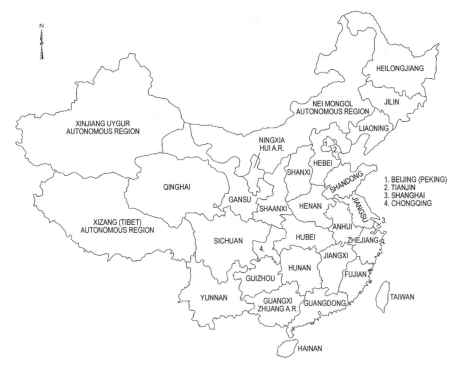

Map 1.3. China's First-Order (Provincial-Level) Administrative Regions

individual provinces. Many of China's provinces and autonomous regions are individually bigger than a number of the larger and most important countries of Europe (see map 1.3). Sichuan province, for example, is larger than any European country except Russia, and with 87 million people in 2003 had more people than Egypt or Vietnam. Guangdong in southeastern China, Jiangsu in East China, and Hunan in Central China, each had more people in 2003 than the United Kingdom, France, or Italy. In fact, the provinces of Shandong, Jiangsu, Sichuan, and Henan all have more people than Germany—Europe's second most-populous nation to Russia (National Bureau of Statistics 2003, 96; *Encyclopedia Britannica* 2003, 480).

China's population of 1.3 billion is very unevenly distributed. Seven of the eleven cities with populations over 4 million within their urban districts are located within East China. Shanghai and Beijing are each home to more than 11 million (National Bureau of Statistics 2004, 362). Of China's largest cities, only Xian and Chongqing are located in the West. As elsewhere, political and economic power tends to concentrate in the most populated regions. Places with greater populations generate more revenues, have better transport, more universities, and have more political representation. All of this confounds the effect on West China of its spatial isolation and higher transport costs, with a parallel increase in costs associated with manufacturing and industrial production—activities that have higher net returns than traditional activities such as agriculture.

Equally significant for China's past and present is the country's location in Asia. China, like the United States, is a middle-latitude land, and its eastern and southern peripheries open onto the Pacific Ocean and adjacent seas. The effect of this is to give the eastern half of the country a high index of accessibility to ocean shipping and international air transportation (see map 1.1). Middle-latitude location and proximity to the ocean and seas help provide a source of moisture and moderate temperatures, and both accessibility and middle-latitude location are great advantages when compared with the relative isolation and extreme climatic conditions of China's northern neighbor, Russia. These advantages resemble, in part, similar conditions found in the United States.

China, however, has the disadvantage of a West that is closed off by a high and extremely dry region of mountains and basins. China's West suffers from inaccessibility and the rigors of a harsh, dry climate. West China, past and present, is sparsely peopled and much of it remains poorly developed. A disproportionate number of China's chronically poor are found within its interior borderland provinces, this being partly a reflection of both their location and environment, but also a testament to their lack of political and economic power. In many of the chapters that follow, contrasts will be made between coastal and interior provinces as new regions emerge and local and regional economies and societies rearrange themselves. Differences in infrastructure, educational opportunities, transport, and central government patronage underlie the current coastal East versus interior West debate. Such palpable differences and inequities no doubt stimulated the contemporary central government policy "Develop the West," which is designed to foster greater regional equity while slowing migration to urban areas and coastal provinces. Regional equity is an important issue in many of our chapters.

It is important to keep in mind the implications of China's great size and the eastern concentration of its population, because these factors relate to past and present development efforts.

China's Political and Cultural Permanence

China's great size and large number of people have been cited as two of the outstanding features of the country and proof of its significance in the panorama of contemporary world events. Another aspect of China that illuminates its importance in world history is its long record of political and cultural tenure. The Chinese people today occupy the original core area (as well as additional territory) that was occupied at the beginning of Chinese recorded history in 1700 B.C. (the beginning of the Shang dynasty). The Zhou (1122–221 B.C.) and Qin (221–206 B.C.) dynasties followed, and signaled an age of cultural development and unification in China. Qin Shi Huang, the first emperor of the Qin and credited with unifying China (see chapter 3), faced many of the problems that, in somewhat altered form, remain today. Imagine the problems facing China's leaders over time, as they sought to manage culturally distinct regions so immense and varied in natural resources. How should the central state deal with and overcome the "friction of distance" among places and regions while establishing effective political control? How and where should investments be made for the construction of public works that would best serve the nation's interest by improving production? These were some of the tasks that confronted Qin Shi Huang in his attempt to unify China and provide an overarching sense of nationhood to *Zhongguo* (the Central Kingdom), or "center of the known universe," as the Chinese refer to their own country.

To achieve his goals, Qin Shi Huang created an imperial dynastic system that exhibited a strong degree of centralized authority. He established a bureaucratic mechanism that used a standardized written language to communicate as it sought to maintain administrative control over the national territory. He standardized currency to promote interregional trade. He also expanded the canal system and road network, investments that aided commerce and were critical for political control of key areas in the early years of the dynastic era. Such accomplishments laid the foundation on which the ensuing Chinese Empire was built.

China expanded its frontiers in subsequent centuries, relentlessly pushing southward and absorbing a great many local tribal peoples and states into the powerful framework of the Chinese cultural system. This was done despite conflict and struggle. By the beginning of the Christian era, China had carved for itself a distinctive national territory, administered by a central political and bureaucratic system and undergirded by a powerful set of shared values and culture. That functioning cultural and spatial system lasted more than two thousand years, until the twentieth century when the traditional dynastic form of governance and administration was overturned by the Republic of China (1911–1949). This twentieth-century revolution later resulted in the establishment of a socialist and communist system of government and national management, the PRC.

Geography, Globalization, and China's Path to the Future

Answers to the why and how of China's political and cultural stability and permanence are historically interesting, and are valuable for the insights they can provide with respect to contemporary visions and plans in China for the future economic development, environmental management, and spatial organization of the nation. These answers and questions are geographic because environment and space (territory), two of the key aspects of the subject matter of geography, are heavily involved in these debates (Tuan 1969). It is for this reason that we have selected the two topics mentioned above (spatial organization, and human occupancy and use of the environment) to follow as basic themes in unfolding and helping to explain the "geography" of modern China.

Parallel to the internal development of China is and has been an accompanying set of forces that are typically identified as global. Yet as Dicken (2003) has forcefully reminded us, these forces are often misunderstood and misinterpreted. He goes on to point out that global forces can best be understood in the context of a series of networks of related production and distribution that operate on a variety of levels from the local to the global. His analysis suggests that power relations vary in different production processes and networks depending on the role of the various actors involved: the multinational corporation, the central state, and the local enterprise and state.

This observation is particularly appropriate to an analysis of China, for as was noted above, the reforms in China have increasingly decentralized power in economic decision making and have led to spatial rearrangements and the emergence of new economic regions based on rapidly changing production activities and behaviors, themselves the results of regional and global economic forces of investment, manufacturing, distribution, and trade. These forces, based on reform and restructuring policies of the central state in place since 1978 and further liberalized after Deng Xiaoping's southern trip in 1992, have been of great benefit to China's economic growth and growing power. Also as noted, the spatial outcomes have largely been in favor of the coastal regions that have been in the vanguard of the new economic shifts. At the same time, however, the tide of economic growth has been so powerful as to lift many other regional vessels, albeit at a lessened rate of advance.

Yet the economic gains have not been matched by political shifts that might lead to a more open and democratic system of governance and to rearrangements in the manner in which political power and regions are constituted. China remains a Leninist state in which the 66 million members of the CCP make the decisions that direct the social, political, and cultural directions of the state as well as play a key role in overseeing the general direction of economic growth and change. In this sense, the forces of globalization are buffered and muted and are not allowed to intrude in ways that might challenge the authority or power of the party and the central state.

The large territory and varied natural environments of China require considerable attention if we are to achieve a real understanding of the manner in which the contemporary Chinese are setting about their goals of economic, social, and political reform. Understanding the interaction of the Chinese and their environment is fundamental to comprehending contemporary China and the steps taken by its leaders to promote development and the well-being of its citizens. At the same time, coming to terms with China as a giant spatial and human system is another intellectual and theoretical challenge that offers us an opportunity to bring the special tools and conceptual approaches of geographic analysis to readers of this volume. Finally, using these themes and approaches will help inform our understanding of how China is increasing its global role as its economy expands rapidly, and as the nation's political, military, and security roles grow in parallel.

References Cited

Blecher, Marc. 2000. The Dengist period: The triumphs and crises of structural reform, 1979 to the present. Chap. 2 in *The China Handbook: Prospects onto the 21st Century*, ed. Christopher Hudson. Chicago: Glenlake, 19–38.

Chow, Gregory. 2002. *China's Economic Transformation*. Oxford: Blackwell.

Chu, David K. Y., and Y. M. Yeung. 2000. Developing the "Development Corridor." Chap. 13 in *Fujian: A Coastal Province in Transition and Transformation*, ed. Y. M. Yeung and David K. Y. Chu. Hong Kong: Chinese University Press, 305–26.

CNNMoney.com. 2003. U.S. trade gap hits record $44B. February 20. money.cnn.com/2003/02/20/news/economy/trade_deficit/ (accessed March 1, 2006).

Croll, Elisabeth. 1994. *From Heaven to Earth: Images and Experiences of Development in China.* London: Routledge.

Dicken, Peter. 2003. *Global Shift: Reshaping the Global Economic Map in the 21st Century.* New York: Guilford.

Duckett, Jane. 1998. *The Entrepreneurial State in China.* London: Routledge.

Dwyer, Denis, ed. 1994. *China: The Next Decades.* Essex, U.K.: Longman Scientific and Technical.

Encyclopedia Britannica. 2003. New York: Encyclopedia Britannica Educational.

Fan, C. Cindy. 1995. Of belts and ladders: State policy and uneven regional development in post-Mao China. *Annals of the Association of American Geographers* 85 (3): 421–49.

———. 1997. Uneven development and beyond: Regional development theory in post-Mao China. *International Journal of Urban and Regional Research* 21 (4): 620–39.

Garnaut, Ross. 2001. Twenty years of economic reform and structural change in the Chinese economy. Chap. 1 in *Growth without Miracles: Readings on the Chinese Economy in the Era of Reform,* ed. Ross Garnaut and Yiping Huang. Oxford: Oxford University Press, 1–18.

Gipouloux, Francois. 2000. Declining trend and uneven spatial development of FDI in China. In *China Review 2000,* ed. Chung-ming Lau and Jianfa Shen. Hong Kong: Chinese University Press, 285–305.

Hart, John Fraser. 1982. The highest form of the geographer's art. *Annals of the Association of American Geographers* 72:1–29.

Hinton, Peter. 2000. Where nothing is as it seems: Between Southeast China and mainland Southeast Asia in the post-socialist era. In *Where China Meets Southeast Asia: Social and Cultural Change in the Border Regions,* ed. Grant Evans, Christopher Hutton, and Kuah Khun Eng. New York: St. Martin's, 7–27.

Huang, Xiyi. 1998. Two-way changes—kinship in contemporary rural China. Chap. 8 in *Village INC.: Chinese Rural Society in the 1990s.* Honolulu: University of Hawaii Press.

Jefferson, Gary H., and Thomas G. Rawski. 1999. China's industrial innovation model: A model of endogenous reform. Chap. 3 in *Enterprise Reform in China: Ownership, Transition, and Performance.* Washington, D.C.: World Bank.

Lardy, Nicholas R. 1992. *Foreign Trade and Economic Reform in China, 1978–1990.* Cambridge: Cambridge University Press.

———. 2002. *Integrating China into the Global Economy.* Washington, D.C.: Brookings Institution Press.

Lin, George C. S. 1997. *Red Capitalism in South China: Growth and Development of the Pearl River Delta.* Vancouver, B.C.: UBC Press.

Lippit, Victor D. 2000. The Maoist period, 1949–1978: Mobilizational collectivism, primitive accumulation, and industrialization. Chap. 1 in *The China Handbook: Prospects onto the 21st Century,* ed. Christopher Hudson. Chicago: Glenlake, 3–18.

Liu Suinan, and Wu Qungan, eds. 1986. *China's Socialist Economy—an Outline History (1949–1984).* Beijing: Beijing Review.

Lyons, Thomas P. 2000. Regional inequality. Chap. 14 in *Fujian: A Coastal Province in Transition and Transformation,* ed. Y. M. Yeung and David K. Y. Chu. Hong Kong: Chinese University Press, 327–51.

Ma, Laurence J. C., and Gonghao Cui. 2002. Economic transition at the local level: Diverse forms of town development in China. *Eurasian Geography and Economics* 43 (2): 79–103.

Mok, Ka-ho. 2000. *Social and Political Development in Post-reform China.* New York: St. Martin's.

Moore, Thomas G. 2002. *China in the World Market: Chinese Industry and International Sources of Reform in the Post-Mao Era.* Cambridge: Cambridge University Press.

National Bureau of Statistics. 2003. *Zhongguo tongji nianjian 2003* [China statistical yearbook 2003]. Beijing: China Statistics Press.

———. 2004. *Zhongguo tongji nianjian 2004* [China statistical yearbook 2004]. Beijing: China Statistics Press.

Perkins, Dwight. 2001. Completing China's move to the market. Chap. 3 in *Growth without Miracles: Readings on the Chinese Economy in the Era of Reform*, ed. Ross Garnaut and Yiping Huang. Oxford: Oxford University Press, 36–53.

Rural Cadre Handbook. 1981. The correct handling of love, marriage, and family problems. Reading no. 81 in *Chinese Civilization and Society: A Sourcebook*. New York: Free Press, 371–77.

Shieh, Shawn. 2000. Centre, province, and locality in Fujian's reforms. Chap. 4 in *Fujian: A Coastal Province in Transition and Transformation*, ed. Y. M. Yeung and David K. Y. Chu. Hong Kong: Chinese University Press, 83–117.

Studwell, Joe. 2002. *The China Dream: The Quest for the Last Great Untapped Market on Earth.* New York: Atlantic Monthly Press.

Tuan, Yi-fu. 1969. *China.* Chicago: Aldine.

U.S. Census Bureau. 2006. Foreign Trade Statistics. www.census.gov/foreign-trade/balance/c5700.html#2005 (accessed March 1, 2006).

Veeck, Gregory. 1991. *The Uneven Landscape: Geographical Studies in Post-reform China.* Baton Rouge, La.: Geoscience Press.

———. 2005. From Communism to the World Trade Organization: The remarkable transformation of China's agricultural sector. *Focus on Geography* 48 (3): 1–9.

Walcott, Susan M. 2002. Chinese industrial and science parks: Bridging the gap. *Professional Geographer* 54 (3): 249–364.

Wei, Dennis Yehua. 1999. Regional inequality in China. *Progress in Human Geography* 23 (1): 48–58.

Williams, Jack F. 2002. Geographers and China. *Issues and Studies* 38:4; 39 (1): 217–47.

World Bank. 2004. *World Development Indicators.* Washington, D.C.: International Bank for Reconstruction and Development.

Xinhua News Service. 2005. China remains developing nation despite GDP increase. dailynews.muzi.com/news/ll/english/1395738.shtml?cc=22181&ccr= (accessed March 1, 2006).

Xue, Muqiao. 1986. *China's Socialist Economy.* Rev. ed. Beijing: Foreign Languages Press.

Zhao, Quansheng. 2000a. The China-Japan-US triangle and East Asian international relations. In *China Review 2000*, ed. Chung-ming Lau and Jianfa Shen. Hong Kong: Chinese University Press, 77–103.

———. 2000b. China in East Asia: Changing relations with Japan and Korea. Chap. 5 of *The China Handbook: Prospects onto the 21st Century*, ed. Christopher Hudson. Chicago: Glenlake, 69–80.

CHAPTER 2

China's Natural Environments

Territory and Location

China's territory encompasses approximately 9,600,000 km² and is roughly the same size as the United States and smaller than only Russia and Canada. Among these very large nations, China is exceptional in that its land and resources must support and provide for more than 1.3 billion people—approximately 21 percent of the world's population—on only 6.5 percent of the earth's land area (National Bureau of Statistics 2004). Its sheer size has many implications, and China exhibits a number of similarities to the United States. For example, both countries are situated in the middle latitudes of the Northern Hemisphere and both have extensive coastlines fronting on middle-latitude oceans and seas. Approximately 98 percent of China's land is located between latitudes 18°N and 50°N, and the densely settled eastern half of the country is mainly a temperate and subtropical land. Physically, the southeastern United States and southeastern China are very similar in their soils, climate, and topography. Although China has approximately 18,000 km of coastline and is easily accessible by water from the east and south as is the United States, the great northern and western portions of China are enclosed and isolated by massive mountain systems, great deserts and basins, and high plateaus (see map 2.1).

The Implications of China's Physical Landscape

The barriers represented by the rugged terrain of China's western regions were historically very significant, isolating China from neighboring nations and cultures. Even at present the formidable terrain and great distances of its West hamper China's westward connections with the remainder of Asia. Unlike Europe, whose mountains are clustered in its center, China has mountains that encircle the country and encourage development within the more accessible eastern alluvial and coastal plains. Historically China's developmental energy has been focused on overcoming the challenge of its internal physical geography, and through the centuries, China's governments have expended considerable time and energy melding the country's various cultures and regions together rather than promoting its external expansion. In this respect, China's experience is in marked contrast to that of Europe, where maritime colonial expansion beyond traditional borders made small nations such as England and the Netherlands, in their heyday, among the most powerful in the world.

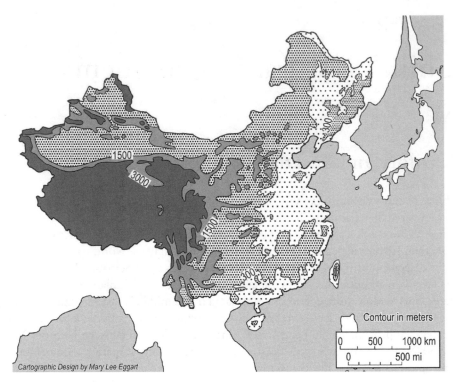

Map 2.1. China's Topography. **Source:** Wu Yuanli 1973. Cartographic design by Mary Lee Eggart

Western China generally is high and mountainous, although the center of the Turfan Basin in Xinjiang is a remarkable 505 m below sea level, and parts of the Tarim Basin are only 1,000 m above sea level (ASL). The vast remainder of West China, however, is well over 2,500 m ASL, and the massive Tibetan-Qinghai Plateau is mostly over 4,000 m ASL. Because of its interior location within the great Eurasian landmass and the orographic effect of these great mountain systems that block out moisture, West China tends to be extremely dry. For three millennia, this western region has remained sparsely populated, despite ever-growing population pressures in East and Southeast China. Spatial isolation, coupled with an inhospitable climate, has given this region a very distinct developmental and cultural history when compared with the remainder of China.

This isolation has created problems of national integration. Traditionally, West China has been viewed by most Han Chinese (the ethnic group comprising 97 percent of China's population) as a remote and desolate frontier region. All of China's provincial-level autonomous regions (offering, in theory, some measure of political autonomy for minorities) are in the West and Southwest. To some extent the stereotypes of the early American frontier parallel those held by the majority of Chinese regarding China's Far West. As in America, the frontier in China projects a range of cultural images from the romantic and free to the wild, unsettled, and remote. Further, like the American Wild West, these regions are contested space where local ethnic-minority traditions, growing Han Chinese intrusions, and conflicting perceptions of modernity have yet to reach a balance. Millennia-old conflicts between West China's indigenous groups and the growing numbers of Han Chinese settlers or migrants arriving to exploit its great natural resources are on the increase. This is but the first example of many in this book of how demands placed on China's environment have shifted dramatically in response to China's changing economy and society.

A country with a large area characteristically has a large resource base. Although precise identification and surveys of China's mineral resources remain incomplete in a few difficult cases such as petroleum, natural gas, and precious metals, it is clear that China has vast reserves of most major minerals, including tungsten, coal, antimony, tin, zinc, iron sulfide, vanadium, molybdenum, titanium, mercury, salt, fluorspar, and magnesite (Zhao 1994). China also has substantial reserves of iron, manganese, aluminum, limestone, and petroleum. Its reserves of tungsten and antimony are believed to be the world's largest. Only in nickel and aluminum, among the most commonly used and requisite minerals for modern industrialization, is China seriously deficient. China's supply, production, and use of mineral resources will be examined in greater detail in chapter 10, but from the outset, it is important to realize that China's mountainous topography is both a blessing and a curse. The mountains and plateaus have restricted economic development, transportation, and national integration, but they are also rich in the mineral resources that are vital for China's continued economic development.

Another consequence of China's size and location is the great diversity of its regional and local climates. In West China, *continentality* is the most important climatic factor because the dominant westerly winds from Central Asia render the northern and western interior regions cold and very dry throughout winter. Precipitation in the North and West is limited as is that of the Great Plains and basins of the western United States. On the other hand, Central and South China are heavily influenced by summer monsoon systems from the Pacific, and the climate of these regions ranges from temperate to tropical, with typically 1,000 mm or more of rainfall per year (see map 2.2).

Monsoon influences are also found throughout eastern China, although northern China receives much less precipitation than does the South. A major environmental distinction may be made between humid, subtropical central and southern China, and dryer, more continental western and northern China. In part, this division follows the east–west trend of the Qinling Shan (Qinling Mountains), which extend eastward to the East China Sea along the Huai River. This mountain chain divides China into regions of water surplus and deficit—a critical issue for agriculture and settlement (see map 2.3). Based on such a division, southern China and the southern parts of the North China Plain and the Northeastern Plain (Dongbei Pingyuan) are regions where rainfall generally refreshes annual groundwater supply. In sharp contrast, all of western China and the remainder of China north of the Qinling Shan are water-deficit regions—where groundwater is but inconsistently replaced by precipitation. Not surprisingly, some of China's worst environmental problems have emerged in the dry, ecologically unstable regions of the North and West.

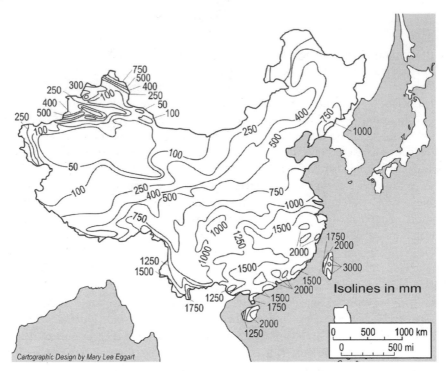

Map 2.2. China's Annual Precipitation. **Source:** *Zhonghua renmin gongheguo dituce*. 1983. Cartographic design by Mary Lee Eggart

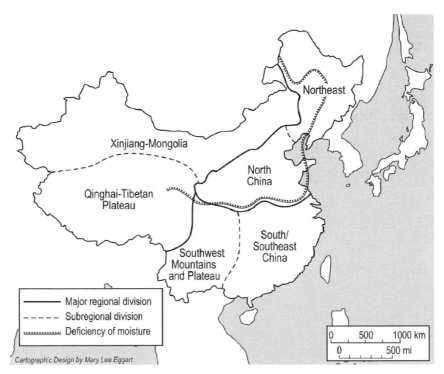

Map 2.3. China's Major Environmental Regions. **Source:** After Pannell and Ma 1983, 16. Cartographic design by Mary Lee Eggart

As this survey of the spatial organization of China's economic activities and population distribution unfolds in subsequent chapters, the environmental advantages or constraints of any given region will be seen to take on great significance. The two major themes of this text—spatial organization, and human-environment relations—provide a geographic explanation of the challenges of modernization, development, and cultural and economic change in contemporary China.

For much of its long history, China has been a nation of farmers. China's great environmental diversity permits the use of a broad range of agricultural environments, resulting in a comprehensive array of agricultural products. This environmental diversity also offers some measure of insurance against local or regional natural catastrophes, because these can be absorbed by the country's larger environmental and economic systems. The summer floods on many of China's rivers in 1998 were the worst in almost fifty years, yet the national summer grain crop that year was one of the largest on record because conventionally dry, interior grain areas recorded unusually high yields. Protected in this way by its sheer size, China is able to meet upwards of 95 percent of its citizens' food requirements while producing an ever-expanding variety of different commodities— grains, fruits, vegetables, commercial and industrial crops, and livestock—for export as well as domestic consumption (see chapter 8 for more on food security).

In all large nations, some regions are more favorably endowed than others. Typically, inhabitants of resource-rich regions become wealthier than their counterparts in poorly endowed or isolated regions. For the successful and ecologically sound development of resources, capital is also a prerequisite. As a consequence of limited capital, many parts of West China remain relatively poor, despite significant subsurface resources. On the other hand, degraded environments in China, as elsewhere in the world, are frequently associated with poverty. Regional inequities in quality of life and income levels result from environmental degradation, and social problems of many types generally follow quickly on the heels of uneven economic growth. Often the poor make improper environmental decisions concerning land and water resources. Just as poverty results from degraded environments, degraded environments often are a result of poverty. Recent high-level government decisions to protect China's beleaguered environment offer hope, but the past fifty years of economic expansion have caused myriad environmental problems that will take many decades to reverse (McElroy, Nielson, and Lydon 1998; Smil 1993). The litany of the environmental problems in most industrial nations, which is all too familiar, holds for China as well. The following chapters will introduce many different types of environmental problems in detail, but a brief overview of China's differing regional problems is warranted here.

China's environmental challenges can be broadly classified into two categories: (1) pollution problems resulting from point-source pollution (e.g., industrial effluents, air-born releases from factories, and power plants), and (2) ecological problems such as deforestation, desertification, salinization, pollution from fertilizers and farm chemicals, and erosion brought about by uninformed and avaricious land-use practices (Smil 1984; Edmonds 1994). Point-source pollution problems once originated largely in urban areas because up until the reform era, major cities (over 500,000 persons) claimed the lion's share of industrial production and coal consumption. After the 1978 reforms, the problems associated with point-source pollution spread throughout much of eastern

China (and even into some urban and suburban areas of the West). Township and village industrialization now accounts for more than 29 percent of rural employment, and too often local government officials and agencies favor growth-at-any-cost policies that ignore pollution and the environmental degradation that can result. Water quality in many areas of rural China has deteriorated rapidly in the past twenty years due to the dumping of industrial chemicals, waste water, salts, bleach, and other toxins into rural China's rivers, ponds, and canals. Ecological problems associated with agriculture, husbandry, and forestry have also impacted much of China, but the most pressing challenges are found in the western regions. Here the use of rangeland for farming, unregulated logging, and the careless disposal of mine tailings associated with mineral extraction have resulted in many tragic, local, ecological disasters that are only now being identified. And farm-chemical abuse throughout the nation has resulted in polluted ground and surface water, causing many types of illnesses in vulnerable populations.

Surface Structure and Geomorphology

The structure and landforms of China are very complex. If viewed in the context of continental drift, the tectonic structure of China has resulted from the gigantic eastward- and southward-moving Eurasian continental plate colliding with the westward-moving Pacific plate. In addition, southwestern China came into contact with the Indian Ocean plate moving northward. The intersection of these gigantic plates, or what is called the *geotectonic structural platform* of China, explains the major structural surface features of China's diverse contemporary landscapes. On the macroscale, the progressive decrease in elevation from western to eastern China is most important for the purposes of this text. Elevations of the higher mountain systems in China, such as the Kunlun and the Himalayas, average over 6,500 m ASL. These elevations in the Far West decline to about 5,000 m on the eastern face of the Tibetan Plateau and eventually drop to sea level near the coast of the Yellow Sea. The Tibetan Plateau, a huge and high *massif,* or primary mountain mass, is rimmed on the north and east by the remainder of China. The eastward descent from this landmass is much like coming down the steps of a gigantic staircase. In proceeding from west to east, one descends several ranges and plateaus, each time discovering lower mountain systems and elevated basins (Pannell and Ma 1983).

In sum, the country may be divided between East and West for physiographic comparison. In both parts, its structure is composed of several giant *geosynclines* and related *geanticlinal* features, which are the result of the tectonic movement described above. China's synclinal structure is made up of alternating ridges and plains. In the East, the *strike* (or directional axis) of these is generally northeast–southwest. Moving from east to west, the most conspicuous features of this structure are the Changbai Mountains of northeastern China that form the country's border with Korea, the Northeast and North China Plains, the Taihang Mountains, the Inner Mongolian Plateau, the Loess Plateau, the Sichuan Basin, and the Yunnan-Guizhou Plateau.

Cutting across these features almost at right angles and on an east–west strike in the East are the Qinling Mountains, the Dongnan Hills (Nanling Mountains), and

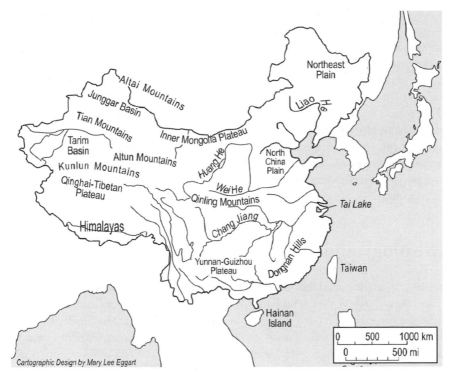

Map 2.4. China's Physical Features. **Source:** After Zhao 1986; C.S. Hammond and Co. N.Y., map 47. Cartographic design by Mary Lee Eggart

many other smaller systems (see map 2.4). In the Far West, the strike of most of the major geomorphologic features is again east–west. Here are the truly great mountains and basins of China. Indeed, these are some of the most extensive physical features on earth—the Himalayas, the Tibetan Plateau, the Kunlun Mountains, the Tarim and Junggar basins, the Tian Shan Mountains, the Junggar (Dzungarian), Basin, and the Altai Mountains (see map 2.4). Massive in scale, these features combine to isolate East and Southeast China from the remainder of Asia. It is this crisscross arrangement of major structural features, east to west and north to south, that results in China's topography being referred to as a "Chinese checkerboard." Almost 58 percent of China's territory lies 1,000 m or more above sea level, and only 25.2 percent is below 500 m (Zhao 1994, 17).

Geologically, much of today's China was formerly under the sea, although three ancient granitic massifs (one in southeastern China, one in Tibet, and one in Mongolia) formed huge stable islands of ancient Precambrian rock (prior to 620 million years ago). Movements against these massifs created the various series of parallel ridges, basins, and plains described above. In addition, a subsequent submergence of troughs and basins during the Paleozoic era resulted in the formation of vast quantities of coal and natural gas.

Variations in the geomorphological structure of China's regions and the resultant surface land forms have shaped and molded the distinctive and complex drainage system of China. At the same time, this drainage system has attracted, but also challenged, the energy and imagination of China's people as they have gone about settling and exploiting the land's many regional environments. It is important to realize that the complex patterns and processes of China's contemporary river and drainage systems are not merely a result of China's physical geography. Rather, current surface conditions are also the result of thousands of years of complex interactions between these landscapes and the people who have occupied them. These "feedback" systems have always yielded both sweet and bitter fruit: greater prosperity, but more environmental degradation. From this long-term perspective, the supporters of the controversial Three Gorges Dam project, unprecedented in human history for its sheer size, are simply the latest of countless generations in China who have undertaken massive landscape transformations by damming rivers, building terraces, and flooding land for rice cultivation.

Hydrology and River Systems

One geographer estimated that China has over fifty thousand rivers with drainage basins of over 100 km^2 (Ren, Yang, and Bao 1985). Thirty-six percent of China's territory has *interior drainage* (rivers having no outlet to the sea), and the remainder drains into the oceans and seas around China and Southeast Asia. China has a number of very large and famous rivers within its boundaries, as well as the headwaters of several other major rivers of the world (see table 2.1 and map 2.5). Most of China's major rivers originate on or near the Qinghai-Tibetan Plateau and flow south or east, emptying into different seas associated with the Indian or Pacific oceans. China's three major self-contained rivers that flow east are the Huang He (Yellow River), the Chang Jiang (Yangtze River), and the Xi Jiang (West River). Of these, the Chang Jiang (see photo 2.1) is easily the largest in terms of length, area of drainage basin, and volume of discharge (see table 2.1). The Huang He is next in length and area of drainage basin, although its discharge is modest compared to the Chang and the Xi because of the dry lands through which it flows. The Heilong Jiang (Black Dragon River, or the Amur in Russia), along with its largest tributary, the Songhua, is the most important river in Northeast China and

Table 2.1. Drainage, Length, and Flow of China's Major Rivers

River	Drainage Area (km^2)	Length (km)	Annual Flow (100 million m^3)	Drainage Area (% of China total)
Chang (Yangtze)	4,638,994	6,300	9,513	18.92
Huang (Yellow)	1,948,818	5,464	661	7.87
Songhua	1,443,090	2,308	762	12.15
Zhu (Pearl)	1,175,052	2,214	3,338	6.07*
Heilong	888,502	3,101	1,181	9.16
Huai	697,440	1,000	622	3.44*
Hai	682,801	1,090	228	3.33*
Liao	593,804	1,390	148	3.61*

* includes major tributaries.
Sources: National Bureau of Statistics 2004, 7; Zhao 1986, 47; Zhao 1994.

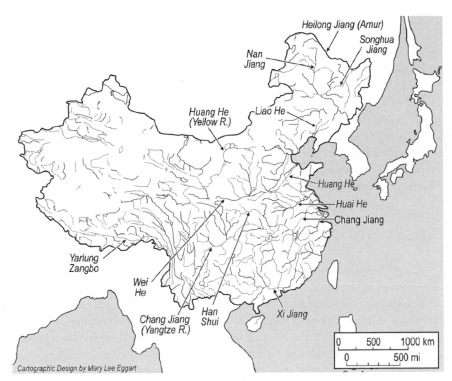

Map 2.5. China's Rivers. **Source:** After Pannell and Ma 1983, 26. Cartographic design by Mary Lee Eggart

Photo 2.1. The Chang Jiang (Yangtze River) near Nanjing, the capital of Jiangsu province, taken in spring 1987. Photo by Gregory Veeck

forms the boundary between China and Russia for part of its course. Perhaps because the Northeast was only integrated into China during the Manchu-controlled Qing dynasty (A.D. 1644–1911; see chapter 3), the Heilong figures less in the history and cultural evolution of China, and is often overlooked. Given that the Northeast is one of the most important new agricultural and industrial regions of China, the ecological health and well-being of this river, along with that of the Songhua, the Nen, and the Liao (its major tributaries), has become of critical concern. International issues complicate environmental protection of the Heilong because it flows through Russian territory to eventually drain into the Sea of Okhotsk just west of northern Sakhalin Island.

THE HUANG HE: CHINA'S SORROW

The Huang He and some of its tributaries, such as the Wei, Fen, and Luo, are of special interest because of their role in the evolution of Chinese civilization. The middle part of the drainage system of the Huang He cuts through the Loess Plateau, as do a number of the river's important tributaries. It is the enormous quantities of yellow loessal silt eroded from the plateau that gives the river its name and characteristic color (*loess* being the German term for loamy, yellow deposits of windblown soil). Uncontrolled logging over the centuries has resulted in extreme erosion in many parts of China, but the problem is particularly severe within the Loess Plateau. As the Huang He descends onto the North China Plain, its gradient is reduced sharply and river velocity slows—limiting its ability to transport the silt in suspension. The result is gradual deposition along the riverbed and the accumulation of large quantities of loess. The *aggradation* (building up) of the riverbed in turn has led to a perennial threat of floods that through the centuries were only ameliorated by building levees. As the riverbed rose in any given location, so did the height of the levees built by farmers to protect their land and homes. In many areas, as a result of centuries of levee construction, the bed of the river is now high above the surrounding agricultural plains (see figure 2.1). Whenever the levees breach, the river pours down onto the plains, causing massive property damage and loss of life—thus, the river's other ancient name, "China's Sorrow."

Beginning in the 1970s, the Chinese government launched a major program to tame the Huang He and utilize the river more effectively, but just as with the more publicized conflicts over the Three Gorges project, these projects remain highly controversial. The large dam and reservoir at San Men Xia (Three Gates Gorge) near the Tongguan elbow of the river began to silt up almost immediately after construction, and technical problems limit its power generation. Overall the river has been contained, but at high cost. There is something akin to squaring the circle in all of these efforts. In order to obtain funding from Beijing, every water-control project must serve many masters. Water and waterways are scarce in North China, and so each project must have multiple goals to receive funding. Ideally, a successful project will control flooding, generate hydroelectricity, expand irrigated area, provide industry and urban consumers with clean, sediment-free water, and offer improved navigation. A compromise dam is often not very successful in meeting any of these goals. And water quality must be improved, before it gets to the river, through the promotion of sound farming practices.

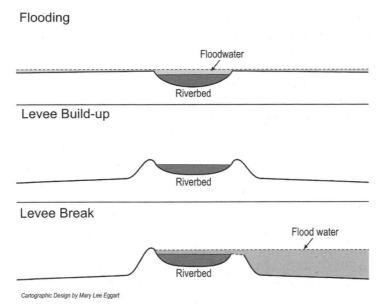

Flooding

Floodwater

Riverbed

Levee Build-up

Riverbed

Levee Break

Flood water

Riverbed

Cartographic Design by Mary Lee Eggart

Figure 2.1. Flooding and Levee Construction on the Huang He (Yellow River). Cartographic design by Mary Lee Eggart

In 1999 a series of logging bans and mandatory reforestation projects went into effect on the upper and middle stretches of the Huang He, and these will eventually reduce erosion and improve water quality and flooding issues. Environmentalists see control of deforestation and erosion on the Huang He as one of the major policy battles that illustrate the importance of environmental policy and regulation in China's continued economic development. There must be better enforcement of and compliance with these environmental regulations. This means more compliance officers are needed, officers who will be able to assess steep fines and provide other coercive measures for noncompliance that will convince local officials to protect the environment. Passing a law is the easy part; enforcing it is much more difficult.

THE CHANG JIANG: CHINA'S MIGHTIEST RIVER

China's largest river is the Chang Jiang (Long River), which drains over 1.8 million km^2 of Central China. Not surprisingly given its name, it is also China's longest river (6,300 km). Rising in the rugged mountains of the Tibetan Plateau, the river flows generally eastward to empty into the East China Sea at Shanghai. The importance of the river cannot be overstated. By draining the central part of China, it has provided water for irrigation to generations of farmers, and has served as the nation's major west–east transit route for three thousand years. The river has, by far, the largest annual discharge, with an average discharge at its mouth of 31,055 m^3/sec. (Zhao 1994, 18). This compares with an average through-flow for the Mississippi River near Vicksburg, Mississippi, of 18,000 m^3/sec., or with 1,822 m^3/sec. at the mouth of the Huang He. The average discharge rate of the Chang Jiang near its mouth, then, is about seventeen times greater than that of the Huang He (18).

As with the Huang He, deforestation in the upper reaches of the Chang Jiang has exacerbated the dangers of flooding on the river. The floods of the summer of 1998 saw the river's water level at its highest since 1954. These floods were blamed, in part, on the flouting of environmental regulations and on illegal logging by local government-owned companies. Unlike the Huang He, the Chang Jiang forms a major access corridor for maritime transportation into the heart of Central China. As Shanghai reasserts its role as the major port of Central China, better management of the river and improving water quality is vital.

For many years the Chinese have discussed diverting water from the Chang Jiang and routing it north to the water-deficient areas of the North China Plain and especially to Beijing and Tianjin. Three routes are generally cited, but none has been fully implemented—due as much to funding and jurisdictional issues as to the engineering challenges these projects present. These projects (*nanshui bei dao*) have been debated in China extensively, and construction is essentially complete on an eastern route. Low water levels on the Huang He that limited irrigation in Shandong in the late 1990s lent support to proponents of the eastern route. This project uses a series of pipelines to pump Chang Jiang water north through the Grand Canal, but also uses four lakes (including shallow Hongze lake in Jiangsu) as portions of the system. A telling stalemate, however, between the provincial governments of Jiangsu and Shandong provinces has frustrated national planners who are unused to taking "No" for an answer. The massive task of constructing a viaduct below the Huang He was a significant engineering challenge, but technical difficulties are overcome faster than political disputes. As a measure of the increasing power of the provincial governments vis-à-vis Beijing, Jiangsu province refuses to allow the project to begin operation unless more water is allocated to its northern portion. Further north, Beijing and Shandong province claim their water needs are more critical, particularly for urban and industrial uses. Potential western and central routes would be more expensive but would traverse less-populated areas, thereby encountering less political resistance (see map 2.6). There are also a number of important water-control projects in the area where the Chang Jiang emerges onto the lower alluvial plains of southern Hubei province. Gezhouba, the most famous of these, is China's second-largest hydroproject. At maximum, the dam produces 14 billion kilowatt hours (kWh) per year. The significance of this Chinese-designed and Chinese-built project is that it served as a pilot project for the vastly larger Three Gorges project. Currently, China's largest dam is on the Yalong, another tributary of the Chang Jiang, in Sichuan province. For a variety of reasons, the Yalong dam has never attracted the attention of the environmental movement in the same way as the Three Gorges project.

THE THREE GORGES DAM PROJECT

The impoundment of the Chang Jiang at Three Gorges (San Xia) is among the largest and most controversial construction projects ever planned in human history. Damming the Chang Jiang in proximity to the gorges near Yichang has been considered for at

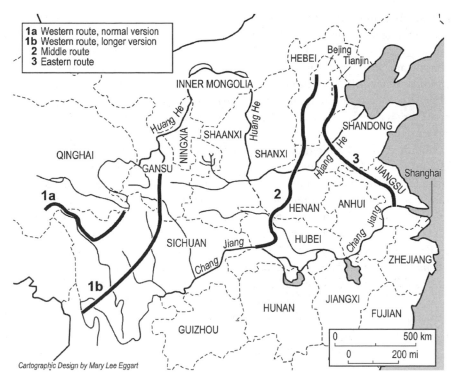

Map 2.6. Four Potential Water Diversion Routes. **Source:** "Nan Shui Beidao: China's South-North Water Transfer Project," presented at the East Asian Research Conference, University of Sheffield, July 1999. Cartographic design by Mary Lee Eggart

least seventy-five years. Sun Yat-sen, in his plan for China's industrial development, proposed a dam in this general area in 1929. There is more to this controversy, however, than the construction of a super-size dam. Since 1949 the dam has come to stand for modernity, symbolizing China's return to its rightful place among first nations. More importantly, the resulting hydroelectric power would provide for more effective economic development of all of Southwest China, an area currently among China's poorest. This region has been neglected despite its considerable contributions to the country, and the dam represents a political commitment to the region's future, as well as to its integration into a more prosperous future China, because low-cost power is seen as a critical input if this once-remote area with its lower wages and tax revenues is to attract manufacturing. Further, low-cost, hydro-generated power will reduce the use of low-quality coal, providing a health dividend to a region where lung-related illness is a major cause of death. These intangibles must be factored in when understanding the unswerving commitment of China's top leaders to the project despite a range of very sound arguments against construction made by virtually every Chinese and foreign environmental expert consulted.

The increasingly public controversy that has arisen over this project derives from a variety of reasons including the project's construction cost, its displacement of farms and farmers and destruction of historic and prehistoric artifacts, and its potential environmental impact (Nickum 1998). As many as 1.2 million people will eventually be relocated, and more than 23,000 ha of agricultural land will be inundated if the dam height reaches 175 m as planned. Resettlement, mostly complete, has not gone smoothly and many rural citizens feel disenfranchised and powerless. Funding for relocation and new village and town construction has not met expectations. Corruption and graft cases are common, and several high-profile corruption cases related to the Three Gorges project were recently settled as the government sought to shore up public support.

Hundreds of archaeological sites, including portions of the famous Town of Ghosts (Fengdu) will also be inundated. The ecological and environmental consequences of the project include its impact on local climate, flora, fauna, soils, geology, and agricultural ecology. In addition, the potential impact of the dam on human health through an increased incidence of malaria and schistosomiasis, due to slower water velocity in the massive reservoir in front of the dam, is thought to be potentially very serious. Downstream effects on the middle Chang Jiang Basin in terms of changes in water discharge, sedimentation rates, and nutrients for aquatic life are also possible problems. The possibility of a wholesale failure of the dam, as a result of structural failure or a military attack, should also be considered, because the resulting flood and subsequent destruction and loss of life would be of unimaginable proportions. While no one outside the government really knows, some foreign experts estimate that the eventual cost of the project could reach US$50 billion.

THE XI JIANG

Of China's three major rivers, the Xi Jiang (West River) is the smallest in length and size of drainage basin, but its position on China's southern coast and the influence on it of the summer monsoon give it a larger discharge than the Huang He. It also serves as an important inland waterway for the rich Pearl River Delta. The Xi Jiang and its tributaries drain 448,000 km^2, an area that supports more than 115 million people. The river and its tributaries provide an easily accessible and almost limitless supply of water for irrigation and urban or industrial purposes to the many major cities of the Pearl River Delta and China's southeast coast. The Pearl River Delta is one of China's fastest growing urban and industrial regions, and conflicts over water use, pitting farmers against urban and industrial concerns, are increasing.

Climatological Patterns and Resources

Climate is as much a part of China's resource base as its land and subsurface resources. Moisture and radiation patterns are quite varied across the nation. Northern areas tend to be dry, with distinct seasons much like the temperate regions of the United States. The more humid southern parts of China are generally monsoonal in character. Precipitation

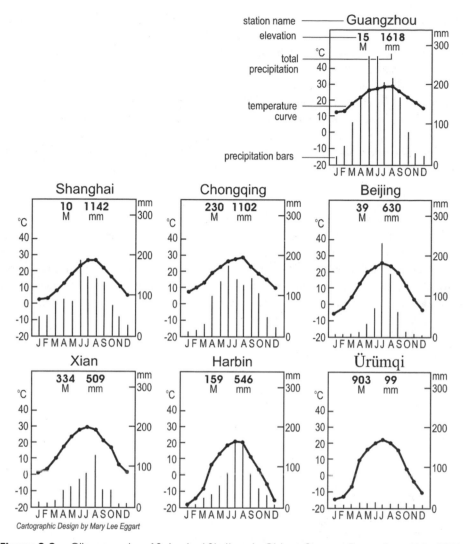

Figure 2.2.   Climagraphs of Selected Stations in China. *Source:* Pannell and Ma 1983

tends to concentrate in the spring and summer months. Figure 2.2 provides typical rainfall and precipitation rates for a selection of China's major cities.

Many parts of southern China, represented by Shanghai and Guangzhou (Canton) in figure 2.2, record around 1,500 mm of rain annually.

In contrast, 500–650 mm of precipitation is common throughout much of North and Northeast China (e.g., Shenyang, Beijing; Zhang and Lin 1992). Without irrigation water, much of North and Northeast China is of marginal utility for intensive agriculture. At present, water shortages are a serious environmental handicap in the improvement and continued development of sustainable agriculture systems throughout the North and West. A report published by the World Bank in 2001 (*Economist* 2005) notes that one in three rural Chinese lacks access to safe drinking water, and more than one hundred large cities are "severely" short of water. The solution of the past fifty years, ever-expanding irrigation systems and deeper and deeper well drilling, has brought the water crisis to a head. In 2005, per capita water resources in Beijing was a very low 300 m³. Further, as discussed in chapter 8, irrigated rice production in the Northeast (Dongbei) has increased faster than in any part of China. Defying ecological logic, northernmost Heilongjiang is now a major rice-producing province. The use of irrigation has also expanded on the North China Plain, and the water table there is falling in many locations as consumption rapidly outpaces replacement through precipitation. In part, support for the water-transfer projects discussed earlier is due to these shortages and to the looming threat of extensive arable land loss due to widespread salinization.

Western China has an even more severe annual moisture deficit, with annual rainfall in some areas averaging a mere 100 mm (see figure 2.2). Initially, most of the settlements in far western China developed around sources of reliable ground water. At present, efforts to capitalize on Xinjiang's long growing season and the intense radiation associated with cloud-free skies (no moisture), has led a drive to expand irrigation through melt-water transfers and tube-well irrigation. Cotton and fruit production has expanded dramatically, and there is considerable concern among China's ecologists that groundwater reserves are being depleted too quickly throughout the Northwest (Zhang and Lin 1992). As oil production and refining has also increased in Xinjiang, so have water shortages (see photo 2.2).

Temperature regimes in China typically vary by north–south location, although there are some deviations from this pattern south of the 16°C isotherm (map 2.7).

Photo 2.2. Desert encroaching on a stand of trees in the northern edge of the Taklamakan Desert in Xinjiang Autonomous Region, 2002. Photo by Gregory Veeck

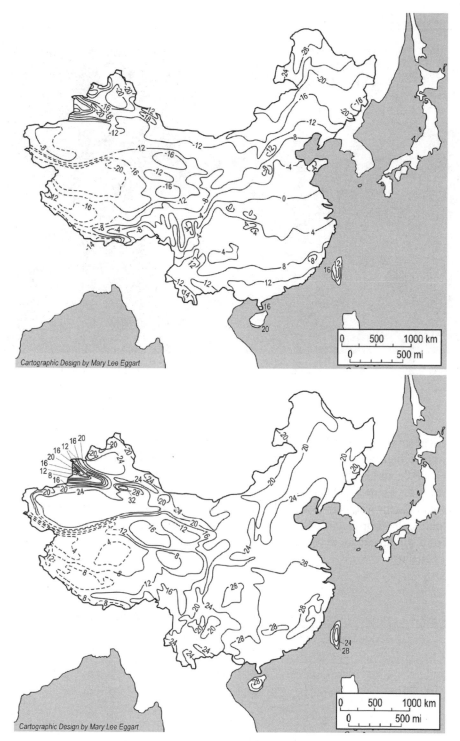

Map 2.7. China's Mean Temperature (°C) in January (top) and July (bottom).
Source: Zhang and Lin 1992, 38, 47. Cartographic design by Mary Lee Eggart

Photo 2.3.   Canal feeding into the Grand Canal in Suzhou, 2002. Photo by Gregory Veeck

South of this isotherm, which runs roughly along an east–west axis, average annual temperature is high, with generally mild winters and sufficient precipitation (see photo 2.3). The middle and lower Chang Jiang Basin region has similarly hot summers and mild winters (see figure 2.2, Shanghai). South of the Chang Jiang, average temperatures increase gradually as one moves south into the tropical coastal areas. North of the 16°C isotherm, the drop in average annual temperature is steeper, and the effects of a continental climate are more prominent (see table 2.2 and climate data for Beijing, Xi'an, and Harbin).

Table 2.2.   Temperature and Precipitation for Selected Chinese Cities

City	January Temp. °C	July Temp. °C	Annual Average	January Precip. (mm)	July Precip. (mm)	Annual Total (mm)
Beijing	−5.4	27.3	12.9	12.2	128.6	338.9
Chongqing	8.3	27.2	18.8	40.2	92.9	814.8
Guangzhou	15.4	28.2	22.5	67.3	415.4	2,678.9
Harbin	−22.8	24.5	4.8	7.1	146.8	385.2
Shanghai	5.9	29.7	17.2	105.9	80.9	1,276.8
Ürümqi	−11.8	23.4	7.7	25.9	61.7	277.7
Wuhan	4.7	31.8	18.0	106.9	39.6	899.8
Xi'an	1.1	29.1	15.0	13.6	96.6	405.9

Source: National Bureau of Statistics 2004, 11.

Soils of China

Soils are an extremely important, if overlooked, resource for a major agricultural country such as China, and greater efforts must be made in China to protect these vital resources. Vegetative and climatic factors are most important in soil formation. Soil formation is dependent on the nature of the underlying rock type or *parent material*, seasonal temperatures, the amount of rainfall and drainage, and the character of the relief on which the soils are formed. The unusual effects of more than twenty-five centuries of cultivation on some of China's soils must also be considered. In China, more than in any other nation, *anthropogenic* (human-induced) effects associated with wet-rice cultivation and terrace construction have formed distinct and extensive groups of soils that are rare in most other temperate nations.

China is fortunate in having a large and diverse stock of soils that are suitable for intensive agricultural development. Equally significant is China's long peasant tradition of manipulating and improving the available soil in order to increase agricultural output. In large part, it is this tradition of intensive cultivation on paddy and terrace that led the Chinese to develop their own classification system, a system that allows greater differentiation among types of anthropogenic soils, or *Anthrosols*. Given the unique characteristics of the order of Anthrosols, it is interesting to look briefly at their classification in the Chinese system, which is more refined than the systems used in other nations, because these soils have been more important to the Chinese both in the past and at the present time.

Anthrosols can be broken down into two suborders: *Hydragic Anthrosols* and *Dryagic Anthrosols*. The suborder Hydragic includes soils that are submerged for a significant portion of each year (e.g., for rice production). The period of annual inundation and the length of cultivation impact the resulting soils differently according to their parent material and the volume of compost that has been applied. Annual field inundation periods vary by available radiation, water supply, and the frost-free period. Variations result in very different types of anthropogenic soils with different concentration of metals in the *gley* layer (a level of soil or *pan* below the surface cultivation zone that ultimately retains the water due to its high clay content; Xu, Yanchun Lu, Yuanchang Lu, and Zhu 1980). For example, farmers in the Lake Tai region of southern Jiangsu and northern Zhejiang provinces have used an anaerobic, water-logged composting system (*oufei*) since before the Song dynasty (A.D. 960). Denied oxygen by a more than two-hundred-day submergence in water, composted material is reduced to ammonium—the ideal fertilizer for paddy rice. Sadly, as farmers in this emerging industrial area concentrate on factory work, composting rates have declined along with the natural fertility of the soils, and the excessive amounts of inorganic fertilizers used extensively in their stead result in polluted runoff and eutrophication in lakes, rivers, and canals (Zhao 1986).

The second suborder, the Dryagic (Orthic) Anthrosols, is less intuitive. There are four groups within this suborder, designed to incorporate dryland soils (or periodically irrigated dry crops) that have been terraced or subjected to heavy applications of manure, compost, and crop residue over long periods of time. These soils, which receive less attention in the academic literature than paddy soils, tend to be located in the old farming regions of North China or in hilly areas in the South and Southwest. Over the decades, the high level of composting in these dryland soils has also altered their soil structure and chemistry to the extent that they no longer fit into traditional classifications of natural soils.

At the macrolevel, China's soils can be differentiated in a manner that correlates to the country's different climates and vegetation, that is, to the high or dry western and northwestern regions, the humid central and southeastern regions, and a zone of transition between the two (see map 2.8). In general, this basic regionalization follows a

I East-Southeat Udic Soil Division
I-1 Boric Luvisols and Udic Isohumisols dominant
I-2 Udic Luvisols and Aquic Cambisols dominant
I-3 Hydragic Anthrosols and Udic Luvisols
I-4 Udic Ferrisols and Perudic Cambisols dominant
I-5 Udic Ferrisols and Ferralisols dominant

II Central Ustic Soil Division
II-1 Ustic Isohumisols and Ustic Sandic Entisols dominant
II-2 Loessal or Orthic Entisols, Ustic Luvisols
II-3 Ustic Isohumisols and Ustic Cambisols

III Northwest Aridic Soil Division
III-1 Cyric Cambisols and Halosols dominant
III-2 Mixed Aridisols and Halosols dominant
III-3 Orthic Aridisols dominant
III-4 Cyric Aridisols dominant

Map 2.8. China's Soils. **Source:** Simplified from Gong Zitong 1999, 860–70. Cartographic design by Mary Lee Eggart

fundamental division in soil science based on processes of soil chemistry (Gong 1999). One process concerns calcium and magnesium carbonate concentration (pedocal formation) in dryer areas. The other process involves leaching and eluviation of aluminum and iron oxides from the upper part of the soil and the deposition and concentration of these oxides (pedalfer formation) in the subsoil. This latter process is common in more humid areas of southern, central, and eastern China. There are many further refinements and complicating factors, which become important in considering subregions within each zone. Gong (1999) divides China into three macroregions: the Southeast Udic (moist) Soil Division (*Dongnan Bu Shirun Turang Quhua*), the Central Ustic (transitional with limited moisture) Soil Division (*Zhongbu Ganrun Turang Quhua*), and the Northwest Aridic Soil Division (*Xibei Bu Ganhan Turang Quhua*; see map 2.8). The Udic division (41.6 percent of national area) typically includes soils that occur in climates with well-distributed rainfall or areas where summer rainfall plus stored moisture equals or exceeds evaporation. The Ustic transitional zone (22.7 percent of national area) typically features soils formed under circumstances dryer than for most of the soils found in the Ustic division, but with sufficient moisture for the regular cultivation of crops in most years. Finally, the Aridic division (35.7 percent of national area) incorporates the driest areas of West and Northwest China where soil formation is severely hampered by limited moisture.

The Natural Vegetation of China

China, as befits a large country that stretches from 18°N to 53°N latitude, has a great range of natural vegetation. Included in this range are most of the vegetative types native to the Northern Hemisphere except for those varieties found in arctic regions. For example, in Hainan Island and along the southern coastal littoral of the country are tropical rain forests and other plants indigenous to the tropics. In the high mountains of western China and Tibet, alpine and subalpine plant communities may be found. The rest of the country holds vegetation communities common to deserts, steppes, savannas, prairie meadows, or coniferous evergreen and deciduous forests (see map 2.9).

Generally, the classification of vegetation in China can be first grossly divided between a humid South and East China and a dry North and West China along the lines for rainfall surplus and deficiency discussed previously. The eastern humid region of the country must be further subdivided into a tropical southern area that supports a tropical rainforest; a subtropical southern and central area of broad-leaved evergreens, pines, and many varieties of bamboo; and a humid but cooler North and Northeast where evergreen conifers and other northern deciduous species such as birch are common.

In discussing natural vegetation in China, it is useful to remember that in the densely populated eastern part of the country, which has been settled for thousands of years, it is now actually somewhat difficult to identify native vegetation. China's farmers have been hard at work for several millennia cutting and burning trees, shrubs, and grasses and farming the cleared fields. In addition, new species from other portions of China and Asia have been introduced extensively for slope stabilization and forestry, as well as for cultivation. Fuel for cooking and heat has long been scarce, especially in North

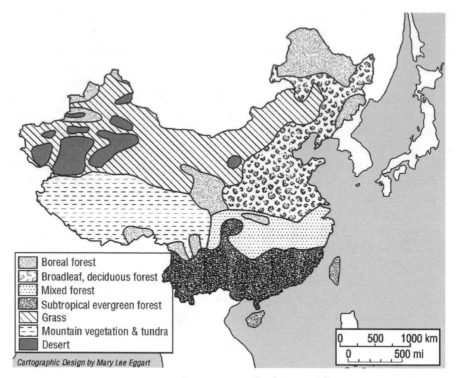

Map 2.9. China's Major Vegetation Types. **Source:** Pannell and Ma 1983, 34. Cartographic design by Mary Lee Eggart

China, and the local peasants have devastated forests and grasslands in their search for both fuel and construction materials (see Coggins 2003 for an excellent case study). Great pressure has been placed on forest resources, therefore, altering their original vegetation. Most remaining old-growth forests are in the Northeast, in the Daxing'an and Xiaoxing'an mountain chains, but there are scattered reserves such as in the Wuyi Mountains of Fujian in the Southeast. The commercial forests first extensively exploited after 1949 are also found in the Northeast, but in the last twenty years commercial timber operations have gradually shifted to the southern portions of the nation where longer growing seasons increase annual production by a factor of two or three. The great forests of the Northeast represent a significant portion of China's remaining old-growth forests. There are also a few much smaller reserves scattered throughout the Southeast.

International support and funding for forest biopreserves in Heilongjiang province has played a critical role in the protection of these areas. Fantastic stands of conifers, birch, ash, and other northern species are still found on the picturesque slopes of the mountains that rim the Northeast Plain (see photo 2.4). Logging bans, increasingly stringent in the past decade, may protect the forests for posterity, but unemployment in the region is as high as in any rural area in China. Conservation, while a good idea, creates a hard and bitter life for many of the unemployed loggers and related workers in cities such as Yichun, the once-heralded "Wood City" sited within the foothills of the Xiaoxing'an Mountains. There are also fairly extensive areas of old-growth forests

Photo 2.4. Fenglin Forest Preserve in northern Heilongjiang province, 1998. Photo by Gregory Veeck

in Tibet, western Sichuan, and Yunnan. It is no accident that most of these areas may be characterized as poor and isolated. This isolation, although a major impediment to improving the living standards and economies of such places, has also protected their forests to an extent not possible in more accessible areas.

In eastern China, Chinese researchers have identified four main vegetational zones from south to north: (1) tropical forests and savanna, (2) subtropical evergreen forests extending north to the Chang Jiang and west to the Qinghai-Tibet Plateau, (3) mainly deciduous forests extending from the Chang Jiang far northward to the Song-Nen Plain, and (4) taiga in the Heilong Jiang Basin. In general, plant communities change with their location from south to north as well as with elevation. However, tropical-plant communities are found as far north as 28°N in the river valleys of Yunnan province and southeastern Tibet. Likewise the Sichuan Basin, characterized by a humid, mild climate and associated thermophilic plant species, does not exhibit the vegetation regimes suggested by its latitude.

The dry, western part of the country is similar to Central Asia, a land of very dry deserts, grasslands, and steppe, again mostly at great elevation. Its vegetation is monotonous and is composed predominantly of several species of grasses and hardy shrubs. The composition of its flora and the character of its vegetation along with its ecological conditions permit dividing this vast region into three major vegetation zones: (1) Mongolia, (2) Dzungaria and the Tarim Basin, and (3) Tibet.

Within these three zones, the flora varies according to local ecological conditions and altitude rather than as a result of shifts in location north and south. Thus, trees will be found where precipitation is greatest and average annual temperatures permit their growth. For example, extensive forests of spruce, birch, ash, and aspen may be found on the windward northern slopes of the Tian Shan, which rise to more than 7,000 m in height. There is, however, great variation in the extent and type of tree cover owing to differences in terrain and climate. At higher elevations and in drier steppe locations, a variety of grasses and sedges are common throughout western China. Ecologically, the most severe region in western China is the western part of the Tibetan upland, a high, cold desert over 4,500 m ASL.

Regional Challenges to Sustainable Development and Resource Use

EASTERN CHINA

An interesting and significant feature of China's physical and cultural landscape is that most of its people are concentrated in the eastern third of the country. This relates partly to the availability of sufficient water for intensive agriculture, particularly in Central and southern China. The agricultural environment in eastern China also prospered from the extensive flat and low-lying alluvial plains in Central, North, and Northeast China and the Pearl River Delta. In turn, the economy at large has benefited from capital flows derived from agricultural surplus and a high return on transportation investments in the alluvial plains precisely because the land there is flat, the roads are cheaply constructed, and much of the soil is fertile due to many thousands of years of flooding. The alluvial plains of the Huang He, Huai, Chang, and Xi rivers and their tributaries constitute China's greatest agricultural resource.

Most of China's greatest cities are located in eastern China, and are within rich agricultural areas. As these cities and their associated transport systems grow rapidly in the reform era, however, much high-productivity cropland is being lost. National environmental protection laws enacted in the late 1980s have helped to stem this loss, but as noted earlier, enforcement is weak and politically difficult when jobs are at risk.

SOUTHWEST CHINA

In contrast to eastern China and the Sichuan Basin, many other areas of China are not especially suitable for intensive settlement and development. The latter includes extensive areas of karstic limestone found in southwestern China (see photo 2.5). Other locations throughout the world possess similar features, but nowhere is the tower karst as extensive, nor is the impact of humans on these landscapes as long established, far-reaching, and striking. Covering much of the area of the three southern provinces of Guangxi, Guizhou, and Yunnan are massive beds of limestone, or *karst*, created when the entire region was part of the southern oceans. These karstic landscapes have been dissolved and eroded by very high annual temperatures and frequently extreme precipitation events. The result is some of the most beautiful and bizarre karstic landscape found

Photo 2.5. Karst (limestone) landscape in Guangxi Autonomous Region (near Liuzhou City) in Southwest China, 1996. Photo by Gregory Veeck

anywhere in the world. Limestone towers and domes abound, with some rising 200 m above base level. These are the major terrain features of the Southwest. Other specialized karst features, such as *dolines* (solution valleys), sinkholes, caves, and underground watercourses, are also present. The scenery is spectacular, but as is often the case, this remote yet beautiful and rugged environment also signifies considerable poverty. To be farmed the steep terrain must be terraced, or alternately, farming must be confined to the narrow stream valleys. Soils throughout are geologically new and thin, with low levels of organic material and nitrogen, except in the river bottoms. But even where the landscape is level or near level, it is difficult to keep water on the surface because of the solubility of the limestone. Enough level land amid the mountain systems within the karstic region is available nonetheless to support a modest level of agricultural development and population density. Particularly since 1978, tourism has become an important mainstay of many local economies here, but the long-term environmental impact of mass tourism on the region is only now being systematically studied.

NORTHEAST CHINA

Although the Han Chinese have occupied and farmed most of Northeast China for less than one hundred years, agricultural and industrial development and population growth in the area have been very rapid during the reform era, especially in the two southern provinces of Liaoning and Jilin. The Northeast's major port city, Dalian, has increased in size many times over as capital from nearby Korea and Japan has poured into the city for industrial joint ventures. Increased industrial production has taken people from the land, and at the same time the region's farms have increased in size and efficiency. The state farms that mostly disappeared from the rest of China with the end of the commune era in 1978–1979 remain quite important in the Northeast. Wheat, corn, barley, millet, gaoliang (sorghum), and soybeans are grown on farms of thousands of hectares on the calcium- and humus-rich *Isohumisols* and *Luvisols* (the *chernozems* in the Russian system). In the northern province of Heilongjiang, however, much of the arable land still remains under grass or tree cover. A very active land reclamation program (particularly in the Sanjiang Plain), which began slowly in the 1950s, has recently clashed with a growing ecological protection agenda that has increasing domestic support both within and beyond government agencies. Certain areas have already benefited from designation as national biopreserves, and in 1991 UNESCO recognized the 18,000 ha Fenglin Forest Preserve as such a site. As ecological research increases, it is hoped that sustainable agricultural developments can coexist with nearby protected environments. Again, it is vital that China use regulation and enforcement to preserve its scarce natural land for future generations.

WESTERN CHINA: XINJIANG, QINGHAI, AND TIBET

The western Chinese regions of Xinjiang, Qinghai, and the Tibetan Highlands account for about half of China's area. Western China is a land of extremes, of very high mountains and plateaus, great basins, and arid deserts. Its physical features, however, offer extremely serious environmental problems for human occupancy and sustained agricultural development. A large portion of this region—the Tarim, Junggar, and Qaidam basins as well as much of northern and western Tibet—are extremely dry. Seasonal rivers fueled briefly each year from snowmelt and the occasional intense rain drain to the centers of these basins. The headwaters of several great rivers—the Huang He, Chang Jiang, Mekong, Salween, Brahmaputra, and Indus originate on the eastern and southern faces of the Tibetan Plateau.

Xinjiang's most imposing physical feature is the Tarim Basin, one of the driest places on earth. Rimmed by tall mountains, most of the basin is uninhabited desert (*Takla Makan*) with very little vegetation. Only along the foothills of the bordering mountains is there opportunity for human occupancy. This is due to the presence of mountain streams fed by snowmelt and to the easily worked alluvial soils that fan out into the basins for short distances. North of the Tarim Basin, the Tian Shan rise to elevations over 7,000 m ASL. Noteworthy among the growth centers of this region has been Ürümqi (Urumchi), an administrative and industrial city of 1.6 million now refining much of the oil in the region and surrounded by a thriving, irrigated-oasis farming system. Based on improved control and management of streams that empty from the adjacent mountains, extensive land reclamation and cropping have proceeded throughout the southern and western margins of the Junggar Basin. (See Toops 2004 for an excellent summary of Xinjiang.)

The Tibetan Highlands (including the Tibet Autonomous Region and Qinghai province) represents more than one-quarter of China's area. Three main physical divisions make up these highlands. The first of these, the large Qianzang Region in the North and West, is an area of mountain ranges, valleys, and plains. Owing to its great elevation, coldness, and aridity, most of this region has only sparse vegetation and human habitation. Second are the alluvial river valleys of the South and Southeast, generally with elevations below 4,000 m, that contain most of the developed farmland and much of the Tibetan population. Here along the Yarlung Zangbo (Brahmaputra) River and its tributaries is the heartland of Tibet and its capital, Lhasa. The third division comprises the older districts of Tibet that are now located outside the boundaries of the autonomous region and include the grasslands in Qinghai province and the rugged mountain systems in western Sichuan and northwestern Yunnan. Although much capital has been invested in building roads in the southwestern mountains, this has been aimed at territorial integration through spatial linkages rather than at extensive agricultural development. The Tibetan Highlands are likely to remain marginally developed and sparsely populated. Isolation and the region's rugged environment offer little incentive for significant investment and developmental commitment. Programs directed at poverty alleviation have centered on improvements to infrastructure and the introduction of new varieties of spring wheat and local traditional crops.

Conclusion

China's physical environments are exceptionally diverse, but much of China is also ecologically fragile. Current challenges to long-term national development can only be understood if this fragility is taken to heart. This is not environmental determinism, but recognition of the simple fact that the land is the foundation for all that follows. In less-populated, land-extensive nations such as Australia, Canada, and the United States, significantly lower population pressure limits the use of the most marginal ecological regions, and much of these are given over to national parks. In contrast, despite the dangers of continued exploitation of these regions, China will probably press ahead, simply because there are few alternatives. Efforts to develop these peripheral lands have many implications, and many environmentalists bemoan the seemingly relentless onslaught of development in these fragile environments.

However, there is more reason for optimism at the present time than at any time in the past five decades. There is a growing awareness worldwide that resources must be used more effectively, and many manufacturing processes and agricultural technologies (including forestry and range-land management) have been transformed with an eye toward lower costs and greater efficiency in resource use. There is a growing awareness among China's leaders that further growth must be sustainable. Of course, the future is uncertain, but at the beginning of the new millennia, the costs of previous mistakes and growth-at-any-cost policies are clearly apparent. The costs of reversing environmental damage from decades of careless actions now often exceed the benefits of these short-sighted activities. Many of China's leaders recognize this simple but powerful economic fact, and support environmental protection.

Despite its current problems, China's recent efforts in environmental protection should not be dismissed out of hand. Rapid economic development can be more blessing than curse, if greater prosperity results in greater awareness and in expenditures directed at protecting the environment and replacing dated technologies. On the other hand, massive public works such as the Three Gorges project raise parallel questions about China's long-term priorities. A prosperity based on environmental exploitation in the absence of sustainable practices will be short-lived.

References Cited

Coggins, Chris. 2003. *The Tiger and the Pangolin: Nature, Culture, and Conservation in China.* Honolulu: University of Hawai'i Press.

Economist. 2005. China and water: Drying UP. May 21, 46.

Edmonds, R. L. 1994. *Patterns of China's Lost Harmony: A Survey of the Country's Environmental Degradation and Protection.* New York: Routledge.

Gong Zitong, ed. 1999. *Zhongguo turang xitong fenlei* [Chinese soil classification system]. Beijing: Science Press.

McElroy, Michael, Chris P. Nielson, and Peter Lydon, eds. 1998. *Energizing China: Reconciling Environmental Protection and Economic Growth.* Cambridge, Mass.: Harvard University Committee on Environment.

National Bureau of Statistics. 2004. *Zhongguo tongji nianjian 2004* [China statistical yearbook 2004]. Beijing: China Statistics Press.

Nickum, James E. 1998. Is China living on the water margin? *China Quarterly* 156 (December).

Pannell, Clifton W., and Laurence J. C. Ma. 1983. *China: The Geography of Development and Modernization.* New York: Halsted Press.

Ren, Mei'e, Renzhang Yang, and Haosheng Bao, eds. 1985. *An Outline of China's Physical Geography.* Beijing: Foreign Language Press.

Smil, Vaclav. 1984. *The Bad Earth: Environmental Degradation in China.* Armonk, N.Y.: M.E. Sharpe.

———. 1993. *China's Environment: An Inquiry into the Limits of National Development.* Armonk, N.Y.: M.E. Sharpe.

Toops, Stanley. 2004. Demographics and Development in Xinjiang after 1949. Washington, D.C.: East-West Center Washington working paper. Project on Internal Conflicts.

Wu Yuanli. 1973. *China: A Handbook.* New York: Praeger.

Xu, Qi, Yanchun Lu, Yuanchang Lu, and Hongguan Zhu. 1980. *The Paddy Soil of Tai-hu Region in China.* Shanghai: Shanghai Scientific and Technical.

Zhang, Jiacheng, and Zhiguang Lin. 1992. *Climate of China.* Trans. Ding Tan. New York: Wiley.

Zhao, Songqiao. 1986. *Physical Geography of China.* New York: Wiley.

———. 1994. *Geography of China: Environment, Resources, Population, and Development.* New York: Wiley.

Zhonghua renmin gongheguo dituce [Atlas of China]. 1983. In Chinese.

CHAPTER 3

Ancient Roots and Binding Traditions

HISTORICAL GEOGRAPHIES OF CHINA

In considering China's contemporary development from a geographic perspective, it is important to start with the simple fact that China's present is based on the nation's long and complex history. This chapter reviews China's past in light of the two interrelated, principal themes described in the introduction: spatial organization of people and activities in China and the implications of human-environment interactions throughout China's long history. Through the centuries, the complex tapestry woven from these interactions and implications has influenced how society and polity were organized, how both functioned over time, how environments were exploited differently across both space and time, and how the production of goods and services took place. China's history extends from a time when the territory was shared by hundreds of kingdoms to that when it was an empire, then a nation, and finally to today with the country's present status as an emerging global power.

Early Humans in China

The origins of China and the Chinese people are not as clear as one might think given that China's civilization has long been studied and venerated for its age, sophistication, and achievements. The territory that is now China was home to at least three distinct Neolithic cultures and probably more. The archaeological record remains surprisingly incomplete for many regions. While many questions remain, it is clear from archaeological finds and related evidence in *palynology* (the study and analysis of pollen samples) that prehistoric humans, initially *Homo erectus* and later *Homo sapiens sapiens,* lived and maintained a presence over extensive areas of contemporary China for at least 1.5 million years (Wu and Poirier 1995). Most archaeologists feel that additional archaeological sites will be discovered within Chinese territory as more time and resources are devoted to larger-scale systematic excavations. China's prehistory, then, is still a story in progress. Pleistocene hominids of one type or another have been found in twenty-three of China's thirty provinces, or first-order administrative regions. The earliest recognized *Homo erectus* fossils found in the Yuanmou Basin in Yunnan province in Southwest China are dated to 1.7 million years ago. A considerable number of other Paleolithic sites have also been found in southern Yunnan and the surrounding provinces of Sichuan and Guizhou,

43

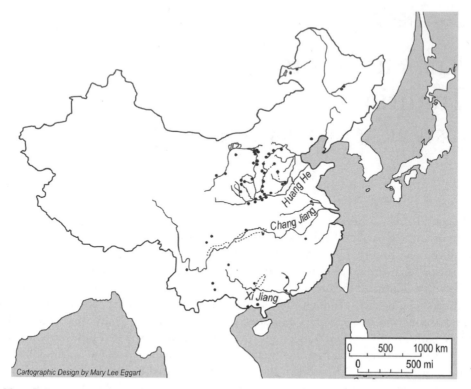

Map 3.1. China's Paleolithic Sites. **Source:** Fumiko Ikawa-Smith, 1978. Cartographic design by Mary Lee Eggart

but there are also important sites in northern China. Major finds, with skeletal evidence in combination with worked stone tools, have been located in Yunxian county, Hubei province; Lantian county, Shaanxi province; Hexian county, Anhui province; Nanjing City (Tangshan Zhen), Jiangsu province; and perhaps most famously, in the caves of Zhoukoudian, which are only 50 km from Beijing (see map 3.1). It is clear that within what is now currently held Chinese territory, there were a number of diverse cultures evolving simultaneously. Less clear are the nature and distribution of common ancestors among these peoples, the times of their separations, and their relationships (genetic and cultural).

A common mistake is to assume the Chinese and Chinese culture emerged from some single ethnic stock, the origins of which could be linked to a particular place and time. But rather than attesting to such a commonality, the evidence points to a pattern in which over time, many distinct groups were blended and absorbed into the composite that we now think of as the people of the Han—named for the dynasty that constituted one of China's golden eras. This blending and amalgamation would be far less complete in the absence of the dynastic system for which China is famous. Military conquest and territorial expansion, however, were but the most visible forces leading to this homogenization. Commerce, exploration, and even religious pilgrimages that fostered the spread of Buddhism all worked to integrate the peoples of China.

Considering China's many environments, the diverse use of plants and animals by early humans throughout China should come as no surprise. Throughout the dynastic era, when new crops, agricultural techniques, methods of manufacture, medicines, architectural designs, or livestock breeds were developed in one region, they were quickly dispersed throughout the empire by imperial bulletins, ambitious court officials, and traders seeking profits. In this sense, it was not until the march of the dynasties that Chinese culture began to approximate the present. And the very foundations of this flexible system of human-environment relations came from the diverse practices of the ancient peoples of the Pleistocene.

As it was in Europe and North America, the Pleistocene epoch in China was a time of dramatic change in many of the country's natural environments. Major natural changes included tectonic shifts and mountain building, changes in climatic cycles with several associated periods of extensive glaciation, and major cycles in fluvial activity with distinct large-scale erosion and sedimentary periods. The Chinese Pleistocene was characterized by several periods of climatic fluctuation accompanied by related changes in landforms, flora, and fauna. Four major cold-moist stages were involved, and these correlated to periods of glacial advance in all the highland areas of northern China.

Although there is some debate about the conditions following the final Pleistocene stage, available palynological evidence indicates a gradual warming trend matched with a considerable increase in precipitation. More rainfall resulted in more erosion, deposition, and the initiation of sedimentary cycles that dramatically altered the topography. During this period, much of the North China Plain (see map 3.2) was either marsh or deltaic swamp. The Shandong Highlands at this time formed a series of islands separated from the Chinese mainland either by the sea or by a series of intermittent saline marshes and lakes. This *ecotone* (the margin between two distinct ecological zones) was ideal for settlement because it provided a wide diversity of useful plants and animals to the early settlers of the region and the areas immediately westward that became the cradle of Chinese civilization.

China's Neolithic Period

The transition from gathering and hunting to the cultivation of plants and the domestication of animals was a turning point in many ancient human societies. The domestication of animals and the adoption of sedentary farming practices and permanent settlement increased the reliability of food supplies and led to food surpluses, which allowed for the specialization of labor. Such specialization was crucial for human progress, and it permitted human groups to turn their energy and creativity to other activities including the construction of cities and states.

Initially, some scholars were convinced that China did not have an indigenous civilization based on the independent development of agriculture (Smartt and Simmonds

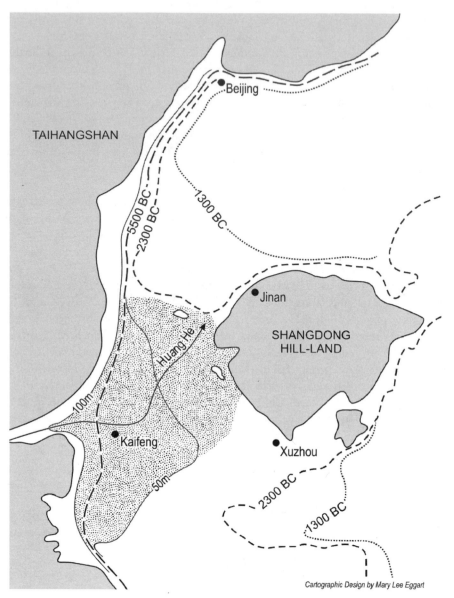

Map 3.2. Deposition and Geological Formation of the North China Plain. **Source:** After Pannell and Ma 1983, 46. Cartographic design by Mary Lee Eggart

1995). For some years it was incorrectly believed that diffusion from western Asia had brought agriculture comparatively late to North China (Fairbank and Goldman 1998, 29). Since the 1940s however, enough new archaeological evidence has been assembled from North China to establish at least one independent center of Chinese agrarian civilization in the region known as Zhongyuan (Central Plain) in the middle Huang He and Wei He basins. More recently, two other areas of China (the southern coastal area

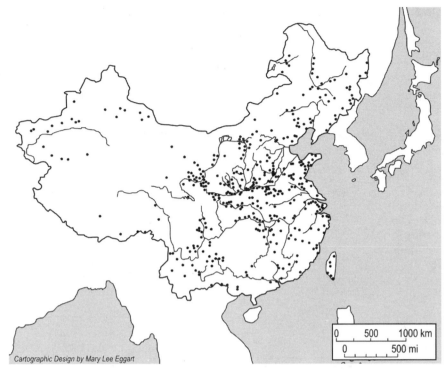

Map 3.3. China's Neolithic Sites. *Source:* Yo Weichao, ed., *A Journey into China's Antiquity*, vol. 1 (Beijing: Morning Glory, 1997), 101. Cartographic design by Mary Lee Eggart

of Taiwan, Fujian, and Guangdong; and Guangxi and the Pacific coastal area stretching from Shandong south to Zhejiang) have been identified as probable loci of other early independent agrarian civilizations (see map 3.3). As the distances between these areas of China might suggest, the prevailing view in Chinese archaeology and prehistory is that the Neolithic farming revolution and its related cultures developed in these three regions at approximately the same time. What remains to be determined are the kinds of interrelationships and linkages that may have existed among parallel groupings of Neolithic development in China. In addition to Zhongyuan, other important Neolithic sites discovered in China include sites related to the Qingliangang culture of the Pacific seaboard and the Dapenkeng culture of the Huai River Basin of Shandong and northern Jiangsu provinces.

Of the three ancient Neolithic cultures in China, the best-known and most important with respect to tracing the earliest threads of Chinese culture to the present is the Yangshao culture of the middle Huang He and Wei He basins (the Zhongyuan region). Based on archaeological records, Yangshao culture appeared by 5000 B.C., and may have existed considerably earlier. Yangshao culture has traditionally been regarded as the source of much of what eventually would come be known as Chinese civilization. In support of this view, it was from this region that the first recorded dynasties sprang

Table 3.1. Population Estimates of Major Chinese Dynasties and Periods

Xia (Possibly Apocryphal)	ca. 2200–1766 B.C.	Population in Millions*
Shang	1766–1122 B.C.**	not estimated
Zhou	1122–221 B.C.	not estimated
Spring and Autumn	722–481 B.C.	not estimated
Warring States	452–221 B.C.	not estimated
Qin	221–206 B.C.	not estimated
Han	206 B.C.–A.D. 220	59.6 (A.D. 2)
Wei, Jin, and Northern and Southern dynasties	A.D. 220–581	16.2 (A.D. 280)
Sui	A.D. 581–618	46.0 (A.D. 606)
Tang	A.D. 618–907	52.9 (A.D. 2)
Five Dynasties and Ten Kingdoms	A.D. 907–959	not estimated
Northern Song	A.D. 960–1126	25.0 (A.D. 1110)
Southern Song	A.D. 1126–1279	not estimated
Yuan (Mongol)	A.D. 1271–1368	58.9 (A.D. 1290)
Ming	A.D. 1368–1644	59.9 (A.D. 1381); 63.7 (A.D. 1562)
Qing	A.D. 1644–1911	102.8 (A.D. 1753); 377.6 (A.D. 1887)
Republic of China	1912–1949	474.8 (1928)
People's Republic of China (PRC)	1949–Present	541.4 (1949) 1.3 billion (2005)

* Estimates prior to 1949 are often widely variable. These are from Zhao 1994.
** Estimates for the beginning of Shang vary widely. The earliest estimate is Zhao 1994, and the later is Sivin 1988.
Sources: Zhao 1994; National Bureau of Statistics 2004; Sivin 1988.

and grew: the apocryphal Xia (ca. 2200–1766 B.C.), the Shang (1766–1122 B.C.), and the Zhou (1122–221 B.C.; see table 3.1).

Yangshao culture was characterized by sedentary farming and village settlements scattered along the loess terraces found in the river valleys of the drainage basin of the middle Huang He. The main crop of the Yangshao cultivators was foxtail millet (*Setaria italica*). A variety of stone tools and implements were employed by Yangshao peoples, the most important of which were hoes, spades, digging sticks, and stone disks, probably for hammering. Knives, axes, adzes, and chisels were also important as well as distinctive pottery jars of many different types and designs, which were used for storing grain, a crucial function in times of agricultural surplus. The pottery was handmade and no evidence of potter's wheels has been found for this early period. Research on Yangshao artifacts indicates that much of the pottery was fired at temperatures approximating 1,000°C. The ability to control and maintain such temperatures within the kilns represents a significant technology.

The sedentary agriculture of Yangshao cultivators was heavily supplemented by wild-grain collecting, hunting, and fishing. Many settlements seem to have been discontinuously occupied, which would be in accordance with the slash-and-burn style of cultivation (resulting in plots known as *swidden*) that is evident at the village of Banpo near modern Xi'an, Shaanxi province (Roberts 1996, 3).

The Chinese Neolithic period extended from approximately 6000 B.C. to 3000 B.C., although the exact period varied from locale to locale. But it was at the next stage of development, commencing at approximately 3200 B.C., that broadly common cultural types emerged. These types are conventionally called *Longshanoid*, and they represent the forerunners of true Chinese civilization.

Longshan and Longshanoid Culture

The Neolithic archaeology of China becomes increasingly complex as it approaches and blends into recorded Chinese historical civilization, which began during the Shang dynasty (1766–1122 B.C.). The painted pottery of Yangshao culture, and the cultures this distinctive pottery represented, was gradually replaced starting around 3200 B.C. by Longshanoid black pottery produced on a potter's wheel. There are close linkages between newer Longshanoid or Longshan-type culture and features of the later Shang period, specifically in symbolism on pottery, the extensive use of oracle bones, and house and village-wall construction techniques.

Features of Longshanoid Culture

Longshanoid culture assemblages have been located in Shandong, Shanxi, and Shaanxi provinces, and along the lower reaches of the Huai and Chang (Yangtze) rivers as well as in several southeastern provinces (see map 3.4). Although these sites may vary in particulars, hence the distinction between "true" Longshan sites and those locations with only some Longshan culture artifacts (Longshan type), they share certain characteristics and features that have allowed their classification as Longshanoid assemblages.

First, all of these Longshanoid cultures were based on subsistence agriculture still supplemented to varying degrees by hunting, fishing, and gathering. Possible proof of rice cultivation has been found in areas of the central and southern region, but current evidence from Longshanoid and Yangshao culture sites suggests that rice cultivation was not important. Yangshao farming, specifically, was based mainly on millet cultivation.

Second, all Longshanoid sites include distinctive types of stone implements useful for carpentry and agriculture. In addition, very distinctive pottery remains have been uncovered that included such diagnostic forms as the *ding* (a tripod vessel for use over an open flame), the *dou* (a vessel with a distinctive ring-foot design), and the *gui* (a tripod jar with handles; see figure 3.1). As noted earlier, the potter's wheel is believed to have come into use in the Longshanoid period.

Finally, the various Longshanoid or Longshan-type cultures occupied distinctive and clear chronological niches that followed the Yangshao and blended into later Longshanoid assemblages. Thus a Longshan-type culture might have been more advanced at a specific time in one place or another, but a steady evolutionary chronology would have developed for each of the Longshanoid cultures. Longshan-type cultures appear to be the main and true prototypes for Chinese civilization as it emerged in the first

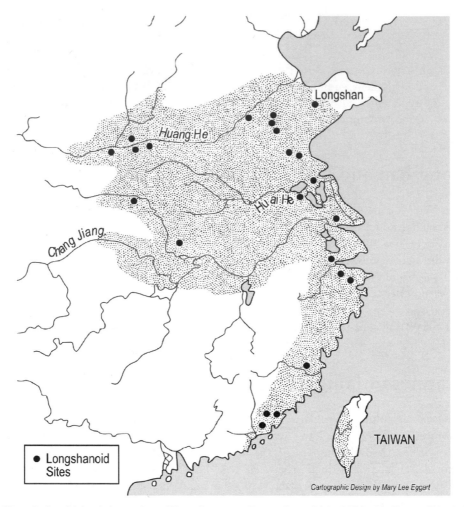

Map 3.4. China's Longshan Sites. **Sources:** Pannell and Ma 1983, 52; Zheng Wenlei 1997. Cartographic design by Mary Lee Eggart

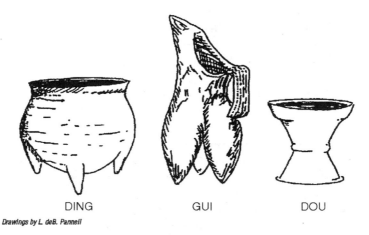

DING   GUI   DOU

Drawings by L. deB. Pannell

Figure 3.1. Examples of Longshanoid Pottery. **Source:** Pannell and Ma 1983. Drawings by L. deB. Pannell

historic period of the Shang dynasty. The occurrences of Longshanoid sites are frequent and common enough, and share a sufficient number of characteristics to indicate that a substantial population sharing this culture occupied a large area of the eastern part of China.

Historic China

The transformation from fragmented, localized, mixed economies based on rudimentary horticulture, hunting, and gathering to a formalized, clearly stratified social system with marked specialization of labor, and an administratively dominant urban center, apparently took place in China sometime between 3000 B.C. and 2000 B.C.

One of the greatest and most enduring figures in China's long cultural history is Huang Di, or the Yellow Emperor, of the fabled Xia dynasty, whose life was acknowledged by the famous Chinese historian Sima Qian in his volume, the Shiji (Historical Records). It is recorded that Huang Di ascended to the throne in 2697 B.C. Tradition holds that he developed writing, established codified rules of conduct, and created a military for enforcing his rule. Huang Di may be apocryphal, but it is important to note that socially stratified groups with a complex specialization of labor and living in spatially differentiated urban centers emerged at this time.

A legendary dynasty mentioned in records written long after its supposed existence, the Xia (ca. 2200–1766 B.C.) has been much discussed by historians, and remains within our idealized lineage of Chinese dynasties despite the lack of definitive archaeological evidence to support its existence as a true dynasty. Based on the presence of several large palace-style buildings of extraordinary size, scholars have suggested that the extensive ErliTou site on the middle reaches of the Huang He might have been the site of the capital of the Xia state. Until proper archaeological evidence is discovered, however, the Xia dynasty must remain a legend with undefined boundaries and uncertain tenancy.

Legend and archaeology do converge in the first archaeologically supported Chinese dynasty, the Shang. Recorded Chinese history begins ca. 1800 B.C. with the appearance of divination records in the form of oracle bones made from cattle and sheep scapula (shoulder blades), or tortoise plastrons (under-shells). It is on these artifacts that the earliest Chinese writing is found. As of 1996, more than 107,000 oracle bone pieces in eighty collections had been assigned to the Shang period (Roberts 1996, 8).

The Shang dynasty (1766–1122 B.C.; see table 3.1) was composed of an established lineage of rulers whose subjects occupied a definite territory (centered in northern Henan). Contemporary written records from a variety of sites support this fact, most importantly the records found at the city of Yin that served as the capital for the last twelve kings of the Shang. Other sites displaying similar material culture as that found in Shang dynasty territory, but spread across a much wider area of China that was clearly not under the control of the Shang kings (see map 3.5), are described as "Shang-type."

Not only did Chinese civilization emerge, in full, from the bloom of the Shang, but a combination of archaeological and textual supporting evidence gives historians a better understanding of the Shang state than they have of the states and kingdoms

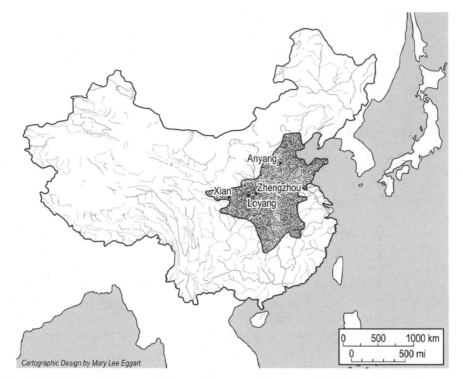

Map 3.5. Shang-Influenced Areas. ***Sources:*** Minneapolis Institute of the Arts, www .artsmia.ORG/ARTS-OF-ASIA/CHINA/MAPS; Cheng Te-k'un 1960. Cartographic design by Mary Lee Eggart

that came before it. And nowhere were the strength and beauty of this civilization and culture more obvious than in the Shang urban capitals, which were, as always, the seats of authority, power, art, and dynastic economy (Wheatley 1971).

A number of Shang urban centers have been found, but three major sites stand out. Two lie along the Huang He in southern Hebei, and the third, Anyang, is north of the Huang He in northern Henan province (see map 3.5). The oldest site is near Yanshi, which contains what is thought to be the oldest palace site in China, and is believed to be the site of the first Shang capital. A somewhat larger and more impressive walled city, rectangular in shape and enclosing an area of 3.2 km², has been found east of Ershi near the present city of Zhengzhou. Artifacts that are characteristic of Shang culture include very high-quality bronze, fine pottery, and oracle bones covered with written records. The Shang bronzes are not only marvels of metallurgy and artistry, they also reflect a benchmark in technology and organization for bronze manufacture. Some of the larger artifacts weigh over 85 or 90 kg. Casting required the orchestrated efforts of a workforce of over three hundred artisans and laborers working to simultaneously lift and pour up to seventy crucibles of molten metal. These early bronzes were some of the hardest bronzes manufactured in China during the entire dynastic era and again reflect a remarkable level of technical sophistication.

The most important Shang capital, serving the last three centuries of Shang rulers, was along the banks of a river near the present city of Anyang. Discoveries in the vicinity provide written evidence of the Shang and indeed provide a surprisingly detailed record of the dynasty's tenure. Thus, the importance of Anyang to early Chinese history and archaeology is unmatched. The stratified nature of its houses and neighborhoods also suggests a far more sophisticated settlement than those of earlier periods. Elite neighborhoods, centers for artisans, and slums for the poor are clearly reflected in the archaeological record.

The Origins of Chinese Cities

Researchers now recognize that North China, along with the ancient Middle East, the Indus River Basin and two locations in Mesoamerica, were the sites of early and independently developed urban civilizations, with settlements of many sizes and purposes joined at times for political and economic purposes. Goods and people circulated easily among these settlements, with a major city overseeing the production and distribution of goods and the defense of the whole. It is now believed that a number of these local systems in China were joined together (i.e., conquered) in the early part of the Shang dynasty to form the core of the fledgling state.

Although the Shang states were allied to defend their northern frontier from barbarian incursions, translations of the oracle bones indicate that the states fought continuously among themselves. Territory and spoils of conquest moved continuously from state to state through the centuries. Eventually these endless wars, both within and without, took their toll, and a rival group, the Zhou, established hegemony over the Shang dominions, while also expanding southward.

Historical accounts of the demise of the Shang dynasty establish a pattern, perhaps also a process, of succession that remained through the dynastic era. The last Shang ruler, Zhou Xin, was thought to be profligate, wicked, and lacking in all of the noble virtues desired of a ruler. This lack of moral leadership intensified the effects of rebellion and external conflicts, and the common people were exposed to constant warfare, high taxes, famine, and pestilence. As a consequence, heaven was said to have withdrawn its mandate (support) from the Shang kings in favor of a more virtuous leader and lineage, thereby ending the Shang dynasty—a victim of antipathy in both heaven and on earth. A better-organized, and presumably more chaste, Zhou dynasty rose from the ashes of the Shang—initiated by the most virtuous King Wu, the first king of the Zhou.

Tradition holds that King Wu, as the first ruler establishing a new dynasty, was only successful because heaven provided support for the transition. This cycle of dynastic loss and gain, commonly called the Mandate of Heaven, was replayed many times—more than the number of China's dynasties, in fact, because often there were two or more competing dynasties operating within what is now China, and all claiming the support of heaven.

The Zhou dynasty has a special place in China's historical geography. Many of China's greatest classical thinkers and philosophers, such as Confucius, Mencius, and

Laozi (Lao-tze), lived during this era. Although the central authority of the Zhou began to break down and become diffused in the middle and later periods of the dynasty, the Zhou dynasty constituted the first classical age for Chinese literature, philosophy, and the arts. The value system set forth in classical literature from the period would not only survive, it would become the philosophy under which China and Chinese culture would flourish for more than two millennia. The Zhou dynasty also saw the further consolidation of institutions and traditions that came to be seen as distinctively Chinese. Agriculture became completely sedentary and considerably more intensive after 700 B.C., eliminating the semisedentary and migratory farming of the late Neolithic and the Shang. Agriculture benefited from technical improvements such as the fallowing of fields to let their soil regenerate and the use of organic fertilizers. Iron plowshares came into common use. Directives regarding the need for the preservation of arable land have also been found in dynastic texts of the Zhou, showing an understanding of previous agricultural problems and the need to protect land resources.

The Chinese Language

Indispensable to an understanding of China's recorded history and development is some knowledge of the nature and working of the Chinese language. Perhaps for no other nation at any time was a written language as critical for nation-building as written Chinese was for Chinese civilization and nation-building. Once standardized, written Chinese served to unify the many disparate groups of peoples and cultures (each with a distinct spoken language) within the territory that would become modern China. Written Chinese has been in use for at least 3,500 years. This tenure makes it the oldest written language continuously in use to the present. The use of written Chinese was critical for homogenizing the many disparate cultures of the Middle Kingdom.

The Chinese language differs from European languages in several significant ways. First, the Chinese language does not employ an alphabet, but relies on the use of Chinese characters that are either *ideographs* (picture symbols) or *phonemic graphs* (sound symbols) that have developed over a very long period to depict objects, actions, and ideas. Each character is unique and varies in its complexity (the number of strokes needed to represent it), but all are composed of combinations taken from a set of standardized strokes. Characters representing similar concepts may often have a common portion, known as the character's *radical.* There are 227 radicals in the Chinese language, including one that represents "metal," one that represents "speech," one that represents "plant," and so on.

While every Chinese character has meaning in its own right (i.e., it is a *morpheme*), in practical terms, most Chinese words are combinations of usually two or three characters. This propensity to combine characters gave written Chinese the flexibility it needed to remain viable. Even so, there are over sixty thousand characters. Most of these, however, are seldom used (Mair 1997). To read a typical Chinese newspaper, for instance, requires knowledge of only two thousand to three thousand characters. And as new concepts, materials, and ideas arise, new characters or combinations of Chinese characters are introduced to produce new words.

In 1956 in order to increase literacy, the Chinese government simplified the writing of a number of characters in common usage (*jianti zi*) by reducing the number of strokes required to write some radicals and complete characters. It is much easier to learn these simplified characters, and literacy in China has increased rapidly. In 2004, 86 percent of the population of the People's Republic of China (PRC) was officially classified by the Chinese government as literate (Heritage Foundation 2004). Overseas Chinese and residents of Hong Kong and Taiwan still use traditional characters.

Another innovation aimed at simplifying the language has been the introduction of systems of standardized romanization (based on the Latin alphabet) for the transliteration of Chinese terms. The most recent of these systems, known as *pinyin*, was designed as an aid in the pronunciation of Chinese characters, particularly in the first and second grades when Chinese students are just beginning to learn to write characters. Pinyin has also been widely adopted as a means of romanizing Chinese outside China. The translation of written Chinese has always posed a problem for foreigners. Prior to 1972 the United States, as well as virtually all other Western nations, used the Wade-Giles system, which was created by Thomas Wade and Herbert Giles, two of the first professors of Chinese at Cambridge University in 1867. After President Richard Nixon's historic meetings with Chinese leaders Mao Zedong (Mao Tse-tung) and Zhou Enlai, the pinyin system was gradually adopted in the United States and most other Western nations. This shift in romanization systems has caused more than its fair share of confusion, despite the fact that pinyin has been used in most cases for more than a quarter of a century. Under the Wade-Giles system, the capital of China was *Peking*. Using pinyin, this became *Beijing*. The Chinese characters that mean "Northern Capital" have not changed; the change is only in the letters of our alphabet that we Westerners use to represent those characters.

Spoken Chinese

China's languages are tonal in nature, and words with the same sound but rendered in different tones have different meanings. This is what made a standardized writing system so critical for holding the Chinese nation together. At the same time, spoken Chinese is represented by many different regional languages and dialects (see map 3.6). That there should be so many Chinese languages is reasonable given China's great expanse, rugged topography, and complex history. These numerous and various regional languages (sometimes inaccurately called dialects), moreover, are generally unintelligible to each other. The most commonly spoken language of the Chinese is still Mandarin (named after the Qing court officials that Westerners first heard speak it in the late 1700s). Mandarin has four tones and is spoken by the largest number of people in China. This official language, also known as *putonghua* (common speech), is the language of North China and is found in its standard, pristine form in and around the city of Beijing. *Putonghua*, or Mandarin, is used throughout North, Northeast, and Central China. Other major language groups are found in the East and South. Among these languages, Cantonese and southern Min (Fujian) are especially significant for overseas Chinese because most of the Chinese emigrating to other countries since the nineteenth

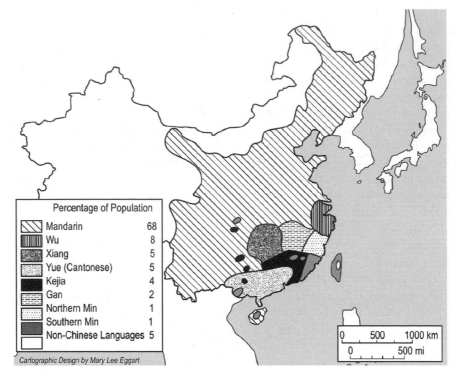

Map 3.6. Chinese Language Distributions. **Source:** After Pannell and Ma 1983, 65. Cartographic design by Mary Lee Eggart

century originated from these areas. Cantonese has nine tones, and is usually considered more difficult to learn.

Because of the tones, Chinese is a difficult language to master. Still, the spoken language in some ways is quite simple in that the verbs have no conjugations and the nouns have no declensions. Beginning in the early 1950s, everyone in the PRC was required to learn Mandarin, and all television and radio broadcasts as well as movies were required to use it. Again, it is the official spoken language of China. However, in the past fifteen years there has been a tendency to return to regional dialects in local television and radio programs, particularly in the southern provinces of Guangdong and Guangxi. This return to local languages, particularly in the public arena, represents a rebirth of regional culture and pride, leavened, some might say, with a safe dose of civil disobedience. The rules that require the use of *putonghua* are still on the books, but people have chosen, en masse, to ignore them.

Imperial China: The Dynastic Centuries

The divisions between competing states in the third century B.C. diminished the power of the remaining Zhou rulers and led to the emergence of a new and powerful state, the

Qin, which through superior military tactics and equipment was able to consolidate power and reunite the country in 221 B.C. The rise of the Qin was improbable. Initially, the Qin was the westernmost of the Zhou states. It started out as a minor royal domain responsible for the defense of the western borders and for the provision of horses to the Zhou army. The ruler of this new state, Zheng, after subduing his foes, later proclaimed himself Qin Shi Huangdi (First Emperor of the Qin) and established many of the structures and agencies that allowed China to become a great empire. Although the Qin dynasty was short-lived (221–206 B.C.), the unified, dynastic-based imperial system that it established lasted as a governing and administrative system without basic changes until 1911 when a republican form of government was introduced. The Qin conquests of many smaller, weaker states started China on its long path to the establishment of the boundaries of the modern Chinese state. The maps of the dynasties included in this section of the chapter, however, clearly show how Chinese territory regularly expanded and contracted over the 2,200 years of the dynastic era.

Exploding from the Qin kingdom based along the Wei River, Qin Shi Huang himself led the Qin armies to battle, first to the East and then more significantly to the rich farms of the South (see map 3.7). Acquiring these rich southern lands, and their associated food surplus, was vital for fueling the massive public works and continued military expansions that marked the dynasty. The Qin dynasty was organized based on

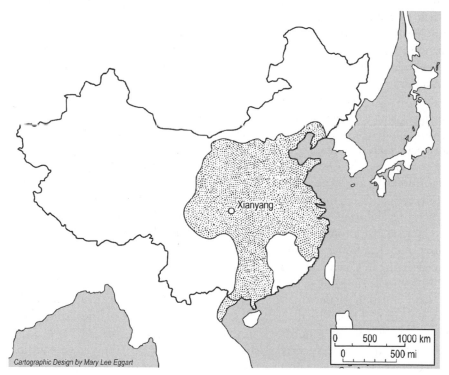

Map 3.7.   Qin Dynasty Territory. **Source:** www.chaos.umd.edu/history. Cartographic design by Mary Lee Eggart

a legalist school of thought best represented by the writings of Yang Kungsun, chief minister of the Qin kingdom from 359–338 B.C., and Han Fei (d. 233 B.C.). The legalists rejected Confucian visions of beneficent government and the moral suasion of citizens in favor of strict legal codes and regulations that addressed virtually all aspects of life.

Qin Shi Huang introduced many policies uniting and governing China, including the establishment of a national civil administration, which divided the country into thirty-six commanderies, further divided into prefectures. This system of politically and militarily organized and united territories was a remarkable departure from the loose alliances and federations of the Shang or the Zhou dynasties. Money, weights, measures, and even the axle-lengths of carts were officially standardized to facilitate trade and transport. Chinese writing was likewise made uniform through the development and promotion of official dictionaries.

The Spatial and Ecological Impact of Qin Shi Huang

Among the many accomplishments of the first emperor of the Qin dynasty in unifying China and in initiating the unified imperial dynastic system, three stand out because of their spatial and ecological ramifications: (1) the most ambitious rendition of the Great Wall to that date, (2) the extension of a national trunk-road network, and (3) the expansion and extension of the national canal network. The Great Wall was for security and boundary-delimiting purposes; the roads and canals improved transportation and communication. Most canals were also designed not only to improve transportation, but to provide irrigation water for farming as well. All of these innovations permitted Qin Shi Huang to acquire more territory and resources (food, lumber, horses, and trade goods). Qin dynasty armies were better supplied, better organized, and capable of faster movement than the opposing forces—armies of the states and kingdoms drawn into Qin control. But the Qin dynasty is regarded as one of the cruelest periods in China's long, storied history. The labor for its walls, canals, roads, food, and above all, the recruits for its armies, came from the weak and the conquered. The Great Wall was an attempt to stabilize an ecological boundary between a zone of sedentary agriculturists, the Chinese, and a zone of pastoral herders including the Xiongnu. The wall created a sharp and clear buffer separating the Chinese farmers of Inner China from pastoral nomads living in Outer China. It was also a symbolic, cultural boundary between the civilized Middle Kingdom in the South and the barbaric regions in the North and West.

Consolidation of the empire in 221 B.C. led immediately to the construction of new roads and highways designed to spatially integrate the political control center at Xianyang (immediately northwest of today's city of Xi'an) with the newly acquired regions. The empire's chief general, Meng Tian, was charged with building a main north–south highway 800 km long north across the Ordos Desert toward the present-day city of Baotou. Other new roads radiated out from Xianyang like the spokes of a wheel. Loewe (1986, 61) estimates that the Qin imperial highway network was approximately

6,800 km. This compares favorably with estimates of the Roman road system of 5,984 km at its greatest extension. This road network continued to expand during the Han period, but after the third century A.D., the road network began to decline, apparently because of the increased importance of rivers and canals for transport. Qin Shi Huang initiated or expanded many extensive canal systems during his reign. In South China, a short but significant canal was constructed in what is now Guangxi province, far to the south. The canal linked the drainage system of the Chang Jiang (Yangtze River) and Central China with tributaries of the Xi Jiang in South China. In this way, Central and South China were integrated more effectively for administrative, military, and economic purposes, and the southern territories were cemented further into Han Chinese territory.

Qin Shi Huang died in 210 B.C., and the collapse of his legalist, authoritarian regime followed soon thereafter, but the tradition of imperial dynasties based on a royal family that changed with each dynasty continued for 2,200 years. The next dynasty, the Han (206 B.C.–A.D. 220) was established after a brief period of instability and fighting. The Han emperor reestablished aspects of a feudal land-ownership system, which expanded the ruling class. The growing power of landed nobles during the Han dynasty, weakened under the Qin, led to a forced policy of subdividing land among all surviving sons. Unlike the European system of primogeniture in which land and titles passed to the oldest son, the Han policy assured the division of land into ever-smaller holdings, often resulting in holdings too small to support a family. This endless subdivision of land had consequences that continued right up to the twenty-first century.

Growth and Change in the Early Dynastic Era

The political and administrative traditions of China established under the Qin and the Han dynasties were durable enough to survive the 360 years of sporadic chaos that followed the collapse of the Han in A.D. 220, as well as the long periods of foreign occupation and domination of China by the Mongols (A.D. 1279–1368) and the Manchu (A.D. 1644–1911).

It is not that there were no changes in China's political system for 2,200 years; certainly there were recurring periods of decisive change, progress, and setback. But while extensive coverage of the dynastic history of China would take volumes, there were some geographical and economic changes that are noteworthy (Huang 1997). Under the Qin and the Han dynasties, territorial expansion was largely to the east and south, but control of key commercial centers in the West along the Silk Road was of equal importance. Once the Chinese gained control over territories in Central Asia and established the overland trade routes that came to be collectively called the Silk Road, great prosperity quickly followed. If the granaries of China were to the south, then the West of China provided the lion's share of profitable trade and access to the distant markets of Persia and Europe upon which the dynastic system was dependent.

Han Wudi, one of the most vigorous of the Han emperors, sent multiple expeditions into the barbarian regions (Xiongnu federations) north and west to pacify its tribes, gain territory, and expand commerce. In 133 B.C., a force of over 300,000 troops was used

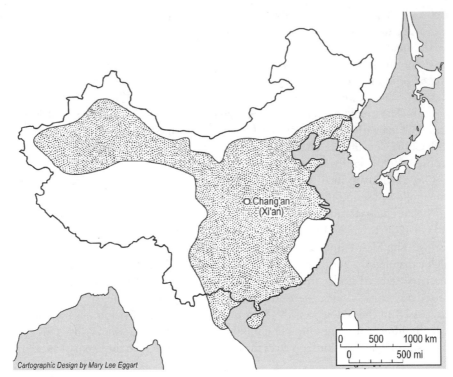

Map 3.8. Han Dynasty Territory. **Source:** www.chaos.umd.edu/history. Cartographic design by Mary Lee Eggart

to establish four commanderies in what is now Gansu province. These troops, and the countless troops that followed, permitted the Han to trade their silk, tea, and porcelain to the great markets of Persia, India, Rome, and the remainder of Europe and Central Asia for centuries. In the Southeast, Han armies finally conquered the Yue and Min peoples of what is now southern Zhejiang and Fujian, giving the empire complete control of the Pacific seaboard (see map 3.8).

The Han dynasty expansions, as the Qin before them, were costly in many ways. Regional conflicts and rebellions were the bitter fruits that sprang from the hardships sowed by court intrigue, bad government, forced conscription into the army, and the high taxes required to support the military. Eventually the empire broke up into minor kingdoms and territories controlled by warlords powerful enough to maintain local control, but incapable of pulling the empire together again.

It would be more than 350 years before China would once again be united under one ruler, with the establishment of the Sui dynasty in A.D. 581. Yang Jian, a Xianbei (non-Han ethnic group) ruler of the Northern Zhou dynasty that gained control of northern China in 577, established the Sui dynasty when his armies finally conquered the South. In the forty years of the dynasty's existence, Sui armies were almost constantly at war or brutally putting down internal rebellions. Appropriately, history treated the Sui and the Qin dynasties in similar fashion; they were both periods of rapid expansion and unification, both very short-lived, and both are now famous for the cruelty and hardship their leaders visited upon the common people (Fairbank and Goldman 1998, 78).

The "Golden" Tang Dynasty

Just as the much-celebrated and relatively long Han dynasty followed the violent and brief Qin dynasty, the famous Tang dynasty followed that of the tumultuous Sui. And just as the high costs of his Korean campaigns helped undermine support for Qin Shi Huang, unsuccessful Korean expeditions during the Sui dynasty so weakened the army that it was susceptible to the attacks of the eastern Turks. This ultimately led to the establishment of the Tang dynasty (Roberts 1996). As with the Han, the key economic and cultural links of the Tang state to other nations and regions were westward. In the early, most vigorous years of the dynasty, Tang armies acquired or regained a remarkable amount of territory in Central Asia after campaigns against the Turks, the Tibetans, the Uighurs, and many other groups (see map 3.9). In A.D. 635, the northern Silk Road route was regained. In A.D. 702, much of what is now Xinjiang province was pacified, and the southern Silk Road route was established as a more defensible option to the northern route.

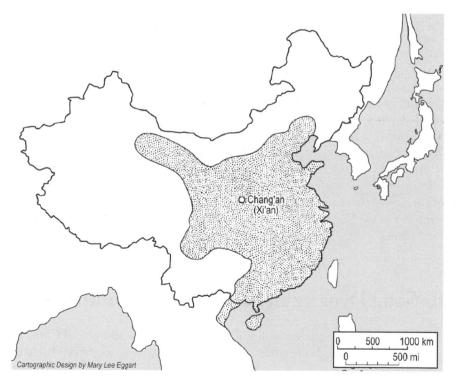

Map 3.9. Tang Dynasty Territory. ***Source:*** www.chaos.umd.edu/history. Cartographic design by Mary Lee Eggart

In the eighth century A.D., the Central Asian trade was so lucrative that Chinese prefectures were established in modern Afghanistan despite the very high costs of maintaining food supplies and troop garrisons. Trade along the Silk Road flourished, bringing not only wealth but also a remarkable array of foreigners, foreign religions, and foreign ideas into China. The Tang dynasty was far more cosmopolitan than any previous dynasty, and culture, high and low, benefited from foreign infusions.

It is important to note that during the Sui and Tang dynasties, the political orientation of the Chinese Empire and its economy remained directed toward the interior of Asia. Wealth and political control came with the maintenance and protection of interior trade routes to Central Asia and Europe. There were many other important and remarkable advances during the Tang dynasty, however. The legal system was completely overhauled, and many of these reforms remained largely in place for most of the remaining dynasties. The code of A.D. 653, which Ebrey notes is the earliest comprehensive legal code to survive as a complete text (1996, 111), contains more than five hundred articles specifying specific crimes and associated punishments. Simultaneously, the government sought to equalize income by confiscating and redistributing land holdings. Equity was promoted not just for the sake of equity, but to minimize rebellions and uprisings, which in all times are bad for business and stability.

Ceramics, poetry, architecture, and the graphic arts all flourished, making lasting impressions on first the ambassadors, and later the peoples of Korea, Japan, Vietnam, and even distant Persia. The cohesion of the cultures of East Asia at the present time is in large part due to the great and pervasive influence of the Tang dynasty upon the material and spiritual cultures of the other nations in the region. Buddhist sects flourished and spread throughout much of Southeast Asia during the Tang.

At its peak during the Tang dynasty, the capital city of Changan had more than 2 million inhabitants. The city walls enclosed more than 90 km^2. The food demands of this city and of many others of impressive size required an extensive canal system for food shipment and distribution. Under the Yuan dynasty (A.D. 1279–1368), the Grand Canal (Da Yunhe) had been extended farther north and east to the vicinity of Beijing, but it was during the Tang dynasty that engineering and excavation techniques were perfected (see map 3.10). The Grand Canal had two critical functions. It served a critical commercial purpose in fostering the exchange of goods and monies between North and South China, and it illustrated, to all, the great military power of the central government in the North and its ability to command grain shipments from South and Central China.

The Song Dynasty and a Turn to the Southern Seas

The western interior orientation (political and economic) characteristic of China from the early dynasties through the golden age of the Tang dynasty was abruptly changed during the Northern and Southern Song dynasties (A.D. 960–1279) that followed. From the outset, it must have been clear the Song dynasty would never regain control over the vast territories held by earlier dynasties (see map 3.11). It never acquired what

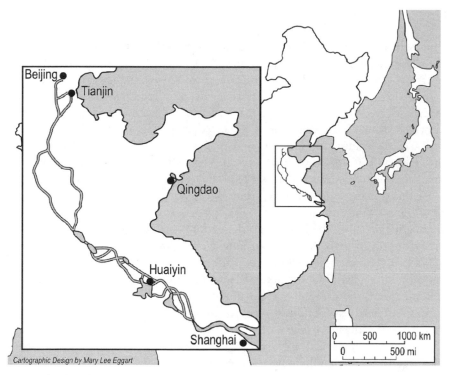

Map 3.10. Grand Canal Routes. Cartographic design by Mary Lee Eggart

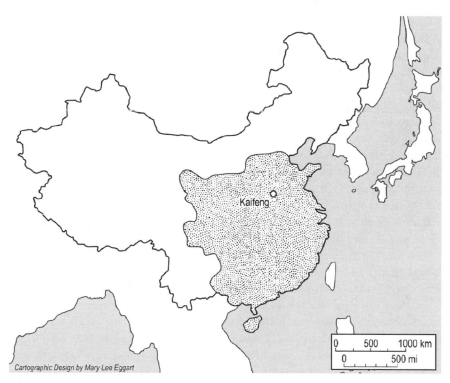

Map 3.11. Song Dynasty Territory. ***Source:*** www.chaos.umd.edu/history. Cartographic design by Mary Lee Eggart

is now Northeast China (Dongbei) where the Manchu Liao dynasty was established in A.D. 916 and remained unconquered until A.D. 1218. To the west, the Tibetan and the Tangut states threatened the frontiers, and along with the Uighurs controlled the Central Asian caravan routes, thus removing a historically vital source of wealth for the new dynasty. Further, the Northern Song dynasty never pacified the northern tribes that had breached the Great Wall. During the most prosperous years of the Song dynasty, North China was under the control of the rival Jin dynasty. The Loess Plateau and the North China Plain regions were lost in A.D. 1126 when tribes of the Jurchen (another nomadic group from Central Asia) sacked Kaifeng after an ill-fated alliance collapsed.

At this juncture, the territory firmly under Song control was but a fraction of that of Tang China, and the riches of the cross-Asia trade had fallen to other hands. One might think that the loss of half the national territory would have crippled the dynasty, but surprisingly the Southern Song dynasty was one of the most prosperous in China's long dynastic history. Only the lands south of the Chang Jiang and eastward from the modern city of Chengdu in Sichuan were secure. In response, however, a new economic geography evolved, made manifest as political and commercial expansions into the southern seas (Southeast Asia). In time, a rise in maritime trade more than compensated for the loss of the northern territories.

In terms of China's future economic geography, this shift to the seas represented a critical change in foreign diplomacy and economic policy. During the Southern Song dynasty, the economic orientation of China abruptly changed from a reliance on domestic trade and the Silk Road, to one dependent on a Pacific orientation, supported by a large merchant marine and defended by a sophisticated imperial navy. Of course, as in Europe several centuries later, this maritime trade also transformed and expanded the domestic economy, while shifting China's core economic region from its interior to the southern and eastern coasts. In measuring this commercial transformation, Ebrey notes that "by 997 the Song government was minting 800 million coins a year, two and a half times the largest output of the Tang" (1996, 142).

The majority of maritime freight, by volume, during the Song dynasty was regional, integrating China with the countries of Southeast Asia, some Indian Ocean states, and many parts of the Indonesian archipelago and the Philippines. During these centuries, China's influence over the economy and cultures of Southeast Asia was at its peak. Of course, there were also important long-distance routes to the Middle East, India, and even the coast of Africa. The most critical commodity in this Arab trade was porcelain, which along with silk and tea brought fantastic profits. There were also the spices, precious woods, and oils that were important in the Indian Ocean trade.

Shipbuilding, fueled by the demands of coastal and canal trade, was far advanced in China relative to Europe at the same time. Levathes reports that imperial revenues from overseas trade went from 500,000 strings of cash at the end of the eleventh century to more than 2 million by the middle of the twelfth (1994, 40). Major maritime ports of the Southern Song dynasty included Guangzhou, Quanzhou in Fujian Province, Xiamen, Fuzhou, and Hangzhou. Ironically, all of these ports became Treaty Ports in the mid-nineteenth century, having been opened to international trade a second time by Western gunboats. To protect its large merchant marine, the imperial Song navy grew to over six hundred ships. The largest merchant ships could carry three hundred tons of cargo (Levathes 1994, 43). Song dynasty maritime innovations included stern-post rudder, multiple decks, and compound composite wooden masts.

In addition to new technologies represented by the flourishing maritime trade during the Song, there were also other technical innovations. Fairbank and Goldman note that in A.D. 1078, northern China was producing more than 114,000 metric tons of pig iron per year, while seven hundred years later England would be producing only half that amount (1998, 88–90). Other important Song dynasty commercial innovations in industrial technology included improved steel production through the use of coal-fired blast furnaces, glass-making, and gunpowder. Papermaking, book printing, and production of ceramics all became established at this time as important commercial industries that relied on exports as well as domestic trade for their profits.

This remarkable boom in technology and innovation, what Elvin (1973) has called China's "medieval economic revolution," did not fuel long-term efforts at combining maritime trade with colonial expansion, however. Unlike Europe, China did not experience an age of global economic and political expansion (which would have been fueled, in part, by commercial applications of the inventions that would prove vital for European influence and control five hundred years later; Fairbank and Goldman 1998, 92). The reasons for this are disputed, but all agree that on the eve of the twelfth century, China was the most technically advanced nation on earth (Needham 1962). Nor did this economic and commercial golden age lead to the great territorial expansions that were characteristic of the early Han or Tang dynasties. The times were different, and China's borders during the Song dynasty were controlled not by the disorganized tribes of the past, but by well-organized states (Khitans, Jurchen, and Tanguts) that demanded treatment as equals. Often bribes of silk, silver, or gold were used to maintain the borders when Song armies, even with 1.25 million men under arms, proved incapable of the task. Just as its absolute extent declined vis-à-vis earlier dynasties, the internal organization of the territory under Song control also changed. Stimulated by increased food production and a growing specialization of labor, China's great cities experienced their own golden era. China now had dozens of cities with more than fifty thousand persons as the specialization of labor attained new levels on the back of increasing control by the central government (Skinner 1977).

In China, and especially South China, farm output increased greatly. Several factors accounted for this, but most important was the widespread use of early-ripening Champa rice varieties acquired from northern Vietnam at the beginning of the eleventh century. There were also technical improvements in the cultivation and irrigation of wet rice, including new methods for leveling and smoothing land for paddy fields, constructing dams, and getting water to the fields by using new types of pumps.

Agricultural and technical primers also became popular in these times with the advent of commercial printing and the promotion of modern agricultural methods by the government. Perhaps the most renown of these primers is the classic *Jiming Yaoshu* (Essential Ways of Living for the Common People), written by Jia Suxie in approximately A.D. 533–544, and promoted by repeated printings and distribution throughout the Tang dynasty as a way to introduce better agricultural practices (Shih 1982, 2–5).

Fairbank and Goldman note that the great paradox of the Song dynasty is that just as China reached its acme of civilization, it was conquered by outsiders (1998,

108). With the exception of the 276 years of the Ming dynasty (A.D. 1368–1644), the remainder of the Chinese dynastic era from the fall of the Song dynasty in 1276 to the 1911 republican revolution is a history of foreign dynasties.

The Mongols and the Empire without End

Mongol conquest of China was substantially linked to China's process of economic reorientation that began at the end of the Tang dynasty as the empire turned slowly from the lands and trade routes of Inner Asia to the southern seas and oceans. As Inner China became increasingly isolated and ignored, the old ties between the states and peoples of the West and the people of Inner China deteriorated. And as trade and mutual strategic interest declined, alliances were increasingly difficult to maintain amid contentious diplomacy that gave way to mutual contempt and conflict. With China's sphere of influence reduced, numerous local states emerged to fill the gap, only to fall to the Mongols. The Ruzhen (Jin), the Tangut, and other states could not match the Mongol's troop strength, strategy, or planning. Eventually all of North China was in the hands of the Mongols. Ogodei, Ghengis Khan's third son, initiated the assault on Southern Song China. Victory led to the establishment of the Yuan (Mongol) dynasty in A.D. 1279 (see map 3.12). The slaughter of civilians associated with these invasions is legendary, and many parts of China were seriously depopulated for more

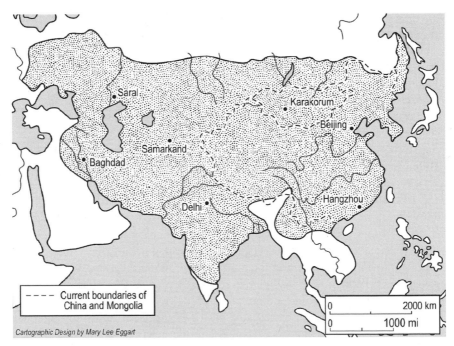

Map 3.12. Yuan (Mongol) Dynasty Territory. **Source:** Minneapolis Institute of the Arts, www.artsmia.ORG/ARTS-OF-ASIA/CHINA/MAPS. Cartographic design by Mary Lee Eggart

than one hundred years by the wanton violence of the Mongols. By way of example, after conquering Sichuan, Ogodei ordered the slaughter of Chengdu's more than 1 million inhabitants (Ebrey 1996, 169–70). The invasion of South China was completed by Kublai Khan, Ghengis Khan's grandson, but only after Kublai Khan had studied China by ruling a prefecture in Hebei for a number of years (Davis 1996, 211–18).

The Mongol conquest (and the resultant Yuan dynasty) represents a benchmark in China's history. While northern China had been under the control of foreigners (non-Han) a number of times, including during the Liao and Jin dynasties, the defeat of the Song dynasty marked the first time that southern China had ever come under foreign control. For the first time, under the Yuan dynasty, all of China was under foreign occupation. Ironically, this was also the first time that all of China had been united since the end of the Tang dynasty (A.D. 907). Mongol control of China was short-lived, though, because rebellions stimulated in part by Song loyalists erupted almost immediately in the South and later in the North (Davis 1996).

The Yuan dynasty had few long-term effects on China's economic geography because most Mongol innovations did not survive beyond the dynasty. In the end, for example, the Song dynasty administrative system remained intact, and Song systems of taxation, currency distribution, and the legal code were mostly unchanged. The Mongols did restore and improve the vaunted transportation systems of the Song and Tang dynasties by using massive amounts of corvée labor for clearing canals and repaving roads. A postal system with relays using 200,000 horses was also set up to further improve communications.

Perhaps the most influential aspects of the Yuan dynasty were cultural rather than economic or political in nature. Contrary to the popular conception of a closed and isolated China, the Yuan dynasty continued a cosmopolitan trend that had begun in the Tang and the Song dynasties. In 1275, Marco Polo arrived in Kublai Khan's summer residence, Shan-tu (this became Xanadu) in the Yuan capital of Cambaluc (later, Beijing), and found visitors, advisors, and ambassadors from many nations. Marco Polo marveled at the wealth and sophistication of China and remained in China for seventeen years, supposedly serving for three years during this time as a tax inspector in the city of Yangzhou in Jiangsu on the Grand Canal. Skeptics point out the absence of many commonplace features of life in China that are missing from his accounts, though, and question if he ever actually lived in China or was just reporting the stories of others. This debate may never be resolved. But the cosmopolitan character of the Yuan dynasty was indubitable:

> Arabs, Venetians, and Russians engaged in business in Chinese ports, and one Russian took first place in the metropolitan examinations in 1321 and became a high official in Chekiang [Zhejiang] in 1341. Chinese and Mongols were penetrating Persia and Europe. Chinese engineers, for example, were used to improve irrigation in the Tigris-Euphrates basin; there were Chinese quarters in Novgorod, Moscow, and Tabriz. As envoy of the Mongol [leader], Rabban Sauma, a Nestorian born in Peking about 1225, visited Byzantium and Rome in 1287–88, saw the King of England in Gascony and Philip the Fair in Paris, and left a description of his visit to the Abby of Saint-Denis and Saint Chapelle, among other places. (Goodrich 1969, 178–79)

The Yuan dynasty collapsed as much as a result of the disintegration of the Mongol empire as of events in China proper. Still, a nascent Chinese nationalism next helped usher in the start of the Ming dynasty, despite the dynasty's lowly origins.

The first emperor of the Ming dynasty, once an indigent peasant, led a rebel army that razed Nanjing in 1356, and finally captured Beijing from the Mongols in 1368. The Mongol court fled northward and regrouped. The Ming armies never conquered the Northeast (modern Dongbei) or the Far Northwest (Xinjiang). Oriented to the coasts as during the Song dynasty, the Chinese economy under the Ming flourished, predicated in part on improvements to the national transportation system completed by the Yuan. The first several Ming emperors were just as ambitious, however, and quickly expanded public works to include massive urban construction projects that resulted in the contemporary layout of many cities, including Beijing and Nanjing. The Great Wall was completely renovated and reached its greatest extent under the Ming (see map 3.13), and Beijing also became the permanent national capital after the death of the first Ming emperor in Nanjing.

A very brief return to long-distance maritime trade and exploration marked the most interesting era during the Ming dynasty. This small sliver of China's long history (A.D. 1403–1433) best represents China's early interest in the remainder of the world.

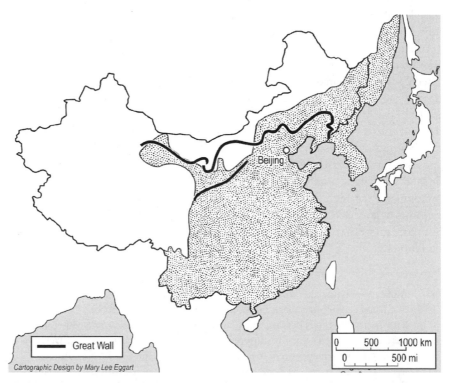

Map 3.13. The Great Wall with Ming Dynasty Territory. **Source:** Minneapolis Institute of the Arts, www.artsmia.ORG/ARTS-OF-ASIA/CHINA/MAPS. Cartographic design by Mary Lee Eggart

Everything about the seven major voyages of the Ming fleet was fantastic. The ships were massive, the distances incredible, and the treasures collected rivaled those of any of history's greatest treasure troves. Predating Vasco da Gama's African explorations by eighty years, the fleet that set out in 1405 from Nanjing to explore the western oceans had 317 ships with a total crew of 27,000 men. The largest of these ships, the *baochuan* (treasure ships) were from 118 to 127 m long and 48 to 50 m wide, and displaced around 3,000 tons. The largest ships measured more than four and one half times the 26 m length of Columbus's largest ship on his 1492 voyage, the Santa Maria (Levathes 1994, 80–83). Led by the eunuch admiral Zheng He, a Muslim intent on visiting the Holy Land, the seven voyages were meant to be as much diplomatic and exploratory as mercantile. In the course of the voyages, Zheng He was to map all of the northern shores of the Indian Ocean, the coast of Africa as far south as Madagascar, and much of the Indonesian archipelago (see map 3.14). From all of the nations encountered, the great Ming fleet exacted tribute and exchanged court officials, and when possible it forged advantageous trading concessions, breaking the Arab lock on the cross–Indian Ocean trade. Giraffes, rhinoceroses, and many other animals, along with exotic products, plants, jewels, and curiosities flowed back into China along with an ever-increasing knowledge of the world. Given the tremendous capital required to construct and maintain such a fleet, it is surprising that in thirty years, the great Ming navy was allowed to disappear. There were many sadly mundane reasons for its demise, including court grumbling about

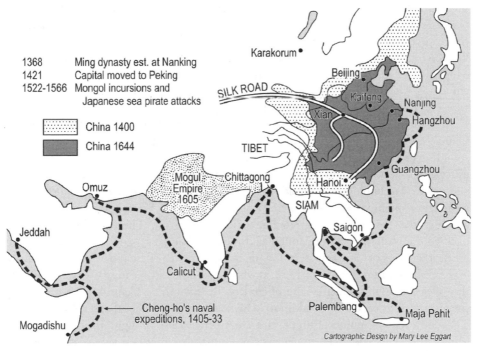

Map 3.14. Ming China Maritime Explorations 1368–1644. **Source:** www.chinapage .com/zhenghe.html. Cartographic design by Mary Lee Eggart

its cost, increasing internal rebellion, and the completion of Grand Canal renovations, which made defense of the coastal trade from pirates (both Chinese and Japanese at this point) less necessary. The most important reason, however, was one that continues to influence China to the present: political rivalry between feuding leaders. Court conflicts between eunuchs and Confucians in the 1430s erupted as a struggle for control of the throne. Since the maritime trade was under the control of the eunuchs, the Confucians continuously advised against investments in maintenance of the navy and the merchant marine. For these reasons the Ming navy, at its peak consisting of three thousand ships, went into fast decline. Unprotected, much of China's vitally profitable coastal trade with Southeast Asia died along with the disappearance of its navy.

Although the Ming dynasty continued for more than two hundred years after the last of the great treasure ships was cut from its stays in Nanjing, its vigor was lost long before its final demise. The greatest days of the dynasty corresponded to periods of expanding global and regional trade. The collapse of the Ming dynasty was due as much to internal problems associated with more than eighty years of peasant rebellion, indifferent government, and profligate spending, as to the invasion by the Manchu, who established the Qing dynasty.

In 1644 and after many years of war, the Manchu, based in Northwest China (hence the name *Manchuria*), overthrew the declining Ming dynasty. The Manchu originated as a Tungic tribe from Central Asia and did not have the maritime interests of the Song and the Ming dynasties. Crossley estimates that the invading force of Manchu numbered only 120,000–150,000 bannermen (1997, 81). This small force would not have been successful if Ming China had not been ripped apart by rebellions and famines occurring concurrently in many of the provinces. Just as the Mongols before them, the Manchu's small force, supported by foreign mercenaries but also including no small number of Chinese, was able to overcome Ming resistance. Again, following the methods of the Mongols, the Manchu used fear and stunning violence to acquire what their soldiers could not. After the siege of Yangzhou (in central Jiangsu province) over 800,000 corpses were cremated in mass graves outside the city walls.

For most of the 267 years that the Manchu ruled as the Qing dynasty (see map 3.15), China's economy prospered in direct proportion to the expansion of its trade. Corresponding to the European mercantile era, the Qing dynasty supplied the world with tea, porcelain, silk, pepper, and many other products. Qing manufactures were traditional, and few new technological innovations contributed to this prosperity. Agriculture grew more labor-intensive, and there were critical adoptions of Western crops such as corn and potatoes, but beyond this, few innovations were made. The Manchu successfully pacified the western tribes of Mongolia, Turkestan (Xinjiang), and Tibet, securing the greatest territory of China's history. Commerce between the East and West continuously expanded from around 1680 to 1820, at which point the Europeans grew avaricious and the "illegal" opium trade grew out of control. Reestablishing Central Asian trade with the modern state of Russia, in addition to maritime trade with Southeast Asia (especially Thailand), the Philippines, Europe, and the Americas, also brought great wealth to the Qing court. Unfortunately, much of it was squandered. When the Western powers challenged, China was ill-prepared to mount a viable defense.

The early Qing dynasty was a time of prosperity that would not continue given the lack of innovation and a rapidly growing population. The population doubled or

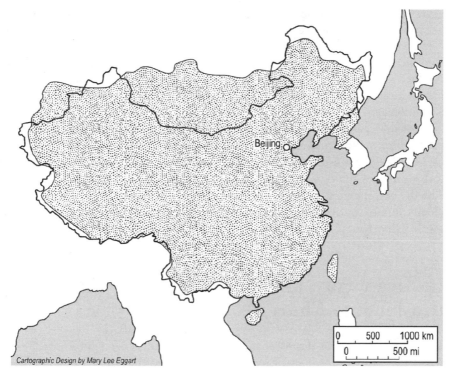

Map 3.15. Qing Dynasty Territory. **Source:** www.chaos.umd.edu/history. Cartographic design by Mary Lee Eggart

perhaps even tripled from 1600 to 1911. This led to ever-increasing pressure on the land, and the internal rebellions that were spawned by environmental collapse and natural disasters at the end of the Qing dynasty clearly contributed to the overthrow of the dynastic system in 1911.

Modern China

China's modern era, as delineated by most historians, begins with the Treaty of Nanking in 1842 that ended the First Opium War between Qing China and Britain. The lost war failed to regulate the trade in opium, and for the Chinese people, the Treaty of Nanking was the first of many so-called unequal treaties. These treaties opened up China to commercial exploitation by Western powers and resulted in significant geographic and economic consequences. The treaties provided extraterritorial privileges to foreigners, thereby making these foreigners immune to local Chinese law and custom.

Signs of internal weakness had already been evident before the Opium Wars. Explosive uprisings occurring during the late eighteenth and early nineteenth centuries, such as the White Lotus Rebellion (1795–1804) and the Taiping Rebellion (1850–1864), attested to the seriousness of many domestic problems under the Qing dynasty. The

Opium Wars and their denouement then set in motion a series of events that were cataclysmic and led to the overturn of a whole political, social, and economic system.

The forces unleashed by the Treaty of Nanking upon China after 1842 were social and political on the one hand—a basic challenge to the old order—and economic and technological on the other hand, and marked an aspiration for industrialization and modernization among forward-thinking Chinese nationalists. These latter economic and technological forces had important ecological and spatial ramifications as well. In the nineteenth century, it was becoming obvious that the combination of an increasing population and the prevailing systems of farming and industrial development were unable to provide a satisfactory life and livelihood for all of the Chinese people. It was also obvious that China's vast territory suffered from inadequate surface transportation, and by the mid-nineteenth century remained a poorly integrated spatial system. Consequently, administrative control of the national territory and economic growth were seriously hampered.

The Treaty Ports and the Western Intrusion into China

One of the significant spatial consequences of Western intrusion in China was the emergence of the Treaty Ports. The Treaty of Nanking forced the weak Qing government to allow Western commercial interests to operate in select cities along China's coasts and major rivers, essentially without control. Tens of thousands of Westerners established export and import businesses in coastal cities. Initially, five ports were opened. Eventually there were more than one hundred, and a whole new stratum of commercial and industrial centers then overlapped the preexisting urban system of traditional and largely interior administrative and marketing centers. The Treaty Ports also introduced new technologies for manufacturing and developing tools, instruments, and weapons; new techniques for assembling, storing, processing, and distributing goods; and modern means of doing business and managing accounts and commercial affairs. Modern scholars differ on the impact of the Treaty Ports on Chinese values and the economy. These changed values would shake China to its very foundations before a new and revolutionary order gained control of China in 1949, but one of the most significant economic consequences of the establishment of the Treaty Ports was the spatial reordering of manufacturing toward export products. Development spread along the eastern coastal periphery of China, where the Treaty Ports attracted large numbers of industrial and service workers in addition to those seeking to improve their life. The transport system of China reoriented itself toward these new commercial centers, especially after the beginning of rail construction in the late nineteenth century. American, German, and British firms built the first rail systems, followed by the Russians and Japanese. These systems were designed to expedite trade in areas nominally controlled by foreign commercial interests, and most of the routes ended at the coasts. As a consequence, new regional and local foci of growth emerged, and the economic and political control mechanisms of the country gradually began to shift to incorporate these new forces and realities.

Ultimately, amid rebellion and nationalist sentiments, the Qing dynasty was overthrown and a republican government emerged, based loosely on the democratic principles and ideals of Chinese nationalist Dr. Sun Yat-sen, partly educated in Hawaii. The Republic of China, established in 1911, was weak from the outset. A period of factionalism followed in which powerful regional warlords fought for territorial control, and Western nations tended to recognize whoever controlled Beijing (then Peking). During this time of confusion and instability, two important events occurred. First, in 1921, the Chinese Communist Party (CCP) was founded in Shanghai. While it took a number of years for the CCP to grow, many urban intellectuals were drawn to its platform of renewed Chinese nationalism and independence from foreign control.

The second important event surrounded the rise to power of Chiang Kai-shek. During the early 1920s, the Nationalist Party (Kuomintang or KMT; also Guomindang or GMD), originally founded by Sun Yat-sen and his associates to guide the republic, was reorganized with the help of Soviet advisers, fresh from the overthrow of czarist Russia. This reorganization was along the authoritarian lines of the Soviet Communist Party. Shortly thereafter a new revolutionary army was created with Chiang Kai-shek as its head. Sun Yat-sen died in early 1925, and Chiang Kai-shek took over the reins of power in the KMT. Almost immediately, he launched military campaigns against local warlords and the newly formed CCP. This conflict, so long ago, remains important because the split between Chiang Kai-shek's KMT and the CCP is at the root of the separation of Taiwan and mainland China today.

China's Communist Revolution

The story of the rise and development of the CCP and its famous leaders has been told often, and the details need not be repeated here. It will be sufficient to review briefly a few highlights and then explore the significance and effect of China's communist revolution on the country's physical environment and spatial organization and orientation. The CCP was initially conceived of as an urban-based movement that sought support from the urban proletariat (factory workers and service workers). After a period of little success, some of its leaders turned to rural areas and focused their attention on the disenchanted peasant masses. The leading proponent of this rural-based strategy was a Hunanese cadre with a middle-class peasant upbringing, Mao Zedong. The man who eventually became Chairman Mao worked hard in his native Hunan and Jiangxi provinces in Central China to organize poor and middle-class peasants during the 1920s and early 1930s, achieving considerable success especially in these poor and isolated regions. He and his cohorts became so successful at promoting a rural communist base of support that power and control in the party soon shifted away from the urban cadres to the charismatic and well-spoken Mao.

Eventually competition between the Nationalists and Communists erupted into open conflict, and Chiang Kai-shek and his forces almost eradicated the communist forces in southern and Central China. In 1934–1935, Mao and his peasant forces (85,000 soldiers, 15,000 government and party officials, and 35 women, mostly wives of leaders) managed to escape through a long and harrowing migration to an isolated area of northern Shaanxi province—the epochal 12,500 km Long March. Only 8,000 survived the journey and arrived in Paoan county in northern Shaanxi, and established a remote base area with its headquarters in the loess hills of remote Yan'an. From this isolated base, the CCP gradually expanded its influence. The survivors of the Long March proved to be the key leaders of China well into the 1990s.

The Sino-Japanese War and World War II provided the CCP with new opportunities to grow, and the Communists exploited these cataclysmic events very effectively. Wisely, communist leaders focused their efforts on the patriotic struggle of the Chinese against the Japanese invaders rather than dissipating their strength against their domestic antagonists, the Nationalists. By the end of the Second World War, the CCP and its military arm, the People's Liberation Army, had grown tremendously in North China. Efforts to mediate the political struggle between the Nationalists and Communists failed, and a civil war followed. The Communists, with their strength in the rural areas, were able to dominate that struggle and isolate the nationalist forces easily and quickly in the North. By 1949, the Nationalists had fled the mainland and set up an exile, rump government on Taiwan (see chapter 13).

On October 1, 1949, the PRC was established with Mao Zedong as its first chairman. This marked the end of a century of domestic turmoil and foreign intervention. And more than two thousand years of an imperial dynastic system had been replaced by a truly revolutionary system that was committed to changing China fundamentally and modernizing its society, economy, and politics. A strong, new central government with a firm and definite ideological foundation and position, supported by a powerful army and civil administrative apparatus, took over China. A new age had arrived. The CCP has led Chinese economic and social development to the present and there is little reason to assume that the party will not remain the dominant decision-making political organization in China for years to come.

In the following chapters, we will discuss the kinds of changes that have resulted from the establishment of a communist system in China. One of the goals of this geographic study of China is to provide at least partial answers to some of our questions concerning the spatial organization of this nation's politics, economy, people, and culture in the past, present, and future.

This spatial approach links the past to the present via an examination of the spatial distribution of resources, people, industry, and other economic activities that are currently observable in China, but have been derived from the complexities of three thousand years of human-environment relations (see Sands and Myers 1986).

References Cited

Cheng Te-k'un. 1960. *Shang China*. Vol. 2 of *Archaeology in China*. Toronto: University of Toronto Press, 14–16.

Crossley, Pamela Kyle. 1997. *The Manchus*. Cambridge, Mass.: Blackwell.

Davis, Richard L. 1996. *Wind against the Mountain: The Crisis of Politics and Culture in Thirteenth-century China*. Cambridge, Mass.: Harvard University Press.

Ebrey, Patricia Buckley. 1996. *The Cambridge Illustrated History of China.* Cambridge: Cambridge University Press.

Elvin, Mark. 1973. *The Pattern of the Chinese Past.* Stanford, Calif.: Stanford University Press.

Fairbank, John K., and Merle Goldman. 1998. *China: A New History.* Cambridge, Mass.: Belknap Press.

Fumiko Ikawa-Smith, ed. 1978. *Early Paleolithic Sites in South and East Asia.* The Hague: Mouton.

Goodrich, L. Carrington. 1969. *A Short History of the Chinese People.* London: George Allen and Unwin.

Heritage Foundation. 2004. *U.S. and Asia Statistical Handbook.* Washington, D.C.: Heritage Foundation.

Huang, R. 1997. *China: A Macro History.* Turn of the Century Edition. Armonk, N.Y.: M.E. Sharpe.

Levathes, Louise. 1994. *When China Ruled the Seas: The Treasure Fleet of the Dragon Throne, 1405–1433.* New York: Simon and Schuster.

Loewe, Michael. 1986. Introduction to the Ch'in and Han Empires. In *The Cambridge History of China,* ed. Dennis Twitchett and Michael Loewe. Vol. 1. Cambridge: Cambridge University Press, 2–19.

Mair, V. H. 1997. Script reform in China. In *China Global Studies.* 7th ed. Guilford, Conn.: McGraw-Hill Duskin, 175–79.

National Bureau of Statistics. 2002. *Zhongguo tongji nianjian 2002* [China statistical yearbook 2002]. Beijing: China Statistics Press.

———. 2004. *Zhongguo tongji nianjian 2004* [China statistical yearbook 2004]. Beijing: China Statistics Press.

Needham, Joseph, et al. 1962. *Science and Civilization in China.* Vol. 4, pt. 3. Cambridge: Cambridge University Press, 1–16.

Pannell, Clifton W., and Laurence J. C. Ma. 1983. *China: The Geography of Development and Modernization.* New York: Halsted Press.

Roberts, J. A. G. 1996. *Prehistory to c. 1800.* Vol. 1 of *A History of China.* New York: St. Martin's.

Sands, Barbara, and Ramon Myers. 1986. The spatial approach to Chinese history: A test. *Journal of Asian Studies* 45 (4). 721–43.

Shih Sheng-han. 1982. *A Preliminary Survey of the Book Ch'i Min Yao Shu: An Agricultural Encyclopaedia of the 6th Century.* Beijing: Science Press.

Sivin, Nathan. 1988. *The Contemporary Atlas of China.* Boston: Houghton Mifflin.

Skinner, G. William, ed. 1977. *The City in Late Imperial China.* Stanford, Calif.: Stanford University Press, 211–49.

Smartt, J., and N. W. Simmonds. 1995. *Evolution of Crop Plants.* 2nd ed. Essex, U.K.: Longman Scientific and Technical.

Wheatley, Paul. 1971. *The Pivot of the Four Quarters: A Preliminary Enquiry into the Origins and Character of the Ancient Chinese City.* Chicago: Aldine.

Wu, X. Z., and Frank E. Poirier. 1995. *Human Evolution in China: A Metric Description of the Fossils and a Review of the Sites.* New York: Oxford University Press.

Zhao, Songqiao. 1994. *Geography of China: Environment, Resources, Population, and Development.* New York: Wiley.

Zheng Wenlei. 1997. *Paleolithic Age.* Vol. 1 of *A Journey into China's Antiquity,* ed. Weichao Yu. Beijing: Morning Glory Publishers.

CHAPTER 4

The Political Geography of Emerging China

A POLITICAL GEOGRAPHY FOR THE TWENTY-FIRST CENTURY

The political geography of a country as old, large, and diverse as China is both very broad and very complex. China has traditionally referred to itself as *Zhongguo*, meaning "Central Kingdom," a term that connotes an ethnocentric bias and indeed a superior attitude toward the rest of the world. Throughout much of its history, the country clearly perceived itself in a central, pivotal role, wherein its relations with other countries, and especially those on its immediate periphery, were typically those of a superior to an inferior. This was the self-view of Chinese culture and civilization even when its military forces were inferior. What does this mean for China's role in global politics and the security environment of the twenty-first century, and how does it affect China's behavior within the community of nations? A brief historical review will help inform our understanding.

In China's relations with other countries, there evolved over time political and diplomatic relationships that are best described as sovereign state to tributary state or patron to client. Until the nineteenth century, even when it was ruled by non-Han emperors as in the Yuan and Qing dynasties, China was always a great Asian power. In part, or perhaps because of its ethnocentrism, China tended to be inward-looking and self-satisfied with its position and role. Historically this may have resulted from China's preoccupation with the internal consolidation of its national territory and its leaders' enduring struggle to keep their various regions tied and loyal to the center.

Related to this was the symbolic role of the Chinese emperor (the "son of heaven" as he was known), who sat in the sacred center of this great empire. This locus of power became what Paul Wheatley (1971) called the "axis mundi," the center of the known universe for all Chinese. Yet there were times when China did in fact look beyond its land frontiers. As early as the eighth century A.D., landless peasants, traders, fishermen, and pirates looked to the sea and places beyond the Chinese ecumene, and many set sail for distant lands to seek their fortunes and enhance their opportunities and livelihoods. Thus began an exodus and dispersion of the Chinese people first to Southeast Asia or the South Seas (the *Nanyang* as the Chinese refer to it) and later to more distant places, an exodus and spread that continues to this day (Wiens 1967).

During the Song dynasty beginning in the tenth and certainly by the late twelfth century A.D., China began to launch trading expeditions into the South China Sea

(Fairbank 1992). By the fifteenth century, this tradition had expanded to the sending out of the great Ming dynasty maritime expeditions headed by Zheng He, and a number of these reached the coast of Africa. An especially extensive network of trading ports was established during the thirteenth to fifteenth centuries in the South China Sea (Nan Hai) area. Cartier (2001) has provided a recent review and analysis of this early Chinese maritime activity and trade that offers a useful perspective on the advances in Chinese overseas exploration and involvement. Yet paradoxically, in late Ming times maritime policy was reversed, and China turned away from sailing and maritime trading activities just at the time when the age of great European exploration was getting into high gear. This change occurred, among other reasons, because of the high cost of fleet construction and also because of a decline in the dynasty and its fiscal control and an increase in its instability. Whatever the causes, the results were an inward reorientation, rapid population growth, and stagnating per capita output.

From a twenty-first-century point of view, these early Chinese maritime forays were important events for they showed the real and potential power of the empire, despite their somewhat abrupt termination. Of great current interest and symbolic significance even today was a recent expansion of the Chinese navy and that navy's first circumnavigation of the globe, which a small fleet of warships made in 2002 by visiting a number of countries in a global showing of the flag of the People's Republic of China (PRC). Such an expedition brings to mind, for the first time since the voyages of Zheng He, the interest of the modern Chinese state in and its commitment to displaying its growing military and technological prowess to the world.

The Chinese Geopolitical View

In evaluating what this process of self-image formation has meant for China and the world, Ginsburg (1968) described the traditional model in which a Sinocentric view was clearly paramount in China when it knew little about the rest of the world—except for those peripheral neighbors with which it had traditionally sought to establish a superior-tributary relationship—a policy that served reasonably well for two millennia despite the vagaries of dynastic effectiveness. According to Whitney (1970) and Ginsburg, the Chinese placed a different value on far-flung national territory. Therefore, the eighteen traditional provinces in the eastern half of the country represented a more-valued national core, and the worthiness of China's remaining national territory declined as a direct function of its distance from this core (see map 4.1). Parts of Southeast and Central Asia as well as Mongolia and parts of Siberia were inside the traditional frontiers of the area over which China had some kind of control or loose tributary relationship.

After the onset of European incursions and especially after the Opium Wars, this traditional view and approach was under serious challenge. China, perhaps because of external threats, began to assume much more interest in its peripheral territories and to issue more direct claims of territorial sovereignty to frontier regions. However, during the nineteenth century as the Qing dynasty became increasingly weak and ineffective,

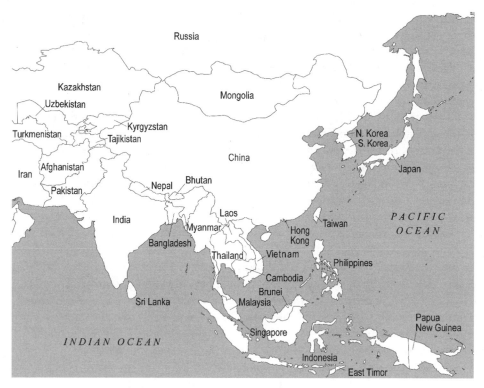

Map 4.1. China and Its Asian Neighbors

China had to yield considerable territory to other countries such as Russia, Japan, and British-controlled South Asia.

As David Shambaugh (2000) recently noted, few issues in modern Chinese studies excite the imagination of scholars as much as the recent evolutionary trajectory of the Chinese state. As he goes on to point out, in the modern period this evolution proceeded from "imperial system to republican to revolutionary communist to modernizing socialist, and in Taiwan to democratic phases" (1). At the same time, he noted three enduring characteristic missions or goals of the Chinese state over the last century: "modernization of the economy, transformation of society, and defense of the nation against foreign aggression" (1). As we proceed with our discussion of China's development, it will be useful to consider the changes in how these missions were approached during the socialist period since 1949 and what methods or paths to their resolutions were followed.

One goal that China has clearly and tenaciously sought and partially succeeded in gaining is restoration to the state territory of those areas of greater China that lay outside the territorial sovereignty of the PRC in 1950. The obvious territories were Hong Kong, Macao, and Taiwan. Hong Kong was returned to China in 1997 by the British according to an agreement signed in 1984 that allowed the territory of Hong Kong to exist as a special administrative region (SAR) of China for fifty years, with many of its existing commercial practices and civil rights as well as its political democracy intact during that period (*Basic Law* 1991). The Portuguese and Chinese agreed to a similar arrangement for Macao, and it was restored to China in December 1999. Taiwan remains outside China, and its reintegration as a part of greater China has become a particularly contentious and volatile issue.

Greater China (*da Zhonghua*) as defined here is simply those areas of the national territory peopled by Han Chinese or linked historically with it through tributary relations. In fact, the conceptual idea of a Greater China is slippery, complex, and subject to a variety of interpretations and designations (Harding 1993).

In the twentieth century after the establishment of the PRC in 1949, the country moved quickly to establish full and sovereign control over many of its outlying territories such as Tibet, Xinjiang or Chinese Turkestan, Inner Mongolia, and all of Manchuria. In addition, serious border conflicts and fighting occurred with India (1964), the Soviet Union (1969), and Vietnam (1979). The PRC has also laid claim to virtually all of the archipelagos in the South China Sea, thereby essentially asserting that the South China Sea is in fact territorial water and an economic resource zone of China. While these geopolitical claims are to some extent problematic, this activist and aggressive approach, as Samuels (1982) has noted, indicates that China has continued to shift from its early Qing dynasty inward-looking posture to a more outward policy that has sporadically been aggressive in asserting claims.

While there are many different interpretations and conclusions that may be offered about China's role in world affairs since 1950, it is clear that the country intends in the future to play a major role in East Asian and global affairs. As China's economic development progresses, its ability to develop a powerful military and political presence will continue to grow. To what extent this will be translated into challenges to those neighbors with whom it has territorial disagreements is difficult to predict. Goldstein (2001) provides a balanced and thoughtful assessment of China's future diplomacy and possible military activity. Such growing power could indeed presage a period of growing conflict. On the other hand, the presence of many ethnic nationalities in China's current frontier territories represents a threat to internal stability. Domestic stability, history suggests, will remain China's first priority. Further, China's historical record with its Tibetan and Central Asian minority nationalities is such that continuing conflict and internal instability here seem likely, and this will require the continuing attention and resources of the central state.

EMPIRE OR NATION-STATE: CHINA'S GOALS FOR THE TWENTY-FIRST CENTURY

One of the more interesting and controversial questions often invoked as a result of China's rapid ascendancy toward global superpower status is how China should be viewed as a nation and country. Given the huge size of its territory and the diversity of its people, should it be considered an empire, reconstituted in a new, twenty-first-century political guise and form from the old Chinese imperial structure and system? Or should it more appropriately be considered a nation-state, despite the many minority and ethnic groups that make up its population, including those various linguistic groups among the mainstream Han Chinese majority? Arguments can be made for both points of view, and in the discussion of minority nationalities that follows, the case for China's behaving like a latter-day empire, and almost in the manner of the Soviet Union, can be seen. Yet the powerful force of Han Chinese assimilation as a mode of long-term nation-building can also be seen at work in the manner in which groups on the margin of Han civilization have progressively been brought into the greater Han fold. Over time some of these groups, especially where *putonghua*, or Mandarin, is the first language, have come to be almost indistinguishable from Han Chinese, despite self-identification (the Manchu or Hui, for example).[1]

In reconsidering China's worldview and global ambitions for the twenty-first century, it is necessary to review China's domestic as well as international situation. Since the late 1970s, the goals of China's restructuring and reforming socialist system were to advance the economic growth and development of the nation while maintaining political and social control through the primacy of the Chinese Communist Party (CCP). Some political liberalization was allowed during the 1980s, but after this liberalization resulted in division and turmoil and the tragic events of June 1989, in which a number of students were massacred in the Tiananmen incident in Beijing, party and government emphasis was placed on maintaining order and control and avoiding what the Chinese perceive as chaos (*luan*) and unstable political conditions. The Japanese specialist on international politics Satoshi Amako (1997) has described as "unified authoritarianism" the political path or political model the Chinese leadership followed after the Tiananmen incident.

At this point a lid was clamped over the domestic political scene, and little changed in Chinese politics for thirteen years until leadership succession was put in motion at the Sixteenth Communist Party Congress in autumn 2002. China then made a transition to a new generation of leaders, and President Jiang Zemin and Premier Li Peng yielded their leadership positions in favor of younger leaders Hu Jintao (president) and Wen Jiabao (premier). Yet how fast this leadership transition will lead to political change remains uncertain, and the particular direction of political evolution in China is unclear. Certainly China's focus on economic growth will continue, and indeed the success of China's economic growth and development are the keys to ensuring the legitimacy and success of the CCP as the sole arbiter of power and control in China.

Modern China since the communist takeover of the mainland in 1949 has been a state and nation that takes its basic direction and guidance for its development and growth from the CCP. Reaffirmed as recently as 2002 at the Sixteenth National Congress of the Communist Party of China, the goal of the CCP is

> to lead the people of all our ethnic groups in a concerted, self-reliant and pioneering effort to turn China into a prosperous, strong, democratic and culturally advanced modern socialist country by making economic development our central task while adhering to the Four Cardinal Principles and persevering in the reform and opening up. (*Xinhua News Agency* 2002)

The "Four Cardinal Principles" refers to maintaining socialism, the people's democratic dictatorship, and the primacy and leadership of the CCP based on Marxism-Leninism and "Mao Zedong thought." The key element in this is the preservation of socialism in whatever form it takes as it continues to evolve and emerge in China, while maintaining the exclusive and primary leadership role of the CCP in the political control of the country.

The same document reaffirms and emphasizes the key role of economic development in leading the cause of socialism: "The Communist Party of China must persist in taking economic development as the central task, making all other work subordinated to and serve this central task" (*Xinhua News Agency* 2002). Such an emphasis suggests that the CCP and its top leadership recognize that domestic economic development and growth underlie their efforts to advance the country, and that the goal of growing the economy is essential to maintaining a stable and productive society and polity in the future. Thus, continued success in political control would appear to hinge on effective efforts in economic growth.

FOREIGN POLICY, INTERNATIONAL RELATIONS, AND THE TAIWAN QUESTION

At the same time that the party regime must focus on domestic control and stability, it must study the forces of international politics carefully to ensure that China's security remains protected, and that the country's ambitions as a growing regional and world power are taken seriously. In the twenty-first century, following the collapse of the Soviet Union and the emergence of the United States as the sole world superpower—and added to this the regional fighting in Afghanistan, South Asia, and Iraq following the events of September 11, 2001—China has sought to establish its proper role as a regional and emerging world power. But how does it deal with its neighbors as well as the United States, and how does it pursue its long-held—almost sacred—objective of reuniting Taiwan with its motherland (Vogel 1997)?

China's foreign policy goals are straightforward and appear reasonable. An official Chinese website sums up the country's goals:

> The basic objectives of this policy are to safeguard the independence, sovereignty and territorial integrity of the country, strive to create a long-standing and favorable international environment for China's reform, opening-up and modernization drive, safeguard world peace and promote common development. (*China through a Lens* 2004)

These are certainly goals that appear reasonable and appropriate in the current global context. China goes further to affirm that it will follow an independent policy and avoid alliances while also opposing what it sees as "hegemonism" in any other state or group of states. Its other general goals are to develop good relations with all its neighbors, strengthen its relations with developing countries, be open to the outside world, and work toward world peace in the framework of the UN.

In China's stated goals of foreign policy and foreign relations, the only place where its current stated position appears aggressive and contentious is in its statements on Taiwan. Here China's policy is clear and unambiguous: Taiwan is part of the integral territory of the motherland, and China seeks Taiwan's reintegration, although under terms that will allow Taiwan some degree of autonomy and time for special development. At the same time, while China calls for this reintegration into the national territory in a peaceful manner, it reserves the right to use force to bring about this territorial reintegration if necessary.

It is the Taiwan issue, China's most contentious and serious goal, that has created ongoing tension, especially with the United States. China views Taiwan as a true and inalienable part of the motherland and will allow no variance from its view that it must reunite the island with the People's Republic. This is in line with the idea that China is a nation-state even though it contains 100 million people who are not Han Chinese.

At present however, despite a rapidly growing defense budget and much progress in military modernization, China does not possess sufficient military power to seize Taiwan. However, its recent accelerated development of military forces clearly appears focused on tactical amphibious, naval, and air weapons that are designed and suited for an invasion of Taiwan and to oppose the likely U.S. forces that would be sent to assist Taiwan in the event of an attack (Shanker 2005). Current insufficiency of forces, however, has not prevented China from issuing periodic threats and conducting military operations in the vicinity of Taiwan that appear to be intended to intimidate the citizens of Taiwan to the point where they will simply yield and capitulate to Chinese rule (Vogel 1997; Goldstein 2001). China has proposed the idea of the "one nation, two systems" principle, wherein Taiwan would be allowed to maintain its own economy and political system for a limited period of, say, fifty years, similar to the model that is in place for Hong Kong. Yet the Taiwanese have resisted this model, and they reject it for now. With support from the United States, they have so far continued to maintain their autonomy from China. However, economic links between China and Taiwan are growing rapidly because many Taiwan industrialists have relocated their production operations to China, taking advantage of China's low-cost labor to keep their products competitively priced. A large number of Taiwan citizens also now live in the greater Shanghai region and are associated with these growing economic ties, ties that may someday help facilitate reconciliation of China and Taiwan based on the mutual benefits.

China and the United States have differed in their view of Taiwan, although both countries continue to support the "one China" policy and the idea that Taiwan is part of China. This was reaffirmed in the Shanghai Communiqué and in related communiqués between the United States and the PRC in the 1970s that set out the framework whereby the United States recognized the PRC as the legitimate government of China and rescinded its bilateral treaty with Taiwan. However, the United States also affirmed its position of rejecting the use of force in the return of Taiwan to China. Through enactment of the Taiwan Relations Act, the United States established the principle that it would provide Taiwan with defensive arms and military equipment to allow it to defend itself against attack from the PRC. While the PRC does not accept the validity of the Taiwan Relations Act and opposes strenuously the sale of U.S. weapons to Taiwan, it has not directly attacked Taiwan in an effort to bring about Taiwan's return. And because the island's population is divided over how to deal with China and how to proceed with Taiwan's political destiny, this matter continues to fester. Not surprisingly, it has soured relations between China and the United States. More discussion on this contentious and complex issue will follow in chapter 13, where we explore the political and social dynamics of Taiwan's people and their recent history.

China's relations with the United States continue to be characterized by uncertainty and difficulty as the two countries seek to engage one another constructively while also continuing to differ and squabble over Taiwan, human rights issues related to Tibet and minority peoples in China, and religious freedom. Military leaders in China remain very suspicious of U.S. goals and the United States' perceived hegemony in world affairs, and they can be expected to oppose any efforts of the United States to establish or maintain outposts of American power in the western Pacific or on the Asian mainland. The United States and Japan in turn both view China's rapid increase in military spending and the modernization of China's military as a dangerous signal of China's long-term intention to establish itself as a dominant military and economic power in East Asia. Consequently, the trajectory of U.S.-China relations in the future must be managed very carefully by both sides to ensure a productive and peaceful outcome despite occasional disagreements and tensions (Vogel 1997; Goldstein 2001).

Internal Political Organization and Administration

One of the basic requirements of any country's political system is the organization of its territory for the most effective and efficient operation of governance. The functions of government and the control and support of the population must be managed effectively if the state is to rule as a credible and legitimate institution. The state must incorporate the territory of the country in a manner that allows that territory to contribute to the national well-being in a positive, economic, and political manner (Whitney 1970).

Traditionally in China, the main goal of the imperial authority was to establish central control, for the task of organizing China's large population and territory was gargantuan indeed. As Hsiao noted:

> The solution as it was worked out in China during the successive dynasties from Ch'in [Qin] to Ch'ing [Qing] consisted essentially in the development of an administrative apparatus which helped the emperors to assure obedience and forestall rebellion, partly by ministering to the basic material needs of the subjects so that few of them would be driven by unbearable hardships "to tread the dangerous path," partly by inculcating in their minds carefully chosen precepts (mostly from doctrines of the Confucian tradition) that tended to make them accept or acquiesce in the existing order, and partly by keeping constant surveillance over them so that "bad people" might be detected and dealt with in time. (1960, 3)

This type of administrative apparatus, supported by the army, permitted a dynasty to maintain control for long periods of time. Indeed, as we noted earlier, the basic system of control and governance in China lasted more than two thousand years. Our goal in analyzing China's internal administrative organization is not to recount the historical method of administrative control, but rather to begin our discussion with the recognition of a significant change in that administrative system after 1949. Our specific goals are to describe the new administrative system and especially its territorial aspects, to explain and evaluate some of the functions and the effectiveness of that system, and finally, to examine the nature of the system's organization of that territory not regarded as traditionally Chinese, that is, the outlying and associated territory peopled by China's ethnic minorities.

GEOGRAPHY OF ADMINISTRATION

The administrative framework of the PRC has undergone significant changes since 1949. Under Nationalist (Kuomintang or KMT; also Guomindang or GMD) rule, China consisted of thirty-five provinces (including Taiwan), one autonomous region (Nei Mongol, or Inner Mongolia), one territory (Tibet or Xizang), one special district (Hainan Island), and twelve centrally governed municipalities. After 1949, major changes were effected.

First, the number of provinces and province-level cities decreased. In 1951 China reduced the number of provinces in the Northeast (Manchuria) from nine to six, and again, in 1954, from six to three, the remaining provinces being Liaoning, Jilin, and Heilongjiang. During 1954–1955, the provinces of Rehe, Suiyuan, and Chahaer were eliminated, with most of their territories transferred to the Nei Mongol (Inner Mongolia) Autonomous Region (AR). In the 1950s too, the number of centrally governed cities was reduced from twelve to three.

Second, autonomous geographic regions in border areas inhabited by minority nationality groups were established. In addition to the Nei Mongol AR, established in 1947, four new province-level ARs were created in the decade from 1955 to 1965. Xinjiang (Sinkiang) province became Xinjiang Uygur AR in 1955. In 1958, Guangxi province was redesignated as Guangxi Zhuang AR, and Ningxia (Ninghsia) Hui AR was created. Finally in 1965, Xizang territory (Tibet) was changed to Tibet AR (see map 4.2). Meanwhile, lower-order minority districts such as autonomous prefectures (*diqu*), counties (*xian*), leagues (*meng*), and banners (*qi*) were established as second- and third-order geographic areas. Minority peoples and areas, as a significant and sometimes contentious issue in the evolving political geography of China, will be discussed in detail in the last section of this chapter.

Third, huge regional administrative units above the provincial level were created and then abolished. During the period from 1949 to 1954, when much of China's administrative power was decentralized, the country was divided into six Great Administrative Areas, plus Nei Mongol (Inner Mongolia) AR. Each area (except for Manchuria and North China) featured a Military and Administrative Committee, which served as the highest organ of political control in charge of several provinces. These regional authorities initially had considerable power and enjoyed a significant degree of autonomy. But gradually, as the political power of the new regime was consolidated, Chinese leaders, perhaps motivated by the fear that the regional governments could become

Map 4.2. China's First-Order (Provincial-Level) Administrative Regions

too powerful for the central government to control, began to increase the power of the central government. In November 1952, the regional governments were stripped of most of their power. Two years later the entire structure above the provincial level was abolished.

Several significant administrative changes have occurred in recent years, and the current administrative hierarchy is comprised of thirty-one first-order administrative regions plus the special administrative regions of Hong Kong and Macao. The thirty-one administrative regions include four national cities (Beijing, Shanghai, Tianjin, and most recently—in 1997—Chongqing); five ARs (Xinjiang Uygur, Tibet, Ningxia Hui, Guangxi Zhuang, and Inner Mongolia) peopled with substantial ethnic minority populations; and twenty-two provinces of which the most recent, Hainan, was separated from Guangdong in 1988. Map 4.3 of the first-order administrative regions indicates the considerable variation in their size. This is paralleled by significant differences in their populations and population densities as well.

Fourth, basic-level administrative units have been established. The most revolutionary changes in China's administrative structure have occurred at the grassroots level. Prior to the revolution, the central government and the basic-level administrative units below the county level were poorly integrated. Although there were administrative systems developed below the county level, such as the *baojia* and *lijia* systems, they were concerned chiefly with taxation, internal security, and corvée functions. Very little of the state's resources for economic development was allocated to villages, where most

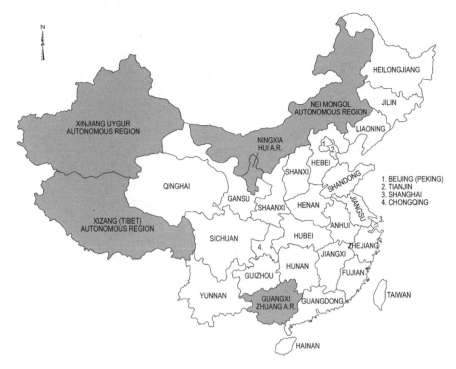

Map 4.3. First-Order Administrative Units for Minority Nationalities in China

people lived, and there was virtually no systematic socioeconomic planning by the state for the masses at the village and urban neighborhood levels. Direct participation by the masses in the political and economic affairs of the state was hampered by a large administrative gap separating the central government from the villages. Members of the rural gentry class almost invariably dominated the affairs of the villages, often at the expense of peasant interests.

All this fundamentally changed after the communist revolution, and new basic-level administrative units were designed that proved to be highly effective. The entire administrative hierarchy in China is now tightly integrated. As a consequence, mass participation in, and state control of, the political, social, and economic affairs of the country at the grassroots level have been much more effective than before, and the authority of the state extends to the level of the household and even to the individual. At the same time, the effects of economic reform and the diminution of state control of the economy have begun to relax the hand of the state in economic activities. Shifting demands in the labor markets have led to a need for the increased migration of rural people to offer needed labor services in cities, and this in turn has led to reduced social controls in administering the *hukou* system of household registration and strict assignment of residential location.

It goes without saying that urban and rural administration at all levels is dictated by the CCP. Once a decision is made by the party, it is put into effect through the various levels of the administrative hierarchy of provinces, prefectures, cities, counties, townships, and villages and is then articulated through the spatial network of these various units.

Two major changes affected urban administration during the 1980s (Ma and Cui 1987). First, economic reforms were applied to cities in late 1984. While the reforms in urban areas did not have perhaps as great an effect as in the countryside, nevertheless some effort at creating a modest private-sector economy with vendors and petty service people had begun. Limited migration of rural people was also allowed to provide service and construction workers in the cities. These migrants were not afforded the conventional subsidies of housing, food, health, and educational services afforded to urban dwellers employed in the state sector of the economy. There are currently estimated to be more than 120 million of these migrants in China's cities, many of whom live in very crude and rough accommodations that are temporary (*Xingbao* 2003). Obviously the government's commitment to and efficiency in providing administrative services and support for these people are different and less than that for long-term residents. Problems of social and political concern such as increased crime, poor health conditions, limited educational opportunities, and crowded and poor housing have increased.

The second major change was a set of political disturbances that occurred in many of China's large cities in the spring of 1989, disturbances known as the "democracy movement." This event had its roots in the general liberalization of both the economy and society that followed the Cultural Revolution and the demise of the Gang of Four in 1977. The violent suppression of this movement in Tiananmen Square in Beijing on June 3–4, 1989, ushered in a period of martial law in Beijing and a severe political crackdown throughout the country. The Department of Public Security (i.e., the *gonganju*, or police) initiated much more rigorous control measures, especially in cities that were seen as the focal points of trouble and dissatisfaction. This was done, in the eyes of the CCP, to prevent any full-blown assault on or threat to Chinese socialism and the integrity of the state. The immediate and direct consequence of these measures was to demonstrate that the CCP, buttressed by the army and its various security forces, was very much in control of China's cities. (For a full and insightful explanation of the Tiananmen incident, see Liang [2001].)

A RETROSPECTIVE VIEW OF CHINA'S ADMINISTRATIVE GEOGRAPHY UNDER COMMUNISM

As we noted previously, the twentieth century brought a fundamental change in the nature of China's political system with the overturn of its long-lived dynastic order. The CCP, which took over in 1949, focused especially on territorial organization and greatly strengthened the administration of territory at the local level. Among the most significant accomplishments of the CCP has been the extended control and involvement of local people at both urban neighborhood and township levels in the affairs of economy and politics. Transforming the economy has strengthened the role of local party cadres as they have embedded themselves more deeply in the expanding economy at local levels. Improvements in the economy have in turn offered greater legitimacy to the CCP at local, regional, and national levels. Yet political reforms have not accompanied these improvements in the economy.

New and younger leaders such as President Hu Jintao and Premier Wen Jiabao have assumed power, but it is uncertain how far they will move in modifying or liberalizing the political evolution of China or at what point the CCP will allow any meaningful competition or opposition to its rule. Until it does, China will remain a Leninist state as defined by the primacy and exclusivity of the CCP. At the same time, its transition from socialism is leading to rapid although sometimes controversial growth in the private economy in which the role of local party cadres in facilitating and indeed in participating in the growing private economy is increasing. The line between socialist "public" and capitalist "private" is becoming less clear as cadres get more and more involved in business and China's dynamic market economic system (Wank 1999). At the same time there is also discussion in the CCP about China's political destiny, and this has led to the study of limited experimentation with local democracy as well as with European-style socialist democracy.

Minority Nationalities

China is a state of many nationalities: fifty-six official ones. Approximately 92 percent of China's total population is composed of *Hanren*, meaning the Han people, an ethnic term that the Chinese have used since the Han dynasty (206 B.C.–A.D. 220) to distinguish themselves from non-Han minority nationalities.

A *nationality* is defined in China as a group of people of common origin living in a common area, with a common language, and having a sense of group identity in economic and social organization and behavior (Dreyer 1976). In 1982 in China there were 67,233,254 people classified as minorities (see table 4.1) who belonged to fifty-five minority nationalities (Banister 1987; Poston and Jing 1987). By the year 2000, this population had grown to 106.43 million, 8.41 percent of China's total population (National Bureau of Statistics 2001). Fifteen minorities in 1982 had a population of more than 1 million each, and the number of groups with more than 1 million has increased to eighteen since then. Although China's minorities constitute only about 8 percent of the national total population, they inhabit about 60 percent of the nation's territory (see map 4.4). While minority groups lag economically behind the Han Chinese majority, their significance is far greater than their numbers would indicate. They receive much attention from the Chinese government, which frequently claims that the minorities are not only politically equal to the Han majority, but also deserve preferential treatment because of their small populations and less-developed economic situations. Efforts have been made by the central government to ensure that the minorities are well-represented at various national conferences. Certain national policies, such as family planning, that might hinder improvement in the socioeconomic level of minority nationalities, are not enforced as rigorously in minority areas (Schwarz 1971; Banister 1987). Yet it is clear that fertility rates among minority women have diminished rapidly in recent years in parallel with those of the Han, although they have not yet declined to the same levels (Wu 1997; Du 2000).

Table 4.1. Population of China's Major
Minority Nationalities in 2000

Zhuang	12,178,811
Manchu	10,682,262
Hui	9,816,805
Miao	8,940,116
Uygur	8,399,393
Tujia	8,028,133
Yi	7,762,272
Mongolian	5,813,947
Tibetan	5,416,021
Bouyei	2,971,460
Dong	2,960,293
Yao	2,637,421
Korean	1,923,842
Bai	1,858,063
Hani	1,439,673
Kazak	1,250,458
Li	1,247,814
Dai	1,158,989

Source: National Bureau of Statistics 2002, 44.

Several reasons account for the special treatment given to these minority nationalities. First, most of the minority groups occupy China's border areas, which are strategically important. Several groups, including the Shan, Koreans, Mongols, Uygurs, Yao, and Kazaks, are also found in neighboring Thailand, Burma, Korea, Mongolia, and the Central Asian republics. If they were hostile to the Chinese central government, these

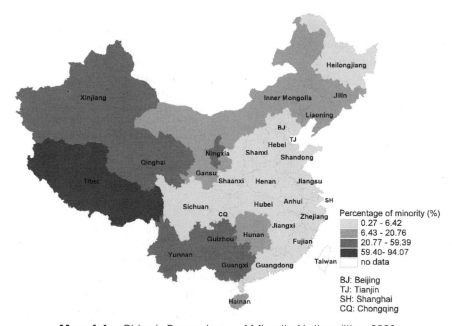

Map 4.4. China's Percentage of Minority Nationalities, 2003

groups could significantly weaken China's border defenses and increase the threat of attack by foreign countries. A significant Tibetan exile group, focused around the Dalai Lama, has been based in India since 1959.

Second, most of China's minority regions are sparsely populated relative to the rest of the country but are richly endowed with natural resources. For example, there are extensive oil reserves in Heilongjiang and Xinjiang, tin and copper deposits in Yunnan and Guizhou, and uranium deposits along the Central Asian border in Xinjiang. The majority of China's forestland is also found in border regions, especially in the northeastern and southwestern provinces. Large numbers of livestock are raised in the arid and semiarid northwestern areas, where more than 80 percent of China's wool and animal skins are produced. In addition, certain minority localities have virgin land that can be reclaimed for settlement to alleviate population pressures in the densely populated regions of China. Extensive virgin land in Heilongjiang, Xinjiang, and other places has been developed by Chinese settlers in the last fifty years for agriculture.

Third is the matter of the political image of socialism. A contented, cooperative, and prosperous minority population is living proof of the superiority of socialism and enhances the political image of the central state. On the other hand, minority problems not only tarnish the image of the government, they also generate domestic and international crises. China's record toward its minority nationalities, though, is mixed and has not always been clear. Moreover, government policy, despite its polite, upbeat rhetoric, has been ambivalent and at times harsh and repressive, as in Tibet and Xinjiang in 1988 and 1989 (Gladney 1995).

HAN EXPANSION

Historically, the Han Chinese were never isolated from the peoples who inhabited the areas surrounding the Chinese cultural realm. Interactions between the Chinese and the non-Han groups were already extensive as early as the Zhou dynasty (ca. 770–221 B.C.). Frequent invasions of the Chinese territories by the non-Han peoples along China's northern borders necessitated the construction of defensive walls against these nomads by various states as early as the Zhou period. Although built primarily for defense against nomadic invasions from the north, the Great Wall was not always militarily effective. Its symbolic significance, however, never changed. For the Chinese, it symbolized a line of demarcation separating the steppe from the sown field, nomadism from agriculture, and barbarism from civilization (Fairbank 1992).

Chinese civilization primarily spread from the Huang He Basin toward the south, a region that offered the Chinese a favorable agricultural environment. Before the establishment of the first empire of the Qin in 221 B.C., most of South China, including the middle Chang Jiang (Yangtze River) region, was inhabited by various Tai peoples, many of whom were displaced, absorbed, or acculturated in later centuries by Han colonizers.

The tempo of the southward spread of the Chinese varied considerably. During periods of nomadic invasions from the northern border regions, alien governments were established in North China and large numbers of Chinese were pushed to the Chang Jiang valley areas. There were, of course, gradual shifts of population to the productive Chang Jiang Basin, where the alluvial soil has always been fertile and the amount of precipitation normally adequate. Further southward expansion took place along the tributary river valleys of the Chang Jiang, notably along the Gan, Xiang, and Yuan rivers. The highly fertile farming region of the Guangzhou (Canton) Delta began to grow rapidly after the eighth century (Wiens 1967).

With the exception of the Mongols during the Yuan dynasty (A.D. 1279–1368), virtually all of the non-Han peoples who had established alien states on Chinese soil, including the Xianbei, the Jurchen, the Khitans, the Tanguts, and the Manchus, were in the end assimilated by the culturally more advanced and numerically greater Chinese. Over the centuries, intermarriage between the Han and other groups has made the population of China genetically heterogeneous. Genetically, there is no such thing as a Chinese race. Authoritative sources have indicated genetic differences, for example, between northern and southern Chinese populations (Cavalli-Sforza, Menozzi, and Piazza 1994). Alien groups, once they had been sinicized, were readily accepted by the Chinese. The term *Chinese* appears to be a cultural rather than a racial term.

The spread of Chinese culture was confined primarily to areas where agricultural cultivation based on lowland rice was possible, leaving the more hilly, arid, and nonproductive border regions largely to non-Han peoples. Although some of the border areas, such as Xinjiang and Tibet, were nominally Chinese provinces, they existed largely as de facto kingdoms, frequently challenging Chinese control until after the communist revolution.

Gaubatz's (1996) description and analysis of Chinese colonization of frontier areas through the establishment and growth of urban garrisons that later grew to full-blown cities provides an insightful interpretation of the growth and spread of the Chinese ecumene and cultural area on the western frontier margins of the national territory. Continued rapid growth of the Han population in these peripheral areas indicates this process of sinicization of frontier areas remains an active policy of the current government of the PRC.

AUTONOMOUS AREAS

The special status of minority groups in the PRC is manifested in its administrative system. Parallel to the Chinese provinces are the five leading minority nationality ARs: Uygur, Mongol, Hui (Chinese Moslem), Tibetan, and Zhuang (see map 4.4). In the ARs where minority groups concentrate, as pointed out earlier, there are second-order administrative units known as autonomous prefectures (*zhou*) and autonomous leagues (*meng*), which are the equivalents of Chinese prefectures. Third-order minority units are autonomous counties and banners (*qi*), which parallel the counties in Han areas. An AR usually carries the name of the largest minority group living there. For example, in Xinjiang Uygur AR, the Uygurs are the largest minority group. Where no single group predominates, an area is named after its two or three leading minorities, such as Jiangzheng Hani-Yi Autonomous County in Yunnan, and Haixi Mongol—Tibetan—Kazak

Autonomous Zhou in Qinghai. Not all minority nationalities have their own ARs, however, and no AR may be established for the Han, even in places where they are a minority. Table 4.1 provides a list of the largest minority nationalities and their populations according to the 2000 census report.

According to the Chinese government, the purpose of this regional autonomy is to guarantee political equality for national minorities and to give special consideration to the development of minority areas. In these ways, the government indicates, the policies and principles of the CCP can be implemented more effectively. It would seem then that minority nationalities are entitled to the right of self-government in their own areas. In reality, however, political administration in such areas is identical to that in Han regions, and the minority nationalities must conform to the rules established by the CCP. Yet although political autonomy exists in name only, there is a considerable degree of cultural autonomy. Comparatively greater freedom is given to peoples who work to retain their ethnic customs and beliefs and to use their native language to conduct such official business as public meetings and legal proceedings. Although the Chinese language (Mandarin) is taught everywhere in China, serious efforts have been made by the government to create new scripts or to improve the written languages in minority areas. Of the fifty-six officially recognized nationalities, at least twenty-five now have their own written languages (Ma 1962; Zhang 1984).

XINJIANG UYGUR

Xinjiang, meaning "New Territory" in Chinese, used to be known as Chinese Turkestan. With more than 1,600,000 km^2 of territory, it is the largest among China's provinces and ARs. Aside from Tibet, Xinjiang is the only AR where minority nationalities outnumber the Han Chinese. Thirteen nationalities are found in Xinjiang: Uygur, Han, Kazak, Mongol, Hui, Kirgiz, Russian, Uzbek, Xibo, Tajik, Tartar, Daur, and Manchu. In the mid-1960s there were about 4 million Uygurs and 500,000 Kazaks. By 1982 the Uygur population had grown to almost 6 million, and Kazaks numbered over 900,000. The total population of Xinjiang in 1987 exceeded 14 million. Less than two decades later in 2001, the Uygurs were estimated at approximately 8.4 million and the Kazaks at 1.3 million. The total population of Xinjiang in 2001 was 18.76 million. Han Chinese numbered 7.42 million in 2001, and had increased their share of Xinjiang's total population to 40 percent (National Bureau of Statistics 2002).

The population of Xinjiang has been increasing steadily as a result of improved healthcare services. Smallpox has been eliminated, and leprosy, malaria, typhoid, venereal disease, and other infectious diseases have been brought under control. Infant mortality rates and postnatal deaths have been greatly reduced. Birth control is not enforced rigorously in ARs because their populations are generally much smaller than in other parts of China, but family-planning guidance and assistance are readily available.

Another factor of population growth in Xinjiang has been the large-scale immigration of Han Chinese. The majority of these migrants were demobilized troops and their families, young people recently graduated from secondary schools, groups sent out from large cities, and civil administrators (Husayin 1966). The rate of Han influx was particularly high during 1957–1958. By the end of 1958, some 556,000 Han Chinese had settled in Xinjiang (Lal 1970); and as noted above, the Han numbered over 7 million in the year 2001 and accounted for approximately 40 of the total population.

The Production and Construction Corps of the People's Liberation Army formed the basis of Chinese colonization of Xinjiang. The size of the corps increased from 100,000 in the early 1950s to more than 500,000. The troops reclaimed more than 700,000 ha (more than 1.73 million acres) of virgin land in Xinjiang for cultivation (Heaton 1971). In addition to reclaiming land, the army also developed mines, built railroads and factories, and operated more than one hundred military farms. The in-migration and growth of the Han Chinese population has been remarkable. Many of them are concentrated in industrial regions and cities such as Shihezi at the northern foot of the Tian Shan Mountains.

For many centuries Chinese Turkestan, as Xinjiang was called, was a politically contested and unstable area. More recently, Xinjiang has been a politically sensitive area because of its proximity to the former Soviet Union, now the Central Asian republics (Pannell and Ma 1997). Several minority groups, including the Uygurs, Kazaks, Hui, Uzbeks, Tajiks, and the Kirgiz, inhabit both sides of this international border. Isolated rebellions by the Kazaks here against the Chinese government took place in the late 1950s and the early 1960s when China's relations with the Soviet Union became strained. Since then, Uygur separatists have created serious problems, and there have been bombings and other incidents involving Uygurs (Gladney 1990). The terrorist attacks of September 11, 2001, further heightened Chinese anxiety and resulted in the dispatch of increased numbers of Chinese troops to the region to counter the perceived threat of a link between Uygur separatists and forces from outside China such as any members of al-Qaeda trained in Afghanistan. Chinese concerns were also raised over an increase in the military activity of the U.S. Army and Air Force in Afghanistan and nearby Uzbekistan.

TIBET (XIZANG)

Until the 1950s, Tibet was largely isolated from other parts of China and experienced only variable Chinese influence. The Tibetans are culturally distinct from other nationalities of China. Prior to the entry of the CCP, Tibet was a traditional theocracy of about 3 million people living in an area approximately twice the size of Texas. Tibetan politics were dominated by a small group of nobles and by the powerful Lamaist monasteries. The best agricultural land belonged to the monasteries, whose members in the upper clergy were drawn from the noble class. Approximately one-third of male Tibetans were monks, and political and religious powers were centralized in the hands of the Dalai Lama, traditionally a king, god, and high priest in one, who was believed to be a reincarnation of the Buddhist deity of Avalokitasvara. When a Dalai Lama died, his successor was sought from among the children who were born shortly after his death. The new leader was then identified by a complicated religious ritual. The present Dalai Lama is the fourteenth in succession and, as noted, is in exile in India.

Much publicity was given by the Western press to Tibetan resistance against Chinese control in the 1950s. The relationship between China and Tibet in historic times remains confusing. In Tibet there were periods of tributary relations with China and periods when China had little or no influence. In the eighteenth and nineteenth centuries, Chinese officials in Lhasa were known as Ambans, or Residents, and were appointed by the Chinese government. The Chinese government regarded the Residents as Chinese governors, a status the Tibetans never accepted. However, Tibetans periodically made gestures of accepting Chinese overlordship, mainly for the sake of furthering their independence. In the waning years of the Qing dynasty, Tibet almost completely broke away from China. After the downfall of the Qing, regional autonomy in Tibet existed for about four decades while China proper was torn by Chinese warlords and Japanese invaders, and by the civil war between the Nationalists and the Communists. The Nationalists never had an opportunity to deal effectively with the Tibetan question.

Tibet has never been recognized by any country as an independent state. The Dalai Lama readily acknowledged in 1950 that there were times when Tibet sought, though rarely received, the protection of China. According to the Simla Convention of 1914, which was signed by Tibet and British India and was designed to reduce Chinese involvement in Tibet, China was to recognize Tibetan autonomy, to accept the so-called McMahon Line delimiting the border between Tibet and India, and to station no more than five hundred troops in Tibet. The Tibetan authorities, on the other hand, agreed to a statement to the effect that Tibet was under Chinese suzerainty and that it was part of Chinese territory. In the following years, British India, when dealing with questions involving Tibet, made clear to the Chinese that Tibet was under Chinese suzerainty, although in reality India almost invariably dealt with Tibet as an independent state. China, however, has never accepted the Simla treaty, and some Tibetans have argued that they themselves are not bound by it.

As far as the Chinese are concerned, Tibet is a Chinese territory. All of the maps published in China in the last one hundred years showing China's ARs invariably include Tibet, as do all Chinese school textbooks published after the fall of the Qing dynasty. So when the CCP came to power and sent its armies to occupy Tibet in 1950, it saw this not as invading a foreign country but merely as establishing political control over an area traditionally considered Chinese territory. In 1954, India and China signed a treaty that accepted Chinese sovereignty in Tibet.

There were frequent reports in the late 1950s of Tibetans defying Chinese rule. The rapid and forceful introduction of a socialist system in Tibet was accompanied by the simultaneous abolition of traditional Tibetan socioeconomic institutions such as monasticism, serfdom, slavery, and forced labor. These institutions had been deeply rooted in Tibet for centuries. The nobles and monastic orders resisted the new measures by armed rebellion, which culminated in the well-known 1959 uprising. In March 1959, Tibetan rebels seized the Tibetan capital of Lhasa for several days, only to be driven out by the Chinese troops stationed there. The Dalai Lama and many of his followers fled southward to India, where he still resides. The Chinese dissolved the Dalai Lama's government and handed over the administration of Tibet to the Preparatory Committee for the Tibetan Autonomous Region, which had been established in 1956. However, autonomy was not formally granted to Tibet until 1965.

Although very little is known about conditions in Tibet after the uprising, much time passed before Tibet became an AR. The granting of autonomy implies that the

Chinese government has some degree of confidence in its control in a specific minority area, and the lengthy time that elapsed before the government granted autonomy to Tibet suggests that establishing Chinese rule in Tibet was not an easy matter. Not surprisingly then, the administration of the Chinese in Tibet in the last three decades has produced mixed results. Although secular schools, health facilities, modern postal services, airlines, roads, industries, newspapers, radio, and so forth have been introduced into a region where none existed, and whereas a railroad linking Tibet with Qinghai is now under construction, the standard of living of the Tibetan people has not improved much.

China continues to have a serious problem with Tibet and the Tibetan people. Serious uprisings in 1988 and 1989 were brutally suppressed by public security forces and the army (Avedon 1989). Not since the Cultural Revolution have such repressive measures been used against Tibetans. These events demonstrate the failure in Tibet of China's minority policies and also suggest that China's long-term approach and solution to minority dissent may be simply one of eliminating minority peoples through forced acculturation and sinicization, the ultimate solution and outcome of Great Han chauvanism. Today the Tibetan AR represents only about half of the territory that traditionally was peopled by Tibetans and traditionally considered Tibetan territory. The remainder has been transferred administratively and incorporated into the territory of the neighboring provinces of Sichuan and Qinghai.

MINORITIES IN SOUTH AND SOUTHWEST CHINA

Of the fifty-five officially recognized minority nationalities in China, twenty-five are found in the provinces of Guangxi, Yunnan, and Guizhou. Perhaps as many as 50 percent, or more than 50 million of China's current minority populations inhabit these three provinces. Two large nationalities, the Zhuang and the Yi, with a combined 1990 population of 22 million, are concentrated in Guangxi and its neighboring provinces, while a substantial number of Miao, Bouyei, and Shui live in Guizhou. At least fifteen small minorities with a total population of more than 3 million are scattered in the hilly regions of Yunnan.

Because of the lack of historical data, it is extremely difficult to clarify the pattern of sequential occupation of China's southern and southwestern border regions by diverse minority groups. Before the establishment of the first Chinese Empire of the Qin dynasty in 221 B.C., much of South China, including the middle Chang Jiang valley, was inhabited by various groups of Tai (Moseley 1973). Subsequently, the Tai moved southward as a result of Chinese expansion into the Chang Jiang valley. Gradually over the centuries, many Tai peoples migrated, primarily in small groups, into Yunnan and various parts of Southeast Asia.

China's largest minority nationality, the Zhuang, are believed to be ethnically a mixture of the Yue people, who were indigenous to the southeast coast of China, and a Tai group. By the time of the Song dynasty at least, the Zhuang had already settled in today's Guangdong and Guangxi areas, and the Tai had also established communities in southern and western Yunnan. The Mongol conquest of South China in the mid-thirteenth century prompted a massive migration of the Tai farther south into the territory of the Khmer Empire of Angkor in Southeast Asia. In the fourteenth century, the Tai founded the kingdoms of Siam and Laos in the valleys of the Chao Phraya and Upper Mekong rivers. Today there are more than 500,000 Tai in China who live mostly in the Xishuangbanna Tai Autonomous Zhou in southern Yunnan and in an autonomous zhou established for the Tai and the Jingpo peoples in western Yunnan.

Large-scale settlement by the Han in Yunnan and Guizhou did not begin until the Ming dynasty (A.D. 1368–1644) when the Chinese government encouraged the people in the Chang Jiang valley to migrate southward. Displacement of indigenous ethnic populations by the Han took place during the course of this southward migration. Many ethnic groups were forced into remote hilly regions that were much less attractive to the Han, who preferred a natural environment suitable for wet-rice paddy farming. In the lowlands where rice cultivation was possible, the indigenous peoples, such as the Zhuang and the Yi, were largely assimilated rather than displaced by the Han.

The consolidation of the southern border provinces by the CCP in the early 1950s was largely a peaceful act. Since then, some industrial enterprises have been introduced, and the region's traditional slash-and-burn agriculture has become a special target for reform. Increasingly, the Chinese way of farming—characterized by intensive cultivation, multiple cropping, vegetable gardening, and systematic application of animal and human manures—is replacing traditional shifting agriculture. As a result, the productivity of the land in the Zhuang areas in Guangxi has greatly increased, contributing directly to a higher standard of living (Moseley 1973).

EFFORTS AT NATIONAL INTEGRATION

China's minority nationalities have enjoyed considerable cultural freedom and experienced significant changes in their traditional ways of life. The ultimate goal of the Chinese ruling authorities appears to be the integration of the minorities into the national socioeconomic and political systems. Several methods of integration have been used by the government. One is the settlement of millions of Han Chinese in minority areas where they then help develop the local resources and bring about a firmer Chinese control. Efforts at integration also include the recruitment of young minority people who are sent to centers of higher learning for education. After graduation, they are sent back to their homelands to assume leading positions. This policy has had very little success, though, with many of the minority nationalities such as the Tibetans.

The development of minorities' written languages based on the pinyin system may be taken as another method of integration. Since all languages used in China employ the same alphabet for spelling, communication among ethnic groups and with the Chinese has become much easier. The introduction of written languages to minority groups and the publication of books and other materials, of course, greatly facilitate the spread of official doctrines.

Our lack of information does not permit us to estimate with confidence the extent to which minority nationalities have been successfully integrated into the Chinese socialist system and to say whether the standard of living of the Chinese minorities today is better or worse than it was prior to 1949. Few objective and in-depth studies, historical or contemporary, exist on these groups. And the Chinese press invariably reports only on the positive accomplishments made in the minority areas. Western journalists, who have recently visited such areas, tend to be extremely critical of Chinese policies and performance there, especially when reporting on Tibet. One Western journalist has reported that there is much mutual distrust between the Chinese and the Tibetans, that the Tibetans resent Chinese incursions into their religious life, that they long for the return of the Dalai Lama, and that there is poverty, starvation, and political imprisonment in Tibet (Kulkarni 1981). The 1988–1989 uprising as reported by Avedon (1989) and others offers very strong evidence that the Chinese goal of integrating the Tibetans into the Chinese system in the last forty years has failed.

Although it appears that the Tibetans, historically a very independent people with a strong and unique religious tradition, have passively and actively resisted CCP rule since the 1959 uprising, we should not automatically infer that the Chinese are having similar difficulties in other minority areas. Poverty is not a problem unique only to minority nationalities; it is, by Western standards, common in many parts of China. There are also indications that many local problems are not always known to the central government in Beijing, and that no large-scale funds have been specially infused into the minority economies.

Today it is clear that the Chinese government is unwilling to grant full political autonomy to its minorities; most of the top political positions in the ARs, for example, are held by the Chinese. Religious worship is now again permitted after it was violently denounced and severely prohibited during the Cultural Revolution (1966–1969) and its aftermath in the early 1970s; nevertheless, active and structured religious propagation is still not acceptable anywhere in China except under careful state control. Such policies and restrictions have made China's minorities unhappy. But with only about 8 percent of the nation's population, and inhabiting largely environmentally marginal areas that require more financial input than elsewhere to obtain the same developmental results, the minorities are in a poor position to dispute and contest the policies of the central state that they oppose. However, with the possible exception of the Tibetans, all of China's minority nationalities, including the Zhuang, the Hui, the Uygurs, and the Yi—which together make up the largest minority groups in China—appear to have at least passively accepted communist rule. Whether or not their full integration with the Chinese can be achieved in the future remains to be seen.

Note

1. The Hui (Moslem) and Manchu nationalities are Mandarin-speaking and are closely associated with the Han people. Together these two groups accounted for about 11.5 million in 1982, about 17 percent of China's minority population. By 2000, the Hui population had grown to 9.8 million, and the Manchu had increased to 10.7 million (National Bureau of Statistics 2002). Such remarkable growth is accounted for in part by reclassification of ethnicity done through individual self-identification that was permitted in the 1990 census count (Gladney 1995).

References Cited

Amako, Satoshi. 1997. Asia since the cold war and the new international order: The historical perspective and future prospects. In *China in the Twentieth Century: Politics, Economy, and Society*, ed. Fumio Itoh. Tokyo: United Nations University Press, 159–67.

Avedon, John. 1989. Tibet today. *Utne Reader* (March/April): 34–41.

Banister, Judith. 1987. *China's Changing Population*. Stanford, Calif.: Stanford University Press.

Basic Law of the Hong Kong Special Administrative Region of the People's Republic of China. 1991. Hong Kong: Joint Publishing.

Cartier, Carolyn. 2001. *Globalizing South China*. Oxford: Blackwell.

Cavalli-Sforza, L. Luca, Paolo Menozzi, and Alberto Piazza. 1994. *The History and Geography of Human Genes*. Princeton, N.J.: Princeton University Press.

China through a Lens. 2004. Foreign policy. August 5. www1.china.org.cn/English/features/38193.htm.

Dreyer, June T. 1976. *China's Forty Million*. Cambridge, Mass.: Harvard University Press.

Du, Peng. 2000. The ethnic minority population in China. In *The Changing Population of China*, ed. Xizhe Peng and Zhigang Guo. Oxford: Blackwell, 207–15.

Fairbank, John K. 1992. *China: A New History*. Cambridge, Mass.: Belknap.

Gaubatz, Piper R. 1996. *Beyond the Great Wall: Urban Form and Transformation on the Chinese Frontiers*. Stanford, Calif.: Stanford University Press.

Ginsburg, Norton. 1968. On the Chinese perception of a world order. In *China in Crisis*, ed. Tang Tsou. Vol. 2. Chicago: University of Chicago Press, 73–91.

Gladney, Dru C. 1990. Ethnogenesis of the Uighur. *Central Asian Survey* 9 (1): 1–28.

———. 1995. China's ethnic reawakening. In *Asia Pacific Issues*. Honolulu: East-West Center.

Goldstein, Avery. 2001. The diplomatic face of China's grand strategy: A rising power's emerging choice. *China Quarterly* (168): 835–64.

Harding, Harry. 1993. The concept of "Greater China": Themes, variations, and reservations. *China Quarterly* (136): 660–85.

Heaton, Bill. 1971. Red sun in Sinkiang. *Far Eastern Economic Review* 71, no. 3 (January 16): 46.

Hsiao, Kung-chuan. 1960. *Rural China: Imperial Control in the Nineteenth Century*. Seattle: University of Washington Press.

Husayin, Abayduila. 1966. The new Sinkiang. *China Reconstructs* 15, no. 1 (January): 26.

Kulkarni, V. G. 1981. Tibet. *Christian Science Monitor*, January 5–8.

Lal, Amrit. 1970. Signification of ethnic minorities in China. *Current Scene* 9, no. 4 (February 15): 16.

Liang, Zhang, comp. 2001. *The Tiananmen Papers*, ed. Andrew J. Nathan and Perry Link. New York: Public Affairs Press.

Ma, Hsueh-liang. 1962. New scripts for China's minorities. *China Reconstructs* (August): 24–25.

Ma, Laurence J. C., and Gonghao Cui. 1987. Administrative changes and urban population in China. *Annals of the Association of American Geographers* 77 (3): 373–95.

Moseley, George V. H. 1973. *The Consolidation of the South China Frontier*. Berkeley: University of California Press, 16.

National Bureau of Statistics. 2001. *Zhongguo tongji nianjian 2001* [China statistical yearbook 2001]. Beijing: China Statistics Press.

———. 2002. *Zhongguo tongji nianjian 2002* [China statistical yearbook 2002]. Beijing: China Statistics Press.

1965 Renmin shouce [1965 People's handbook]. 1965. Beijing: Xinhua shudian.

Pannell, C. W., and L. J. C. Ma. 1997. Urban transition and interstate relations in a dynamic post-Soviet borderland: The Xinjiang Uygur Autonomous Region of China. *Post Soviet Geography and Economics* 38 (4): 206–29.

Poston, Dudley L., and Shu Jing. 1987. The demographic and socioeconomic composition of China's ethnic minorities. *Population and Development Review* 13 (4): 703–22.

Samuels, Marwyn S. 1982. *Contest for the South China Sea.* New York: Metheun.

Schwarz, Henry G. 1971. *Chinese Policies towards Minorities.* Occasional paper no. 2. Western Washington State University, Program in East Asian Studies.

Shambaugh, David, ed. 2000. *The Modern Chinese State.* Cambridge: Cambridge University Press.

Shanker, Thom. 2005. Rumsfeld issues a sharp rebuke to China on arms. *New York Times,* June 4, A1–A7.

Starr, S. Frederick, ed. 2004. *Xinjiang: China's Muslim Borderland.* Armonk, N.Y.: M.E. Sharpe.

Toops, Stanley. 2003. Xinjiang (eastern Turkistan): Names, regions, landscapes, and futures. In *Changing China: A Geographic Appraisal,* ed. Chiao-min Hsieh and Max Lu. Boulder, Colo.: Westview, 411–23.

Vogel, Ezra, ed. 1997. *Living with China: U.S.-China Relations in the Twenty-first Century.* New York: W.W. Norton.

Wank, David. 1999. *Commodifying Communism: Business, Trust, and Politics in a Chinese City.* Cambridge: Cambridge University Press.

Wheatley, Paul. 1971. *The Pivot of the Four Quarters: A Preliminary Enquiry into the Origins of the Ancient Chinese City.* Chicago: Aldine.

Whitney, Joseph B. R. 1970. China: Area Administration and Nation Building. Research paper no. 123. Chicago: University of Chicago, Department of Geography.

Wiens, Herold J. 1967. *Han Chinese Expansion in South China.* Hamden, Conn.: Shoe String Press.

Wu, Cangping, ed. 1997. *General Report on China's Changing Population and its Development.* Beijing: Higher Education Press.

Xingbao. 2003. Migrating to trouble. June 3. www1.chinadaily.com.cn/hk/2003-06-13/119165html.

Xinhua News Agency. 2002. Sixteenth National Congress of the Communist Party of China, 2002. November 18. www.china.org.cn/English/features.49109.htm.

Zhang, Tianlu. 1984. Growth of China's minority population. *Beijing Review* 27 (25): 22–26.

CHAPTER 5

Population and Human Resources

People and human resources are the centerpiece and enduring reality that shape the images and perceptions most of us have of both contemporary and historic China. No theme is more compelling or profound of the mental portrait we hold of China than its people, their remarkable number, and their variation and distribution across its vast and changing landscape. The superlative of the world's largest population in a single country kindles a bright image of a boundless and industrious people that have created an enormous and growing consumer market as well as a powerful economic engine in manufactures and exports. At the same time, the faces of impoverished peasants in remote rural areas and scenes of millions of disenfranchised migrant laborers in the eastern cities remind us that China's huge population remains one of its most daunting challenges.

Throughout this chapter we continue to examine the notion introduced at the beginning of the book that China's population and people are its greatest resource and treasure although representing perhaps its greatest question and problem as well. The latter issue focuses on labor absorption, decline in per capita arable land, future food grain production, insufficient educational investment and resources, and the need for improving the general educational level. The rapidly changing demographic profile of a population that is now growing older, and with a declining share of women, raises very significant social and economic issues that must be addressed in the future. Such changes continue to indicate that China's huge and still-growing population remains one of the most fundamental issues that confront and challenge its drive to develop and modernize.

About 21 percent of the human population lives within the borders of the People's Republic of China (PRC). The State Statistical Bureau (now the National Bureau of Statistics) of the Chinese government has officially reported, based on 2000 census results, that China's population in 2000 was 1,265,830,000 (excluding Hong Kong, Macao, and Taiwan; see table 5.1), an increase of approximately 137 million people or 12 percent more than the 1990 population. The rate of net natural increase (the annual death rate subtracted from the annual birth rate) for 2000 was 7.58 per thousand, or 0.76 percent, and this dropped to 6.01 per thousand in 2003 (National Bureau of Statistics 2004). This 2000 census count continued the accurate enumeration of the Chinese population established in the 1982 midyear census. Together with the census of 1990, these three census counts are probably the most reliable estimates and counts ever taken of the Chinese people. In 2003, the population was reported as 1,292,270,000 (National Bureau of Statistics 2004).

Table 5.1. Demographic and Urban Trends in China, 1953–2003

Year	Total Population (Millions)	Birth Rate (Per 1,000)	Growth Rate (Net Natural Increase Per 1,000)	Urban Population (Millions)	Urban Share (%)
1953	587.96	37.00	23.00	78.26	13.31
1958	659.94	29.22	17.24	107.21	16.25
1964	704.99	39.14	27.64	129.50	18.37
1969	806.71	34.11	26.08	141.17	17.50
1975	924.20	23.01	15.69	160.30	17.34
1978	962.59	18.25	12.00	172.45	17.92
1980	987.05	18.21	11.87	191.40	19.39
1982	1,016.54	22.28	15.68	214.80	21.13
1985	1,058.51	21.04	14.26	250.94	23.71
1990	1,143.33	21.06	14.39	301.95	26.41
1993	1,185.17	18.09	11.45	331.73	27.99
1996	1,123.89	16.98	10.42	373.04	30.48
1999	1,257.86	14.64	8.18	437.48	34.78
2000	1,265.83	14.03	7.58	459.06	36.22
2001	1,276.27	13.38	6.95	480.64	37.66
2002	1,284.53	12.86	6.45	502.12	39.09
2003	1,292.27	12.41	6.01	523.76	40.53

Sources: National Bureau of Statistics 2001, 2002, and 2004.

Counting China's People and Household Registration

For many centuries China has employed various mechanisms to count its households and guarantee the security and behavior of its people. The socialist period brought with it an enhanced administrative capacity and witnessed an intensification of this population checking and control with the introduction of household registration books shortly after the Chinese Communist Party (CCP) took control of China in 1949. In 1958, following a decade of substantial rural-to-urban migration, a household registration (*hukou*) system was instituted through new state regulations that clearly and sharply delineated the population into permanent urban and rural components based on location, employment, and birth. Thereafter, being born a peasant farmer, one was almost surely destined to remain a peasant, and individual mobility and the freedom to move were sharply curtailed until the 1990s (Oi 1999; Solinger 1993, 1999). The *hukou* system of household registration thus until recently provided a means of checking and controlling China's population as well as counting it. Inasmuch as there was close agreement between the 1982 census figures and the figures derived from the official household registration system, the *hukou* system, whatever its alleged shortcomings of over- or undercounting particular groups, appears to have been an accurate and effective means of keeping up with the size of China's population (Banister 1984, 1987). Whether such a system continues to be accurate in the face of the far-reaching economic reforms that have so relaxed the rules on rural migration in China and allowed for a much increased mobility of the rural population remains to be seen (Oi 1999; Solinger

1999). While the 2000 census continues to be built on the earlier model of a close conjunction between enumeration and household registration, its validity is subject to increasing question. The location of people counted through the *hukou* system, as well as recent births and deaths among transients, make the system less than fully reliable as a population enumeration method, given the increased mobility of the population during the last fifteen years, and especially during the 1990s. It has been estimated that there is a so-called floating population of as many as 120 million people living in China's urban centers (*Chinadaily.com* 2003).

China's official population data, both historical and contemporary, should be used with caution, however, because of incomplete coverage. Historically, population data were never collected for the sake of objective knowledge or national economic planning. Population registrations were carried out mainly for the purposes of taxation or conscription of able-bodied males for military corvée duties. To evade registration to avoid paying taxes or the draft was a common practice. Females and children, considered socially inferior and physically unfit for labor services, were largely unreported in dynastic times (Ho 1959). In the early twentieth century, census counts were not sophisticated enough for meaningful analysis of population changes. And until midcentury, data on such demographic variables as age-specific birth and death rates, migration rates, regional demographic characteristics, rural and urban differentials, and sex and age compositions were largely lacking. The figures cited in this book, especially historical figures on China's population, are meant to suggest rough orders of magnitude rather than precise demographic realities.

HISTORICAL GROWTH PATTERNS

Historically, China's population varied greatly (see tables 5.2a and 5.2b), and large discrepancies may have existed between official population data recorded in historical documents and the demographic truths. In addition to the reasons for the unreliability

Table 5.2a. China: Estimated Population, Western Han Dynasty–People's Republic of China

Period	Year	Population
Western Han dynasty	A.D. 2	59,594,978
Eastern Han dynasty	A.D. 156	50,066,856
Three Kingdoms dynasty	220–280	7,672,881
Western Jin dynasty	280	16,163,863
Sui dynasty	606	46,019,956
Tang dynasty	742	48,909,809
Song dynasty	1110	46,734,784
Yuan dynasty	1290	58,834,711
Ming dynasty	1393	60,545,812
Qing dynasty	1757	190,348,328
Qing dynasty	1901	426,447,325
Republic of China	1928	474,787,386
People's Republic of China	1949	548,770,000

Sources: Zhou 1979.

Table 5.2b. Official Data and Estimates of China's Population, Selected Years, A.D. 2–1848 (in Millions)

Year	High	Low
2	59.6	
57		31.0*
105	53.2	
156	56.4	
280		16.2
606	46.0	
705		37.1
755	52.9	
961		32.0*
1109	121.0*	
1193	120.0*	
1381		59.8
1391		60.5
1592	200.0*	
1657		70.2
1776	268.2	
1800	295.2	
1848	426.7	

* Indicates an estimate; other numbers are from official sources.
Sources: Chao 1986, 41.

of data mentioned above, another important factor contributing to the varied historical figures was China's changing national boundaries in different dynastic periods following the rise and fall of the nation's political and military strength.

The earliest national population figures date back to the ancient Han period. In A.D. 2, the Han dynasty reportedly had a population of about 60 million. For the next sixteen centuries there were drastic population fluctuations both temporally and spatially. Population tended to increase steadily during the more peaceful years and to decline in times of war or national disaster, in part also related to the expansion or contraction of the state area and the population under its control.

Chao (1986) explained the growth of China's population based on two main factors. Ever since the Zhou dynasty (770–221 B.C.), China had maintained a traditional culture based on the Confucian values of a male-dominated society. Ideally, virtually all males married and were obligated to produce families with several sons to carry on the family name and to perform rituals associated with the veneration of ancestors. The families in turn were obligated to assist each male in forming his own family, even when resources were marginal, and to help ensure the economic viability or survival of the additional family unit.

Next, population growth and decline tended to parallel the cyclical pattern of dynastic rise and fall, although not necessarily in the same sequence. Chao (1986, 30–31) estimated that under stable conditions and with an average life expectancy of thirty, the historical population growth rates prior to the Ming dynasty (A.D. 1368–1644) were probably between 0.5 and 1.0 percent per annum. He suggested that periods of stable growth were typically offset by extended periods of warfare and instability that saw substantial fluctuations in the population and probably at least until the fifteenth century kept the population more or less near or below the number it reached during the Han period (approximately 60 million; see table 5.2b).

Mallory (1926), drawing on a Chinese study, noted that between 108 B.C. and A.D. 1911 "there occurred 1,828 famines somewhere in China." This averages out to almost one famine a year in China since Han times. Mallory described and analyzed a number of factors, both environmental and human-related, to account for these famines. One may conclude from Mallory's analysis that famine was historically, to a greater or lesser degree, a normal part of the mobility and demographic process in China.

The major exception to this may have been achieved during the Song dynasty (A.D. 960–1279), a period of substantial economic change, extensive trade expansion, and city growth. Although Chinese national territory was split between the Southern and Northern Song along the Huai River line after A.D. 1120, the combined population of the two empires may have been as great as 120 million according to Chao (1986, 36). Thereafter, there was a period of decline during the Mongol invasions and conquest until the establishment of the Ming in 1368. By the end of the fourteenth century, peace and order had been restored, and an unprecedented four centuries of population growth began. During some periods, the annual rate of population increase apparently exceeded 1 percent.

The most rapid growth of population took place during the period from 1657 to 1848 when the population size jumped from perhaps as low as 70 million to 427 million (see table 5.2b). This growth was particularly noticeable during the two centuries from the mid-1600s to the mid-1800s under the benevolent despotism of the early Qing (Manchu) rulers when stable political and favorable economic conditions generally prevailed (Ho 1959). The national economy reached a new stage of development. The dissemination and widespread use of such newly introduced food crops as early-ripening rice, "Irish" potatoes, corn, and sweet potatoes greatly enlarged the nation's capability to produce food. More and more new areas previously unsuitable for agriculture were now brought under cultivation. Perkins (1969) has described the sixteenth- and seventeenth-century arrival of potatoes, corn, and peanuts from the New World. While these were important because they could be grown on upland dry areas previously marginal or little used, Perkins noted the Chinese disinclination to eat potatoes based on taste preference and the modest use of corn prior to the twentieth century. Corn thereafter became more popular, especially as an animal feed, due to its widespread growth in the Northeast, a region little settled by Han Chinese until the twentieth century. Therefore, most improvements in food production likely resulted from an intensified use of improved varieties of rice and better cultivation practices within the traditional horticultural framework. Finally, the trend of population growth was again checked during the last century of the Manchu rule when a series of rebellions, the White Lotus (1795–1804), the Taiping (1850–1864), and the Nian (1853–1868), coupled with widespread floods, droughts, and famines, resulted in millions of deaths. Thus, when the Manchu (Qing) empire ended in 1911, the population was probably around 400 million.

As Perkins (1969), Elvin (1973), and Chao (1986) have discussed, the relationship between food production and population growth after the Ming dynasty was complex. Environmental, cultural, economic, and political factors all came into play in a functionally and spatially variegated web of interrelated strands whose individual causal determinants are virtually impossible to disentangle from one another. Population and growth in food-grain output thus grew together historically but in an erratic, complex, and multifaceted manner, some aspects of which will be discussed further in chapter 8.

Prior to the establishment of the PRC in 1949, the nationalist government made several attempts to come up with a realistic population count. Many government institutions, including the Post Office Department, the Ministry of Internal Affairs, the Bureau of the Budget, and the Maritime Customs Office, carried out enumerations. But political instability, caused by internal warlord politics and the Japanese invasion, hindered them from satisfactorily implementing a registration system. There were conflicting reports regarding the actual size of the population. It is generally believed, however, that in the 1930s and the 1940s the population of China was in the neighborhood of 450 million.

Population Distribution

The present pattern of population distribution in China is a consequence of expansion and migration by the Chinese in historical and recent times. Today the vast majority of the Chinese people are concentrated in the eastern half of the country in several areas where the environment offers the necessary conditions for development of intensive agriculture, relative ease of transportation, and the growth of cities. Within the traditionally densely settled East, four major regions have especially dense populations: the North China Plain (primarily Beijing and Tianjin municipalities, and Hebei, Shandong, Henan, and the southern Liaoning provinces); the middle and lower Chang Jiang (Yangtze River) Basin and Delta (Hubei, Hunan, Jiangxi, Anhui, Jiangsu, Zhejiang, and Shanghai); the Sichuan Basin; and the Xi Jiang (West River) and Zhu Jiang (Pearl River) basins and Delta (Guangdong and Guangxi; see map 5.1 and table 5.3).

Map 5.1. China's Population Density, 2003

Table 5.3. Total Population and Birth Rate, Death Rate, and Natural Growth Rate in China by Region, 2003

Region (%)	Total Year-End Population (10,000 Persons)	Birth Rate (%)	Death Rate (%)	Natural Growth Rate (%)
Beijing	1,456	5.10	5.20	−0.10
Tianjin	1,011	7.14	6.04	1.10
Hebei	6,769	11.43	6.27	5.16
Shanxi	3,314	12.26	6.04	6.22
Inner Mongolia	2,380	9.24	6.17	3.07
Liaoning	4,210	6.90	5.83	1.07
Jilin	2,704	7.25	5.64	1.61
Heilongjiang	3,815	7.48	5.45	2.03
Shanghai	1,711	4.85	6.20	−1.35
Jiangsu	7,406	9.04	7.03	2.01
Zhejiang	4,680	9.66	6.38	3.28
Anhui	6,410	11.15	5.20	5.95
Fujian	3,488	11.43	5.58	5.85
Jiangxi	4,254	14.07	5.98	8.09
Shandong	9,125	11.42	6.64	4.78
Henan	9,667	12.10	6.46	5.64
Hubei	6,002	8.26	5.94	2.32
Hunan	6,663	11.82	6.87	4.95
Guangdong	7,954	13.66	5.31	8.35
Guangxi	4,857	13.86	6.57	7.29
Hainan	811	14.68	5.52	9.16
Chongqing	3,130	9.89	7.20	2.69
Sichuan	8,700	9.18	6.06	3.12
Guizhou	3,870	15.91	6.87	9.04
Yunnan	4,376	17.00	7.20	9.80
Tibet	270	17.40	6.30	11.10
Shaanxi	3,690	10.67	6.38	4.29
Gansu	2,603	12.58	6.46	6.12
Qinghai	534	16.94	6.09	10.85
Ningxia	580	15.68	4.73	10.95
Xinjiang	1,934	16.01	5.23	10.78
National Total	129,227	12.41	6.40	6.01

Sources: National Bureau of Statistics 2004.

In addition to relatively abundant precipitation and level topography, these floodplain areas have fertile alluvial soils produced by the river systems. In the South, the Chang, Zhu, and Xi and their numerous tributaries are navigable. These rivers have greatly facilitated movement and the development of trade. Most of China's major cities are found in these four fertile and productive regions.

Secondary population concentrations of somewhat lower density are found throughout the rugged uplands of much of South and Southwest China; in the remainder of the Songliao Plain of the Northeast provinces of Liaoning, Jilin, and Heilongjiang, which were settled later and where colder climate and extensive marshlands discouraged higher population concentrations; along the Hexi corridor in Gansu province; and in the oases in the Xinjiang Uygur Autonomous Region (AR; see map 5.1), Xizang (Tibet)

AR, Inner Mongolia AR, Qinghai, and other areas of Xinjiang and Heilongjiang, where minority nationalities reside. Insufficient rainfall, extremes of temperature, and poor soils have limited agricultural development and production in much of western China. In such areas, pastoral nomadism predominates.

Population growth during the period of Chinese socialism was highest in percentage terms in some of the sparsely settled interior provinces and regions such as Xinjiang (Pannell 2003). During the reform period, however, migration has been toward the coastal provinces, as rural people have left the farms in search of employment and improved opportunities in the cities and economically dynamic areas of the coastal regions with their expanded and growing ties to the global economy (Fan 2005; see maps 5.2 and 5.3). Growth in the interior may reflect patterns of internal migration of Han Chinese in an effort to populate remote border areas as well as higher birth rates in recent years among minority nationalities (see table 5.3). It is unlikely, however, to result in any fundamental change in the pattern of a densely settled eastern China and a sparsely populated interior.

Since 1983 and 1984, new laws that allow rural people to migrate to cities to work as service, factory, and construction laborers, although without the subsidies normally afforded state-supported urban workers, have further added to the densities of people in the eastern provinces where most of China's large cities are located. Numerous and variable estimates of the number and location of these temporary migrants have been proposed, some claiming more than 120 million in total with large cities such as Beijing and Shanghai having as many as 3 million each (*Chinadaily.com* 2003). As temporary migrants, these workers are not counted as urban residents, and most retain their rural

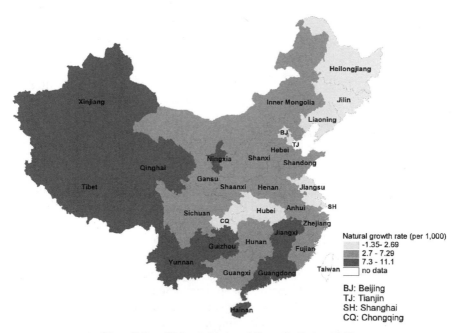

Map 5.2. China's Natural Growth Rate, 2003

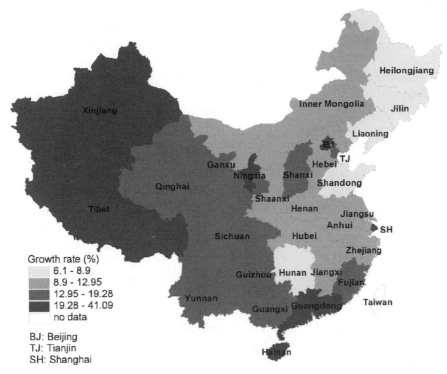

Map 5.3. China's Population Growth Rate between 1990 and 2003

hukou status. Recent policy changes are now altering the rigid *hukou* system of the past to allow rural residents to establish residency status in towns and small cities.

Clearly the rules are changing to reflect the new realities of migrants who perform valuable and needed labor services to allow them to become legal residents where they work. It is becoming abundantly clear that the urban economies in many of China's larger cities and metropolitan regions could not function without the labor services of these migrants. Moreover, urban subsidies are diminishing in importance owing to efforts to improve the efficiency and profitability of state-owned enterprises (SOEs) or by simply allowing those that are inefficient to fail and close. Increasingly, these transient workers are becoming a part of the urban scene, and their temporary status is now evolving over time into a more long-term arrangement as befits their contribution to these burgeoning Chinese urban economies.

Population Size and Vital Rates

When the CCP came to power, it decided to conduct a national census to obtain information indispensable for the preparation of its first Five-Year Plan (1953–1957). The information sought was quite simple: the address of each Chinese household, and the name, age, sex, ethnic status, and relationship to the head of the household of each household member. According to the census results, China in mid-1953 had a total of 582.6 million people, plus 11.7 million on Taiwan. Since this census was the first official population count China has made in the socialist period, it has been used widely as a basis for population estimates and projections, and was a basis for more recent census counts taken in 1964, 1982, 1990, and 2000 (Tien 1983; Banister 1987).

There are indications that even the Chinese leadership was unclear about the actual size of the population. In the 1970s, top-level Chinese leaders and other informed sources used national figures that differed by as much as 100 million. For example, officials at the Supply and Grain departments believed that China's population was 800 million, while the Ministry of Commerce stated that it was 830 million. In 1972, the head of the Chinese delegation to a UN environmental conference in Stockholm said that China had as many as 900 million people, a figure that was then widely used in the Chinese press until mid-1979 when the figure of 975 million (1978 population) was released by the State Statistical Bureau. Recent official information from China indicates that the rate of population growth in the 1950s and the 1960s averaged 2 percent per year.

Since the early 1970s, stringent policies of family planning have been enforced with substantial results. Vice-premier Chen Muhua disclosed in late 1979 that the rate of China's natural population growth had dropped from 23.4 per thousand in 1971 to 12.05 per thousand in 1978. Such a drastic reduction of the net natural increase in a few years is extremely rare in the history of the world's population evolution, outside of catastrophes such as massive famines. As seen in table 5.1 and figure 5.1, the rate

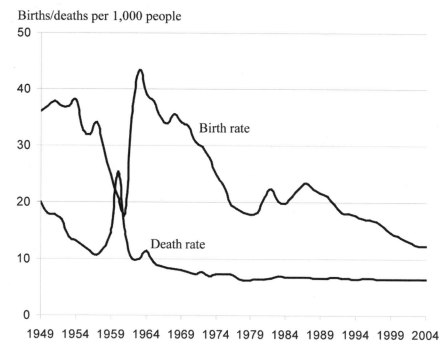

Figure 5.1. Birth and Death Rates in China, 1949–2004. **Source:** National Bureau of Statistics 2004

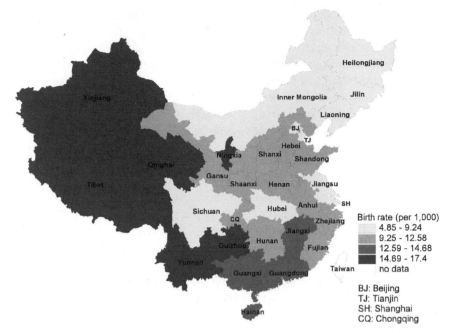

Map 5.4. China's Birth Rate, 2003. **Source:** National Bureau of Statistics 2004

had increased by 1990 to 14.26 per thousand as some relaxation of the one-child policy occurred in rural areas. The Chinese government has since called for a further reduction to zero growth by the early twenty-first century, and a decline in fertility and birth rates has continued to reduce the natural growth rate. By 2000 the birth rate had declined to 1.3 percent with a rate of annual net natural growth of 0.69 percent, a figure that indicates continuing decline toward zero population growth. As seen in table 5.3 and map 5.4, the birth rates continue to vary in different regions of China, with substantially higher birth rates in the western and interior provinces than in the east coast provinces. In 1999 the average fertility rate, based on a less than 1 percent sample, was 1.33 for the nation, well below the replacement level. A 2001 survey indicated a total fertility rate of 1.22 children per woman in urban areas, while the total fertility rate on average among rural women was 1.98. Thus, there is a significant gap between urban and rural families.

This evidence indicates China has gone through much of its demographic transition in a very short period, although whether such progress is sustainable in the absence of firm and coercive central policy remains problematic. A developing country experiencing the process of demographic transition or shift can often be seen to go through three stages of change, beginning with relatively high birth and death rates (say, 30–50 per thousand people per year) and ending with relatively low vital rates (5–15 per thousand per year; see fig. 5.1). The intermediate stage is a period of rapid population growth resulting from declining death rates and continued high birth rates. The rapid population growth in China resulted from good and sufficient nutrition, improved health conditions, and better environmental sanitation, all of which help to reduce mortality. Meanwhile, the birth and fertility rates declined more slowly due to the persistence of traditional cultural values associated with Confucian ideals in favor of male children, and often resulting in larger families, especially in rural areas where the vast majority of China's people have always lived. Fertility reduction is necessarily a slow process, for it involves not only attitudinal changes toward the role of the family in the social fabric of the nation, but also an awareness and adoption of new ideas and techniques of family planning. This parallels improvement in living standards, income, and the educational level of women. Such a reduction proceeds more rapidly and effectively in cities than in rural areas (Hsu 1985). China has been able to enforce compliance with family planning policies more easily in cities where people depend more on state support for housing, jobs, and other benefits.

Both birth and the death rates in China have decreased appreciably since the 1949 revolution. In 1953, the census reported an impressively reduced crude death rate of 17 per thousand and a high crude birth rate of 37 per thousand, leaving a crude natural rate of increase of 20 per thousand (see fig. 5.1). According to official data, between 1954 and 1957, death rates also dropped more rapidly than birth rates, resulting in large natural rates of growth. (Selected data for annual birth rates, death rates, and rates of net annual growth are presented in tables 5.1 and 5.3.)

Aside from the issue of food supply and nutrition, China's mortality and fertility declines are the result of two national programs focused on public health and family planning. The accomplishments of the early years of the PRC in public health are well-known. In a relatively short time, China eliminated or greatly reduced such dreaded diseases as typhoid, smallpox, cholera, scarlet fever, tuberculosis, trachoma, and venereal disease. Parasitic diseases such as schistosomiasis, hookworm, and malaria were brought under control and today pose no serious threat to the population. These accomplishments were achieved through massive inoculation drives, pest-eradication programs, environmental cleanup campaigns, and preventive medicine. Public health programs today are carried out in every province, city, and county in China.

One of the saddest and most regrettable aspects of China's recent demographic history was the catastrophic human suffering that resulted from the late Chairman Mao Zedong's Great Leap Forward policy and program. In 1958, Mao announced a program to push China ahead forcefully through full communization of agricultural lands and property and other radical production and social policies. The peasants reacted unfavorably to these new policies that took private plots and animals away from them, and farm production, including that of food-grains, plummeted in 1959 and 1960 (Ashton et al. 1984; Banister 1987). Bad weather and inaccurate reporting of grain production further exacerbated the production declines. Food-grain shortages followed, and a massive famine swept the country (it was especially serious in 1960). So severe was this famine, coupled with the government's unwillingness to publicize the problem and seek help internationally, that as many as 30 million people may have died as a direct result of the government's failed policies and programs. The tremendous demographic impact and suffering of this famine may be seen in decreased birth and increased death rates (see table 5.3 and figs. 5.1 and 5.2), with their devastating effect on the age cohorts born in 1960 and 1961. Only after the radical policies were rescinded, and small private plots and animals were restored to the peasants, did farm production pick up and return some normality to both the rural economy and way of life of China's rural people.

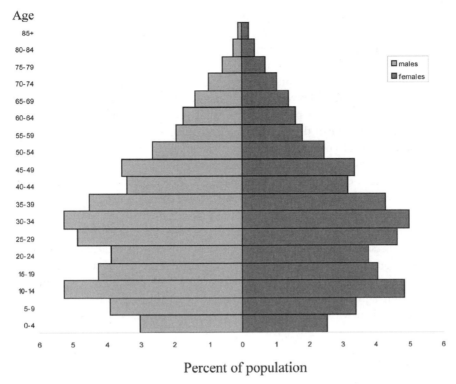

Figure 5.2.   China, a Population Pyramid, 2000. **Source:** National Bureau of Statistics 2004

At an approximate average rate of natural growth of 20 per thousand between 1949 and 1982, China in those thirty-three years had a net gain in population of roughly 480 million (see table 5.1). Another 126 million were added between 1982 and 1990, and still another 137 million between 1990 and 2000. China continues to add about 7 million each year to its population, despite a reduction in birth rates, simply by virtue of its enormous size. These rapid, large, absolute gains are without precedent in China's history. Despite recently declining birth rates, the large number of women in the child-bearing years of fifteen to forty-five will ensure substantial population momentum and growth, but the size of the cohort is diminishing rapidly as relatively low birth rates have been in place now for a generation (see fig. 5.2). So rapid is the reported drop in birth and fertility rates that some observers now foresee a new potential problem in another generation of a rapidly aging population (Kinsella and Phillips 2005).

Family Planning

China expects to reach zero population growth at some point early in the twenty-first century, and 1.6 billion people as a maximum population reached around the year 2030 was a possibility recently discussed (Wu 1997, 6). This goal, of course, remains ambitious, especially considering the fact that the nation has experienced only partial industrialization and urbanization, processes that are just now moving into full acceleration and that are yet theoretically associated with slowdowns in population growth in modernizing economies and societies. In a country where tradition continues to place a high value on male children, the target will be even more difficult to reach. The Chinese government, however, is now firmly committed to limiting the growth of its population, and it has provided effective if sometimes controversial leadership. The new social structure of the nation is such that it greatly facilitates family planning programs, and China continues to promote aggressively a reduction in fertility and births to achieve the goal of zero population growth.

Failure to take effective action before the 1970s to stabilize the rapidly growing population was a shortcoming of Chairman Mao Zedong, who appeared to believe literally in the Marxist notion of surplus labor value and therefore that a large population would bring more producers. The Chinese leadership did not initially recognize the fact that an excessively large population could deter the growth and development of the nation's economy. Serious efforts were not made during the 1950s to reduce the birth rate, although limited proposals for family planning were made. Four separate family planning campaigns operated in China during the socialist period. Each successive one intensified the rigor with which the plans were implemented.

EARLY EFFORTS AND POLICIES

An initially cautious and limited approach to promoting birth control and to producing contraceptive devices was launched in 1956. The Great Leap Forward interrupted this program in 1958 because of its emphasis on late marriages. This was to some extent interrupted by the Cultural Revolution, although it is difficult to establish the Chinese government's official position on family planning during this time (Banister 1987, 148–52).

In 1971 China began to place much greater emphasis on family planning with its third family planning campaign. The Chinese press in the late 1970s carried extensive information on family planning programs and their effects on population growth. All newly married couples were expected and were legally obligated to practice birth control. The drive to lower the nation's fertility rate was implemented through a vast medical and public health system (Chen 1976). It involved extensive face-to-face contact with the people by both trained medical personnel and paramedics, readily available contraceptives, and a variety of incentive programs. More than a million "barefoot doctors," who normally received short-term medical training of between three and six months, and who engaged in farm production while not performing their medical services, worked in China's countryside.

Dedicated medical personnel were then ubiquitous at all levels of China's rural administrative units. In the cities, the urban residents' committees were the basic administrative units where family planning programs were formally structured. At these basic levels of society, nurses, barefoot doctors, and midwives not only provided ordinary health care to the people, they also provided modern contraceptives, sterilization, and abortion services that were readily available and free or at low cost. Contraceptives available to the Chinese are similar to those found elsewhere, and new methods have been frequently reported in the Chinese press. Xie (2000, 58) has noted that according to recent surveys in China, over 80 percent of couples were using contraception methods by the early 1990s. Most common methods included female sterilization through tubal ligation (41 percent), use of an IUD (40 percent), and male sterilization (12 percent). Abortion had declined substantially from 20 million per year in the 1980s to 10 million in 1992.

Family planning, as noted above, has since the late 1950s been openly publicized through the administrative and educational systems. It is organized at the central government level by the Office of Family Planning of the State Council. Since 1981, the State Family Planning Commission is the principal agency responsible for carrying out China's population program (Xie 2000, 52). Leading cadres at the provincial, regional, and county levels transmit the state's policies downward to the rural communities and urban districts for enforcement. Each township has a Family Planning Committee, which coordinates and supervises family planning work. Family planning subcommittees are responsible for such details of birth control as disseminating family planning information and contraceptives, organizing and leading study groups, persuading non-participants to adopt family planning, and checking the results of these programs. In the cities, similar activities are found in offices and factories as well as in residents' committees.

At these lowest levels of family planning, detailed records are kept on the number of the local population, the number of local women of childbearing age and their monthly cycles, the methods of male and female contraception used, and the projected number of births each year. Women who fail to practice birth control, who have too many children, or who get pregnant or give birth at the wrong time, are likely to encounter unpleasant official pressure from cadres and sometimes social pressure from their colleagues and neighbors to conform to the rules.

In the third family planning campaign, three key words characterized the goals of China's family planning education: *late, thin,* and *few*—meaning late marriage, spacing births at intervals of no less than four or five years, and fewer children per couple. In the countryside, the target age for marriage is generally twenty-three for women and twenty-five for men, but there are many different ages used, and early marriage has been preferred. In the cities, the minimum target ages for marriage have been slightly higher: for example, twenty-five for women and twenty-seven for men, but again there have been many variations. There is some evidence that late marriage has been deemphasized with the advent of the one-child policy and because of a strong social preference for early marriage.

THE ONE-CHILD POLICY AND PROGRAM

In January 1979, a fourth family planning campaign emerged, and a one-child policy was formally put into effect for most of China's population. Since then, families have been encouraged to have only one child, and to sign a pledge that they will have only one child. Many places have issued honor certificates to families that have decided to have no more than one child. The certificate provides economic benefits to those who qualify. For example in many urban places, one-child families receive a "monthly health maintenance fee" (it originally amounted to a significant share of an average worker's monthly income) until the child reaches a certain age. Priorities for admitting children to nurseries, kindergartens, and schools are granted to these families, often free of charge. In some cities, such families enjoy priority in housing allocation and receive the same amount of living space as families with two or more children (Jowett 1990). In Shanghai, a retiree with only one child will get an additional pension payment to be calculated on the basis of 5 percent of his wage at retirement. These incentives, however, are cancelled if a second child is born. In most places, families must return these acquired benefits to the state in installments if their one-child pledge is broken.

Education has been assigned a high priority in China's family planning. The masses are taught that there is no need to adhere to the old saying "Grain is stored against famine, and sons are brought up to ensure security for one's old age." Under the communist system, they are told, everyone is guaranteed a certain amount of basic daily necessities (such as grain, cooking oil, and cloth), and there is no need to have several sons and a large family. It is also argued that improved medical care and public health services have greatly increased the probability of infant survival, and there is no need to produce many sons to ensure the survival of a few or even one. The masses are also told that successful family planning will help improve the health of both the mother and the child and will bring about a higher standard of living for the family. Since 1979, population planning has been justified on the basis that the nation's large population hindered the development of the national economy; created serious problems in availability of food, housing, education, and employment; and reduced per capita income and an already low mainland ratio. Yet the policies of economic reform, especially in rural areas with privatization of farms, have worked at cross-purposes with family planning policies. Peasants who work the land clearly see more children as a direct economic benefit (Tien et al. 1992).

Through the mass media, study classes, and small group discussions, reasons for family planning are persistently explained to the people. Furthermore, health workers make frequent home visits, during which pressure to adopt family planning measures is privately exerted. There are indications that the younger generation has been more receptive to family planning than the older generation was, and that the urban population is more actively involved in family planning than the rural people. Local cadres must work closely with women of childbearing age to determine who shall have a child and when. Such intensive family planning programs, of course, affect personal freedom of action and frequently generate dissatisfaction. In the long run, however, a smaller population is seen to benefit the entire nation.

COMPLIANCE AND COERCION

The idea of a single child per family and the rigorous family planning introduced in the late 1970s have been controversial and unpopular in China. Perhaps the most controversial aspect of this are the coercive measures used to ensure compliance of all Chinese. In addition to the economic incentives and official pressures used to promote compliance, cadres and health workers, especially in the early 1980s, carried out forced abortions and sterilizations when family planning policies were violated. This created much resentment and criticism of the policies and their implementation, criticism that sometimes came from foreign sources (see for example, Aird 1990; Mosher 1983, 1993). Another unfortunate aspect of the policies was significant increases in the incidence of female infanticide, especially in rural areas where peasants wanted to ensure the birth of a male heir.

While there may have been some over-dramatization of the significance of this, vital statistics on the sex ratios of China's population in many counties offer direct evidence of inordinately large male populations, which suggests that the practice of female infanticide may have been more widespread than admitted during the 1980s (Li 1987). Other pernicious practices, such as forced abortion during the second or even third trimester of pregnancy, and forced sterilization of women who have already had three or more children, have offended many foreigners, who are concerned by the severity and rigor with which China has gone about its family planning and birth control program. Undoubtedly, freedom of choice has been denied to many if not most Chinese families, and some pain and suffering have been inflicted. Whether or not these severe and draconian policies and actions are justified by the magnitude of China's population problem and its aspirations for future development are complex and difficult questions for policy makers and officials. Thoughtful appraisals of this contentious issue and the related matter of the impact and significance of rapid fertility decline may be reviewed in Tien (1987) and Riley (2004).

As Riley (2004) explains, although economic advance and fertility decline have been closely associated in the traditional economic development literature, recent state policy in China of rigorous family planning and birth control has trumped in part the more conventional forces associated with economic growth. These forces include improved literacy, more education, and higher urbanization. Nevertheless, it remains clear that in China, fertility levels are higher in rural areas, while lower fertility is found in association with higher socioeconomic status in the wealthier, more urbanized regions typical in the eastern provinces.

Perhaps the basic question is whether more pain and suffering will result from too huge a future population—one that may perpetuate economic stagnation and persistent poverty—than from the current rigorous and unpleasant policies that China hopes will help push it more quickly to faster economic growth and a better standard of living for all its citizens.

Advances in Education and Literacy

China is a developing nation undergoing the throes of rapid but sometimes unequal economic growth and change. The nation's large and growing population poses a serious challenge to its hope of lifting itself out of the vicious cycle of underdevelopment. One cause as well as symptom of underdevelopment is that advanced educational opportunities are available to only a small share of the population. This affects directly the quality of the population. China's ambitious plans for the development of agriculture, industry, defense, and science and technology can hardly be achieved without the necessary technical manpower.

The financial resources of the Chinese government are strained to such an extent that the nation can barely take care of its most essential needs. Investment in education in recent years has been low. In 2003 about 99 percent of Chinese children were enrolled in primary schools, and of those graduating, 98 percent advanced to junior middle school. Approximately 53 percent of those graduating from junior middle went on to senior middle or high school. Only a small fraction of these will advance to college or the university, however, and students in higher education constituted approximately 7.3 percent of the total enrolled students in 2003. Further, in 2003 there were 1,552 institutions of higher education in China, and these institutions can accommodate only a small share of the nation's college-age students, compared to 2,600 institutions of higher education in the United States that can take 40 percent of U.S. college-age students. In 2003 in China there were 11,085,642 students enrolled in all institutions of higher education. Of these, 1,877,492 graduated, and of these 34 percent completed degrees in engineering (National Bureau of Statistics 2004).

LITERACY

Adult literacy has increased dramatically during the socialist period from about 25 percent of the population to more than 90 percent today. Although there are varying definitions of literacy, literacy in China today may be defined, for peasants and workers, as the ability to read and write 1,200–2,000 ideographs or characters (World Bank 2000). A substantial effort to make older citizens literate was launched in the 1950s, and it had some success. Yet illiteracy, especially among women and rural people, remains a problem. In 1982, 19 percent of China's male population was classified as illiterate, whereas 45 percent of the female population was so classified, a sex-based difference greater than that found in some Muslim countries. By 2003 this had been reduced to a rate of 6.12 percent for adult males and 13.85 percent for females classified as illiterate or semiliterate.

The disparity in educational enrollments for females at all levels remains, but the difference in percentages has steadily diminished. According to a sample survey, approximately 47 percent of all enrolled students in 2003 were females, and 41 percent of those enrolled in institutions of higher education were women (National Bureau of Statistics 2004). Thus, the earlier disparities in educational levels have changed remarkably, and women have made steady and significant progress at all levels of education in China during the last twenty years. Parity with males seems likely in the near future.

Women's Role in Modern China

The data on literacy and primary education presented above, in parallel with vital statistics on the sex structure of the population, indicate a somewhat lower status for women in China's socialist state. Despite substantial improvements in life expectancy, literacy, well-being, and nutrition under socialism, women lag behind men and continue to have an inferior status, especially in rural areas. While this may be expected in the countryside, given the patriarchal nature of the society and its culture and the established male-dominant position, females must still survive the perils of possible infanticide at birth, and they receive poorer nutrition, family care, medical services, and fewer educational opportunities during childhood. After their own marriages, rural women join new families where they are expected to work hard and contribute to the family economic production system as well as to produce at least one son. While not always relishing this role, nevertheless Chinese women have endured and persevered remarkably well.

China for more than two thousand years has been a patriarchal society in which males have been privileged and have enjoyed a dominant position. Women were subordinate and had few rights. The Confucian canon, on which the Chinese social order and value system have been based since the fourth century B.C., institutionalized this idea of women's inferior role in society. Only in the mid-nineteenth century did things begin to change as new ideas about the role of women entered China and began to effect change. This was seen first in increased efforts to educate women and in early proposals to eliminate such archaic practices as foot binding and female infanticide. By the turn of the twentieth century, women's associations and new schools for women were widespread. In 1907 the Ministry of Education issued a regulation to govern the operation of women's schools (He 2003).

Following the founding of the Republic of China in 1911, a temporary constitution gave all Chinese rights of citizens, and this included women; yet the force of China's long history of social inequality impeded the move to full equality for women. In 1929 a new civil law went into effect that prohibited sexual discrimination and gave women rights to property, a significant advance. The Communists came to power in 1949, and the 1954 constitution guaranteed equal rights for women. Supporting legislation (a marriage law) and related policies were aimed at strengthening and ensuring these rights.

Mao Zedong is credited with the saying "Women hold up half the sky," a slogan that was popularized during the Cultural Revolution (1966–1969) and was designed to show the party chairman's official approval of the idea of full equality for women. Certainly during the Maoist years women entered the labor force in cities and in SOEs in large numbers, and their status was greatly enhanced as full members of the brave, new society. Many also became CCP members and assumed leadership positions at various levels of government. Despite such progress, it remains clear that women have not yet achieved the same status in Chinese society as men, and this is especially true in rural areas. As noted, literacy rates for rural women are lower than male rates, and the daily lives of farm women remain arduous and challenging.

There is also evidence that in recent years women who worked for SOEs were laid off or forced to retire early, and that many of the gains of the Maoist years were lost once the force of economic reforms took hold and layoffs began. There have also been recent calls in the media for women to return to domestic roles, given the reduced need of a large labor force (He 2003). Does this mean that the position of women in China's contemporary society may be retrogressing? Although there continue to be many challenges and difficulties for both urban and rural women in China, it seems unlikely that there will be any serious reversal of the steady advances of the last 150 years. One key contradiction of that advance is the divide between the status of urban and rural women, but one can argue that there is also an equally significant and serious divide between the well-being of rural and urban men.

One of the most serious and vexing issues related to gender in China is the matter of sex selection of fetuses, which is leading in some places to skewed gender distribution with greatly enlarged young male populations. If this is not ameliorated, it will lead to an unhealthy imbalance, and an excess of "missing girls" in the future, with attendant serious social unrest. And if because of the continuing treatment women receive as a result of the one-child policy their numbers diminish to the point where there is a real scarcity of available brides, women may come to be much better appreciated and treated in the future. According to the 1990 census, for every 100 women in China there were 106.6 men, and this number had increased from 106.3 in 1982. Sample survey data from 1999 indicated that sex ratios were improving and adjusting in favor of more women as a share of the total population. The 2000 census report then indicated that the ratio had fallen back to 106.3; however, in the age cohort 0–4 years of age, the male ratio had increased to 120.17, an indication that new technologies that allow for gender identification of a fetus may be encouraging more couples to abort female fetuses so that they may plan a male birth as their first, and perhaps only, offspring. If this is in fact the case, it is a disquieting prospect for China's future and suggests that there may soon be a large number of unhappy and frustrated males who are unable to find mates.

The fact that the national male-to-female ratio in China is not much different from that in other developing countries seems to contradict dire reports of female infanticide and mistreatment. Yet it does indicate that couples are taking advantage of new technologies in planning their families. The national statistics, moreover, mask regional variations that could clearly be seen in county-level data even as early as the 1982 census, where clusters of counties in Northwest China had male-to-female ratios of 112 to 100 or higher (see Li 1987; Skeldon 2001).

Human Resources and Employment

One serious consequence of overpopulation and underdevelopment is unemployment. Firm statistics are difficult to obtain, but unemployment among young people in China is known to be widespread and may be spreading among older, established workers as more and more SOEs are closed or restructured to improve operating efficiencies and profitability. This is especially true in the cities where factory jobs are insufficient to meet the demand for employment and the service sector has not been sufficiently developed to absorb more unemployed.

China's economy has shifted from a system based heavily on agriculture to one more reliant on industrial and service-oriented activities. A parallel shift in employment is also occurring, and the agricultural sector's employment share has declined from 84 percent in 1952 to 49 percent in 2003 (see chapter 7, table 7.2). Yet the problem here is the sheer size of a labor force that had grown to approximately 744 million in 2003 by keeping in step with population growth. Of this total labor force, 365 million (49 percent of the total) were in agriculture. This has resulted in serious under- or unemployment in rural areas as the Chinese economy converts to a greater focus on sideline, industrial, and service activities. Varying reports indicate there may be as many as 100–150 million marginally employed or unemployed people in China's farm economy, and the number may increase as the population grows and the economy continues to modernize (Taylor and Banister 1991). This is truly one of the most serious problems posed by China's huge and growing population, and one that may prove to be the biggest challenge to the future social and political stability of China (see Premier Zhu 2003, 9).

Migration

Migration, both domestic and international, has been largely restricted for most people during China's socialist period. It is true that during the first eight years of socialism there was virtually an open policy on personal movement, and many rural people moved into towns and cities. This came to an end in 1957, and as we previously described, a system of household registration (*hukou*) was implemented that effectively ended internal migration. Although there were subsequent periods of substantial but erratic migrations, such as were seen during the Great Leap Forward and the Cultural Revolution, internal population movements have continued to be controlled, with significant modifications, since 1994 (Goldstein and Goldstein 1985; Chan 2004).

In recent years and with increasing economic growth and demand for labor in the cities, coupled with far-reaching reforms and the evolution of China's market economy, movement of rural people to the cities has increased greatly, and estimates indicate approximately 120 million such temporary migrants (Oi 1999; Solinger 1999; *Chinadaily.com* 2003; Chan 2004). The general policy of the state has been two-pronged: rural folk should remain on their farms or in their villages and townships, and city dwellers should be accorded special privileges by virtue of their household registration in an urban location. Urban dwellers also by virtue of their employment in SOEs or *danwei* (units) thereby have received many special subsidies such as low rents in state-owned housing, health services, low energy costs, and pensions. It is no wonder that many people wished to go to the cities and thus had to be controlled to keep them on the farms (Taubmann 1993). As noted, these policies began to change as the central state increasingly recognized the contributions of rural migrants to the successful economic development of China's growing cities and coastal regions (Premier Zhu 2003, 9).

Yet to understand the real forces driving migration in China, it is necessary to look to the countryside and to consider the demographic and economic processes at work there. China's rural economy has been in rapid transition since 1978, and new methods of earning a living are everywhere as are more efficient methods of cultivation on the farms. The rural areas have far too many people for the available jobs, and there is a serious problem of redundant employment (Taylor and Banister 1991). Somewhere between 60 percent and 70 percent of China's people are farm householders (depending on how these householders are defined), and as we noted above, as the farm economy modernizes and is commercialized, an estimated 100–150 million redundant farm workers will need other employment in order to increase their marginal productivity. Many indeed have already moved to the towns and cities in search of better employment prospects, the major reason why people anywhere elect to move.

The 1980s and 1990s brought rapid economic growth and the fast changes typically associated with economic advancement, both in and around the cities, and especially in the coastal provinces, as China's economic links with the global economy took hold (Fan 2005). Construction and factory workers were needed as were workers to perform a variety of service activities. As these demands accelerated, farmers near and far were allowed to move to take these jobs as transient workers.

In 1984 China's policy makers modified the rules on migration to allow limited temporary migration of those who could provide their own grain rations. This resulted in a remarkable movement, largely from rural to urban areas, but it involved other shifts as well, and these introduced a new pattern of migration in socialist China. Over time more and more people moved as new and better opportunities for jobs became available. Gradually the changing economy and its demand for new workers in the growing cities and towns created a massive flux of human beings with an attendant relaxing and changing of the policies that determined, through enforcement of the *hukou* system, where people might live and work.

Migrants moved from rural areas to towns and cities, and in some cases even to other rural areas that offered new and better-paid opportunities. Rural-to-rural migrants are typically farmers from poor regions who migrate to other, wealthier regions and hire themselves out to farm the land of those villagers who have taken nonfarm employment in burgeoning local industries or other commercial and trading activities. Rural-to-town movement involves those laborers recruited to nearby towns to work in new factories or enterprises or those who go to these towns to open small businesses. Rural-to-city or town-to-city flows involve those who go to the cities to provide labor services as factory, construction, or transport workers, as well as those who go to work as domestics or simply to seek whatever work is available. In addition, there is a flow of permanent migrants from rural areas to the cities who have had their household registration changed by virtue of an official job shift, such as results from entering a university or being assigned to an SOE.

Migrants are typically young and comparatively well-educated. Both sexes migrate, but males predominate, and most are single. There are several variations of temporary migration (Taubmann 1993). These variations are typically based on the migrant's length of stay, although many migrants become permanent residents by virtue of increasing liberalization of government policies and rules on transfer of residence. Others enter the cities without permits and remain there illegally. Migrants in some cities have reached significant thresholds and have created problems, although there is growing recognition of the need to improve the living conditions of these migrants who are providing valuable labor services. Inadequate housing, sanitation, employment, and health services, and a growing crime problem are among the serious issues associated with these temporary migrants in China's cities. As noted earlier, it has been estimated that 120 million temporary migrants are now in China's cities. In many cities, they may account for

10 to 15 percent of the total population. At the same time, the flow and presence of temporary migrants is crucial to China's urban economies, which offer many new employment opportunities in construction, factory, transportation, and service jobs (Chan 2004).

Early on in the economic reforms, government policy was content with the idea of temporary migration because if the economy soured and urban jobs dried up, the migrants could be pushed out and easily returned to their rural areas. Moreover, the state had no obligation to provide expensive subsidies to these temporary residents. Yet the scale of this migration, coupled with an enormous rural surplus labor force, has created the potential for serious social problems and possible political instability in China's cities if no better arrangements are provided to incorporate future migrants in a fairer and more equitable manner. Solinger (1993, 1995) argued poignantly on the fundamental inequity of the urban-rural dichotomy in the household registration system, and lamented the second-class or marginal status to which the transient population was so clearly relegated. Yet given a very large surplus rural population, the economic advantages to the state, and the disincentives to allowing large-scale migration with its so many related social and environmental problems, it is easy to see why China would not allow a completely unregulated rural-to-urban migration. An increased recognition of the economic benefits of free mobility of labor and of more flexible policy and rules regarding such migration led some analysts to argue that the rules no longer mattered (Oi 1999; Solinger 1999). In January 2003, China's State Council issued new regulations and policies that gave rural migrants the legal right to work in cities and to begin to set up official residence in the urban places where they worked (Hutzler and Lawrence 2003, A12). Finally, the government had come to recognize the importance of the contributions of these migrants and their value to the urban economy. This indicates significant progress in the Chinese government's willingness to allow market mechanisms to work, and it is a crucial step forward in social policy and in improving the lives of millions of China's rural citizens.

China's continuing although slowing population growth, coupled with its restructuring and transforming of the countryside, offers evidence for a potential migration to cities and towns on a scale without precedent in human history. The challenge of managing this migration effectively and humanely is likely to be one of the major issues for China's leadership in the twenty-first century.

Population Growth and China's Future

As noted at the beginning of this chapter, China's people and its population are both its greatest resource and greatest challenge, offering the nation's leaders a set of problems as the country seeks to improve its economic condition and boost its standard of living. For more than three decades, China's leaders and policy makers have recognized the significance and scale of this population question and problem, but the demographic momentum built up under the government's variable policies in the periods of political instability during the first two decades of socialist rule have led to such rapid growth that it will require another generation to slow. Tien et al. (1992) has argued that given China's level of economic development, the government has probably achieved about all it can in reducing fertility and thereby advancing the trajectory of its demographic transition. Yet the 1990s proved to be a period of remarkable economic advance for China, and this permitted the central state to proceed to enforce vigorously its one-child policy to the point that China's fertility and birth rates have continued to decline, leading to a rate of net natural increase as low as countries such as the United States.

Further reductions in fertility likely will proceed apace with continued economic growth and accompanying social change, as has been seen in Japan, Taiwan, and South Korea. Yet the draconian measures embodied in the policy of the one-child family cannot go much further without the full-scale national industrialization and urbanization that typically herald modernization and attitudinal changes about family size. These in turn will lead to long-term reductions in fertility and birth rates. If its trajectory of economic growth and related urban and industrial development continues in the pattern of the 1990s, China will likely approach and achieve zero population growth in the next two or three decades. Japan, South Korea, Hong Kong, and Taiwan offer good East Asian and Chinese examples of how this process works. They may, therefore, provide useful portents for the patterns likely to unfold in China should its current process of economic reform and political stability continue through the twenty-first century.

Should China's demographic profile of below-replacement fertility continue, this will raise serious questions about the future of Chinese society and the structure of the Chinese family. A generation of Chinese children will grow up with no siblings and few cousins. The next generation will have no aunts or uncles. Some parents may have little support or connection to their only child once that child marries out to another family, and the dynamics of family life will surely change profoundly as the number of family members contracts sharply (Riley 2004).

Of perhaps even greater significance are the economic questions related to a rapid slowdown in population growth with the future possibility of population decline. While the effects of such a transition are just now beginning to appear, it is clear that even in one decade and certainly in two or three, if present demographic trends continue, China's annual added increment to the national labor force will be much smaller. At the same time, the proportion of its population 65 or older will be considerably larger, with all of the related social and economic consequences. For example, in 2000 approximately 7 percent of China's population was 65 or older compared to 12 percent in the United States. In China this 7 percent share is expected to double by the year 2026, a doubling that will require only twenty-six years, whereas in the United States the same doubling of the senior population will have occurred in the year 2013, but will have required sixty-nine years to do so. This a kind of demographic compression of an older population is similar to what has occurred in Japan. As some have described it, however, there is likely to be a marked difference between Japan and China, for China is projected to be the first country "to get old before it gets rich," a portent of challenging social, economic, and political consequences to come (Kinsella and Phillips 2005).

This possibility might witness a reversal in the proportion of China's working population, with a sharp rise in its dependent population as a proportion of the total. The retirement age of state employees could lengthen, which would probably be a good thing. China conceivably could even enter a period when labor becomes scarce. Both the economic and the social ramifications suggest that China's official policy on limiting families to one child will change in the future, but other development indicators such as improved incomes, higher levels of education and urbanization, and higher costs of living will likely lead to a reduced preference among Chinese couples for more than one or two children. China will then have completed its demographic transition, and it will have entered a phase of long-term no-growth or population decline.

References Cited

Aird, John. 1990. *Slaughter of the Innocents: Coercive Birth Control in China.* Washington, D.C.: AEI Press.

Ashton, Basil, et al. 1984. Famine in China, 1958–61. *Population and Development Review* 10 (4): 613–45.

Banister, Judith. 1984. An analysis of recent data on the population of China. *Population and Development Review* 10:3241–271.

———. 1987. *China's Changing Population.* Stanford, Calif.: Stanford University Press.

Chan, Kam Wing. 2004. Internal migration. In *Changing China: A Geographic Appraisal,* ed. Chiao-min Hsieh and Max Lu. Boulder, Colo.: Westview, 229–42.

Chao, Kang. 1986. *Man and Land in Chinese History: An Economic Analysis.* Stanford, Calif.: Stanford University Press.

Chen, Pi-chao. 1976. *Population and Health Policy in the People's Republic of China.* Washington, D.C.: Smithsonian Institution, Interdisciplinary Communications Program.

Chinadaily.com. 2003. Premier preoccupied with rural areas, unemployment, poverty. June 18. www.chinadaily.com.cn/highlights/nbc/news/318rural.html.

Elvin, Mark. 1973. *The Pattern of the Chinese Past.* Stanford, Calif.: Stanford University Press.

Fan, C. Cindy. 2002. Population change and regional development in China: Insights based on the 2000 census. *Eurasia Geography and Economics* 43 (6): 425–42.

———. 2005. Modeling interprovincial migration in China, 1985–2000. *Eurasia Geography and Economics* 46 (3): 165–84.

Goldstein, Sydney, and Alice Goldstein. 1985. Population mobility in the People's Republic of China. Paper no. 95 of the East-West Population Institute. Honolulu: East-West Center.

He, Pequin. 2003. Women's rights and protection policy in China: Achievements and problems. In *Social Policy Reform in China,* ed. Catherine Jones Finer. Aldershot, U.K.: Ashgate, 203–14.

Ho, Ping-ti. 1959. *Studies on the Population of China, 1368–1953.* Cambridge, Mass.: Harvard University Press.

Hsu, Mei-ling. 1985. Growth and development of population in China—the rural-urban contrast. *Annals of the Association of American Geographers* 75 (2): 241–57.

Hutzler, Charles, and Susan Lawrence. 2003. China acts to lower obstacles to urban migration. *Wall Street Journal,* January 22, A-3.

Jowett, John. 1990. People: Demographic patterns and policies. In *The Geography of Contemporary China,* ed. Terry Cannon and Alan Jenkins. London: Routledge, 102–32.

Kinsella, Kevin, and David R. Phillips. 2005. Global ageing: The challenge of success. *Population Bulletin* 60 (1). Washington, D.C.: Population Reference Bureau.

Lewis, Jane. 2003. Women's rights and gender issues. In *Social Policy Reform in China,* ed. Catherine Jones Finer. Aldershot, U.K.: Ashgate, 215–24.

Li, Chengrui, ed. 1987. *The Population Atlas of China*. Hong Kong: Oxford University Press.

Mallory, Walter H. 1926. *China: Land of Famine*. New York: American Geographical Society.

Mosher, Steven. 1983. *Broken Earth: The Rural Chinese*. New York: Free Press.

———. 1993. *A Mother's Ordeal: One Woman's Fight against China's One-Child Policy*. New York: Harcourt Brace Jovanovich.

National Bureau of Statistics. 2001. *Zhongguo tongji nianjian 2001* [China statistical yearbook 2001]. Beijing: China Statistics Press.

———. 2002. *Zhongguo tongji nianjian 2002* [China statistical yearbook 2002]. Beijing: China Statistics Press.

———. 2004. *Zhongguo tongji nianjian 2004* [China statistical yearbook 2004]. Beijing: China Statistics Press.

Oi, Jean C. 1999. Two decades of rural reform in China: An overview and assessment. *China Quarterly* 159:616–28.

Pannell, Clifton W. 2003. China's demographic and urban trends for the 21st century. *Eurasian Geography and Economics* 44 (7): 479–96.

Perkins, Dwight H. 1969. *Agricultural Development in China, 1368–1968*. Chicago: Aldine.

Premier Zhu. 2003. Government work report delivered at the first session of the Tenth National People's Congress. March 5. www.chinadaily.com.cn/highlights/nbc/news/319zhufull.htm.

Riley, Nancy E. 2004. China's population: New trends and challenges. *Population Bulletin* 59 (2): 1–36.

Skeldon, Ronald. 2001. Personal communication, January, Hong Kong.

Solinger, Dorothy J. 1993. China's transients and the state—a form of civil society. *Political Sociology* 21 (1): 91–122.

———. 1995. The floating population in the cities: Chances for assimilation. In *Urban Spaces in Contemporary China*, ed. Deborah Davis et al. New York: Woodrow Wilson Center Press, 113–48.

———. 1999. Demolishing partitions: Back to beginnings in the cities? *China Quarterly* 159:1–34.

Taubmann, Wolfgang. 1993. Rural urbanization in the People's Republic of China. In *Urban Problems and Urban Development in China*, ed. Wolfgang Taubmann. Hamburg: Institut für Asienkunde, 94–127.

Taylor, Jeffrey, and Judith Banister. 1991. Surplus rural labor in the People's Republic of China. In *The Uneven Landscape: Geographical Studies in Post-reform China*, ed. Gregory Veeck. Vol. 30. Baton Rouge: Geoscience Publications, Louisiana State University, 87–120.

Tien, H. Yuan. 1983. China—demographic billionaire. *Population Bulletin* 38 (2): 2–44.

———. 1987. Abortion in China—incidence and implications. *Modern China* 13 (4): 441–68.

Tien, H. Yuan, et al. 1992. China's demographic dilemmas. *Population Bulletin* 47 (1): 1–42.

Wang, Gabe T. 1999. *China's Population: Problems, Thoughts, and Policies*. Aldershot, U.K.: Ashgate.

World Bank. 2000. Entering the 21st century. *World Development Report 1999/2000*. New York: Oxford University Press.

Wu, Cangping, ed. 1997. *General Report of China's Changing Population and Its Development*. Beijing: Higher Education Press.

Xie, Zhenming. 2000. Population policy and the family planning program. In *The Changing Population of China*, ed. Peng Xizhe and Zhigang Guo. Oxford: Blackwell, 51–63.

Zheng, Wang. 2000. Gender, employment, and women's resistance. In *Chinese Society: Change, Conflict, and Resistance*, ed. Elizabeth J. Perry and Mark Selden. London: Routledge, 62–82.

Zhou, Jinghua. 1979. Interview with a specialist on population. *Beijing Review* 22 (46): 20–22.

CHAPTER 6

Culture and Cultural Change in Urban China

Christopher J. Smith

How do leading cultural critics, both Chinese and non-Chinese, assess what they see happening in the contemporary Chinese city? One answer to this question is offered by Dai Jinhua (2002), who observes that "the image of happy consumers... has replaced that of angry citizens" in Tiananmen Square (221). This would suggest a consensus among city dwellers, at least when it comes to economic concerns. But where some scholars see harmony, others see a dangerous level of fragmentation. Araf Dirlik (1994), for example, describes the "total disintegration of ideological unity" in China, in which "every idea from the most contemporary to the most reactionary... seems to find a constituency" (56). Geremie Barmé (1999) agrees, suggesting that in China by the end of the twentieth century, "fewer people in any group spoke the same language... and despite greater latitude, many were increasingly speaking at cross-purposes" (362). This would certainly have disappointed Mao Zedong, who was hoping that intellectuals, workers, and peasants in the new society would one day all be speaking the same language. It was already becoming clear by the end of Mao's lifetime, and certainly by the time Deng Xiaoping died, that this was not going to happen.

Some China experts have suggested that what they see happening in China today is symptomatic of an entirely new epoch. Scholar and journalist Orville Schell (1999), for example, thinks that the Chinese Communist Party (CCP) is now desperately trying to cling to its rule over a society that is "mutating into an almost uncategorizable form of crypto-capitalism dependent on foreign markets" (74). The effect of this "mutation" is manifested in part as nostalgia for a lost communist past, and in part as ambivalence. Schell takes his argument one step further, suggesting that by the end of the millennium, the Chinese people scarcely knew where to turn for cultural and political guidance, which perhaps explains why so many of them have become avid consumers of popular culture in its various manifestations.

These sentiments are shared by many Chinese scholars and artists, who feel their country is now experiencing a serious "cultural deficit." Beijing artist Ai Weiwei, for example, is repulsed by having to watch other artists "celebrate their craven pragmatism and opportunism... [which reflects their]... degraded standards and... lack of heart-felt values" (quoted in Barmé 1999, 363). Others are much more optimistic than this. Jianying Zha (1995), a Chinese cultural critic now living in the West, thinks that what she sees in contemporary China represents the birth of an entirely new cultural form. Western social scientists have weighed in on this debate, many of them on the negative side. In material terms, contemporary China certainly seems to be exhibiting many of the characteristics of advanced modern societies. Political scientist Gordon White (1996) suggests that in the 1990s China became infinitely more "fluid" and mobile in economic, social, and demographic terms than it had been in the Maoist (pre-1976) era:

> Urban workers . . . left their jobs in the public sector to start small busi-
> nesses; officials and professionals . . . left their secure . . . jobs on the govern-
> ment payroll to seek their fortunes in the private or collective sectors . . .
> [while] . . . peasants from rural hinterlands . . . left for local towns and cities,
> creating a growing "floating population" existing within the interstices of
> urban life. (1996, 204)

As indicated earlier, not all China scholars—and not all Chinese people—find these new trends alarming: in fact some suggest that the trends represent a major step forward in what is still, by many measures, a closed society. From this perspective, it is clearly possible to interpret what is happening in contemporary China as a positive and wholesome force: a virtual explosion of pent-up ambitions and desires among the long-suffering Chinese people. But even this interpretation is tempered by the observation that in the short run, the emerging cultural scene appears to be a complete hodgepodge, with many new voices all talking at once. Throughout the 1990s, experiments in all types of artistic expression were appearing on the streets, in the theaters, on television, and in print. The profusion of new cultural productions has more than matched the situation in the economic realm, which serves to underscore the enduring reality that the only arena where significant experimentation has not been occurring is in the realm of political life.

Our goal in this chapter is to try to make some sense out of the confusing mix of elements that is coming to define contemporary Chinese culture. In simple terms, two trends are observable, both of them tending to push in similar directions. First, in the habits and practices of everyday life, there has been a significant shift away from the heroic and utopian values of the revolutionary era toward the more quotidian pursuit of wealth and the simple pleasures of consumption (Tang 2000). What was starting to happen to Chinese cultural practices in the last part of the twentieth century, in other words, was a process of transition from an era dominated by the aesthetics of socialist realism to the collapse of utopian ideals in the aftermath of the Cultural Revolution, followed by the gradual "cannibalization" of Chinese socialism by consumer culture at the century's end.

The other trend in China, operating within a narrower definition of culture as artistic expression, is a movement away from the "highbrow" to the "lowbrow" end of the culture spectrum, from what are traditionally considered elite and rarified cultural forms, to the mass reproduction of popular culture that (by some accounts at least) has no apparent depth or significance (Kraus 1995). As we survey the contemporary scene in China, there is evidence to support this second observation, as illustrated in table 6.1, which is adapted from Kraus. This categorization allows us to distinguish elite from popular art forms, and traditional artistic practices from contemporary (most of which have been adopted in China during the last century). As this division indicates,

Table 6.1. A Conceptualization of Cultural Change in Contemporary China

	Elite Art/Culture	Popular Art/Mass Culture
Traditional	ink painting landscapes classical poetry calligraphy seal carving	New Year's painting opera novels handicrafts
Contemporary	oil painting symphonies ballet spoken drama avant-garde poetry and painting	pin-ups Hong Kong or Taiwan popular music sex and violence family-life pot boilers disco television and video karaoke

Source: Adapted from Kraus 1995, table 7.1, p. 182.

the Contemporary/Popular Art/Mass Culture quadrant shown in table 6.1 includes the enjoyment of imported (and foreign-influenced) rock music, sex- and violence-rich shows on television and video, and karaoke. It is here that the new urban art productions have had their greatest impact in China, where the demand for new products is highest, and "where potential rewards for artistic entrepreneurs are greatest" (182).

Significant efforts have been made to maintain at least some of the cultural practices within such domains as oil painting, classical music, literary novels, ballet, spoken drama, and avant-garde poetry. The problem in China today, however, is that in spite of these continuing efforts, people attempting to generate a cosmopolitan—and uniquely Chinese—form of art in these realms are finding they are almost as disadvantaged as those trying to maintain a public interest in China's traditional or elite art forms. The major reason for this, and the principal dynamic in the production of cultural and art forms in contemporary China, is the pervasive impact of market forces. To quote Kraus again, "High-minded novelists now have more difficulty finding publishers; ballet and spoken drama troupes and symphony orchestras are forced to cut their payrolls, as well as to find ways of earning additional funds" (1995, 183). The most immediate impact of the reform era on the elite forms of Chinese art (in both their contemporary and traditional manifestations) has been the reduction—and in many cases the complete withdrawal—of state subsidies for the art forms considered most important by would-be cosmopolitans in China.

Changing Cultural Trends in the New Urban China

One way to begin looking at cultural change in China is to focus on the way Chinese people are spending their time and money, in the understanding that this will tell us something about what they consider important in their lives. Luckily, with the relatively recent resurgence of academic social sciences in China, a range of research tools is now available to help in this task.

SPENDING TIME

One specific set of research tools now being used in China involves the use of time budgets and the keeping of daily activity diaries, which allow the researcher to explore different dimensions of everyday life. In a review of such research in contemporary China, Wang Shaoguang (1995) has referred to the notion of "private time" to describe what people do to amuse or entertain themselves when they are not working. In his discussion of trends that were emerging in the early 1990s, Wang reported dramatic changes since the end of the Cultural Revolution, not only in the quantity but also in the quality of private time, and it is reasonable to assume that the context for these changes was a shift in the nature of state control over the lives of the Chinese people. The evidence suggests that beginning in the 1980s and continuing to the present day, the state has no longer felt quite the same need to define what are and are not suitable leisure-time activities for the people. In essence, rather than requiring citizens to toe the line defined by the official state ideology, the Chinese government now allows them to spend their spare time however they want, provided their behavior does not directly challenge the state or threaten the social order.[1] What this means is an effective uncoupling of public and private time: in essence, the people have been liberated, on the understanding that they will exercise restraint, and presumably in the clear knowledge that the state can at any time redefine where the line is to be drawn between what is acceptable behavior and what is not.

Wang's data, collected from a variety of official sources and from research reports compiled by Chinese scholars, suggest that the average Chinese city dweller had significantly more free time in the 1990s than was the case in the previous three decades. The reasons, Wang suggests, include the widespread introduction of household consumer durables that saved time in and around the home; a reduction in the length of the working day, associated mainly with the abolition of political study sessions and voluntary political work; and an increasing efficiency in the reform-era workplace. The average Chinese family in 1980 had two hours and twenty-one minutes of "leisure time" per day; but that had increased to four hours and forty-eight minutes by 1991 (1995, 158). Charlotte Ikels reinforces this observation in her book about Guangzhou, *The Return of the God of Wealth*, where she reports that the official working week was cut in 1994 from 48 to 44 hours, and again in 1995 from 44 to 40 hours (1996, 222). As she observes,

> The amount of discretionary time . . . has increased as people have been relieved of tedious tasks that occupied their non-work time in the past. . . . They no longer have to stand in long lines for rationed goods, struggle to get things repaired, or scout state stores for clothing. . . . The elimination of rationing, the return of the small repair business . . . and the expansion of commerce have made it easier to meet basic needs and still have time left over. (222)

As Ikels notes, the reestablishment of the private sector in the Chinese city has allowed the expansion of a huge variety of commercial and service industries, including fast-food restaurants, home-appliance repair shops, and "decoration" companies that are able to perform a wide range of previously ignored or DIY (do-it-yourself) activities in the home. These new ventures have reduced the burden of shopping, food preparation, repair work, and housing maintenance. The additional time gained by this reduction, combined with a growth in income in some strata of urban society, has increased the demand for new and varied leisure activities.

Two other features of the reform era have had positive effects on the supply and diversity of leisure activities in urban China. One has been the presence of foreign investors who have been willing to pour capital into a variety of new activities or enterprises, including filmmaking, music productions, nightclubs, restaurants, and bars. All of these serve to offer new diversions for the masses, while broadening the range of what is acceptable as cultural production, and expanding the demand for freelance artists, who no longer have to depend on the state for their livelihood. The other important change is in the fiscal situation of what might be referred to as China's "culture industries" (J. Wang 2001). All state units and enterprises involved in cultural production, including those in the communications business (newspapers, magazines, radio, and television), have been forced to become economically self-sufficient, which means they now need to be responsive to market forces and to appeal to new consumer tastes (Smith 2002a). As Ikels (1996) remarks, "Articles or programs with heavy-handed ideological content lack such appeal and consequently have been almost entirely displaced" (261). It is also apparent that Chinese media outlets, television stations in particular, have not been able to respond adequately to the huge increase in demand for new and diverse programming. The outcome is that many of them have been forced to look abroad for suitable material, which usually means the Chinese TV-watcher is exposed to endless reruns of martial arts films, historical dramas, and soap operas, mainly from Hong Kong and Taiwan.

It is worthwhile speculating briefly here on the ideological impact of these trends, and on the reaction of the regime to such new developments, although no hard data are available to temper such observations. Bearing in mind an inherent emphasis on affluence and consumption, and all of the other "bourgeois" traits typically associated with contemporary life in the places where such products originate, we might expect the state to remain vigilant, at the very least, in its overview of such trends. For the most part, however, this does not appear to be the case, although such products are carefully screened for political content (which they rarely have) and for such things as nudity (although not violence). Perhaps in part to counteract the "bourgeoisification" of Chinese television, the state continues to exhort newspaper editors and television producers to include some column space or devote some program hours to issues that promote "positive" moral development (Ikels 1996). Ikels also hints that the state is still relatively intolerant of public events and behavior considered to be related to China's many "feudal superstitions" (262). From the account Ikels provides, in Guangzhou at least, the state tolerates only low-key celebrations of traditional holidays in the public realm, no matter how lavishly families may celebrate them at home.

SPENDING MONEY

In the search to uncover the nature of new cultural developments in contemporary China, it is also useful to investigate how the urban Chinese, or at least those who are doing well in the reform era, spend their new wealth. Obviously, many things that were hard to come by, even taboo, in the pre-reform era, have now become commonplace, as a walk around any of the new supermarkets in Shanghai and Shenzhen will demonstrate. In spite of all that has been written on this topic in recent years, we may reasonably suspect that these changes—the impacts of the reforms—will be nowhere near as pervasive in China's interior regions as they are on the coast. After spending two years in a medium-size town in Sichuan province on the Chang Jiang (Yangtze River), Peter Hessler in his book *River Town* offers some interesting observations on this issue. Hessler and another young American were employed to teach English grammar and literature to a group of students in a small teacher-training college. As a way of getting their students to write in English, they asked them about their lives and their aspirations, and at one point in the book, Hessler describes what happened when his colleague gave an in-class assignment in which the instructions were for the students to "write about anything you want." As Hessler recalls:

> The students wrote. At the end of the hour . . . [he] . . . collected their papers. They had written about anything they wanted, and what he had was forty-five shopping lists. I want a new TV, a new dress, a new radio. I want more grammar books. I want my own room. I want a beeper and a cell phone and a car. I want a good job. Some of the students had lists a full page long, every entry numbered and prioritized. (2001, 26)

What these two young Americans came to realize was that Chinese people living in the interior regions are only just starting to define some of their dreams about being consumers. In the not-too-distant past, such desires would have been muffled, either because there was no chance of becoming wealthy enough to make such purchases, or because the public expression of such desires would have been politically incorrect. Today all that has changed: it is now considered not only normal but positively patriotic to consume at the highest rate possible. What this signifies is that China is experiencing significant changes in the consumption habits that determine and define the practices of everyday life, practices that, as suggested earlier, are equally as important in defining culture and cultural change as the more traditional literary and artistic domains.

The nature of some of these changes is illustrated in table 6.2, which shows the increase in the average level of income and retail sales from 1978 to 1997. The magnitude of the increases is startling: in less than two decades, urban income more than tripled, the amount of living space almost doubled, and the percentage of households using natural gas increased from 14 to 76 percent. Also helping to make life at home much easier and more comfortable were huge increases in the ownership of consumer durables: automatic washing machines, refrigerators, sofas, and color televisions. These upward trends are likely to continue as urban households try desperately to "keep up with the Zhangs," and in real terms, as Tang and Parish (2000) point out, "improved objective

Table 6.2. Consumption Categories and Media Exposure in Urban China, 1978–1997

Category	1978	1985	1997
Disposable income per capita	100	160	312
Per capita living space (m²)	3.9	5.2	8.8
Natural gas (% of homes)	14	22	76
Consumer durables (per 100 households)			
washing machines	6	48	89
refrigerators	0	7	76
sofas	89	132	205
televisions (color)	—	17	100
Media and communication (national)	—		
TV broadcast coverage (%)	—	—	88
Radio broadcast coverage (%)	—	—	86
Copies published (millions)			
newspapers	140	200	187
books	46	67	73
magazines	11	26	24
Urban telephones (100,000's)	28	48	554
Long-distance phone lines (1,000's)	19	38	1,146
Mobile phones (1,000's)	0	0	1,323

Source: Adapted from Tang and Parish 2000, table 2.1, p. 39.

conditions meant that family life was far more comfortable in the 1990s than at the end of the 1970s" (42).[2]

More recent data, released by the Chinese government in 2003, show that the living standards of both the urban and the rural populations continued to improve into the new millennium. The annual per capita disposable income of urban households, for example, was 7,703 yuan in 2002, an increase of more than 40 percent in a five-year period (see table 6.3). The Engel coefficient, which measures the proportion of expenditures on food to the total consumption expenditures, was 37.7 percent for urban households, down from 44.5 in 1998—again this suggests that more of total household income was available for the consumption of "luxuries," or for saving.

Table 6.3. Increases in Urban and Rural Incomes: China, 1998–2002

	1998	1999	2000	2001	2002
Per capita disposable income of urban population (yuan)	5,425	5,854	6,280	6,860	7,703
Per capita net income of rural population (yuan)	2,162	2,210	2,253	2,366	2,476
Engel coefficient of urban households* (%)	44.5	41.9	39.2	37.9	37.7
Engel coefficient of rural households (%)	53.4	52.6	49.1	47.7	46.2

* The Engel coefficient is the percentage of total household income that is spent on food.
Sources: National Bureau of Statistics 2004; statistical communiqué of the People's Republic of China on the 2002 national economic and social development. See www.16congress.org.cn/e-company/03-03-20/page030102.htm.

Tang and Parish (2000) also call attention to a very significant shift in this time period, from what might be defined as an era of scarcity, in which people in China's cities could only fantasize about the things they did not have, to an era of plenty, in which many now have access to almost everything they want. It is surely a fine irony to recall that in the not-too-distant past, the hero or heroine of Chinese urban society was the person with the most effective *guanxi*, that is, the one able to get the best deals, find the real bargains, and generally make the most of his or her connections in an otherwise luxury-scarce environment. Such finely tuned networking skills are no longer as prized as they once were; in fact, the only requirement today for living the good life in China is having plenty of money. More importantly, it is now becoming clear that in contemporary urban China, shortages and underproduction are no longer the problem; the anxiety these days—for the state's economic planners at least—is that demand will not be great enough to soak up all the products being made. This may help to explain why the state seems to be so fixated on increasing the rate of urbanization in China, which—it is assumed—will result in the establishment of new household units that have to be filled and furnished with domestically made consumer durables. All of this is consistent with the state's push during the last decade in the direction of privatized housing, as we will discuss in chapter 9 of this book.

The state's anxiety about consumer spending may also explain in part why it has pushed so hard to promote the domestic automobile industry and increase the rate of private car ownership, as a way of forcing Chinese consumers to spend rather than save their earnings—even in the face of the potentially disastrous environmental consequences of such a policy (Johnson 1997; see also chapter 3). As all of this suggests, the exemplary economic figure in today's China is more likely to be a salesperson or marketing agent, than a peasant or a soldier. The contemporary fantasy—what Elizabeth Croll (1994) has described, although in a different context, as the people's "dreams of heaven"—is for every household to have an array of consumer durables appropriate to its status (Tang and Parish 2000, 43). To make sure they move in the direction of achieving this goal, urban consumers are now surrounded by "wall-to-wall" advertising, on the streets, on television, and in publications of all types.

One new trend that is of obvious importance in a discussion of culture and cultural change in China is the way the Chinese people eat, what they eat, and where they eat it. As urban incomes have risen in China, the structure of spending on food and eating habits, in general, has changed very significantly. In a report commissioned by the Center for Chinese Agricultural Policy (CCAP), residents in five cities were asked how much of their income they spent on food of various types and in various locations (Ma, Huang, Rozelle, and Fuller 2002). The results showed that as incomes rose during the 1990s, households spent a smaller proportion of their total income on food, but there was a corresponding increase in the amount of meat and fish they ate, and a sharp decline in their consumption of grains (mainly rice and wheat—noodles or bread). Not surprisingly, the ratio of meat and fish to grains consumed increased as a function of rising incomes among urban households: in households with per capita incomes below 1,000 yuan, grains represented 28 percent of total purchases, with meat and fish accounting for 21 percent and 6 percent respectively; but in households with per capita incomes above 4,000 yuan, grains made up only 14 percent of the total, while meat and fish accounted for 38 percent and 13 percent respectively.[3] Ma and his colleagues also point out the beginning of a very significant trend toward eating away from the home in urban China, a trend that more than doubled, from 6 percent of all food expenditures in 1991 to 13 percent in 1999; and again this percentage increased with income levels. As the authors suggest, this trend, which looks likely to continue as average urban incomes rise in China, will have a significant impact on the urban landscape. They observe,

> Powerful forces, such as rising income, are not only changing the pattern of people's diets, the new habits of consumers also have their own effect on the nation's urban environment . . . [which has] . . . spawned a huge increase in the catering industry and created a highly visible venue in which people are able to meet, entertain themselves and do business. (7)

In the spirit of the reform era, all of these new "private time" activities have blossomed in response to the changing economic climate. The demand of the newly empowered Chinese consumer for a more varied lifestyle, which includes eating in restaurants, is obviously an important dimension of this new trend.

Also apparent in table 6.3 is an increase in the consumption of media of all types in urban China, and a sizeable increase in the amount of electronic interaction through regular and mobile telephones. Increased media exposure is a sure sign of the coming of a modern age in any country, in part because it allows consumers a greater degree of flexibility in what they can do in their spare time, but also because it offers people a much greater opportunity to imagine different possibilities for themselves and their family members (we are reminded again here of Croll's "dreams of heaven"). Television coverage in all urban areas of China is now almost universal, and the hours of programming (and watching) have increased noticeably. Much of the new programming (on television at least) consists of what many cultural critics refer to as "lowest-common-denominator programming," including soap operas and historical dramas (Dai 2002). Critical dramas, documentaries, and satirical comedies have also been aired over the last few years, with enough intellectual and political content to suggest at least a minor role for television in sharpening the critical faculties of its viewers.[4] The line beyond which such programs are not allowed to go, however, is still drawn by the state, which is not surprising, if we bear in mind that all media and publication outlets are still publicly owned and operated.

The consumption data also show that readership in all contexts (including books, newspapers, and magazines) has increased significantly during the reform era, although it seems likely that in the late 1980s and early 1990s, television began to attract some of those who might have otherwise been readers in the future, or who had been readers in the recent past. The proliferation of newspapers of all types in China during the last decade—including party propaganda outlets, respectable dailies, and a galaxy of tabloids—implies that far more topics and issues are now being covered, including even gossip about the personal lives of some of the country's top leaders. One is tempted to think that this absolute increase in the availability of publications has allowed the Chinese people, or those who live in the cities at least, to voice a greater range of opinions on and about public issues (Lynch 1999). In some spheres, the state has encouraged the press to be hypercritical, especially when such a stance supports official policies—for example, in the state's quest to reduce official corruption; in its position on some environmental issues; in its struggle to oppose certain organizations, such as Falun Gong; and in its attempts to wipe out crime—but in many of the more politically controversial spheres, coverage ranges from the perfunctory to the nonexistent (Smith 2002b).

To old China hands, the expansion of the country's communication capabilities represents one of the most remarkable changes in the new China. In days-gone-by, foreign China scholars kept themselves amused by telling stories about the difficulty of living in China, and one of their most frustrating experiences would be trying to make phone calls, which led to the near impossibility of keeping in touch with the outside world. Just ten years ago, several apartment compounds might have shared a single pay phone. All of this has changed today, with an increase in telephone availability, coupled with rapidly rising use of cell phones and the Internet. Again we might suspect that in the long run this new openness will have an impact on the quantity and the quality of public consciousness about all sorts of issues, including the environment, the abuse of women and children, and the problem of urban unemployment. It is evident, in other words, that people in China not only have much more to do in their spare time today, and much more spare time in which to do it, they also have much more information about the world and whatever interests them. An optimist might suggest that the logical outcome in this situation will be an increase in Chinese awareness about social and economic problems, and a greater concern that the government do more to solve such problems. The next logical question to ask then is whether the government will be likely to listen to such talk, and willing to respond by delivering the goods and services needed in the new era of plenty.

It is appropriate to conclude this section by taking a step backward to consider the magnitude (and the significance) of the cultural changes that have been recorded in urban China during the reform era. In not much more than two decades, China's city dwellers have witnessed a shift from Maoist asceticism to the middle-class enjoyment of capitalist luxuries. As Judith Farquhar (2002) points out, this can be expressed in terms of the satisfaction of new "appetites" that were not only not realizable in the pre-reform era, they could not even be talked about in public. In the mid-1970s it was totally unacceptable to introduce the topic of individual appetites—or their indulgence—into public discourse in China. In the Maoist state, as Farquhar observes,

> It was much more proper to speak of past suffering (in the old society), future utopia (when communism is achieved), and, in the present, work, production, and service. For at least two decades . . . wishes and discomforts could not be spoken of casually and privately, [and] the existence and indulgence of non-collective appetites were almost an embarrassment. (3)

By comparison, in what Farquhar calls the "roaring nineties," the enjoyment of personal appetites was being extravagantly displayed in public places, often with an air of defiance. We should remember here that an excessive concern with individualism and consumerism is diametrically opposed to the principles of orthodox socialism. The fact that the CCP continues to urge the people to consider doing public service, to maintain high standards of morality, and to pursue selfless behaviors (Bakken 2000), serves to highlight the huge disparity that has now emerged between what was acceptable behavior in the past and what is acceptable today. During the last two decades in China, commercialization and entrepreneurialism have resulted in major changes in the traditionally solid ideological facade of the socialist regime, and in the realm of centralized cultural production. As one Chinese scholar suggests, this new development has been met by "an almost visible sigh of relief, a not-so-quiet celebration of the demise of overpoliticization and the end of Ideology" (Tang 2000, 273).

The Politics of Cultural Production in the New China

The evidence we have looked at thus far fills in only one side of the story, however, focusing as it does on the material (and measurable) aspects of cultural change in contemporary China. It appears that artists in China today (defining the term *artist* as broadly as possible) can now begin to dream of a more positive future, after a long period in which they were held captive in a metaphorical space between the old controls of the CCP and the newer mechanisms of the market. As Richard Kraus (1995) explains this situation, "The changing relations between plan and market force[d] changes in the lives and visions of China's artists and in the pleasures offered . . . [to] . . . urban audiences" (173). Although the present (and to some extent the future) looks relatively rosy for cultural and artistic production, with enormous new territory opening up, Kraus also reminds us that there is a downside to these new trends. For some artists, the new era is much less secure, in the sense that state-supported art once offered regular work and certainty, even if the boundaries of what was artistically acceptable were drawn sharply by the state. "The market" on the other hand means excessive competition, a seemingly endless search for new consumers and patrons, and a drift toward what Kraus calls the "coarsening" of public life, in which there is a massive drift toward the "lowbrow" end of consumer preferences. A major problem facing Chinese artists today, in other words, is in deciding what type of art is to be produced (and consumed), and many would-be artists are forced to decide whether they can live with what Kraus refers to as the "cheapening" process associated with this drift toward the lowest common denominator of mass taste. If they choose to shun the path of the market, artists face the prospect of banishing themselves to obscurity and poverty.

As we shall examine in more detail later in this chapter, this dilemma is clearly evident in the production of independent films in contemporary China. To illustrate this point briefly here, it is useful to focus on the controversial film *Frozen* (1996), which was (and still is) banned in China and had to be smuggled out of the country for distribution in the West. The film offers a look at the underground culture in China's cities in the post-Tiananmen era, and provides a window on the world of avant-garde art in Beijing. Most of the cultural productions depicted in the film fall into the category of extreme performance art, which is clearly a fringe activity in terms of drawing crowds and generating income. Some of the performances depicted in the film—including one in which two men eat a bar of soap each, with a knife and fork—are attended only by a handful of other artists and a smattering of baffled passers-by. The antihero of the film is a young performance artist who decides to make his own suicide the object of his last work of art. In the middle of summer he melts a huge block of ice with his own body heat and appears to die of hypothermia. The film's ending is open to different interpretations, and some critics suggest that the artist may actually have faked his death. As an independently made film, *Frozen* is now only legally available outside China, and the filmmaker—although widely acknowledged among those in the know to be Wang Xiaoshuai, who later directed a much more popular and more politically correct film called *Beijing Bicycle*—was forced to use the nom de plume Wu Ming, or "Anonymous," to avoid censure at home and a complete ban on his activities.

In the Maoist era, the arts were regarded primarily as a tool for mass mobilization of the population. The major task for the CCP's propaganda officials was to encourage and provide financial support for artworks that adhered to the party line, and to discourage or censor those works that did not. As Kraus (1995) points out though, propaganda work was never as centralized in China as it was in the Soviet Union, and the job of censorship was often left to writers, editors, and local officials in the hope that they would effectively censor themselves. For the most part this seemed to work reasonably well to suppress unorthodox or dissenting ideas, but only as long as there was (or officials believed there to be) a sense of common cause among the people. As noted at the beginning of this chapter, however, this no longer seems to be the case in contemporary China, and many new films dealing with controversial topics (such as HIV/AIDS, homosexuality, political dissidence, and coal-mining accidents) are almost automatically banned within China.

Surprisingly, this situation has not choked off all of the art and culture operating at the margins of political acceptability, primarily because the huge expansion in all media outlets that has accompanied the economic reforms overloaded the CCP's control mechanisms (Lynch 1999). For this reason, and (according to Kraus at least) because artists' professional organizations began to meet with some measure of success in protecting their members from political criticism, cultural productions and artworks that were far from being politically correct began to appear in many parts of urban China. Although such events were attacked sharply by the government's censors at intervals, most notably immediately after the Tiananmen Square massacre (Kraus 1995, 177), the net result has been the emergence of an impressive new body of artistic and cultural work (J. Wang 2001).

As this brief summary suggests, the primary trend throughout the reform era has been for diminished state control, and as artwork and cultural production have become increasingly commodified, artists of all types have come to rely less on securing financial support from the state and more on the sale of their paintings, books, shows, and presentations. A review of what sells and what does not sell in contemporary China indicates that the market has been kinder to some art forms than others: poetry of all types and classical Chinese artworks for the most part have not sold well. But with these important exceptions, the demand for art and cultural productions is more robust today than ever before in China, and we have witnessed the emergence of a great deal of experimental art and increasingly risqué literature, especially in the big cities of the coastal provinces. It is also worth noting that in the past decade there has been something of a revival of some the old forms of popular culture, including street-level productions of Chinese opera, which meets with broad approval among older people, as does the introduction of foreign innovations such as karaoke, video games, and imported rock music with the younger ones.

In spite of this growth of new market opportunities, some artists have chosen to remain closely tied to the political establishment, preferring to support the regime (or to work quietly or subtly against it), rather than to adopt a deliberately aggressive stance.[5] Overall as the cultural marketplace expands, it is reasonable to expect that CCP control and influence will gradually be eroded even further, primarily by an expansion in the number and variety of opportunities available to artists for boosting their careers and incomes. As this happens, we might expect to see a greater proportion of art and cultural productions becoming apolitical in character, although there is also the distinct possibility that more artists might choose to take what Kraus refers to as "judiciously critical positions against the status quo" (1995, 178) to produce what amounts to a "culture of resistance" (Barmé 1999).

From a historical perspective, it is important to note that a great deal of China's politics during the last century has been centered on the task of reforming culture, based on the belief that traditional Chinese culture is fundamentally feudal and must be radically restructured, often using Western norms as the model. Only this way, so the argument goes, can China be transformed into a modern state. As early as the 1920s, the emerging CCP, believing that modernization could only occur by replacing feudalism with cosmopolitan culture, began to prepare for a broad purge of traditional Chinese culture. Once the party was dug in at Yan'an, however, and later when it finally came to power in 1949, this situation changed somewhat. From that time onward, party leaders realized that the only way to radicalize the peasants was to force urban intellectuals to honor them by developing national forms of culture that were heavily rural-based (Kraus 1995).

A visually stunning example of this trend was portrayed in Chen Kaige's mid-1980s film *Yellow Earth*, which is set in northern Shaanxi province in the late 1930s. Northern Shaanxi, which is part of the dry and barren Loess Plateau, is considered the cradle of Chinese (Han) civilization; but it was also—at the time the film is set—close to the heart of the emerging communist movement, some two hundred miles to the south in Yenan. The action takes place ten years before the revolution, and the Communists are attempting to win over the peasants to their cause, which involves expelling the Japanese, defeating the Nationalists, and bringing about the modernization of China, roughly in that order (McDougall 1991). The premise of the film is that operatives of the Eighth Route (Red) Army are being dispatched into the countryside to collect peasant folk songs, which will be transformed into battle songs for the soldiers as they march to war (see later in this chapter for a more detailed discussion of *Yellow Earth*).

Some of the individuals Kraus (1995) refers to as "radical cosmopolitans" within the CCP were hoping that, after gaining power and mobilizing the peasants, the party would eventually be able to return the country to a May Fourth–type of urban, international culture.[6] With hindsight we now know that this did not happen, not that is, until Mao had been long dead. Ironically, it was market reforms that were to internationalize Chinese culture, and this certainly did not happen in the way CCP intellectuals had anticipated. The huge amount of new popular culture notwithstanding, an argument can still be made that the May Fourth call to bring cosmopolitan culture to China has been reinvigorated in new ways during the reform era. Some examples of this would include the immensely popular but controversial *Heshang* (River Elegy) television series, the introduction of abstract, Western styles of painting and music, and the new vitality of a literary modernism that, according to Kraus, "rejects the . . . [socialist] . . . realism imposed over several decades" (180).

In addition to a proliferation of domestic cultural productions, in the last decade the Chinese public has been exposed to a wide range of foreign art forms—often arriving in a haphazard order, and putting together "high" art (like the ever-popular events featuring the Three Tenors) with more "lowbrow" television dramas and block-buster movies. In his evaluation of these developments, Kraus (1995) concludes that "diversity coupled with diminished political control has freed space for a newly autonomous aesthetic domain in which artists explore the implications of art separated from politics" (178). As the CCP slowly relaxes its grip, artists and critics of all stripes have been involved— without significant input from the state, and for almost the first time since 1949— in momentous debates about what signifies beauty and aesthetic standards in China (J. Wang 1996). Reduced artistic dependence on the state means that instead of focusing on works that are social and political in nature, artists and cultural producers have been increasingly likely to approach the once-dangerous territory of personal exploration into the domains of emotion, sexuality, and psychology.

Contextualizing Cultural Change in Urban China

As a way of exploring some of these contemporary artistic and cultural developments more fully, this chapter examines two dimensions of artistic and cultural production in China by focusing first on literary works, and then on filmmaking. To put these new developments into their cultural and political context, however, we will preface this discussion with an analysis of the role of subjectivity and the self in post-Mao China, a role that is close to the heart of many of China's new cultural trends. It is also appropriate here to explore the emergence of a new and specifically urban culture that has challenged the traditional, rural-based ideas of culture allied to the CCP both before and after 1949.

SUBJECTIVITY AND THE SELF IN CONTEMPORARY CHINESE CULTURE

Insiders and outsiders now generally agree that China's brand of communism resulted in a system of indoctrination that largely deprived its people of authentic experiences and of the ability to express themselves, either verbally or physically (Barmé 1999). In spite of this, some scholars suggest that communism provided the Chinese with powerful and even inspirational interpretations of their world by presenting an attractive, even seductive "story" that many of them—including, significantly, a large number of intellectuals—were able to live with (Rofel 1999). It also provided a structure of belief and an orientation to life that had an appealing simplicity, and with the (often coercive) help of the state, an entire generation became convinced that communism was not just the best but the only way to live.

Literary and artistic output at the time reflected these beliefs, especially in the socialist realism mode that was adopted from the Russians and adapted by the Chinese to their own, more rural-oriented situation. The founding of the People's Republic of China (PRC) in 1949, however, marked a major turning point in China's search for modernity, and from that time onward, discursive authority was placed directly in the hands of the state. Much of the CCP's original rhetoric was inherited from European critiques of bourgeois ideology, which provided China's new leaders with an opportunity to transform the notion of individualism—including concerns with, for, and about the self—into a metaphor for a highly negative and corrupted other, which was generally presumed to reside in the capitalist West. It is important to recall here that historically (or until the beginning of the twentieth century at least), the very idea of a self-actualizing and motivated individual was anathema to the fundamentals of Chinese cosmological and ethical belief systems. As Lu Xun[7] wrote,

> In less than three or four years after the word *geren* [individual] was introduced into China, progressive intellectuals began to shun the idea like leprosy. Whoever had the misfortune of having the label of the individual tagged to his person . . . would be regarded as a scoundrel, for it is commonly believed that individualism privileges self-centeredness at the expense of others. (1957, 186–87)

With its new ideological base, the revolutionary state played an active role in presenting the idea of individualism to its people as decidedly negative and "un-Chinese" (L. Liu 1996). By holding up the image of a debased Other—in the West—the regime was able to launch massive campaigns to rid China of much of what its leaders considered the West's corrupted and corrupting colonial heritage. In the public health realm, for example, this included mass campaigns to clean-up and sanitize the streets of the Western-dominated urban centers, which meant sweeping away traces of the buildings, bodies, and lifestyles associated with the decadent past of urban capitalism in coastal China (Smith 2005a, 2005b; Hershatter 1997).

From a longer historical perspective, it is apparent that what was happening in the revolutionary era was not all that different from what had happened in earlier periods. China's past is in fact dotted with searches for (and abandonment of) universalizing worldviews, most of which were fundamentally different from communism, but which followed a similar trajectory. Historian Jonathan Spence (1996) maintains, for example, that the Chinese, driven by a "frenzied search for security and reassurance" (60), have on more than one occasion supported extraordinary social movements that were based on millenarian dreams. This was especially the case in the middle of the nineteenth century, when millions of Chinese people listened to and largely believed the words of Hong Xiuquan, an educated peasant who had convinced himself he was the son of the

Christian God. Hong claimed that he had been entrusted with the heavenly task of saving the world, and although he failed in the long term to bring about the utopia his Taiping Rebellion had foretold, he was able to lead millions of his followers into a long drawn-out and ultimately deadly conflict with the ruling Qing dynasty.

The demise of orthodox communism—another universalizing worldview—must have been a welcome relief to many Chinese people, whose lives improved significantly thereafter. However, there is clearly another side to this story, one involving the loss of an ideology that initially made sense to many people, and without which many of them may have experienced something approaching feelings of bereavement (Barmé 1999). The loss of its communist worldview may not have caused China as much direct death and destruction as the Taipings did in the nineteenth century, but some China scholars think it helped to create an emotional and spiritual vacuum (Perry and Selden 2000; Liu and Link 1998). As we suggested at the beginning of this chapter, a new and previously unheard-of alliance in reform-era China between political authoritarianism and no-holds-barred capitalism has produced an extraordinary mélange of consumerism and an intensely commercialized popular culture. This has reached such a point that some observers, both Chinese and foreign, are now saying, and only partly with tongue in cheek, that the only ideology now officially sanctioned in China is the desire to get rich. What outsiders now see when they look at China is a bizarre assemblage of images that, when viewed as a whole, seem thoroughly contradictory. One overseas Chinese cultural critic, returning to her homeland in the mid-1990s, described the fragmented and puzzling nature of the new China as "half-baked, sheepish, defensive, cynical, masked, stealthy, and often comic" (Zha 1995, 10–11); and to some extent, it is all of these and more.

At the center of the issue here is the role of the self in the new China. In the Maoist era (1949–1976), the notion of selfhood was sharply circumscribed: an individual subject's identity was fixed (either voluntarily or not) by his or her orientation to an external order and hierarchy that was defined by the state. The moralizing models that Chinese people were exhorted to identify with at that time, and which were represented almost universally in the state-supported art and literature of socialist realism, embodied such concepts as altruism, self-sacrifice, clean and healthy living, and everyday heroism (Bown 1998). To drive home the importance of such concepts, the state embodied them in a small number of simple but larger-than-life (and often too-good-to-be-true) characters that were intended to serve as role models for the populace (Bakken 2000). Social responsibilities and class status consigned people into clearly defined and thoroughly immutable group identities, which existed along a continuum "from the red to the black": from the truly revolutionary but poor peasant class at one end to the rich, landlord class and the even more despicable intellectual at the other end (Blecher 1997). Mao accepted the fact that even with the utmost of zeal, the Communists would not be able to obliterate the "bad" classes any time soon, and in his writings and speeches he made it clear that the revolution had not ended with the victory over the Nationalists in 1949.

In conceptual and emotional terms, Chinese communism in the Maoist years was like a closed box, and the Chinese people had almost no opportunity to question the way events were to be understood and evaluated. As Blecher (1997) has observed, the

Maoist hegemonic project did not so much try to change *what* the people thought, as *the way* they thought, which it did by making the language of class and class conflict a part of the everyday discourse that dominated social and cultural life. This represented a socialist version of modernity that was clearly different from the capitalist version in that it rarely encouraged the subject to be preoccupied with the self. In fact, it was rare to find any discourse, spoken or written, in which there was a conscious awareness of the complexities and contradictions associated with the self.

By comparison, modern literature—as well as art in other cultural realms, including film—embraces vernacular storytelling, in which the subject is free to construct his or her own meaning from an infinite assortment of possibilities. The modern stories that people tell to each other, and the stories they tell about themselves, have increasingly become conceptually open, which implies that the self can live in more than one story at the same time, and that conflicting stories can be acted out, sometimes with no hint of a solution. As cultural historian Mark Elvin (1997) suggests, in fact, in modernist discourse, "there is a feeling of metaphysical loneliness, and an endless testing of possible truths, which is never thought of as final, but at best as only provisional" (207).

In the Dengist era (post-1978), most of the principles associated with Maoist-style communism were discarded. Ideas about a collective utopian future were cast aside, to be replaced with a more mundane concern with everyday life; and there was an increasing emphasis on consumption, getting rich, and the endless expansion of markets. The rigid class identities of the Maoist era disintegrated, and to justify its existence in such radical circumstances, the CCP began to redefine its hegemonic project, effectively replacing class struggle with an all-out attack on China's poverty and backwardness. The only way to do this (which has by now been proved beyond all doubt) was with a many-pronged state-supported effort to stimulate rapid economic growth in China's core regions, in the expectation (or hope) that wealth would eventually "trickle down" to the periphery. This new project—Deng Xiaoping's Four Modernizations—has been popular with the Chinese people, especially those living in the urban areas along the coast, because of the material benefits it has brought them. In addition to the economic improvements in the lives of the people during this period, however, there was a significant psychological and cultural shift from almost blind allegiance to external power to a new situation in which there was a real possibility for individual freedom and autonomous self-expression. These were truly modern—and, previously, exclusively Western—sensations, and they were now possible for many of the Chinese living in urban areas.

If we define culture at least partly in terms of everyday patterns of living, we might be tempted to conclude from the above observations that for the majority of the urban Chinese, the primary goal today is to serve the self exclusively, a goal that is clearly related to a modernist preoccupation with individuality. We need to qualify this conclusion, however, by recalling that the relative freedom of the present era was achieved without the state having guaranteed the sovereign rights of individuals in China. Barmé takes this one step further by suggesting that the new level of consumption in urban China might, in the absence of real political emancipation, eventually enslave the Chinese people as much as the old authoritarianism did. In his words, the individual, "increasingly freed from subservience . . . to the party-state . . . discovered the heady delights of individual identity, of feeling special because he or she was being appealed to through advertising rather than simply propagated at by the state" (1999, 238). What Barmé is getting at here is that commercialization and advertising may have resulted in a materialist liberation of the Chinese, but at the same time may have produced another form of subjugation and passivity—consumerism and a slavishness to fashion—that in the long run will turn out to be "just as beguiling as the utopian dialectical materialism of high Maoism" (238), although the cynic could justly add here that no one will be killed or have their human rights denied solely because of their pursuit of the former.

Moving closer to a more traditional—and narrower—definition of culture as the production and consumption of art and art works, we find also an ongoing healthy debate about whether the new trends evident in urban China are entirely wholesome. One side of this argument involves the suggestion that in spite of the material advancements being made, and in spite of an incredible increase in the range and diversity of the new work, literature and art in the contemporary era are involved in what amounts to a downward spiral: a transition from an archaic and once "noble" vision of what should be produced and consumed to one in which standards are set (or not set) according to the baseness of self-centered artists and writers (Elvin 1997). One cultural critic puts this argument nicely by suggesting that artists and writers in today's China are now wallowing in "a sea of self-determining freedoms" (Zhang 1997). Another suggests that debates about individualism, the role of the self in literature, and the notion of subject-making in general had, by the 1990s, become "tantalizing national hobbies" in China (J. Wang 1996, 245).[8]

It is from this perspective that critics interpret the currently widespread phenomenon of cynicism, alienation, and thoroughly self-serving behavior being reported in contemporary urban China. The self, in this analysis, is like a mask of cynicism: behind it we expect to find another, more humane self concealed. The problem (or perhaps the fear) in this case, is that the promised self—that which is hidden behind the mask—could turn out to be a moral void. The danger is that the mask may be transformed into something that cannot be lifted, so that whatever was hidden behind it "becomes a moral lacuna" (E. Y. J. Wang 1996, 42). The mask, in other words, becomes intransitive; it is "a mask of nothing, of emptiness." This line of critique suggests that in spite of the obvious material benefits that have been experienced by many Chinese in the reform era, and in spite of the expanded production and consumption in China of art and literature of all types, many Chinese people are now feeling they no longer belong to any larger entity, whether it is a nation, a community, a work unit, or a class (Anagnost 1997). These feelings might have been first encountered during the alienating years of the Maoist purges—especially during the chaotic and, for many, traumatic years of the Cultural Revolution—but the process of loss has been accelerated in the reform era to such an extent that any shared feelings of belonging that may have existed in the past have now almost totally evaporated, along with the values of social commitment, political solidarity, and moral integrity.

In contemporary discourse focusing on a wide range of social issues that are thought to be symptomatic of this new, modernist "emptiness" in China—including rising crime rates, government corruption, public immorality, pornography, and the spread of sexually transmitted diseases—the CCP has become almost obsessed with the idea that it must try to maintain control if China is to stay on the desired trajectory of its modernization drive (Bakken 2000; Perry 1999). As anachronistic as it may seem in the neoliberal climate of contemporary Chinese capitalism, the state is still trying to use its own moral authority to influence social trends. The goal of such campaigns is not just to modify Chinese ways of thinking, but also to produce healthier and more morally upstanding Chinese citizens, in the face of what are officially defined as unhealthy and immoral practices. The irony of this situation, of course, is that such practices—which were once thought to be coming ashore in "waves" of Western (and Western-style) "spiritual pollution"—are now also being produced at home, as the direct and indirect result of the state's own modernization project.

THE DOWNSIDE OF CHINA'S NEW COSMOPOLITAN CULTURE

From a geographical perspective, these new cultural trends, which for the most part have been driven by the economic reform process, have had a significant visual and environmental impact on China's biggest cities (see also chapter 9). A visitor to China in the early 1980s who returned today would be shocked by the transition: from the stark monotony and Spartan nature of the cities of the past to the dazzling postmodernity of the contemporary city (Smith 2000, 2002b). In most cases, the advent of the market has been welcomed by writers and artists as a liberalizing agency, allowing a new sense of personal freedom or space, which has resulted in a spate of "young and restless" literary productions that are far removed from the moralizing and heroic works of the socialist realism era. Xiaobing Tang (2000) argues that the sheer "shock value" of much of the new work has helped in the marketing process.

Behind the facade of appearances, however, a more significant transition is also taking place: from the socialist city—which was characterized by full employment, secure jobs with fringe benefits, and minimal income and lifestyle differences—to the post-socialist city of the new millennium that is beginning to experience some of the anxieties and negative externalities of the reform era, including the disappearance of state-employment security, threateningly high unemployment rates, rising crime statistics, and new and previously unimaginably high levels of income polarization (Solinger 2000). As Tang casts his eye across these new urban landscapes, he observes that what has happened is not just a transformation of the built environment, but more importantly, the

> institution of . . . [new] . . . social values, such as personal mobility, privacy, and diversity, that are associated with life in the modern city. The consumer city, in place of the discredited model of producer cities . . . [has] . . . reasserted itself as the dominant center of a new political economy and should offer us a clue to the logic of Chinese culture in the age of global capitalism. (2000, 276)

Life in these new cities is much changed from the boring fare offered to China's urban residents in the past. Leisure time quickly turns into a busy search for entertainment and diversion. Tang (2000) writes that as evening approaches, "loud and color-splashing karaoke bars dutifully supply sentiment and expression to the fashionable and adventurous, and the milling crowds, as in all big cities, take pride in being indifferent and anonymous" (276). But closely allied to this new urban excitement is another view of the contemporary city, and one that is much more negative, a scenario that Tang describes as a "nightmare" city, bursting at the seam with millions of recently transplanted peasants, some of whom are clustering in ethnic ghettos that are serving as "vast breeding grounds of urban unrest" that may become a "brewing area for new forms of class, gender, and ethnic conflicts" (277). Tang concludes his dystopic evaluation of the new urban situation in China with an observation that harmonizes with an argument that will by now be familiar to readers of this book: that the market is Janus-faced, serving both as a liberating angel *and* as a destructive devil by transforming the urban world into a more lively and colorful place, while at the same time throwing existing values into disarray, and threatening to bring an end to the much-vaunted promise of urban social order. James Farrer covers some of the same territory, although in much greater detail, in his book *Opening Up: Youth Sex Culture and Market Reform in Shanghai* (2002).

An outsider visiting the new urban China might wonder what the impact of all these changes must be on the residents of these cities as they make their explosive transition toward market culture and commodity relationships. What, our visitor might reasonably ask, has been lost in this transition? A reflection along these lines may help us understand one of the more bizarre cultural trends to have emerged in China in recent years: the so-called Mao Craze of the early 1990s (in which images and representations of Mao Zedong became commercially popular among a broad segment of the population). Tang (2000) describes this phenomenon as "a good sign of the collective anxiety" that the market economy has generated (283). In other words, it is only after revolutionary mass culture has already disappeared that it reveals itself—or is reinvented—as a "heroic effort to overcome a deep anxiety over everyday life, often at the cost of impoverishing it" (283).

Another response to this new set of urban landscapes and lifestyles is to use it as part of a more widespread critique of the new era. In this sense, what we see today in China's booming cities is the visible manifestation of exactly what their urban residents consider to be of most importance, and this tells us quite a lot about the nature of new cultural values in China. What we see is a seemingly endless concern with the events of everyday life, translated into decisions about where to live, what to eat, how to dress, what sort of car to drive, and how to position one's children for similar success in the future—none of which people used to have to worry about in the Maoist city of the past. This represents a situation in which, to use Tang's terminology, "everyday life is affirmed," and has assumed a new hegemony.[9]

What Tang is suggesting here allows us to examine the extent to which new art and literary productions can be interpreted as anything other than simple—and lowest-common-denominator—products of the new consumption era. To put it differently, is there anything out there that has deeper meaning, or is all popular (mass) culture devoid of significance completely? Tang argues that some new artworks should be taken seriously, realizing that it is both too simplistic and the height of cultural snobbishness to reject all new works of art out of hand. To illustrate his point, he discusses two novellas written about urban life in contemporary China: one depicting life in Changsha city, He Dun's *Life Is Not a Crime*, and the other following the life of a mainland Chinese woman who moves to Hong Kong, Wang Anyi's *Love and Sentiment in Hong Kong*. He Dun's story describes a seemingly never-ending life of consumption and new opportunities in a reform-era city, but it ends with the hero feeling lonely and lost, and realizing that all the new things he can and does enjoy in the city have no real meaning. In the second novella, Hong Kong is described as having been, until quite recently, the ultimate dream city for most Chinese people. Beneath the spectacle of the city, however, and the perception of Hong Kong as an enormous postmodern shopping mall where "everything is for sale and all anxieties can be shopped away" (Tang 2000, 290), is the realization that the city is full of lonely people living out intense human dramas. Again quoting from Wang Anyi, Tang notes that Hong Kong "throws an inclusive party by inviting all kinds of loneliness, and arranges a grand re-union by bringing together all moments of solitude" (290). In this way, the new urban literature offers the Chinese a glimpse of a future that has already been clearly visible in places like Hong Kong for some time now, and which serves as a model for the way many Chinese cities are now developing. As Tang claims, the story tellers in this new urban genre

> grasp the city as central to a post-revolutionary reality, and, in doing so, they make representable an age in which the emergent hegemony is no longer Ideology or Collectivity, but rather everyday life. Also, in this sense, they blend mass culture and high literature and directly participate in the making of a new urban culture, the historical function of which is to help absorb the shock of urbanization and ultimately to legitimate modernity. (2000, 290)

A similar conclusion may be reached from an analysis of Hong Kong through the lens of filmmaker Wong Kar-wai, especially in his film *Chungking Express*. This film, which has become something of a cult classic in the West—in part because of its endorsement by American director Quentin Tarentino—portrays how the hectic pace of life in Hong Kong makes it increasingly difficult for people to connect with one another in meaningful ways. As Wong shows in the film, people can coexist geographically without forming any lasting emotional bonds, a point that is made explicitly at the start of the film when one of the characters remarks that "every day we brush past so many other people . . . people we may never meet, or people who may become close friends." Spatial coexistence in the city is insufficient to bring people together in meaningful ways.

The idea of missed connections becomes a structuring principle of *Chungking Express* when Wong follows up in the second part of the film the lives of two of the incidental characters introduced in the first half of the film. (Here we see a possible link to the structure of some of Tarentino's films, especially *Pulp Fiction*.) The two major characters in the second part of the film—a young woman, played by Hong Kong rock-star Faye Wang, and a local policeman—effectively share an apartment for some time without ever actually meeting. She gradually appropriates the apartment space (which belongs to the policemen) and makes it her own, but their cohabitation is based upon the assumption that they will never meet.

An analysis of Wong's filmmaking suggests that he is extremely successful at convey-ing the frenzied nature of life in Hong Kong, which he does "through his manipulation of camera speed, editing rhythms, and other special effects that alter our perception of the rapidity of events" (Rowley 1998). In the opening scene of *Chungking Express*, for example, Wong uses a camera style that alternately produces freeze frames then rapid motion, which has an effect similar to the way in which our eyes switch from one object to another as our attention shifts. Rowley also claims that Wong goes further than simply depicting the difficulties of urban life in the postmodern age. In *Chungking Express* the main characters are, according to Rowley, able to make use of their living spaces as a means of resistance against the chaos of postmodern urban life, and to some extent at least their strategies are successful, even though at the end of the film, the viewer believes that the main characters have drifted apart. Wong's characters, Rowley suggests, are not disconnected in emotional terms; in fact, he argues that the film's greatest strength is its ability to evoke the emotional agonies produced within the tortured relationships that are depicted.

Chinese Literature in the Reform Era

After the death of Mao Zedong in 1976, there was a gradual relaxation in the state's hold over literature (and the arts more generally) in China. Memories of earlier repression and even of the murder of artists during the anti-Rightist movement of 1957 and throughout the Cultural Revolution helped to produce what began as a trickle and ended up as a torrent of the so-called literature of the wounded (sometimes also referred to as "scar" literature). Some of this literature has been marketed outside China, with one or two authors becoming household names; but much of it is either too repetitive for Western tastes or, in the case of exiled Nobel Prize–winner Gao Xingjian, too obscure to sell well.

The third plenum of the eleventh party congress in 1978 invited China's intellectuals and artists "to liberate their thoughts, to break into previously forbidden zones, and not to fear a return to repressive policies" (Link 1983, 20). In spite of these words, the state has seen fit to tighten up on writers at intervals, as was the case in the early 1980s, and again in the period after the Tiananmen massacre in 1989, when there was a shift back to the "pre-thaw" climate that had formerly faced intellectuals and artists.

Also emerging at about the same time as the scar literature was a new genre sometimes referred to as "reportage": writing that was more confrontational in its efforts to expose government corruption and official instances of wrongdoing. Much of this work was intentionally direct, but sometimes writers tried to be more elliptical in their work, in part, perhaps, as a deliberate tactic to confuse the state's censors. In one section of a poem called "Reply," for example, Bei Dao refers obliquely to the dark days of China's recent past (referring to them as the "Ice Age"), and at the same time he asks why the aftereffects of such darkness have lasted for so long.[10] Bei Dao's work is often interpreted as a deliberate example of resistance literature. In a poem published on the cover of an issue of *Tintian* (Today), a literary journal published in exile by Tiananmen-era expatriates, Bei observes that "Power depends on yesterday" but "Literature always stands facing Today."[11] And in the opening stanza of what is now considered to be his most famous poem, "The Answer," which has become something of a rallying call for the Tiananmen protestors, Bei writes that "the gilded sky is swimming with undulant reflections of the dead."[12]

We can assume that from the safety of exile, Bei Dao feels free to say what he really means, and as Jing Wang (1996) observes, his words here tell us "worlds about the antagonistic and agonistic relationships between 'Power' and 'Literature,' and about how Chinese literati are constantly mapping out, consciously or unconsciously, their own positionality against a rival who is both real and imaginary" (197).

Among the prose writers most closely associated with the reportage literature of the late 1970s and 1980s, and writing in a much more journalistic style than Bei Dao, is Liu Binyan, who was a former *People's Daily* correspondent and whose best-known work is *People or Monsters*; and the one-time minister of culture for China, Wang Meng. Wang—often writing under a pen name, but well-known to most of his readers in official circles—produced many stories dealing with different types of official corruption, arrogant officialdom, and party factionalism; and he continued writing into the 1990s, supporting humanism and criticizing the authoritarian nature of the Chinese state. The fact that he was allowed to continue writing throughout this period was indicative of the new era's tolerance and acceptance, but in the mid-1990s, ironically, critics began accusing him of abandoning his earlier principles and selling out to market forces.

The first decade of the reform era (the 1980s) was marked by an often seething conflict between those writers who relied on the new commercial culture, and others who felt Chinese literature had strayed too far from its own culture. The struggle between these two positions has been described as a culture war (Schoppa 2002, 431), and also, as part of what Jing Wang (1996) calls China's "High Culture Fever," a "post-revolutionary fever about knowledge and enlightenment... an era in which miracles and superstitions triumphed over rational forces" (38). Wang also observes that the early and mid-1980s ushered in a "symphony of unmitigated optimism" in China (37), accompanying the state's modernization program, which was steering the country toward previously unimagined prosperity. She argues that during this period, China's intellectuals "not only collaborated with the Party in its reconstruction of the socialist utopia, but... busily proliferated their own discourse on thought enlightenment" (37). She concludes her interpretation of this period by suggesting that there was movement toward the perfection of the "twin projects of modernization and enlightenment" in China, a movement that was to some extent halted by the more dystopian views of the future that dominated cultural productions at the end of the decade (views that were both manifested in and represented by the Tiananmen Square tragedy).

China's literary critics seem to agree that the period from the late 1980s to the mid-1990s was dominated by the works of Wang Shuo, who has been described as the epitome of the individualist in a nation caught up in the often sordid business of getting rich. Wang became an icon of popular culture in the new China, and a continuous best-seller; many of his books were translated into television series and movies (often with himself as the scriptwriter). One view of Wang's literary output was that it "captured the crude vitality of the entrepreneur unbound, the loose world of the modern criminal, and the boredom and amorality that occasionally led good girls into the arms of bad men" (Barmé and Jaivin 1992, 217). His stories are usually populated by marginal characters who are street smart and who operate at the very border of respectability, which explains why they are referred to in Chinese as *liumang* characters, the word *liumang* translating roughly to "hooligan."

Barmé (1999) suggests that Wang Shuo's writing serves as "shorthand for certain urban attitudes that have been quintessentially expressed not in the tones of overt dissent but more often in the playful and ironic creations of popular culture" (63). In spite of his appeal to the masses, Wang clearly has a serious side; Barmé in fact refers to him as "a playful writer of serious intent," arguing that he has a perceptive knack of being able to see the funny side of the current situation. Wang's Shuo's books, and the films and TV shows made from them, offered popular entertainment for the masses throughout the 1990s, and he is still popular today, although primarily as a scriptwriter or occasional film director. It is also apparent that Wang's work is a form of "coded" political writing, which generally remains acceptable to the censors, in spite of its satirical edge. In this sense, his books represent a more compelling form of art than much of what is currently available in the mass market, primarily because they have acted as a "literature of escape" during the upheavals of the reform era (63).

One way to interpret the popularity of the *liumang* culture is in the context of the constant turmoil the Chinese people have been living through during the past two decades. In spite of an expanding economy throughout the 1980s and the obvious fact that the power of the CCP had been undermined on several fronts, the evidence suggests that many Chinese people were at the time still confused by the seeming contradictions surrounding them. In many ways, and especially in the economic realm, people were much freer than before, but their words and actions were still closely supervised by the state, and in reality they still had no political freedom. The Chinese were living in two very different worlds: the openness of the capitalist marketplace had been superimposed on what was still a secret society dominated by an authoritarian elite. This resulted in what Barmé (1999) calls an "existential malaise" that was accompanied by significant psychological tensions (62). The cultural uncertainty this produced was, according to Barmé, "part and parcel of the existential sociopolitical crisis that the Communist Party variously attempted to ignore, escape from, avert, and even co-opt" (62). Unlike the situation in the recent past, however, today it is no longer an option for the state simply to squash all potential dissidence by military action, or to counter it with traditional party propaganda, and it is this new space of uncertainty that is inhabited (and exploited) by Wang Shuo and his motley crew of characters.

The stereotypical *liumang* character is a person who rides around the city on his bicycle (later such characters were more likely to be on motorbikes, as with the courier Mardar in Lou Ye's 2000 film *Suzhou River*; today the *liumang* is no doubt driving a car!) The *liumang* is constantly on the lookout, although lethargically, for any action that might be shaping up or going down, and all the time he is made to look even more sinister by his reflective sunglasses, ensuring that no one can see his eyes. As harmless as this character may seem, there is, just below the surface perhaps, the possibility of a much darker persona within, consistent with a suggestion by John Minford (1985) that the *liumang* is more than just a shady character; he is in fact, or he may be, a

> rapist, whore, black-marketeer, unemployed youth, alienated intellectual, frustrated artist or poet—the spectrum has its dark satanic end, its long middle band of relentless grey, and, shining at the other end, a patch of visionary light. It is an embryonic alternative culture. (quoted in Barmé 1999, 63)

Barmé also points out that the *liumang* personality has a history in China's urban culture and dates back to the late Qing dynasty, when the term was first used to describe the petty criminals and minor hooligans who hung around the dockland areas in Shanghai as the city's underworld culture expanded (Barmé 1999, 64). Also originating in this era was the connection between the *liumang* and a variety of sexual misdemeanors, ranging from premarital sex all the way to gang rape. Barmé even notes that the phrase "to play the *liumang*" is still sometimes used in everyday Chinese speech today to describe overt sexual harassment (64).

It is also possible to expand on the notion of the *liumang* and to apply it in a more directly political way, either as a form of resistance, or as a way of describing the malaise that is rampant in the contemporary Chinese city, as manifested in its growing rates of urban crime and corruption (Farrer 2002). Wang Shuo, however, seems to be using the term more loosely than this to label the often unscrupulous and unprincipled activities of entrepreneurs in new China. *Liumang* characters seem to have no time for cultural pursuits; they operate at the fringes of and sometimes just beyond the law; and in most cases, they appear to have no moral or social conscience. Wang's usual hero is not a rapacious capitalist who reinvests profits to expand production, however; more likely he is the type who takes all he can find and squanders it until it is all gone—acting as if there was no tomorrow. In some circumstances, he might behave like the small-time crook or entrepreneur who skims off a percentage of everything that passes through his hands, takes every opportunity to eat and drink lavishly at someone else's expense, and exploits every bit of power that is available.[13]

In a typical Wang Shuo story, all of these themes may be intertwined, and according to Barmé (1999), Wang also makes skillful use of the *liumang* personality to do some subtle satirizing of CCP officialdom, which occasionally results in his works being banned by the censor. In Wang's 1989 story "An Attitude," for example, the hero is arraigned in court for "practicing literature without a license" (an obvious parody). The judge asks him how he would behave if he someday became king of the cultural world in China, to which the hero answers that he would allow those who submit to him to prosper, but those who cross him would perish. Presumably with tongue in cheek, he also says he would be loyal to his partners whatever happened, and even if he were forced to purge them, he'd be sure to let them down gently! We can assume here that Wang is referring to the situation that existed in China before and during the Cultural Revolution, when writers could be censored, excommunicated, and even jailed for what they wrote.

In other works, Wang pokes fun at China's past, and even at important elements of Chinese culture and nationalism. In what might be seen as an allegory of China's obsession throughout the 1990s with hosting the Olympic Games, his novel *Please Don't Call Me Human* mixes historical fact and sheer fantasy to create a bizarre mockery of China's past and present. A group of profiteers in contemporary Beijing are searching for a new athletic hero to restore China's damaged pride after a humiliating defeat in an international wrestling competition. The person they eventually select—a character by the name of Tang Yuanbao—is by no means a warrior; he is in fact a simple Beijing pedicab driver who just happens to be related by birth to one of the leaders of the

Boxer Rebellion (the pun is probably intended here). One problem the group faces is to prepare Tang for his first competitive bout. As the leader of the group points out:

> My primary concern is with the image of Tang Yuanbao. He'll be representing the entire Chinese race, and just winning a match won't be enough. This must be a rout in every sense of the word. That way he takes glory with him wherever he goes, the subject of veneration every step of the way, a national hero.... Comrades, we must act prudently. Just beating up some foreigner won't do it. Our ultimate purpose is to establish a national model. Do not, under any circumstance, underestimate the importance of our work, for what we are engaged in now is an enterprise of historic proportions—the mere thought makes me shudder. (Wang Shuo 2000, 45)

Once he has been selected, Tang is introduced to the public in a parade, followed by a banquet at a special restaurant, where the food is considered to have special qualities. Wang here manages to poke fun at the Chinese obsession with banqueting and feasting. In preparing the diners for their meal, one of the group leaders notes that

> every dish on today's menu has profound ties to Chinese culture, and will cause us all to ponder our great nation. Why not call it "cultural cuisine," the partaking of which can be the equivalent of completing a spirited course in Chinese culture. In the history of the world, ours is the only civilization whose food has been passed down without change for generations, which is why for millennia China has stood tall among the nations of the world. We can cut off our queues, unbind our feet, even change into Western suits, but we cannot stop eating. That has formed a national characteristic, instilling pride in us as descendants of China's earliest rulers. Our ancestors took great pains to keep us from forgetting our roots. Now dig in. (73)[14]

Wang Shuo's work has been heavily criticized on a variety of counts, including charges that his views on the new sexual culture in China effectively act as a call for Chinese people to abandon all forms of sexual inhibition. Miraculously, over the long haul he has been able to stay out of real trouble, and has even become something of an urban legend: quotations from his books have been mass-produced and printed on t-shirts.[15]

An essentially positive picture of Wang Shuo and his work is put forward by Chinese cultural critic Dai Jinhua (2002), who argues that Wang's heroes may actually represent a new type of Chinese person (*xinren*) at the end of the millennium who was able to come to grips with living in a society in which ideologies were clearly in a state of flux. The benefit to Wang's readers, according to Dai, was that almost for the first time a modern writer was telling them stories they could relate to, and which allowed them some release and satisfaction.

Toward the end of the 1990s, young writers in urban China began to explore new territory, with some of the most popular and talked-about works steering clear of Wang Shuo's fondness for hoodlum life and choosing instead to explore the once-forbidden topics of sex and sexuality. Earlier in the decade, the publication of Jia Pingwa's *The Abandoned Capital* (1993) caused a sensation, selling more than 500,000 copies in just three months, and although the story would be considered relatively tame by Western standards, being cast in what amounts to soft-pornography, it is a description of the sexual exploits of a middle-aged writer. In his interpretation of Jia's book, Barmé (1999) suggests that it offers a reasonably representative reflection of what any Chinese person could see happening during the 1990s, when life in the new cities had obviously left behind most of the former values of Chinese civilization and communism, and was focusing instead on a new era of urban experimentation and alienation. Barmé quotes what one Chinese cultural critic said in describing this situation in the reform era: "All we dream of now and hope for in the future are money and sex. The unprincipled process of moneymaking and sexual gratification has gravely undermined the pillars of civilized society" (184).

In spite of this advance warning, most Chinese readers were probably unprepared for the next development in this direction, when new books written by young, sexually liberated women began to appear in the bookstores (Jiang 2003). The most popular example of this genre is Zhou Weihui's blockbuster novel *Shanghai Baby*, which was officially banned in China but was widely available through blackmarket outlets (the ban on the book no doubt contributed significantly to its vast popularity). As one critic commented, more significant even than the heroine's detailed exploration of her sexual exploits was "the novel's examination of life, freedom, love, and death" in the new Shanghai. This same critic ultimately questioned whether China's women could, in real life, hope to find anything like the sexual and emotional liberation enjoyed by Zhou's heroine. Other critics panned Zhou's book, describing it as derivative and shallow. In a review appearing on the Amazon.com website, one reader found the book problematic, suggesting that it "wants very much to be ... shocking ... [but] ... it contains little more ... than some random sex scenes." On the other hand, the same reviewer felt that the book did "accurately portray how beautiful, cold, and ultimately helpless it feels to be young."

Other China scholars have attributed much more significance to Zhou's journey of self-discovery, arguing that it can be interpreted as a metaphor for the ongoing struggle of young people in China and their need to reconcile their own personal desires with the collectivist orientations of Chinese culture. Weber (2002), for example, suggests that *Shanghai Baby* illustrates some of the important dimensions of what amounts to a process of identity construction in the new urban environment. Weber identifies seven dimensions of this new identity that are clearly exemplified in Zhou's book:

- the desire for self-expression
- the drive to be economically successful
- the generation gap between youth and their parents (and China's leaders)
- the attraction of hedonism, consumerism, and the apparent need for immediate gratification
- the call for female sexuality and empowerment
- an admiration of all things foreign
- a desire to express criticism of the party and state in public

Weber concludes that Zhou's book offers a "powerful metaphor" for the dilemmas facing China's young people, who are trying to deal with the multiple demands associated with rapid social change (2002, 366). He takes this conclusion even further by extending it to the realm of political life in the new urban China.

> [China's youth] . . . suffer from a peculiar form of impotence experienced under a "one-country, two-system" structure—a willingness to push the parameters of acceptable behavior and the accompanying guilt (and retribution) when they do. . . . This type of duality hits the young hardest, in part because of youth's willingness to embrace functional individualistic values that provide them with the basic survival skills in a materialistic world and partly the underlying cultural heritage that defines how they should act. The result of these shifting lines of acceptable behavior and form of expression is seen as youth rebellion, which raises concern of a potentially destabilizing force as feared at Tiananmen. Subsequent censorship of . . . [Zhou's] . . . novel illustrates the periodic political fits of the Communist Party at what . . . [the] . . . authorities deem youth decadence and youth sees as another inconsistency frustrating their spirit of idealism and cultural independence. (2002, 366)

More sensational still has been the reaction to Hong Ying's novel *K: The Art of Love*, which is set in China in 1935, and contains long and very explicit descriptions of the lovemaking between a Westerner and a Chinese woman (similar scenes also figured largely in *Shanghai Baby*). The woman, Cheng Lin (*K*), is the wife of the head of the English Department at a major Chinese university. It turns out that she is adept in the "Daoist art of love," and because her husband is impotent she begins to coach a junior member of the faculty, who happens to be a British visitor to the university. The most startling thing about the book, described on the cover as "the Chinese *Lady Chatterley's Lover*," is that it was based loosely on the lives of real characters, and in 2001 a Chinese woman living in London actually filed a lawsuit against Hong Ying, claiming the book had caused her significant "spiritual damage" by libeling her late parents (the fictionalized head of the department and Cheng Lin). As was the case with Zhou Weihui's book, publicity (generated by the lawsuit) guaranteed that Hong Ying's book would be a big seller. The main title of the book, *K*, is the same in the Chinese edition as in the English edition (even though the letter *k* is both unpronounceable and incomprehensible in Chinese). What all of this amounts to, in the words of one reviewer, is "a kind of avant-garde trifecta, combining experimental gestures, sex, and the glamour of fact" (Lanchester 2003, 25).[16]

Chinese Filmmaking in the Reform Era

Since the Cultural Revolution, China's film industry has experienced a major transformation, both qualitatively and quantitatively, as part of the nation's push toward modernization. From 1949 onward, the CCP exercised significant control over all films that were made. For the party, film was considered more than just art—it was an integral part of what Mao Zedong referred to as "cultural work," which he considered "a forceful weapon to unite and educate the people as well as to fight against and annihilate the enemy" (Mao Zedong 1975, 111). Mao believed that literature and the arts needed to be evaluated from the perspective of the "two services" (serving politics on the one hand, and the "two hundreds" (letting "a hundred flowers blossom" and "a hundred schools of thought contend"). In both cases, the former of these considerations was considered the primary goal, with the latter representing the means of achieving those goals. With the establishment of class struggle as the party's major task before and during the Cultural Revolution, greater emphasis came to be placed on a film's political orientation than on its artistic merit or its aesthetic quality. Naturally, what suffered during this era was both the quality and quantity of films produced, and the diversity in the type of films that could even be considered. Relatively few films were produced during the Cultural Revolution, and those that were released were stamped with a uniformity dominated by the dictates of socialist realism.

As the reforms took hold, however, China's leaders seemed to accept that political correctness need not be the only or the major criterion for determining the merit of a film. There is still in China the threat of censorship for films that are directly critical of the government and its policies, or for films that deal with topics the government feels are either potentially damaging to the social order or "unhealthy" in some way—as is the case for films made about homosexuality in China, like *Lan Yu* (directed by Stanley Kuan, a Hong Kong–based director), and *East Palace, West Palace* (directed by Zhang Yuan). Filmmakers are no longer required to sing the praises of the CCP to get their films approved, and some have actually been very skillful at using their work to send out a quasi-political message. Sometimes, however, even the most subtly portrayed political criticism is detected by the censor.

One example of this is a film mentioned above, Chen Kaige's *Yellow Earth*, which paints a striking picture of peasant life in northern Shaanxi province before 1949. Some scholars believe the film was criticized because it portrays peasants as being unable (and unwilling) to grasp the modernization message of the Communists, preferring instead to rely on their ancient behaviors and beliefs (for example, praying to the gods for rain on the barren lands of the Loess Plateau). Another possible reason for the censorship of *Yellow Earth* was that Chen hints at the unbending nature of the Communists, who at the time in which the action takes place were encamped at Yanan, some two hundred miles south of where the film is set. At one point the film's heroine, an impressionable fourteen-year-old girl, asks the Red Army soldier who is staying with her family to take her with him when he leaves for Yanan. The soldier refuses to take the girl with him, blaming the party's inflexible rules about signing up new conscripts. Subsequently the girl, desperate to leave home because she has already been betrothed to a much older man, drowns while attempting to cross the Yellow River and follow the soldier south to Yanan.

Yellow Earth was filmed in 1984, and is generally recognized to be the first film of a new wave of Chinese filmmakers, the so-called Fifth Generation, who were graduates of the Beijing Film Academy in 1982 (the first class to graduate after the academy reopened in 1977, following the Cultural Revolution). As McDougall (1991) has pointed out, the film raised a storm of criticism at the time of its release, in part because of the time and the place in which it was set. To make a film in the present would limit its significance to only the present; but to set it in the late 1930s implied that the most fundamental policies of the CCP were being brought under the microscope. At the same time, the backwardness of the peasants was highlighted in the film, and as McDougall argues, the combination of the period and the locality suggests that this backwardness was intended to characterize the entire Chinese peasantry and, by extension, all of China. As she notes, "To stress the local peasants' backwardness and ignorance . . . was to suggest the failure of the . . . Party to transform the condition even up to the present time" (4).

In addition to the controversy surrounding its political message, and in comparison to the unambiguous moviemaking of the recent past in China, *Yellow Earth* represented a breath of fresh air in the filmmaking industry. This was in part because it broke so dramatically with the propagandist paradigm that had dominated filmmaking in the pre-reform era. But it will also be apparent that in comparison to the world of literature, the transition in filmmaking after the Cultural Revolution occurred more slowly, in part because of the collective and highly capitalized nature of filmmaking in China. The result was that filmmakers were a long way behind writers, who first began to pour their hearts out in the so-called scar literature, which was followed by a shift toward a romantic encounter with rural Chinese primitivism, and then by a critical examination of China's rustic cultural roots (sometimes referred to as "roots-searching" literature).

Silbergeld (1999) has suggested that the making of *Yellow Earth* represented a shift away from a focus on the Cultural Revolution to a focus on China's cultural roots, following a trend set in the literary field. More importantly perhaps, *Yellow Earth* was the first "independent-minded cultural critique of the entire socialist experiment in China" (14). In 1984, *Yellow Earth* departed in almost every possible way from the formulaic films of the recent past; shifting from the determined and heroic human characters of socialist realism filmmaking, to the vaguer, ambiguous uncertainty of the modern era. The film only won one award in China, for photography (the cinematographer was Zhang Yimou), and it failed miserably in its first domestic showings, in part because it was considered by Chinese audiences to be impenetrable. After the film created a sensation at the Hong Kong Film Festival in 1985, however, it was rereleased in China and became one of the most popular films of the year.

As McDougall (1991) suggests, *Yellow Earth* represented an entirely new era in Chinese filmmaking, in part because of its sharp reversal from and rejection of the canon of socialist realism. In the past, anything in filmmaking that smacked of art for art's sake, ambiguity, or abstraction had to be eliminated if the film was to escape the censor's knife. Central to the Maoist aesthetic standard during the revolutionary era was the purging from film (and in fact from all forms of artistic production) of the so-called middle characters (Silbergeld 1999, 18), which meant characters that a Western audience might think of as real people, or as people with complex and unresolved motives and attitudes. In *Yellow Earth*, this would describe *all* of the characters: the peasants, for example, are portrayed not as the vanguards of the revolution, but as near-silent, superstitious victims of their environment. In most films made in China before the early 1980s, the peasants were depicted as heroes; they were usually tall, uncomplicated people, strong and resolute, always looking ahead, never looking sideways. Much of this was also to be found in the socialist realism posters and artwork that were common in China before the coming of the reforms. As Silbergeld notes, "If an actor wanted to praise, it was done with an arm outstretched to the sky. If he despised something, he pointed to the earth strongly. If he got excited, he put his hand to his heart" (19).

In *Yellow Earth* there are no such characters; there are in fact no heroes, no villains, and no theatrics—only ambiguity and lengthy silences, and probably for that reason, public reaction to it was underwhelming, to say the least. Most Chinese filmgoers found the peasants portrayed in the film to be sullen, and their silences too long to be interesting. *Yellow Earth* in other words, looked too much like a foreign art film to please Chinese audiences! Ever since its release in China, cinema critics have argued with each other about the meanings of the film. Among the most popular debates are those that focus on what the death of the girl signifies, why the peasants are so passive, and whether Chen Kaige was implicitly criticizing the CCP. Silbergeld (1999) raises the issue of whether the film's ambiguity is its means or its end. As he suggests, if Chen had wanted to launch a criticism, the only way he could do it—and get away with it—was to try to fool the censor by making the whole thing hopelessly ambiguous, which he apparently succeeded in doing.

Silbergeld also makes an interesting point at the end of his analysis of the film, noting that in many ways *Yellow Earth* can be considered a thoroughly postmodern film: it expresses viewpoints other than the filmmaker's own; it emphasizes the signifying capacity of passing details, multiple allusions, and possible meanings in the narrative; and it portrays the shifting spatial and temporal nature of the environment. All of this, as Silbergeld (1999) notes, "may seem beholden to the world of academic postmodernism" (52). Not content with such a conclusion, however, Silbergeld resorts to the idea of "path dependency" to suggest an alternative interpretation, arguing that much of what we see in *Yellow Earth* has actually appeared before in the long history of Chinese art and literature. As he suggests, all of the seemingly postmodern stylistic devices of the film

> depend on and grow right out of the Chinese tradition itself, indirect and layered with alternative meanings like those created and exploited by Chinese artists, writers and politicians since ancient times . . . [which represent] . . . a native-bred "semiotics" that matured in Chinese art and literature long before the Western term . . . [*postmodernism*] . . . was invented. (52)

It is this fact, according to Silbergeld, that allows *Yellow Earth* to appear avant-garde—or postmodern—by contemporary Chinese standards, while at the same time admitting it to the ranks of traditional Chinese art, which would be a truly cunning accomplishment, if in fact that was Chen's objective.

In some ways, the transition that occurred with the making of *Yellow Earth* reflected a similar transition that was taking place in the world of art in China during the reform era. The mid-1980s marked the appearance of a wide range of avant-garde works produced by Chinese artists, some of which were funded and exhibited by foreigners (including Hong Kongers) who were willing to invest in up-and-coming artists from the mainland.

After *Yellow Earth*, cinematographer Zhang Yimou branched out on his own and within a few years had become the most successful and internationally best-known of China's Fifth Generation filmmakers. He exhibited a fondness for exotic scenes, peopled either by barbaric or tragic characters with exhilarating or suffocating stories behind them. Although much of his output met with mixed reviews in China, internationally his films have won him more awards than all other Chinese film directors combined. One of Zhang's most common themes is primitivism, which is evident in the films he made during the late 1980s and early 1990s. Primitivism as a literary mode expresses a form of nostalgia for a pre-civilized way of life (see Silbergeld 1999), and is analogous in some ways to the "roots-searching" genre of post–Cultural Revolution literature and poetry (J. Wang 1996). The assumption is that there was a paradise-like era some time in China's past—a golden age when innate instincts and passions prevailed over the dictates of reason. This is akin to our idea of the good old days, during which time life was lived more spontaneously and instinctually, with no trace of the anxieties and frustrations we associate with the modern world.

A primitivist plot generally features characters who have escaped from the complications and alienation of modern civilization into the simplicities of a long-lost and presumably idyllic life. Zhang's masterpiece, *Red Sorghum* (1987), is such a film, presenting the audience with a sparkling example of primitive, natural existence. The film is populated with simple, lusty characters who lead unrestrained, almost barbaric lives, but who are portrayed as somehow heroic and admirable. The boy narrating the story in the film tells how his grandfather rescued his grandmother from bandits, how they later consummated their relationship in the sorghum fields, and then how they took over a winery, making liquor from the grain (sorghum). All the men in the film, from the sedan-chair bearers to the workers at the winery, are rustic and uninhibited. They drink to their heart's content, sing loudly, and behave badly (it is also a very modern film in this sense!).

In their remote and primitive land, the characters revel in being free from social restraints, as if they have reverted to the innocence of wild animals, satisfying their no-longer hidden urges without taking social values into consideration. In the second part of the film, these instinctual characters come into close contact with Japanese invaders, whose savagery makes the instinctual heroes, with all their faults, look like saints. In the face of the bloodthirsty invading army whose soldiers loot, burn, and kill everything and everyone in their path, the Chinese patriots are portrayed as simple country folk prepared to give their last drop of blood in the name of resistance. Both of the boy's grandparents and most of the film's characters are killed in battle, but they have died for a just cause. With the presentation and affirmation of the life and death of these men and women, Zhang might have been demonstrating a longing for a way of life in which it was still possible to enjoy gratification of natural, innate instincts and passions. This is famously illustrated when one of the film's characters urinates in the fermenting wine, producing what will become the factory's successful "secret" recipe!

In Zhang's next films he replaced the charm of the simplicity and masculinity characterizing *Red Sorghum* with a much more depressing human landscape. In *Judou* (1990), instead of the wide-open spaces and carefree lives of his former protagonists, Zhang now presents the audience with the claustrophobic atmosphere of a dye-works, an atmosphere that has a suffocating effect on the characters who work in the factory. The heroine is deprived of the freedom the grandmother in *Red Sorghum* enjoyed, though Zhang, by presenting modern life and progress so negatively, may again be showing his nostalgia for a life unfettered by restraints or traditions—a life that has long since disappeared in China. Inside the factory compound, that primitivism is still in evidence, but this time it takes on the dimensions of ignorance and decadence. Instead of the noble savage types of *Red Sorghum*, the characters here are shown as frustrated, incomplete, and unfulfilled individuals. In *Judou*, Zhang moves to the other extreme: from the triumph of primitivism to a scathing criticism and denunciation of the evils this primitivism is associated with. It is perhaps significant to note that this shift made Zhang's later films both more controversial and less commercially successful at home; *Red Sorghum* was an immediate success, both in China and overseas, but *Judou* was banned in China for some years. In *Raise the Red Lantern* (1991), another later film, instead of showing the glories of primitive ways of life, Zhang points out the wretched existence women endured under the oppression of Chinese feudalism and patriarchalism. Again he is presenting a longing for a simple, more primitive way of life, but this time he is demonstrating the hopelessness of those who seek such freedom in a world of structural and permanent inequality.

Chinese cultural critic Dai Jinhua (2002) has been scornful of the movies and the motives of the Fifth Generation filmmakers in her discussions of postcolonialism in contemporary China. In their discussion of Dai's work, editors Wang and Barlow in turn suggest that Dai is using the term *postcolonialism* in this instance to describe the peculiar cultural conditions that existed in China during the 1980s and 1990s, and that she places the burden of Western imperialism on the directors themselves (she would mainly be referring here to Zhang Yimou and Chen Kaige). Dai argues that these two directors have effectively been captured or "colonized" by Western cinematic aesthetics, which have trapped them in "an orientalism that internalizes the fantasy of the Other/West for an imaginary China that is premodern, a splendid spectacle of exoticism and an ancient land ruled by repressed desire" (Dai Jinhua 2002, 14).

In the post-socialist era of state-subsidized filmmaking, China's budding directors faced a serious obstacle: the realization that although filmmaking is an art form, it is also a part of everyday commerce and industry. Put simply, making a film good enough to sell at home and abroad is an extremely expensive and financially risky business. Some of the Fifth Generation filmmakers rejected the avenue of pure artistic narcissism that was beginning to characterize Chinese art and literature in the 1980s and 1990s, choosing instead to focus their work on the Western (especially European) market for art films, much of which was channeled through a series of international film festivals. The assumption (and the reality in many cases) was that a good review, and preferably a prize at one of the many summer film festivals, would not only increase sales abroad, it would also attract future investors willing to encourage the making of new Chinese films. In Dai's words,

> Initially an indicator of the success of Chinese art films, winning awards soon also became a means of survival, providing a chance to secure foreign investment, co-production, or other forms of assistance. Ironically, this narrow gateway became the sole opening for directors who wanted to keep a cultural foothold in art, evade the commercial tide . . . and thus avoid the mainstream model. (Dai Jinhua 2002, 50)

Dai suggests that this strategy worked; in fact it may have worked too well, because as filmmakers were fleeing through "the narrow gateway" they often fell into a different trap: "Since securing foreign investment . . . had become the . . . focus, the prerequisite for filmmaking became the representations of an Orient that was palatable and intelligible for Western viewers." By internalizing this Western cultural perspective, China's filmmakers were forced, or forced themselves, to reconstruct their narrative subjects according to Western expectations. As Dai reports, "Films . . . that managed to squeeze through these narrow gateways . . . simply fell under the yoke of one discursive power in their attempt to escape from another" (Dai Jinhua 2002, 50).[17]

Zhang's films might have been unpopular with the censor because they occasionally clashed with changes (or, reversals) in state policy. The early 1980s saw the resurgence of nationalism in China, patriotic sentiments being expected from people who had just emerged from the devastation of the Cultural Revolution. Economic restructuring (after 1978) in the rural areas turned out to be a great success; then reforms began in the urban areas, and it started to look as if political change was just around the corner. If we evaluate a film like *Red Sorghum* in this light, in other words, as the product of a highly successful reform era, it is easy to see how it reflects and speaks to the hugely optimistic tone of the times; and even though there was some criticism about its boldness in depicting female sexuality, the stature of *Red Sorghum* as a first-class film was guaranteed. Of course, we now know that political democratization did not follow the opening up of the economy, and that by the end of the 1980s, disappointment, despair, and even resentment were in the air. Rising expectations and finally bloodshed in the spring and summer of 1989 (in Tiananmen Square) plunged the nation into a period of disillusionment and uncertainty. The power of the CCP seemed to be overwhelming, and the future once again looked grim.

As we came to realize with the massacre in Tiananmen Square, outright resistance on a mass scale in China was not to be tolerated, so it might be realistic to suggest that in *Judou*, Zhang was making a veiled political criticism of the status quo. The film features a wealthy but miserly old man who owns and operates a small textile factory. He buys himself a young bride to make sure he will have an heir; at the same time, he hires his poor nephew to help him run the business. In the household, an ancient drama is being played out: the old man is unable to produce a child, but he entertains himself by tormenting and torturing his bride, in part because he thinks the problem is *her* infertility. The young wife is eventually driven into the arms of the nephew, with whom she finally has a child. The film won Best Director award for Zhang at Cannes and in Chicago, but the Chinese censors prevented the film from being shown at home. If we look for reasons, it is possible to interpret the film as a political parable, the old man being a symbol of the socialist order of Maoism, which was still able to inflict cruelties, even in its dying days.

The 1990s saw a more balanced development in economic growth in China, but it was now quite clear to all potential opponents of the CCP that any hasty political moves would be dealt with swiftly and decisively. The people, under such circumstances, needed to be patient and determined, rather like Wei, the young teacher in Zhang's film *Not One Less* (or like Qiu Ju in Zhang's *The Story of Qiu Ju*). Wei's and Qiu Ju's patience and waiting pay off eventually, and this may also be the message Zhang was sending to the Chinese people through these new films. What is also apparent about the 1990s is that market forces were coming to play an increasingly important role in the business of filmmaking in the new urban China. Potential box-office appeal quickly became one of the most important criteria of a film's value, with artistic merit coming onto the radar screen as a clearly second-place consideration.

Although the state still determines the total number of films to be made domestically each year in China, and also how many films will be imported, there have been some important structural changes in the industry. Film studios, for example, are now treated as enterprises, with the director rather than the party secretary overseeing production and being responsible for all financial affairs. Studios now have to raise all of their own revenues, rather than relying on the state for support, and although the film distribution companies are still state-run, they now pay the studios according to sales rather than a fixed allocation as in the past. As their contribution to the reform-era restructuring process, filmmakers are now required to form their own groups to contract with the studios if they wish to make a film, and from that point onward all executive decisions are their own. This also allows directors to seek out potential investors, which may include entering into joint ventures with overseas film interests, with other film studios, and with nonmedia enterprises. In 1993, films that had begun life with direct investment from the state-run studios made up less than 20 percent of the total number produced in that year.

In the past, films were mainly shown to the public free of charge or for very low admission prices, which meant that producers and directors in the film industry did not have to work particularly hard to make a film popular; the only real requirement was that the state's censors be happy that the state's political message had been presented. Today by comparison, the box office is directly in control of a film studio's future, and as the costs of filmmaking have increased, so have ticket prices. Audiences have also become more discriminating, and with growing competition from television and other cultural or recreational outlets, film studios have had to pay special attention to their potential viewers. Going to the movies has increased in price significantly in the reform era, from an average of 0.2 yuan in the 1970s, to close to 20 yuan or more in the late 1990s, which puts it in the category of luxury entertainment for many urban residents. Over time this has meant that the primary demographics of film audiences have shifted: urban film markets used to be dominated by young people and migrant workers, with better-educated residents mainly staying away (at least until the early 1990s). The result was that the tastes of the young and the less well-educated city residents influenced what films were shown (and therefore, what films were made). Not surprisingly, kungfu-style films dominated throughout the 1980s, with suspense films based on police and crime stories the second most popular. By the mid-1990s, however, the kungfu market appeared to have peaked, with more and more viewers wanting to see comedies, thrillers, and "real life dramas" (Lin 1996).

In a study analyzing the content of all feature films produced in China between 1979 and 1993, Hao (2000) reported that "life dramas" accounted for more than 40 percent, which was more than twice the number of suspense films produced. Interestingly, films described as "propaganda films"—with plots centering on such themes as party history, exemplary or model citizens, and party politics—were still being made, and were in fact the third most frequently produced category. But as the reforms progressed, and especially after Deng Xiaoping's tour of South China in 1992, fewer films in the propaganda category were being produced as the film industry increasingly attempted to cater to the tastes of its audiences.

The rising popularity of crime stories as film plots may indicate both that viewers were interested in topics that were very different from their everyday lives (escapism), and that the public was well aware of the growing prevalence of crime in Chinese society, especially in the cities (i.e., realism; see Chan 1995). Other significant trends in the contemporary Chinese film industry have been the production of films that encourage individuals to change their lives and social status, often with characters that "jump into the sea" (that is, plunge into the world of private business); and films that focus on marriage and sexual relationships, or on other themes familiar to Western filmgoers such as love triangles and extramarital affairs, themes that were strictly taboo in the old pre-reform days.

One consistent trend running through the reform era to the present day has been the Chinese film industry's focus on film scripts depicting social and interpersonal struggle. Earlier, such films would probably have originated or been inspired by issues of class conflict or questions of political belief; but in the contemporary era, filmmakers have been freer to focus on social or psychological dramas, individual quarrels between citizens, and conflicts between citizens and the state—which is the situation so poignantly portrayed in Zhang Yimou's much acclaimed *The Story of Qiu Ju*. It is also important to note a shift away from the depiction of traditional families in Chinese films, with an increasing prevalence of single people as heroes and heroines, which would be consistent with the industry's shift toward investigations of the self and personal issues. Also to be noted is an increase in the portrayal of divorced people in post–Cultural Revolution films, reflecting an increase in the divorce rate throughout contemporary urban society. Foreigners are also much more likely to appear in Chinese films today than in the past, which reflects the reality of China's new open-door policies of the 1980s and 1990s, although as Hao's data show (2000), there is still a tendency in many Chinese films to portray foreigners as unsympathetic characters.

The huge potential demand (and ability to pay) of urban Chinese audiences has also resulted in a significant shift toward films that have an urban focus, with a corresponding shift away from films set entirely in rural areas. In addition, a new genre of filmmaking involves the issue of rural-urban interactions, focusing on some of the problems and frustrations encountered by rural people when they travel to cities (or when they do a significant amount of business in nearby cities). This is the situation in Zhao Xiaowen's film *Ermo*, which features a determined rural woman who sells her home-made noodles in a nearby city. Her dream is to earn enough money to buy the biggest television for sale in the city, and to this end she spends much of her free time gazing enviously through the window of the TV shop. It seems obvious that such a storyline could be interpreted as a critique of urban China's post-socialist infatuation with consumption, noting that the character Ermo's "unwitting desire . . . for freedom from poverty and rural isolation" drives her "pursuit of modernity in a box" that has been "earned with her feet and her blood" and which subsequently "enslaves her body and soul" (Silbergeld 1999, 91).

Another film set within and dealing with the rural-urban transition is Zhang Yimou's *Not One Less* (1999), which was his first film to deal with contemporary China. The film was notable at the time because it was set in a poor village in a remote and mountainous part of the countryside, and because the actors in the film were mostly local people playing themselves. Wei Minzhi is a thirteen-year-old girl who is called upon to teach the grade-school class when the village's only teacher is called away to visit his sick mother. The village is desperately poor, and Wei has only one piece of chalk for every day the teacher is away. Because the school is funded on a per capita basis, she is told that she must try to keep all of the students at school (hence the film's title). In poor areas it is not unusual for parents to take their children (especially the girls) out of school, either to help at home, to work in the fields, or to be sent to the city in search of a job, so Wei becomes convinced that keeping all her students in class is more important than anything she can teach them.

Unlike other films Zhang has been involved in over the years, this one is not a melodrama or a tearjerker (like *To Live*); it does not have gorgeous scenery and evocative colors (like Zhang's primitivist films *Judou*, *Red Sorghum*, and *Yellow Earth*); and it does not feature glamorous lifestyles and elements of high fashion (as in *Shanghai Triad*). It is rather a matter-of-fact look at a desperately impoverished area, in the shadow of a city that becomes increasingly attractive to the local people. As such, the film looks at a way of life that is very far removed from the new wealth associated with the cities and the coastal regions of China. As the plot develops, one of Wei's students, Zhang Huike (played by himself), runs away to look for work, so she sets off for the city, determined to get him back in the classroom. Again unlike almost all of Zhang Yimou's earlier films, this one has a Hollywood-style happy ending, but even so it is also able to insert some sharp social commentary. When the girl finally arrives in the city—after walking most of the way—she searches for several days unsuccessfully, but by sheer perseverance manages to get herself on a local TV news show, which helps her to find the boy and bring him back home safely. The village is then showered with goodwill and gifts from city people and the television station, and the film ends with a statement about the importance of keeping schools open in poor parts of the countryside—a direct reference to the growing disparity between the city and the country in reform-era China.

As mentioned earlier, another popular theme in recent Chinese filmmaking has been its near obsession with issues of urban crime and corruption, with the result that some of the most popular characters are portrayed either as law enforcement officials or as criminals—in both cases, male and female—which represents a shift away from characters playing the part of peasants and military personnel, as was the case in many of the films made in the pre-reform era. Other films focus on life within a criminal or semi-criminal urban environment, which would include the film voted as outstanding Chinese language film at the 2000 Hong Kong International Film Festival, *Suzhou River*. This was the only entry from mainland China, and the second film of a young director, Lou Ye, who is one of the so-called Sixth Generation of Chinese filmmakers, these being graduates of the Beijing Film Academy who began making films in the 1993–1995 period. The film resembles a contemporary film-noir (Hitchcock-style), set in the ugliest and most rundown neighborhoods of present-day Shanghai. Most of the action takes place along foul Suzhou Creek, which winds through decaying warehouses and decrepit factories on its way to Shanghai's glittering waterfront. Some film critics have recognized a connection between the characters of *Suzhou River* and those who normally inhabit Wang Shuo's stories—marginal, *liumang*-like characters. *Suzhou River* has also been described as a brooding tale of love and loss. It is set in Shanghai, but certainly does not portray any of the glamour usually associated with that city's rapid economic modernization. In sharp contrast to such glamour, the film shows Shanghai as a dark and dangerous city where its inhabitants strive endlessly for fulfillment in the liminal world of the riverside.[18]

Although *Suzhou River* is a unique film in a number of ways, it shares some characteristics with other films made by Sixth Generation directors. As one reviewer has commented,

> In general, the Fifth Generation made pretty films set in the rural past; the Sixth Generation makes gritty films set in the urban present. Emperors and concubines have been replaced by the grungy malcontents of Zhang Yuan's *Beijing Bastards*. . . . Its anomic punksters spit out obscenities in sync sound and groove to hard rock. A night at the Peking Opera gives way to an all-nighter in the Beijing mosh pit. (Corliss 2003, 1)

Although they make or have made very different films, Fifth and Sixth Generation filmmakers have at least one thing in common: their uneasy relationship with the censor, which has helped to create a truly independent film culture in China. Further, the Sixth Generation is a group of new young directors who don't sit around waiting for the censor to do his or her work; they go out and raise their own funds to make whatever films they want to make. It is not surprising, therefore, to find that their major characters are often silent, sullen resisters, who refuse to give in to the system. In Jia Zhang-ke's film *Pickpocket*, for example, the leading character is a thief with scruples who, unlike some of his old burglar friends—*liumang* characters again—is unable to parlay his talents into economic success in the new era. He is spurned by an old gangster friend, harassed by the police, and cursed by his father, who says he should have drowned him when he had the chance! When he is finally arrested for theft, he is handcuffed to the cable of a telephone pole in a public square, and left there to be stared at like a creature behind bars in a zoo (Lu 2003). Sometimes the heroes of Sixth Generation films are loveable villains, as in He Jianjun's film *Postman*, which begins with the leading man reading the letters he should be delivering. When he learns that many of the letters are heartfelt pleas for human contact, he starts to write replies to those same letters; it is an illegal act, but one with a pro-social message.

Dai Jinhua suggested in 1994 that there really never was such a category as Sixth Generation filmmaking in China (2002). She argued this for a number of reasons, including her belief that the new school of directors had not (at that time) produced enough good work that was clearly categorizable as a new genre of filmmaking. At the time, she also hoped that when (or if) a new group of filmmakers emerged in China, they would be able to claim something more original than just being the next group of graduates from the same institution as their predecessors. As she put it, "I harbored the optimistic, perhaps chimeric, expectation that when social transformations shattered cultural heroism, a new generation of filmmakers might be able to appear in their own names, rather than in the name of any new 'generation'" (78).

Later on Dai reluctantly admitted that a Sixth Generation of filmmakers had in fact emerged in China, but she suggested that their appearance was particularly badly timed. With the exception of Wang Shuo's work, the climate of opinion in China in the early 1990s was clearly not favorable to the type of films these new directors wanted to make. What the people wanted to see was dictated by the new norms of mass culture, which in the visual domain included only what Dai referred to scornfully as "quasi-film" phenomena (television and video). At that time, Dai claimed, art films were "box-office poison." The better works of the more-famous Fifth Generation filmmakers had been able to sidestep this problem because they were often generously funded by international investors who had a specific idea of the Chinese films they wanted to see being made. In Dai's words, "Riding high on the crest of the wave of orientalism, the Fifth Generation undoubtedly produced a China fever . . . a hunger for Chinese film in European and American art film festivals" (2002, 80), but there was little left in the way of funding for the younger hopefuls. When these young directors learned that no one was willing to fund their film projects, they were forced into the margins of artistic space; in fact, many of them "ended up in various venues, joining the nomadic Beijing artist groups, or making their living with TV programs, advertisements, and MTV, or doing temporary work on various film production teams, yet still committed to their dreams" (81).

The first filmmaker to break out of this predicament was Zhang Yuan, who managed to scrape up just enough cash to make what would become the first Sixth Generation film, *Mother*. The film was so poorly funded that Zhang ended up shooting most of it crudely in black and white. It was also produced entirely on location, and all of the actors were amateurs. Zhang followed this with his better-known film *Beijing Bastards*, in which he collaborated with China's rock-star Cui Jian, and then later with his tour-de-force *East Palace, West Palace*, which dealt with the topic of homosexuality in Beijing. These were all entirely self-financed productions, and they represented a new genre of films in China that would become known primarily as "independent productions." Another of the pioneering Sixth Generation films was Wang Xiaoshuai's *The Day in Winter-Spring*, which was also shot in black and white, and was financed for a total of 10,000 yuan (compared to Zhang Yimou's standard budgets of 6–10 million yuan).

Dai Jinhua's version of the troubled history of the Sixth Generation leaves the impression that these were a small number of young film directors who wanted to remain independent of both state funding and global capital, and who would eventually "break away from commercial culture's ambush of art film" (2002, 84). Although the nature and the content of the new films was a subversion of the official system of film production in China, the creative styles adopted by the new directors, Dai argues, were forced upon them more by circumstances than by actual artistic choice, and in this sense the new independent filmmakers were operating very much in the style of many young filmmakers outside Hollywood, especially in the third world.

In spite of this, quite a few of these new films actually made it to the important art film festivals around the world, and some of them did well. Dai suggests, however, that their success was in part a result of the thirst or demand for Chinese films that had been started by the Fifth Generation directors, and in part a result of the fact that most of the films were labeled as "underground films" (2002, 90). She argues that the reviews of these films tended to bypass their actual artistic qualities (or lack thereof), concentrating only on their political significance. (This would be similar in a number of ways to the warm reception the West gave to films from Eastern Europe at around the time of the demise of the communist ruling powers.) What Dai concludes from all of this, rather cynically, is that the filmgoers and critics at art film festivals around the world were more interested in where the films had come from, and in the fact that they had been shot "underground" or independently, than in their actual artistic merit.

According to Dai, because the films of Zhang Yimou and his imitators had satisfied the West's "old orientalist" mirror image, the West again privileged the Sixth Generation as the Other, reflecting Western liberal intellectuals' anticipations or expectations of the 1990s Chinese cultural condition. Created as a mirror image, this expectation again validated Western intellectuals' mapping of China's democracy, progress, resistance, civil society, and marginal world position. Western intellectuals disregarded not only the cultural reality displayed directly in these films, but also the filmmakers' cultural intentions (2002, 90).

What Dai is suggesting here is that Western critics—or some body of film appreciators masquerading as such—used the work of these new directors to create an imaginary China, a China they wanted and hoped to see emerging (but which was in fact not emerging). The result was that the films of the Sixth Generation became what Dai calls "scenes in the fog," in the sense that they were highly exposed in the outside world, but little-known and little-seen inside China. Dai reports that even she, one of China's best-known film critics, only heard about most of the films in question from overseas publications and reports sent to her by friends from abroad. But there were, on the other hand, some benefits that would accrue from this situation, in that a path had been paved for the new young directors of the future to follow. As Dai concludes, "If the 'Zhang Yimou style' used to be a narrow door through which Chinese directors could move on their 'march toward the world,' independent filmmaking now became a shortcut to the powerbase in Western cinema" (2002, 91).

Conclusion

Perhaps the most obvious way to interpret cultural change in contemporary urban China is to think of it as a series of transformations, working somehow in unison. The first of these is the shift from the "plan" (socialism) to the "market" (capitalism). As artistic and cultural productions are liberated from one source of domination (the state), they are captured by another equally powerful source (the market). In this chapter, by looking at changes in the way people are now spending their time and money, we have seen how this shift has been manifested in the pattern of everyday life in urban China; and the same holds in case studies of the developments occurring in the world of literature and film in the new urban China. The second transformation involves the downward movement from "high" to "low" forms of culture, as market-share and profits become the primary standards of appraisal for new cultural forms. The third transformation involves the notion of convergence, as art and culture in China are assumed to become increasingly Westernized through the mechanisms of transnationalism and globalization.

As attractive as such simple notions of transformation may be, in truth they do not have much explanatory value, immersed as they are in cold-war ideology, permeated with elite notions of cultural aesthetics, and insistent on simple binaries such as plan/market, high/low, and East/West. As Jing Wang (2001) articulates, dichotomies of this type are based on clichés, and she is convinced that further exploration will reveal many divergent trends within Chinese culture during the last two decades. Wang's major criticism, however, is that all three interpretations of what has happened in urban China fail to take into consideration the vastly important role the state still plays in determining culture and cultural trends. The CCP has, at least from the early 1930s onwards, been concerned about developments in popular culture, has clearly realized the importance of using culture for propaganda purposes, and has seen the need to control the form and expression of culture (Goodman 2001). In the contemporary era, the CCP has certainly adjusted some of its perspectives, but it is still fundamentally concerned with the management and articulation of popular culture—although as Jing Wang (2001) suggests, this has involved a subtle shift away from the coercive control of culture (of the pre- and post-1949 era) in the direction of greater legal regulation during the reform era.

In making this argument, and as an alternative to the simple dichotomies mentioned above, Wang identifies two significant trajectories along which we can see the notion of "culture" traveling within the last decade in urban China. One of these she refers to as the "popularization of the discursive construction of *xiuxian wenhua*," or "leisure culture" (J. Wang 2001, 71). This is a situation in which the state has effectively been able to create a new nation of consumer-citizens, as a result of very well-calculated policies. What Wang argues is that, freed from the need to mobilize the people through its own political ideology, and refusing to allow any significant democratization that would capture the imagination of the people, the CCP has invited—and, she argues, has enabled—the Chinese people to become members of an egalitarian consumer (re)public. This has been part of what Wang describes as a determined state campaign to "democratize society's access to cultural goods" (71). It has been achieved, she argues, in a number of ways, including using a transformation of the system of socialist legality to accommodate a modern culture of consumerism—for example, by implementing a Customers' Civil Statute, a Tourists' Civil Statute, and a Law of Consumer Rights Protection. The state also passed into law a 40-hour workweek in 1994, which effectively created the reality of a two-day weekend for the first time in China—the so-called double leisure day (*shuangxiu ri*). What the people could or should do with their new-found leisure time became the hottest topic in newspaper and magazine columns, and the state, at all levels, was not hesitant about making its own recommendations. On the streets, in factories and offices, and even in government departments, "a leisure culture fever swept over all major cities" (75).

To help provide the wherewithal for leisure consumption, interest rates were lowered several times between 1996 and 1998, encouraging the people to spend more and save less. This was seen as a part of the state's larger goal of boosting China's "spiritual civilization" to keep it in line with obvious advances that had already been made in China's "material civilization" (Bakken 2000). The state, in other words, was busy trying to get the people to be more modern and civilized by teaching them how to spend their leisure time profitably (with an emphasis on "spend"). These policies had multiple goals: in addition to helping build the Chinese character and develop a modern state, they were also part of a deliberate attempt to increase consumer demand for commodities as varied as automobiles, computers, and sporting gear of all types.

As intuitively attractive as Wang's idea is, it suffers from an exposure to the realities of urban China in the late 1990s (see chapter 9). The most obvious contradiction of Wang's argument is that in spite of the state's attempts to "democratize" consumption, its own economic reform policies have worked to increase the extent of inequality in China. This has been the case not only between the cities and the countryside, as foreign investment and state policies continue to favor the coastal provinces, but also, more disturbingly, within the cities. Behind the facade of appearances, a much more significant transition is taking place in urban China: the socialist city, which was characterized by full employment, secure jobs with fringe benefits, and minimal income and lifestyle differences (Solinger 2000, 2002), has been transformed into the post-socialist city. This new city has for some time now been experiencing the negative "externalities" of the reform era, including loss of state-employment security, dangerously high unemployment rates, rising crime rates, and new and previously unimaginably high levels of income polarization. Millions of workers are being laid off from their jobs in state-owned enterprises, and at the same time millions more poor peasants are entering the cities in search of jobs, and are willing to accept those jobs at lower than market rates, without any benefits. It is not clear exactly how or when such people will be able to enjoy the benefits of what Jing Wang calls the new "egalitarianism" of consumption.

A second trajectory that Wang points to, and one that seems to offer a more robust account of cultural change in urban China, is the emergence of a new cultural economy (*wenhua jingji*), which has resulted in the "collapse and convertibility of cultural capital into economic capital" (J. Wang 2001, 71). In addition to its focus on increasing leisure pursuits among the Chinese people, all through the 1990s the state concerned itself with turning culture into capital. A distinct pattern for this was established in Guangdong province after 1994. Guangdong had been traditionally known as a place to get rich, but as most of the guidebooks indicated, there was very little in the province to attract tourists (especially domestic tourists). In just a few years, however, the province succeeded in reinventing itself as a cultural vanguard by launching a range of shows and festivals—featuring both "high" and "low" culture—under the auspices of the Guangdong Provincial Institute of Cultural Development Strategies. This link between culture and business, which is what Guangdong was traditionally famous for, was made effectively, and the new catchphrase became "Utilizing culture to promote business." A levy was imposed on major entertainment venues in the province, as well as on TV stations, newspapers, and magazines, which was earmarked as a "construction fee" for the building of cultural enterprises; and philanthropic donations to opera houses, symphonies, and ballet troupes were made tax deductible.

Another key innovator in this regard was the city of Beijing, where an explicit link was forged between cultural history and tourism, with the preservation (and often the entire rebuilding) of key historic sites. Huge new investment projects were announced, with plans to construct large-scale cultural establishments such as museums, libraries, and culture-focused shopping malls. The Department of Culture in Beijing publicized plans to rebuild or recover lost cultural venues such as run-down theaters and cinemas; and a plan was announced to build a special cultural zone composed of five locations of major historical significance across the city. As bold as these plans were, it is worth noting that Beijing—and other Chinese cities, especially Shanghai—was simply being more entrepreneurial and image conscious in its search for new investment funds and tourists, a strategy that it learned from many other cities around the world. In the process, however, the redevelopment of historical sites and scenery has helped Beijing to buck the trend toward cultural homogenization and globalization.

There is a danger, perhaps, when discussing changes in Chinese culture, of assuming too great a role for the state in the control of culture during the pre-reform era, and too little a role during the reform era. As Goodman (2001) points out, "Even at the height of the Mao-dominated era . . . creators of culture did not have to be previously state-sanctioned in order to have access to public outlets such as museums, journals, or publishing houses" (247–48). This was clearly a different situation from that in the Soviet Union; writers in China were not required to be members of an official writers' association, and the initiative for writing and translation was never fully monopolized by the state. In the reform era, by contrast, it is unusual to find agents of popular culture that have had *no* contact at all with the state and its infrastructure. Many of them have previously worked for the state, and have taken their *guanxi* (connections), as well as their training and expertise, with them into their cultural exploits. In countless instances, new cultural activities have close structural relationships with the state, and this is especially true in the new era of decentralizing decision making down to the local level. As Goodman notes,

> Local government provides access to capital (funds, equipment, and build-
> ings), labor, and political protection. . . . The booming collective sector of
> the economy is largely at the level of local government and ensures financing
> and a network of influence to support . . . [cultural] . . . activities that want to
> grow beyond the small scale of private enterprise. (249–50)

Goodman uses such evidence to suggest that rather than being created from below, much of the development of new cultural trends in China today is better described as having been subverted "from above" (2001, 250). In this sense, he is agreeing with Jing Wang's claim that the state has developed a new ruling technology that is not content to let popular culture go its own way. As Wang argues, and as has been emphasized in this chapter, "leisure and pleasure" in China, even in these days of market triumphalism "are not easily disentangled from politics and state sponsorship" (2001, 99).

Notes

1. Another way to put this is to say that today the state no longer has an "official state" ideology, over and above exhorting the people to produce and spend as much as possible. As we have seen throughout this book, in the Dengist era (post-1978) most of the principles associated with Maoist-style communism were discarded: ideas about a collective utopian future were replaced with a quotidian concern with everyday life, while at the same time economic reforms increasingly stressed the importance of consumption, getting rich, and the endless expansion of markets. The rigid class identities of Mao's time disintegrated, both informally as a result of new

economic and geographic freedoms, and formally, as an edict of the regime. To justify its existence in such circumstances, the CCP started to redefine its hegemonic project as a determined attack on China's poverty and backwardness, which was to be achieved primarily by stimulating rapid economic growth (Smith 2000; Blecher 1997).

2. A recent survey revealed some very expensive tastes among Chinese business people, at least when it comes to cars. The magazine *Zhongguo Qiyejia* (Chinese Entrepreneurs), which is affiliated with the Economic Daily News Group, recently conducted a survey of two hundred entrepreneurs. Twenty-eight percent of those surveyed said that Mercedes-Benz tops all brands and is their first choice when it comes to purchasing their own cars, with BMW close behind, followed by Audi and Lexus (see http://ce.cei.gov.cn/enew/new_f1/fk00fb40.htm [accessed December 2000]). Another recent survey that had interesting results in this context was conducted during 2001 by the *Far Eastern Economic Review*. The survey interviewed over one thousand respondents in three Chinese cities: Guangzhou, Shanghai, and Beijing. Most of these respondents were relatively wealthy citizens (reflecting, we must assume, the *Review*'s readership, and making up a group the *Review* refers to in its published articles as "China's Elite"). One of the most interesting findings was about a generation gap that now exists in China within this "elite" group, and in a variety of areas, for example, in a preference for fast food or in the use of computers. Within the latter category, people under 55 were enthusiastic users of computers, but those over 55 rarely were. Further, the majority of respondents under 35 (55 percent) regularly used credit cards, while only a minority of people over that age (41 percent) even owned credit cards. The group in the age category 45–55 spoke significantly less English than any other group, and tended to earn less as well. The household income of the wealthy Chinese surveyed in this study averaged more than 8,000 yuan (US$967) a month, but those with a household head aged 45–55 earned only 6,909 yuan a month. In an attempt to explain some of these discrepancies, Vittachi (2002) suggests the following: "People aged 45–54 went through their key years of education between 1960 and 1970, when Chinese society was in turmoil [because of the Cultural Revolution]. . . . Teachers were denounced, libraries were burned and peasantry was celebrated over intellectualism. It appears evident that their careers have never recovered."

3. A survey conducted in 1998 by the State Statistical Bureau (now the National Bureau of Statistics) and covering twelve cities and five thousand people provides a snapshot of urban Chinese consumer habits. Somewhat unexpectedly, spending on food was above the national average, with 56 percent of the households surveyed spending US$36–US$84 a month on food. The major break with the past, it seems, was in some of the food items that people were spending money on. Ready-to-eat frozen Chinese dishes were consumed by 54 percent of households (refrigerator ownership was 88 percent). Instant noodles were another favorite, with a consumption rate of 73 percent (one-fifth of those surveyed ate at least ten packs of instant noodles a month). Coffee drinking was also on the increase, with just over one-third of those sampled drinking two to six cups a week, while 8 percent were daily coffee drinkers. Another dramatic break with the past was in the new popularity of bottled water, which was drunk by 65 percent of the respondents (for a further discussion of these trends, see www.apfoodonline.com/magazines/2000/mar/art02.html [accessed November 2000]).

4. The most significant of these was a 1988 multiseries documentary called *Heshang* (River Elegy), which was probably the most watched and debated series in the history of Chinese television (according to Barmé 1999, 23). The main impetus behind the *Heshang* series was a conclusion reached by its producers that China's traditional culture, and its long history (symbolized by the Huang He [Yellow River]), was acting as a drag on the future, and that what China really needed was to abandon the traditional, inland, earth-bound worldview, which it had had for so long, and to substitute for it a new orientation toward the sea (the "deep blue") and the outside world. For details about the series, see Su and Wang (1991).

5. This is true, for example, of the darling of Western filmgoers, Zhang Yimou, some of whose films have been banned by the CCP, but who for the most part has been able to stay out of trouble, perhaps because he directs films that are hugely popular (and therefore highly commercial) in the West, and especially in Europe, although they are not as popular at home. For a detailed examination of Zhang and his career, see Zhang (1977); as well as a highly critical view by Dai Jinhua (2002).

6. The May Fourth movement of 1919, which was the culmination of more than two decades of intellectual ferment and debate over China's perennial weakness internationally, gave birth to modern Chinese nationalism. Some scholars refer to it as China's equivalent to the European Enlightenment (see for example, Hutchings [2001, 306–7]).

7. Lu Xun is generally considered to have been China's greatest twentieth-century literary figure, and was later to become one of the chief proponents of Chinese modernity.

8. Outsiders have jumped into this debate. Literary critic Jonathan Arac, for example, observes that contemporary Chinese fiction has achieved more than the obvious shift from an omniscient (author) to point-of-view (individual) narration; it is now evident that "the voice of fiction . . . [in China] . . . is no longer understood to be speaking authoritatively for the people as a whole collectivity . . . but simply for a sole self" (1997, 274). Arac suggests that this represents a transition from the "sentimental utopia" of the Maoist era, to the "chaos" of the 1990s. A conclusion to be drawn from this debate is that one of the costs associated with life in contemporary China is a modern sense of meaninglessness, lack of purpose, and emptiness, more generally described by E. Y. J. Wang (1996, 40) as the "loss of frameworks in which to situate oneself."

9. Tang appears to stretch this point beyond credibility, however, when he suggests that the new urban malaise results from a conflict between adherents to the new urban culture—which represents the present and the future—and a desire among some who would prefer to return to China's rural past. Tang argues that "while an apparently amorphous everyday life becomes the norm and an alienating institution, rustic simplicity and authenticity seem to possess a greater peculiar attraction." He is saying, in other words, that revolutionary mass culture, replete with all the familiar images of the rural collectives of the past, still has an appeal of wholesomeness, against which the new urban culture offers a secular existence that is thoroughly routine (and certainly vacuous), but is also full of concrete expectations that, for many, can never be fulfilled.

10. This poem is quoted in J. Wang (1996, 197–98).

11. J. Wang (1996).

12. This is reprinted in Damosh (2003); see also, pup.princeton.edu/chapters/i7545.html (accessed March 1, 2006).

13. In a more nuanced *liumang* performance—such as Mardar's role in the film *Suzhou River*—the character is dragged rather reluctantly into illicit activity, in this case kidnapping, by the people he hangs out with. Mardar's particular transgressions have a high price, however, when his girlfriend apparently drowns herself and he is sent to prison for his role in the crime.

14. On the subject of food obsession in China, see also Mo Yan's often hilarious but sometimes quite shocking book *The Republic of Wine: A Novel* (2001). For a review of the book see Goldblatt (2000).

15. In 1988 alone four of Wang Shuo's stories were made into feature films (see Barmé 1999, 67). Popular magazines came to describe this as "Wang Shuo Year."

16. Lanchester also suggests that such a lawsuit could only have been filed in China, which is one of the few places where the law allows for dead people to be libeled. The impact of this law on historical fiction in China, however, could be devastating because, as Lanchester notes,

the one thing Chinese intellectual life certainly does not need at this time is a new way for books to be banned! Hong Ying lost the lawsuit and was ordered to pay damages and make a public apology in the press. Lanchester concludes on the absurdity of this situation,

> A lawsuit heard in Manchuria, between two people who live in London, over a novel published in Taiwan, giving a fictionalized version of events which happened three quarters of a century ago between people all of whom are dead—welcome to the world of the twenty-first-century Chinese literary novel. (2003, 25)

17. If we accept Dai's interpretation, it may be seen as a gesture to his audiences, or perhaps as just a way to become more commercially successful at home, that Zhang Yimou's more recent films (for example, *The Story of Qiu Ju; Not One Less; The Road Home;* and *Happy Times*) have contemporary themes, with stories that are less obviously obsessed with primitivism. The first three of these films are set in remote parts of rural China, with images of the starkness and remote beauty of the land and of settlements that are clearly premodern. In these barren landscapes, the people are often shown as being close to nature, hard-working, uncomplaining, and basically content with a life that offers little more than getting enough to eat. Life in such villages is depicted as congenial; the people are for the most part kind. Zhang then switches his locale to urban China, in *Happy Times*, but he remains consistent in sticking with the themes of poverty and a concern for China's underclasses.

18. The film begins as the narrative of a lonely videographer who makes a careful study of the human traffic passing along the river in front of his balcony. He falls in love with a young woman who performs as a mermaid swimming in a giant tank in a seedy bar down by the riverside. Despite his initial euphoria, the narrator is deeply troubled by his lover's unexplained silences and periods of absence. She slips in and out of his life, leaving suddenly to lose herself in the human traffic of the city streets. At this point another story is blended in, and a young man appears, claiming that the mermaid character is actually his former lover (who had jumped into Suzhou River from a bridge and drowned). To make matters more confusing, the two women are actually played by the same actress, so there is some real basis for the confusion—the audience is left at the end of the film asking whether there were in fact two women or just one!

References Cited

Anagnost, Ann. 1997. *National Past-Times: Narrative, Representation, and Power in Modern China.* Durham, N.C.: Duke University Press.

Arac, Jonathan. 1997. Chinese postmodernism: Toward a global context. In *Postmodernism and China*, a special issue of *Boundary* 224, no. 3 (fall): 261–75.

Bakken. 2000. *The Exemplary Society: Human Improvement, Social Control, and the Dangers of Modernity.* London: Oxford University Press.

Barmé, Geremie. 1999. *In the Red: On Contemporary Chinese Culture.* New York: Columbia University Press.

Barmé, Geremie, and L. Jaivin, eds. 1992. *New Ghosts, Old Dreams.* New York: Times Books.

Blecher, Marc. 1997. *China against the Tides: Restructuring through Revolution, Radicalism, and Reform.* London: Pinter.

Bown, M. C. 1998. *Socialist Realist Painting.* New Haven, Conn.: Yale University Press.

Boym, S. 1994. *Common Places: Mythologies of Everyday Life in Russia.* Cambridge, Mass.: Harvard University Press.

Chan, T. C. 1995. Call the tune without paying the piper: The reassertion of media control in China. In *China Review 1995*, ed. C. K. Lo and M. Brosseau. Hong Kong: Chinese University Press, 1–21.

Chen, N. N. 2001. Health, wealth, and the good life. In *China Urban: Ethnographies of Contemporary Culture*, ed. N. N. Chen et al. Durham, N.C.: Duke University Press, 165–82.

China Cinema Press. 1984. *China Film Yearbook*. Beijing.

Chow, R. 1995. *Primitive Passions: Visuality, Sexuality, Ethnography, and Contemporary Chinese Cinema*. New York: Columbia University Press.

Corliss, R. 2003. Bright lights. *Time Asia*, January 31.

Croll, Elizabeth. 1994. *From Heaven to Earth: Images and Experience of Development in China*. London: Routledge.

Dai Jinhua. 2002. *Cinema and Desire: Feminist Marxism and Cultural Politics in the Work of Dai Jinhua*, ed. J. Wang and T. E. Barlow. London: Verso Press.

Damosh, D. 2003. *What Is World Literature?* Princeton, N.J.: Princeton University Press, pup.princeton.edu/chapters/i7545.html (accessed March 1, 2006).

Dirlik, Araf. 1994. *After the Revolution: Waking to Global Capitalism*. Hanover, N.H.: Wesleyan University Press.

Dutton, M. 1999. *Streetlife China*. Cambridge: Cambridge University Press.

Elvin, Mark. 1997. *Changing Stories in the Chinese World*. Stanford, Calif.: Stanford University Press.

Farquhar, Judith. 2002. *Appetites: Food and Sex in Post-Socialist China*. Durham, N.C.: Duke University Press.

Farrer, James. 2002. *Opening Up: Youth Sex Culture and Market Reform in Shanghai*. Chicago: University of Chicago Press.

Goldblatt, H. 2000. Border crossings: Chinese writing, in their world and ours. In *China beyond the Headlines*, ed. T. E. Weston and L. M. Jensen. Boulder, Colo.: Rowman and Littlefield, 327–46.

Goodman, D. S. G. 2001. Contending the popular: Party-state and culture. *Positions* 9, no. 1 (spring): 245–52.

Hao, X. M. 2000. The Chinese cinema in the reform era. *Journal of Popular Film and Television* (spring), www.findarticles.com (accessed March 1, 2006).

Hershatter, G. 1997. *Dangerous Pleasures: Prostitution and Modernity in Twentieth-Century Shanghai*. Berkeley: University of California Press.

Hessler, Peter. 2001. *River Town: Two Years on the Yangtze*. New York: Perennial.

Hutchings, G. 2001. *Modern China: A Guide to a Century of Change*. Cambridge, Mass.: Harvard University Press.

Ikels, Charlotte. 1996. *The Return of the God of Wealth: The Transition to a Market Economy in Urban China*. Stanford, Calif.: Stanford University Press.

Jiang, H. 2003. The personalization of literature: Chinese women's writing in the 1990s. *China Review* 3, no. 1 (spring): 5–27.

Johnson, Todd. 1997. *Clear Water, Blue Skies: China's Environment in the New Century*. Washington, D.C.: World Bank.

Kraus, Richard. 1995. China's artists between plan and market. In *Urban Spaces in Contemporary China: The Potential for Autonomy and Community in Post-Mao China*, ed. D. S. Davis et al. Washington, D.C.: Woodrow Wilson Center Press, 173–92.

Lanchester, J. 2003. Looking for trouble in China. *New York Review of Books* 50, no. 4 (March 13): 25–27.

Lee, L. O. F. 1999. *Shanghai Modern: The Flowering of a New Urban Culture in China, 1930–1945*. Cambridge, Mass.: Harvard University Press.

Lin, H. 1996. On China's urban consumption of films. *China's Film Market* 66:26–28.

Link, P., ed. 1983. *Stubborn Weeds.* Bloomington: Indiana University Press.

Liu, B. Y., and P. Link. 1998. A great leap backward? *New York Review of Books* 65 (15): 19–23.

Liu, L. 1996. Translingual practice: The discourse of individualism between China and the West. In *Narratives of Agency: Self-Making in China, India, and Japan,* ed. W. Dissanayake. Minneapolis: University of Minnesota Press, 1–34.

Lu, T. L. 2003. Music and noise: Independent film and globalization. *China Review* 3, no. 1 (spring): 57–76.

Lu Xun. 1957. On the misorientation of culture. In *The Complete Works of Lu Xun*, vol. 1. Beijing: Renmin wenxue chuban she, 186–87.

Lynch, D. C. 1999. *After the Propaganda State: Media, Politics, and "Thought Work" in Reformed China.* Stanford, Calif.: Stanford University Press.

Ma, H. Y., J. K. Huang, S. Rozelle, and F. Fuller. 2002. Getting rich and eating out: Consumption of food away from home in urban China. Working paper 02-E11, June 3. Center for Chinese Agricultural Policy (CCAP).

Mao Zedong. 1975. *Selected Works of Mao Zedong.* Hong Kong: Modern Chinese History Archives.

McDougall, B. S. 1991. *The Yellow Earth: A Film by Chen Kaige*, with a complete translation of the filmscript. Hong Kong: Chinese University Press.

Minford, John. 1985. Picking up the pieces. *Far Eastern Economic Review*, August 8, 30.

Mo Yan. 2001. *The Republic of Wine: A Novel.* New York: Arcade Publishing.

National Bureau of Statistics. 2004. *Zhongguo tongji nianjian 2004* [China statistical yearbook 2004]. Beijing: China Statistics Press.

Perry, E. J. 1999. Crime, corruption, and contention. In *The Paradox of China's Post-Mao Reforms*, ed. M. Goldman and R. MacFarquhar. Cambridge, Mass.: Harvard University Press, 308–32.

Perry, E. J., and M. Selden, eds. 2000. *Chinese Society: Change Conflict and Resistance.* London: Routledge.

Rofel, L. 1999. *Other Modernities: Gendered Yearnings in China after Socialism.* Berkeley: University of California Press.

Rowley, S. 1998. *Chungking Express, Happy Together*, and postmodern space. www.werple.net .au/~lerowley/postmod2.htm (accessed February 2000).

Schell, Orville. 1999. The Jiang Zemin mystery. Review of *Tiger on the Brink: Jiang Zemin and China's New Elite*, by Bruce Gilley. *New York Review of Books* 46, no. 14 (September 23).

Schoppa, R. K. 2002. *Revolution and Its Past: Identities and Change in Modern Chinese History.* Upper Saddle River, N.J.: Prentice-Hall.

Silbergeld, J. 1999. *China into Film: Frames of Reference in Contemporary Chinese Cinema.* London: Reaktion Books.

Smith, C. J. 2000. *China in the Post-utopian Age.* Boulder, Colo.: Westview.

———. 2002a. From "Leading the masses" to "Serving the consumers"? Newspaper reporting in contemporary urban China. *Environment and Planning A* 34:1635–60.

———. 2002b. Postmodernity in new millennium China? *Asian Geographer* 21, nos. 1–2, pp. 9–32.

———. 2005a. Examining the connection between temporary migration and the spread of STDs and HIV/AIDS in China. *China Review* 5, no. 1 (spring): 9–137.

———. 2005b. The social geography of disease transmission: Migration and sexually transmitted diseases in China. *Asia Pacific Viewpoint* 46, no. 1 (April): 65–80.

Solinger, D. J. 2000. The potential for urban unrest. In *Is China Unstable?* ed. David Shambaugh. Armonk, N.Y.: M.E. Sharpe, 79–94.

———. 2002. Labour market reform and the plight of the laid-off proletariat. *China Quarterly*, 170.

———. 2003. Chinese urban jobs and the WTO. *China Journal* 49 (June): 304–26.

Spence, Jonathan D. 1996. *God's Chinese Son: The Taiping Heavenly Kingdom of Hong Xiuquan*. London: HarperCollins.

Su, X. K., and L. X. Wang. 1991. *Deathsong of the River: A Reader's Guide to the Chinese TV Series "Heshang,"* trans. R. W. Bodman and P. P. Wang. Ithaca, N.Y.: Cornell University Press.

Tang, W. F., and W. L. Parish. 2000. *Chinese Urban Life under Reform: The Changing Social Contract*. Cambridge: Cambridge University Press.

Tang, Xiaobing. 2000. *Chinese Modern: The Heroic and the Quotidian*. Durham, N.C.: Duke University Press.

Vittachi, N. 2002. China's elite getting ready to lead. *Far Eastern Economic Review*. October 4, December 5, and December 12. www.feer.com/cgi-in/prog/printeasy?id=76959 .5381178991.

Wang, E. Y. J. 1996. Samsara: Self and the crisis of visual narrative. In *Narratives of Agency: Self-Making in China, India, and Japan*, ed. W. Dissanayake. Minneapolis: University of Minnesota Press, 35–55.

Wang, Jing. 1996. *High Culture Fever: Politics, Aesthetics, and Ideology in Deng's China*. Berkeley: University of California Press.

———. 1998. *China's Avant-Garde Fiction: An Anthology*. Durham, N.C.: Duke University Press.

———. 2001. Culture as leisure and culture as capital. *Positions* 9 no. 1 (spring): 69–104.

Wang Shaoguang. 1995. The politics of private time: Changing leisure patterns in urban China. In *Urban Spaces in Contemporary China: The Potential for Autonomy and Community in Post-Mao China*, ed. D. S. Davis et al. Washington, D.C.: Woodrow Wilson Center Press, 149.

Wang Shuo. 2000. *Please Don't Call Me Human*, trans. Howard Goldblatt. New York: Hyperion East.

Weber, I. 2002. Shanghai baby: Negotiating youth self-identity in urban China. *Social Identities* 8 (2): 347–68.

White, G. 1996. The dynamics of civil society in post-Mao China. In *The Individual and the State in China*, ed. B. Hook. Oxford: Clarendon, 196–221.

Zha, Jianying. 1995. *China Pop: How Soap Operas, Tabloids, and Bestsellers Are Transforming a Culture*. New York: New Press.

———. 1997. China's popular culture in the 1990s. In *China Briefing: The Contradictions of Change*, ed. W. A. Joseph. Armonk, N.Y.: M.E. Sharpe, 109–50.

Zhang, X. D. 1997. *Chinese Modernism in the Era of Reforms: Cultural Fever, Avant-Garde Fiction, and the New Chinese Cinema*. Durham, N.C.: Duke University Press.

Zhou Weihui. 2002. *Shanghai Baby*. New York: Pocket Books.

Zweig, D. 2002. *Internationalizing China: Domestic Interests and Global Linkages*. Ithaca, N.Y.: Cornell University Press.

CHAPTER 7

A Preface to China's Changing Economic Geography

Central Planning, State Policy, and the Transition to a Market and Global Economy

China, the world's most populous country, today has one of the world largest economies as well. After several centuries of stagnant or slow economic growth, China in the twentieth century ushered in a cataclysmic period of revolution, strife, and far-reaching and radical political change. Finally, after a time of intense internal struggle and the death of party chairman Mao Zedong in 1976, more moderate leadership emerged and reform of the economy soon followed.

After twenty-seven years of erratic political change and sometimes chaotic economic performance during the Maoist period (1949–1976), China changed dramatically once its leaders decided at the Eleventh Communist Party Congress in 1977 to proceed with economic reforms and to allow market incentives to help stimulate economic growth. In 1977 at the beginning of these economic reforms, the size of China's economy as seen in its gross domestic product (GDP) was approximately US$38.6 billion (National Bureau of Statistics 2002). By the year 2003 this had increased almost fortyfold to US$1.4 trillion, and the per capita GDP had increased twenty-six times to approximately US$1,100 (see table 7.1 [in yuan]).[1] This kind of remarkable economic growth has improved and transformed profoundly the lives of hundreds of millions of Chinese while also altering dramatically the landscape of city and countryside and reorienting the regional framework of production and distribution.

The remarkable renaissance and rise of China as a global as well as regional economic engine must be considered and examined in the context of a rapidly changing world economic system based on new technologies of production and distribution that both lead to and reflect new spatialities in the framework of China's economic geography. These new spatialities, as Dicken (2003) describes them, reflect the distinctive locational and functional elements of production in an economic system that itself is shifting in response to the ebb and flow of relationships between the state and enterprise as seen on a variety of levels and scales.

In the case of China, once the reforms of the late 1970s and 1980s began to take hold, a fundamental spatial redeployment of production and distribution was set in motion. New economic regions emerged that sought to link China's new production centers, which were geared toward the global exchange economy, as the country began to alter its economy from a command and direct system to one that was designed

Table 7.1. China: Growth in Gross Domestic Product, 1952–2003 (Current Prices)

	GDP 100M (Yuan)	GDP/Per Capita (Yuan)
1952	679.0	119
1960	1,457.0	218
1970	2,252.7	275
1975	2,997.3	327
1977	3,201.9	339
1978	3,624.1	379
1980	4,517.8	460
1985	8,964.4	855
1990	18,547.9	1,634
1995	58,478.1	4,854
2000	89,442.2	7,084
2001	95,933.3	7,543
2002	107,640.0	8,280
2003	115,920.0	8,916

Note: U.S. dollars converted at the rate of 8.28 yuan/US$1 from 1998 to 2005. In mid-2005 China's government allowed a modest increase in the value of the yuan relative to other major currencies. In May 2006 the rate was approximately 8 yuan/US$1.
Source: National Bureau of Statistics 2004.

to employ market forces and incentives to advance the rate of economic growth and accelerate trade with the global trading system. These new policies and the resultant economic production coincided with extraordinary advances in technology both in production and in transportation and logistics. Some of these transport and shipping systems were already in place in Hong Kong, for example, in what was emerging as one of the world's largest container ports, and China moved quickly to take advantage of the existing modern transport infrastructure in the Pearl River Delta region. In retrospect, it is no surprise that the first new Special Economic Zones (SEZs) were all located in that region, and that these have served as a model for China's spatial reorientation from interior China to the coast as the country reorganizes its regional and distribution focus toward a rapidly growing global economic system.

STRUCTURAL SHIFT AND SPATIAL OUTCOMES

Structural shift or change of China's economy was put in motion during the early stages of communist rule in 1952. However, the pace of the change was muted and modest owing to erratic policies, political events, and related economic performance. This is evident in the slow pace of the shift in farm workers to nonfarm activities in the period 1952–1975 (see table 7.2). The reforms of 1978 accelerated the structural shift. This shift may be tracked in two simple ways. One way is to consider the structure of production or output by comparing the percentage share of production attributed to different sectors of the economy. A glance at table 7.3a indicates a continuing decline in the share of the value of output accounted for in the primary sector, mainly agriculture, of the economy since 1985, to the point where this sector accounted for only 14.6 percent

Table 7.2. China's National and Agriculture Labor Force, 1952–2003

Year	Population (Millions)	National Labor Force[a] (Millions)	Agricultural Labor Force[b] (Millions)	(%)	Value of Output of Sector (% Share of GDP) Primary	Secondary	Tertiary
1952	574.82	207.29	173.17	83.5	50.5	20.9	28.6
1957	646.53	237.71	193.09	81.2	40.3	29.7	30.1
1975	924.20	381.68	294.56	77.2	32.4	45.7	21.9
1978	962.59	401.52	283.18	70.5	28.1	48.2	23.7
1980	987.05	423.61	291.22	68.7	30.1	48.5	21.4
1985	1,058.51	498.73	311.30	62.4	28.4	43.1	28.5
1990	1,143.33	647.49	389.14	60.1	27.1	41.6	31.3
1995	1,211.21	680.65	355.30	52.2	20.5	48.8	30.7
1999	1,259.09	713.94	357.68	50.1	17.6	49.4	33.0
2000	1,265.83	720.85	360.43	50.0	16.4	50.2	33.4
2001	1,276.27	730.25	365.13	50.0	15.2	51.1	33.6
2002	1,284.50	737.25	368.70	50.0	15.3	50.4	34.3
2003	1,292.30	744.32	365.46	49.1	14.6	52.2	33.2

[a]all individuals employed or self-employed in urban or rural areas
[b]all individuals working in agriculture, forestry, animal husbandry, and fisheries
Source: National Bureau of Statistics 2004.

of the value of China's total production by 2003. Paradoxically, almost half of China's employed population continues to work in this sector (see table 7.3b and figure 7.1), a matter that will be taken up later in this chapter as we discuss the importance of the primary sector of the economy in absorbing labor.

While the value of agricultural production as a share of total production has declined steadily, there has been significant growth in both the secondary and tertiary sector shares in their contribution to the value of total output, and the secondary sector, led by manufacturing, now accounts for more than half the total value (52.2 percent). This will not come as a surprise to anyone who has been following China's economy in recent

Table 7.3a. China's Structure of Production, 1985–2003 (% Share of Output)

Economic Sector	1985	1990	2000	2001	2003
Primary	28.4	27.1	20.5	15.2	14.6
Secondary	43.1	41.6	48.8	51.1	52.2
Tertiary	28.5	31.3	30.7	33.6	33.2

Source: National Bureau of Statistics 2004.

Table 7.3b. China's Employment Structure, 1985–2003 (% Share of Output)

Economic Sector	1985	1990	2000	2001	2003
Primary	62.4	60.1	50.0	50.0	49.1
Secondary	20.9	21.4	22.5	22.3	21.6
Tertiary	16.7	18.5	27.5	27.7	29.3

Source: National Bureau of Statistics 2004.

Percent of labor force

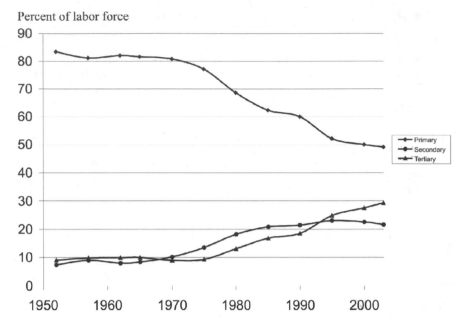

Figure 7.1. China's Employment by Sector, 1952–2003. **Source:** National Bureau of Statistics 2004

years, or indeed anyone who shops in a Wal-Mart or Target store. China has become over the last decade the manufacturing center of the world for a host of products, initially producing low-value consumer goods such as textiles and garments, shoes, sporting goods and equipment, small tools and hardware items, lamps, fans, and light fixtures.

Increasingly, however, the complexity, value, and sophistication of these products has increased, as China attracts more investment from abroad to take advantage of the country's low-cost and relatively productive labor by setting up manufacturing plants. Thus computers and peripherals and a large array of electronic products are being increasingly produced in China, along with auto parts and equipment. Auto assembly plants of many global firms based in major industrial countries such as the United States, Germany, and Japan are rapidly expanding their production in what is increasingly being perceived as the world's most rapidly developing automobile market. This outsourcing of manufacturing came initially from China's nearby neighbors such as Hong Kong and Taiwan, but more recently it has come from Korea, Thailand, Japan, Mexico, and the United States. China's tertiary or service sector has also grown and now accounts for roughly one-third of the value of its production, and the trend can be expected to continue as the economy grows and matures to the point where producer services increase in importance relative to other activities.

By any standard this growth and structural shift is a remarkable accomplishment and has had the effect of transforming the lives and well-being of hundreds of millions of China's citizens. The number of citizens in China who have been pulled out of abject poverty is startling, and may be in the tens if not hundreds of millions. Moreover, the Chinese worker's ability to seek new employment and to shift locations to where the jobs are has become an increasingly important part of the evolving economic and social scene in contemporary China. At the same time, it is certainly true that this new wealth and economic growth has not been shared equally among China's people or its regions.

The Chinese government's decision in the late 1970s to introduce far-reaching economic reforms had an especially dramatic effect on the coastal regions of China, as noted, where incomes have grown rapidly and the cityscapes have come to resemble those in Japan and Korea. In addition to these changes in the structure and growth of the economy, there have also been significant, related outcomes in the geography of this economic growth and change.

IS CHINA'S ECONOMIC GROWTH AND TRANSITION DIFFERENT?

It is the goal of this chapter to examine and explain the character of China's recent remarkable economic growth, to describe and provide insight into the spatial changes and outcomes related to this economic growth—that is, China's changing economic geography—and to examine the various scales on which this has occurred. As with so many other aspects of change in China, the story of this economic change must be viewed in the context of political change and within an evolving framework of policy and the implementation of that policy at the level of the central state, of the larger regions (such as the provinces), and perhaps most significantly, at the local level. All of these levels and scales matter, but to local people, it is perhaps what is happening in their city, town, or neighborhood that matters most. It is at this level that life is lived and business is done. In this chapter, we shall try to include discussion of economic change at all of these levels and on all of these scales.

One of the more challenging yet intriguing issues in pondering China's economic growth and geography in the twenty-first century is the lack of an adequate theoretical framework for examining and analyzing the processes of Asian economic growth and change. As Yeung and Lin (2003) have discussed, mainstream economic geographers have sadly ignored for the most part the remarkable economic advance that has occurred in Asia in the last quarter century, thus leaving a kind of conceptual vacuum in which those interested in understanding the processes of Asian economic advance, especially in spatial terms, have had to use conventional, theoretical "lenses" derived from Western experience. Yeung and Lin do note the recent emergence of what may be called China's economic transition theory, although they argue it has not been extended into economic geography studies of Asia.

In this chapter we use Western conceptual approaches to economic change, such as the conventional notion of structural shift in an economy, as well as the idea of comparative advantage and regional specialization of production. The reader should keep in mind this conceptual approach and perhaps ask if this is the best and most appropriate means of seeking to understand recent change in China.

China's economic advance continues in a manner that has had and is likely to continue to have an enormous impact on the lives not only of the Chinese but of all people in the world. China's immense size makes it a key player on the global stage, and as its economy grows, the impact of China's size will become ever clearer to people everywhere. One example is China's increasing participation in various international organizations such as the UN and its various subagencies. China's entry into the World Trade Organization (WTO) in 2002 provides the most striking illustration of international recognition of China's growing economic power and its role as a key player in the world economy. The enormous growth in China's trade and its activity as an export powerhouse, especially its enormous export surplus with the United States, testifies to its might. This huge trade surplus has allowed China to accumulate more than US$800 billion in foreign currency reserves, a situation that makes China a key player and not far behind Japan in its impact on global capital markets and the world economy. At the same time, such a trade imbalance is becoming an increasingly contentious political problem between the United States and China.

As the twenty-first century unfolds, China's role as a powerful economic engine as well as a major political and military force will become increasingly evident. Its economic role will be seen in its commercial power as market, producer, and, more recently, investor; in its industrial role as manufacturer and innovator; and in its service role as collector, distributor, and processor of goods, services, and information. China's economic power is growing, and the next half century will likely witness an extraordinary increase in the commercial and industrial force exerted by this rising power.

Chinese Socialism and Central Planning

Following a successful communist revolution in 1949, China emerged as a Marxist state and brought with it a radical new vision for the planning and operating of its national economy. Its model at the time was the Soviet Union, which had evolved a highly centralized mode of economic operation. In this model, the central state, through a State Council and various ministries, created a centrally planned economic system in which bureaucrats in central offices drew up plans for allocating resources, thereby determining the structure of economic production as well as the location of that production.

Such planning and production could not be achieved overnight, so a phased approach was adopted, but clearly the ultimate goal was full ownership of the means of production by the state, by which the state would centrally plan and direct the economic system for the entire nation. As Eckstein (1977) explained in his study of the Chinese economy, the Chinese Communist Party (CCP) leadership in 1949 initially had three main options in operating China's economy following the successful 1949 revolution: (1) a free market option, in which prices would be set and resource allocations would be made based on market forces in equilibrium, more or less based on supply and demand for products; (2) a market socialism option, wherein the state would own and control the means of production and provide central planning, but would allow some other pricing system based on market forces to determine the allocation of some resources or segments of the economy; and (3) a command economy option, in which the allocation of goods, services, and factors of production would all be determined by central planners (party bureaucrats) through an administrative bureaucratic apparatus rather than by market forces. As we shall see in a brief chronological survey of actual events, all three of the options have been in play at various times during the more than half century of communist rule in the People's Republic of China (PRC).

CHRONOLOGY OF PLANNING

Following a brief period of rebuilding and restoration of economic production in the early 1950s, the leadership of the Chinese central state began to move toward a centrally planned model, based largely on the Soviet approach to economic planning. In 1953, the first Five-Year Plan was introduced with the trappings of a command economy in which the central state, through its State Council and State Planning Commission and various ministries and bureaus, planned and organized production, allocated resources to support this production, and began to set prices.

Initially things went reasonably well owing to good weather and a surge in farm production. The communist revolution appeared to have been a good thing, and conditions were improving for many people, most of whom lived in rural areas. This initial success emboldened the communist leadership and especially Party Chairman Mao Zedong to seek more radical approaches to advancing the cause of socialist egalitarianism in Marxist China. Beginning in late 1957 and proceeding rapidly thereafter, Mao promoted radical new policies in an attempt to move Chinese society to the left to fulfill his vision of a Marxist revolution, and to move away from what he perceived to be the more conservative, technocratic approaches to economic growth that other senior leaders such as Liu Shaoqi were advancing. In this way, China's economic planning shifted to the Great Leap Forward, a mass social and political movement that sought to propel China to a stage of economic production that would rival that of Great Britain, and to do this very rapidly as a demonstration of the power of a people's revolution.

The Great Leap Forward involved a sharp advance to full socialism in which all of the means of private production were eliminated, including the private plots and farm animals that the Chinese peasants had been allowed to keep. It also involved the formation of communes in rural areas in which all farming was done in teams and brigades, and wherein the labor and output were shared by all based on their need as well as, or perhaps rather than, their effort. In addition, production of all kinds of locally needed goods such as farm machines, iron, cement, and fertilizer was to take place locally, regardless of local conditions and realities of comparative advantage. In some cases, actual output of these locally produced goods increased, but the quality of the products was frequently so poor that they could not be used and were therefore discarded. Moreover, when the incentives of private plots and animals had been removed, farm production collapsed owing to the inability of the peasants to grow crops and husband animals for themselves and their families. For example, farm pigs had formerly been an important source of organic manure and mulching materials in the Chinese countryside, and much of this was lost with the disappearance of the peasants' pigs and other farm animals. A severe famine ensued (see chapter 5), and as many as 30 million people starved to death in what can only be described as one of the great catastrophes of the twentieth century. This was in fact a policy-induced famine of enormous proportions and one of the greatest human cataclysms of the socialist period.

Chairman Mao was heavily criticized by other top leaders in China, and the Communist Party Central Committee moved away from the most radical aspects of this leap to socialism. It allowed some restoration of private plots and animals in an attempt to restore farm and food production and to avert a more serious crisis. Yet Mao was not finished, and by 1964 he set about galvanizing the young people of China to counteract what he regarded as the too-conservative members of the CCP and the educated elites of the party, especially those in the party leadership who opposed his idea of continuing revolution. In 1965, in a mass movement involving millions of young people, Mao sought to gain firm control of the CCP by unleashing these young people to renew the revolution through a program known as the Great Proletarian Cultural Revolution, or simply, the Cultural Revolution.

Massive social protests and chaos ensued, and the country was plunged into disarray as schools and universities closed, ports were shut down, and factories boarded up. In this movement, the peasants were left alone, although many urban elites and intellectuals were sent to rural areas for "thought reform" and "rehabilitation." The education of a generation of students was interrupted, and the country's planned economic production was seriously disrupted.

This event also coincided with geopolitical circumstances that pitted China against the United States during the Vietnam War, and China moved many of its new industrial enterprises into remote areas of the interior, places such as Sichuan that were believed to be less vulnerable to attack from the coast. This policy of locating new industries away from the coastal regions and into the deep interior for security reasons was termed the *san xian*, or Third Line, a reference to the movement away from an earlier and more vulnerable coastal First Line (Naughton 1988; Cannon 1990). While such industries may have been more secure against external attack, the irrationality of their location relative to markets and shipping points created highly inflated costs for their products on the way to markets and thus represented an enormous misallocation of scarce capital and resources based on a perceived and perhaps unrealistic appraisal of the security threat.

The more radical phases of the Cultural Revolution began to subside by 1971, but an actual shift to reforms and a restructuring of China's economy did not begin until after Mao's death in 1976, an event that was followed by a leadership succession struggle that culminated in the arrest of Mao's wife, the infamous Jiang Qing, and her radical cronies in 1977. Shortly thereafter, a new group of leaders led by Deng Xiaoping took over and adopted major reform policies for the economy at the Eleventh Communist Party Congress.

In 1978, far-reaching reforms were therefore put in motion that would lead to a remarkable shift in the manner in which China's economy was planned and operated. It is these reforms that have led to a whole new way of doing business in China for they have sought to take advantage of market forces in allocating resources and determining prices. Yet the Chinese government was careful to implement the reforms gradually, first in rural areas and then in the cities and towns with their extensive network of state-owned enterprises (SOEs). Moreover, it proceeded differently in different regions of the country, because some regions responded to the use of market forces much more readily and vigorously than others.

New Economic Reforms

Much has been written about the economic reforms initiated following the death of Mao and the ascendance of the so-called second generation of leaders assembled around paramount leader Deng Xiaoping. They were initially implemented in agriculture through a responsibility system of household production (see chapter 8), and the effect of this system was to return the farm land to the farmers through leasing arrangements and to allow the farmers to take advantage of incentives on raising food-grain and cash crops as well as on related sideline activities. Output of farm products rose immediately as the farmers responded, and there was a dramatic rise in crop and animal production as well as in farm family income.

However, the new prosperity was not universal; as more enterprising farmers or those farming in more advantageous locations benefited greatly, others languished or lagged behind in the new drive to riches. In conceptualizing how these reforms were proceeding, we may refer to the three alternative systems Eckstein identified and postulate that these reforms were attempting to use aspects of a market system to rationalize the allocation of resources and to raise production based on incentives and on a regional specialization of crop production based on comparative advantage. Yet the role of the central state remained an active one, especially in the matter of continuing to levy requirements and quotas on farmers for the production of food-grain.

REFORMS EXTEND TO THE STATE SECTOR AND URBAN AREAS

In 1984 a policy decision was made to extend these reforms to the state sector of the economy and to apply them extensively within urban areas. However this was not intended as a full-blown reform, and it was meant to take effect once the basic production quotas of the SOEs had been met by what were still enterprises of the central state. The SOEs, however, had serious problems. First, such enterprises typically had large numbers of redundant employees, and their efficiency and productivity was low. Many also had enormous debts to state banks or credit institutions, and this debt was increasing, as was long-term financial liability. There was little likelihood that these debts would ever be paid off (Lardy 1998, 2002). Moreover, during the first decade of the reforms, these SOEs continued to add substantial numbers of employees, and thus their problems of low productivity and efficiency continued, and the red ink associated with them increased (see table 7.4).

In the state sector of the economy, SOEs typically operated housing estates for their employees, provided health and hospital services, and operated schools for the children of their employees. They also had pension liabilities in their responsibility to provide housing and health services to all their employees throughout their lives. As was becoming increasingly clearer, however, and also more ominous in its long-term outlook, the prospects and fate for most of these SOEs were not sustainable. Yet in a socialist system, it is difficult to face the reality of impending financial failure when so many in the system have become accustomed to the entitlements of their jobs and positions (Lardy 1998).

Table 7.4. China's Urban and Rural Employment (in Thousands), Selected Sectors, 1952–2003

Urban Employment Year	Business Sector		
	State-Owned Enterprises (SOEs)	Collectively Owned	Individual/ Private[a]
1952	1,5800	230	8,830
1957	2,4510	6,500	1,040
1965	37,380	12,270	1,710
1975	64,260	17,720	240
1980	80,180	24,250	810
1990	103,460	35,490	6,710
1994	112,140	32,850	15,570
1996	112,440	30,160	23,290
1999	85,720	17,120	51,020*
2000	81,020	14,990	51,900*
2001	76,400	12,910	56,539*
2003	68,760	11,730	76,380*

Rural Employment Year	Business Sector	
	Town and Village Enterprises (TVEs)	Individual/Private[a] and Self-Employed
1995	128,620	35,250
1999	127,040	47,960
2000	128,200	40,730
2001	130,086	38,160
2003	135,730	40,140

[a]includes individual-, private-, and foreign-funded sources
*includes private corporations of various types as well as foreign-invested units
Source: National Bureau of Statistics 2004.

REFORMS AND SPATIAL REDEPLOYMENT

In parallel with the growing problems of the SOEs, the CCP had decided to accelerate economic growth in coastal areas and to seek to take advantage of the global marketplace. Thus, locations such as the Pearl River Delta, which is proximate to Hong Kong, were allowed to establish SEZs, where the more rigid rules of the central state would be relaxed to encourage foreign investors to commit their resources to production facilities that would take advantage of the very low cost of Chinese labor and related positive factors in construction, land, waste removal, and transportation. At the same time, many local entrepreneurs in China took advantage of the new more relaxed rules and environment for doing business, and a number of township-village enterprises (TVEs) were created. Nominally part of the collective economy and owned by a village or township, many of these TVEs were in fact private in all but name because many were funded by private individuals but were operated under the guise of public ownership by a township or village (this is known as "wearing a red hat"). Such enterprises flourished in the more independent atmosphere of Southeast China where the entrepreneurial spirit of family

Map 7.1. Special Economic Zones (SEZs) and China's Open Coastal Cities. **Source:** Modified from Cannon 1990; Marton 2000; Wei 2000

capitalism had had a long tradition of success, especially in connection with family relatives and common-surname clansmen in Southeast Asia.

The four initial SEZs (Shenzhen, Zhuhai, Shantou, and Xiamen) were successful, and other regions clamored for equal status; thus numerous other locations, including Hainan along China's coast, were quickly awarded similar status (see map 7.1). A kind of free-wheeling, capitalist-oriented market socialism spread to other coastal cities. Some developed their own special style and set of products that were distinctive, and the Wenzhou model, so named for a small city on the coast of Zhejiang, became well-known for its independent mode of operation as well as its remarkable success. Clearly a major spatial reordering with a strong coastal orientation of production and distribution was underway, and it was leading China toward much closer links to the global economy.

GROWING REGIONAL DISPARITIES AND SOCIAL UNREST

Yet all was not well. As the success of many of the TVEs grew, the economy heated up to a point of almost unsustainable growth. Moreover, there were now rapidly growing disparities between those who were earning lots of money and those who were falling behind. Inevitably, the new wealth quickly attracted the attention of local and higher officials, who insisted on their share of the loot in order to approve of virtually any transaction. Thus, levels of corruption throughout the bureaucracy grew to egregious heights, and the problem of unequal incomes became more obvious. Economic growth was palpable, and the prosperity it brought was obvious, but so too was the greed of some officials and of those who were paying the bribes. In an emerging new spatiality of production and consumption, regional disparities in income were also becoming increasingly apparent between urban and rural areas as well as between coastal and more remote interior areas.

In the spring of 1989, a broad movement erupted among students and young people that was a mixture of efforts to liberalize the politics of China and to create a society that shared its wealth in a more equitable and fairer way. In fact, a precedent for this movement was the May Fourth Movement of 1919, a mass movement led by patriotic students and intellectuals that had the goal and ideal of rejecting foreign imperialism and Japanese intrusion into China while promoting a strong, modern, and democratic China (Fairbank 1992). It is difficult to pinpoint precisely the causes and objectives of the 1989 movement, yet clearly one of the key elements of dissatisfaction was a result of the intolerable levels of corruption and greed that permeated Chinese society and the bureaucracy. The movement resulted in a brief uprising in Tiananmen Square, Beijing, with a subsequent crushing of the uprising by the People's Liberation Army on June 4, 1989. International outrage followed, and there was a reduction in trade and international transactions that reduced the rate of economic growth in China. Political repression came next, and China entered a period of relative calm (Liang, Nathan, and Link 2001).

Three years later, Deng Xiaoping made his epic trip to South China during which he unleashed a new wave of relaxed rules and proclaimed that to get rich was good and that the accelerated model of market socialism as practiced in the Pearl River Delta was an admirable thing for China. A modern emperor, in so many words, had put his imprimatur on an open, relatively unrestricted, aggressive, and market-oriented approach to doing business. It was now OK to be a capitalist, although this was described as "socialism with Chinese characteristics."

Deng Xiaoping's trip also validated the value of regional location vis-à-vis the Pearl River Delta and the various scales at which the new production and ties to the global economy were taking place and being formed. China is a vast spatial system, and its different regions were advancing under the new rules at different speeds and by building on different sets of comparative advantages in restructuring their production and distribution systems. Hong Kong and its already established networks for shipping and trading gave the Pearl River Delta an early start and an enormous advantage. Money from overseas Chinese in Southeast Asia as well as Hong Kong and Taiwan was flowing in and being invested in factories producing consumer goods for the domestic and foreign markets. Local and regional Chinese economies were booming as they began to reshape themselves.

Deng Xiaoping's southern trip also resulted in a new wave of reforms, beginning in 1993, and these are the policies that have continued to the present. In conceptualizing this growth since 1993, it is useful to invoke the analysis of Barry Naughton (1995), who has described a kind of "dual-track" system and approach that has sought to maintain some elements of traditional central planning, especially in the energy and key infrastructure sectors, while simultaneously encouraging and allowing the full impetus of market forces to propel rapid economic growth and to assist in making SOEs more efficient. China's recent efforts have placed the most emphasis on the market track, in what Naughton and others have described as "growing out of the Plan."

SIGNIFICANCE OF EMPLOYMENT GROWTH, AND ESTABLISHING THE MARKET ECONOMY

One of the significant components of the approach of growing out of the Plan is to use the private sector to offset job losses in the state sector of the economy as it is restructured and downsized, and to make creation of new jobs one of the highest priorities of the central state. Arguably then, job creation might be seen as a key government policy goal throughout the reform period. In fact, it could be seen as the key policy goal, given its link to social and political stability and the maintenance of public order as a high priority of the central state. As the reforms proceeded—and it can be argued that they became more flexible in their use of market approaches with the transition to more pragmatic CCP leadership—the role of the private sector grew and became an increasingly more important driving force in labor absorption. In the early reforms of the late 1970s and early 1980s, private enterprise and private entrepreneurs (*geti hu*) were allowed into the marketplace; however, they were subject to many rules. As Han and Pannell (1999) explain, there developed a pattern of geography from the manner in which rules and acceptance of private sector enterprise spread over China, and some areas of the country were much more receptive to the use and growth of the private market economy than others. Especially prominent among the faster and steadier promoters of private enterprise were the coastal provinces from Jiangsu south, as well as some border areas such as Inner Mongolia and Xinjiang.

Yet even while the central state was liberalizing policy on private workers during the first two decades of economic reform, significant growth in employment continued in SOEs, as the central state strove to ensure employment for the large number of new workers entering the marketplace each year. From 1980 to 1994 there was an increase of more than 30 million workers in SOEs even after new policies in the early 1990s had been put in place to reduce such employment (see table 7.4). It was only after 1996 that the central state and Premier Zhu Rongji got serious about reforming the SOEs and reducing the redundant employees in these units. Thereafter there began a severe reduction, and within four years more than 30 million workers had been cut from the state sector in urban areas.

The pattern of employment and the balance between the state and the private sector in China, however, is complex and varied. For example, there is also the collective sector of the economy, and in rural areas the TVEs have been a key component in accounting for rural employment (see table 7.4). In urban areas up to the mid-1990s, the collective sector grew substantially, but began to shrink markedly thereafter. Meanwhile, the individual private sector grew rapidly during the 1990s as the rules governing it became increasingly flexible and controls on its activities were eased (see table 7.4). By the year 2000, private employment, including various corporate and foreign enterprises in urban areas, had reached more than 50 million, and it was clear that this was a crucial element in the employment equation for China's economic growth and social stability.

Job creation in rural areas also witnessed substantial growth in the private sector; moreover, it was clear that many of the jobs in what were described as TVEs were in fact disguised private jobs. Much private and indeed foreign investment was cloaked under the guise of collective ownership to give it greater political protection in case of a reversal of state policy and a reversion to the more rigorous socialist policies of the past. Investors were ensuring that they would be protected in the event of a shift in political currents that might take China back to a more orthodox period of socialism!

Yet it had become increasingly clear that a return to such policies was highly unlikely given the transition in government leadership to a younger group that was less ideological in outlook and more prone to pursuing policies that would work based on practice and an increased involvement with the global economy. What began in earnest with Deng Xiaoping's southern tour in 1992, and was enshrined at the Fourteenth Communist Party Congress in the same year as a key feature of the socialist market economy, came to be regarded as an increasingly liberal and friendly period for the market economy with its emphasis on individual and private commerce. Moreover, as Han and Pannell (1999) have documented, the regions of China where private economic activity was strongest also were associated with the highest rates of economic growth. This established an even stronger imperative for advancing the private economy as an engine of growth, and as one that was likely to benefit all of China through its impetus for faster growth.

Premier Zhu Rongji in his final report in 2003 at the conclusion of the ninth Five-Year Plan (in effect from 1998 to 2003) offered the following thoughts on the continuing success of the reforms and opening up of China and the establishment of a socialist market economy:

> The ownership structure was further readjusted and improved. The public sector of the economy grew stronger in the course of readjustment and reform, and efforts to diversify ways of realizing public ownership were successful. The state sector of the economy went through accelerated restructuring, and markedly enhanced its dominance and competitiveness. . . . The collective economy in urban and rural areas made new headway. The joint-stock company sector of the economy expanded continuously. Individually-owned businesses, private enterprises and other non-public sectors of the economy developed fairly fast and played an important role in stimulating economic growth, creating more jobs, invigorating the market and expanding exports. (Premier Zhu 2003, 2)

Premier Zhu went on to applaud the success of the market economy in propelling China's economic growth through its role in allocating resources and in instituting price reforms in such sectors as public services, energy, and transportation. Such a testimonial from a leading technocrat of the retiring administration in 2003 set the stage for continuation of a market approach to economic growth in China, and provides a positive outlook for the continuation of economic liberalization and commitment to involvement in the global trading system. China has committed itself to a fast economic growth approach as a means of meeting its labor demands, while it continues to reduce its population growth for future posterity and prosperity.

Regional Development: Spatial Outcomes of Economic Reforms

China is an enormous country and a huge and ever-changing spatial system. This historical reality has presented its people with a continuing challenge, which its imperial system and bureaucratic structure and apparatus have struggled to counter, even as the central state has sought to control the country and keep its peripheral regions under Chinese hegemony. This has been an enduring theme in Chinese history, given the rugged surface geography of China and the many formidable physical barriers and impediments it offers to movement. Only in the twentieth century had improvements in transportation and communication advanced to the point where China truly could begin to integrate its many regions and outlying territories in an effective and meaningful manner for governance, as well as to make this territory economically contributory to the well-being of the central state. Certainly one of the key economic tactics of the socialist administration of the PRC has been to invest heavily in transportation and in this manner to better integrate the country, while also seeking to promote a more balanced regional development.

Dr. Sun Yat-sen had a plan for China's development, and he wrote of it in a book that outlined a variety of things needed to advance the country (1953). One of these was promotion of greater spatial integration through a national network of railways that would link all the provinces of China. Now many years after the publication of Dr. Sun Yat-sen's plan, the central state in its tenth Five-Year Plan is finally completing a major goal of this plan with construction of a long-planned rail link to Lhasa in Tibet, the last remaining province of China with no rail link. It is the recognition of this kind of commitment that helps us understand the enormous challenges facing China in its effort to create a fully integrated modern state and spatial system that can provide for the movement and linkage of goods, people, ideas, and innovations. This is a recent accomplishment, and indeed continues apace as China pushes ahead aggressively in building not just railroads but also a new and expanded highway network, more airports and harbors, and more power and telecommunications grids for all its people. Regional development in China, then, is in part a story of building and linking the various regions of China and of seeking to provide a scheme and means of doing this to accelerate economic growth while bringing the advantages and benefits of this growth to all citizens.

REGIONAL INTEGRATION IN CHINA'S HISTORY

Pannell (1992) has argued that we may distinguish three main periods of spatial development in China's history. The first was a traditional imperial period that lasted for many centuries but which saw China's development focused on the interior of the country, and in which typically the impetus for urban and regional growth focused on administrative functions supplemented by economic activities. Over time these economic activities increased in importance, especially with the Song dynasty (A.D. 960–1279), and these gradually assumed primacy. Yet China for most of its history has been a nation that

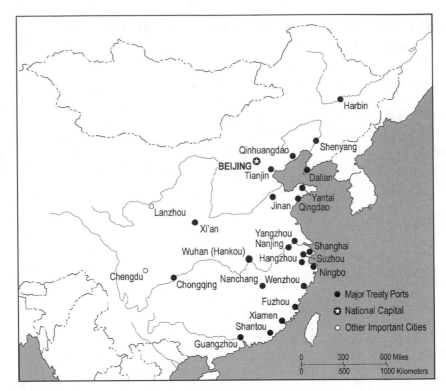

Map 7.2. Treaty Ports and Other Major Cities in China. **Source:** Modified from Murphey 1974

focused on its internal development and seemed to stress trade among its regions rather than abroad. These regions, as noted earlier, operated to some extent as discrete entities and were not always well-connected or responsive to the center, but the extent to which they were so linked to the center reflected the strength and effectiveness of the central state as a governing and functioning polity. Thus, there was a waxing and waning of the roles of China's regions and its center state over time, which paralleled the waxing and waning of dynastic authority and effectiveness (Fairbank 1992; Skinner 1977).

This began to change in the nineteenth century following the arrival of Western colonial powers and especially after the first Opium War (1839–1842) by which the British formally colonized the island of Hong Kong and expanded to a small adjacent territory. This was quickly followed by the establishment of a host of Treaty Ports that were mini-colonies, and that served as outposts of an evolving global economy that witnessed the establishment of numerous European and some Japanese colonies (see map 7.2). The function of these colonies essentially was to serve the interests of a home country through a mercantilistic system of trade in which natural products from the primary sector of the local economy were exploited and sent to the home colonizing country, which in turn sought to return low-end manufactured products to the colony and to maintain terms of trade that were skewed to enrich the colonizing country. At the same time, some modest manufacturing was established in many colonies to begin to take advantage of abundant and low-cost labor and to produce products that could be sold in the local economy but would not be a threat to the economy of the colonizing power.

What this meant for China was not only the introduction of new industrial methods and the true beginning of modern industrialization, but also a remarkable and far-reaching spatial reorientation of its economic and urban structure. In this spatial reorientation and redeployment, the most advanced, dynamic, and rapidly growing urban centers, with clusters of new industries and improved transportation, emerged in coastal or riverine locations where they could connect more easily to an emerging global trading and economic system.

The great port of Shanghai, gateway to the Chang Jiang (Yangtze River) Basin and a quarter of the Chinese population, was the epitome of this new urban center. It quickly became both symbol and archetype for the new, foreign-influenced China—admired for its dynamism and modernity, yet despised for its subservience to Western foreign "devils," and seen as a center of wealth and power that was far too "perverted" from Chinese cultural roots and ethnocentrism to be acceptable as truly Chinese. Numerous other Treaty Ports such as Canton (Guangzhou), Amoy (Xiamen), Fuzhou, Ningbo, Nanjing, Hankou (Wuhan), Qingdao, Tianjin, and Dalian followed suit and attempted to mimic Shanghai. Thus, along China's coast and greatest river were clustered the key economic centers of the late nineteenth and early twentieth centuries, for here were easy links to world shipping and the international marketplace.

Meanwhile, the vast body of China with its huge rural population was not profoundly affected, and rural life continued apace much as it had for many centuries (Murphey 1974). Unfortunately, this growing population was placing increased stress on the environment to the point that food production was hard pressed to keep up with growth, and calls for change added to the pressure to modernize. China's old regime ended, a new era began with the creation of the Chinese Republic, soon followed by civil war, World War II, and a communist victory in 1949. The communist victory would lead to a significant spatial reorientation and a new effort to redirect development to the interior.

Regional Development in China

In 1949 when the Communists assumed power, Mao Zedong and the new leadership sought to shift the emphasis away from the coast and back to China's interior, the traditional regions of the country's seats of power. This was also an effort to reduce the power and influence of centers of capitalism and global or colonial influence. Thus, cities like Shanghai were seen as sources of funding to be exploited so that capital could be transferred to other cities and regions, and in this way to fulfill the promise of a nationalist revolution that would restore traditional centers of development and return China to its earlier focus on interior places and development (Wu 1967).

The extensive literature on regional policy and development in China during the first two and half decades of socialist rule, 1949–1976, clearly indicates this focus on restoring more regional balance through the transfer of investment to interior locations (see for example Wei [2000] for a good review of this literature). At the same time, the communist regime built on industrial bases in places like the Northeast where the earlier investments of Japanese colonialists in a dense transport network linking a cluster of industrial cities had accelerated the rate of industrial production in China. Other centers like Beijing were supposed to become both industrial and administrative in function to justify their proper role in a people's republic as "producer" rather than "consumer" cities. The putative "consumer" role—that had previously prevailed in such capitalist outposts as Shanghai and Canton, both former Treaty Ports and trading centers—was seen as evil.

As noted earlier, this regional policy was accelerated by so-called Third Front industrial development during the Vietnam War era, when key industries and new rail lines were constructed in the deep Chinese interior in such provinces as Sichuan, Guizhou, and Yunnan to protect them from possible attack from the coast or from the Soviet Union. While such investments may appear irrational in pure economic terms owing to their distance from appropriate market centers and low-cost shipping locations, they did have the effect of stimulating development in China's interior and acted as an impetus to provide some corrective to existing regional inequalities.

A number of scholars have written extensively on regional development in China, and there have been a variety of opinions offered as to the trajectory and effectiveness of regional development policy during the last half century in remediating spatial inequalities in income and well-being (Fan 1995; Marton 2000; Lin 2000). Wei (2000) has summarized well the conceptual approaches and contrasted them in the context of mainstream neoclassical theory on regional development and economic growth. As he notes, while there have been varying opinions, the consensus viewpoint suggests that during the Maoist years there appeared to be a pattern of declining regional inequality as the state directed more of its investment to the interior. After the beginning of the reform period in 1978, however, the pattern was reversed, and there is now more evidence of a growing regional inequality as the coastal regions benefit from state policy to advance their growth. The idea in China, in part derived from Western economic theory, is that the coastal regions should be allowed to grow faster owing to their locational advantages and connections to the global economy. Theoretically, as Wei points out, this should follow more or less an inverted-U model of regional development, with the idea of a spatial "trickle down," by which "some regions advance that others may follow"—if put in a more benign context (see also Veeck 1991). How well this is working in China is open to debate, but there is substantial evidence of very rapid growth in some, if not all, of the coastal provinces. Per capita income figures continue to provide a quick regional descriptive picture of this reality (see map 7.3).

Promotion of coastal development was first enacted in policies on the establishment of SEZs in the 1970s, and SEZs have since spread from the Southeast to other coastal provinces and then into interior locations. China in its seventh Five-Year Plan in 1986 laid out a regional scheme that divided the country into three main regions—coastal, central, and western—and these have remained a convenient if sometimes difficult-to-interpret mechanism for describing the manner in which the country has been allowed to develop (see map 7.4). Wei (2000) in his study tracked and mapped both per capita GDP as well as growth in GDP in the provinces. He concluded that while there were

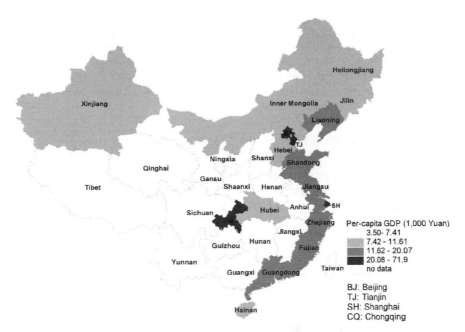

Map 7.3. China's Per Capita GDP, 2003

Per-capita GDP (1,000 Yuan)
- 3.50- 7.41
- 7.42 - 11.61
- 11.62 - 20.07
- 20.08 - 71.9
- no data

BJ: Beijing
TJ: Tianjin
SH: Shanghai
CQ: Chongqing

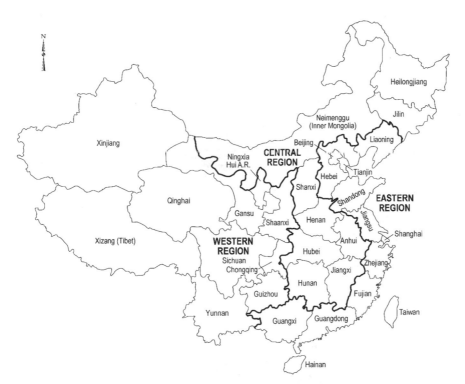

Map 7.4. China's Regional Scheme for National Development. ***Source:*** Wei 2000, as derived from Chinese official sources

sporadic investments in the interior provinces for various reasons such as security or to promote industrialization during the 1950s, there was a decrease in regional inequalities. In the 1960s and 1970s, however, while there was some industrial investment owing to Third Front development, the impact was spotty, many of the interior provinces did not benefit, and regional inequalities increased.

With the recognition of a new regional scheme in 1986, there was also the recognition that a greater policy commitment to the coastal regions would result in these advancing faster than the interior provinces. Yet this was considered appropriate because China now accepted the use of market mechanisms—such as the principle of comparative advantage and the role of regional specialization of production—that were likely to favor the coastal regions. The regional pattern of growth and well-being quickly revealed much more rapid development in the coastal areas, especially of the Southeast but also in Zhejiang, Jiangsu, Shanghai, and Shandong (Cartier 2001). As a result of complaints from other regions and with a concern for satisfying other regional interests, the regulations on foreign investment and other incentives for regional growth were modified. This allowed for faster growth in the interior provinces, with a special focus on remote border regions such as Xinjiang (perhaps for geopolitical as well as economic reasons). These steps appear to have had some success, for per capita income in Xinjiang has grown rapidly (see map 7.3). Yet this may also reflect rapid growth of the Han Chinese population in that region, especially in the industrial centers with their focus on oil and gas development.

As a spatially uneven pattern of development evolved and disparities in regional income and well-being became increasingly visible, the issue of social and political stability in interior regions became more serious. Owing to this concern, by the late 1990s there were increasing calls to develop the western regions of China, and indeed a commitment to increased funding emerged (Loughlin and Pannell 2001). In March 2003 at the Tenth National People's Congress, Premier Zhu Rongji in his main report on the work of the government gave a review of the program to develop the western region.

> Over the past three years since the introduction of the western development strategy, the government has given a powerful push to the region's development by increasing investment, stepping up transfer payments and introducing preferential fiscal and taxation policies. Work was begun on 36 new key projects, which called for a total investment of over 600 billion yuan. (Premier Zhu 2003, 2)

While it is clear that a much intensified effort has been made to create a more spatially balanced development policy in recent years, the data continue to demonstrate the enormous advantage of the coastal provinces as seen in virtually all indicators of well-being. Moreover, despite efforts to counter this as described above, the disparity is already great, and the advantages of these coastal locations so linked to world trading and financial systems is only likely to intensify.

Another way to judge the enormous and growing power of the coastal provinces is to note the migration streams in China and to see where these migrants are going. While there is cross-migration throughout the country, the main migration streams are from the interior provinces, such as Sichuan, to the east and especially to the dynamic coastal provinces and cities where the jobs in manufacturing, construction, and service trades are located (Fan 2005). These regions are powerful magnets and will no doubt continue to be so for the foreseeable future as growth regions that represent the leading edge of China's fast economic growth and dynamic structural transformation.

Trade and China's Future Economic Growth

China's trade involves both domestic and international trade, and for much of China's history, domestic trade among the various but sometimes spatially discrete and functionally separate regions of the country made up the great bulk of trade and the exchange of goods and money. As Pannell and Ma (1983) note, domestic trade was traditionally composed of both local and regional exchange, and the main exchange of goods was at the local level where peasants and petty merchants traded commodities for tools, clothing, and other needed items, virtually all of which were derived from or related to the rural economy. Regional exchange involved the movement of grain from the grain-surplus regions of Central China to political control centers of the North, as one key example, but there were many patterns of movement of bulk commodities drawn from the primary sector along with selected flows of precious goods, salt, and even money. Such flows, however, had little effect on the daily lives of the peasants who made up most of China's population.

Foreign trade for most of China's history was very limited and involved the sale and export of costly goods such as silk, porcelains, fine handicrafts, and teas that were much in demand outside China. China's traditional posture, as noted above and in chapters 3 and 4, was one focused on internal development, and for much of its history it was largely closed to foreigners and to trade. China took the position for much of its history that it did not need foreign products. Western interest in China, however, began early and in earnest as explorers and traders from Europe penetrated beyond South and Southeast Asia, and the Portuguese set up a small enclave on the southeast coast of the Pearl River estuary at Macao as early as 1557. Trading with czarist Russia began in the seventeenth century, but all of this trade was regulated, and the Chinese continued to seek to control its trade and contact with the West and to keep foreigners out. In South China, a guild system, the *cohong*, was established at Canton to oversee and control this trade, and it worked reasonably well as a regulating and control mechanism that tightly restricted the access of Western traders.

The British, who were very interested in the China trade and who were looking for something to sell China to help pay for the Chinese goods that were increasingly in demand in Britain and Europe, seized on opium, grown in India, that could be purchased cheaply and sent to China where it would fetch a good price to balance the terms of trade. The Chinese resisted, and in 1839 the British initiated hostilities in the First Opium War, which led to China's defeat. This military conflict was followed by the Treaty of Nanking in 1842, a humiliation for China, that ceded the port of Hong Kong to the British and opened certain Chinese cities, designated as Treaty Ports, to foreign commercial and diplomatic activities, and in which foreigners were given immunity from Chinese laws. As foreign powers rushed to China to share in the new access, the number of these Treaty Ports expanded rapidly, and by the turn of the century they numbered almost one hundred (see map 7.2). As a result, foreign trade grew rapidly, and China began to import a variety of foreign manufactured goods as well as foodstuffs while exporting valuable commodities such as silk, tea, and other foodstuffs and goods from the rural economy. By the end of the nineteenth century, China's key trading partners were Hong Kong, Japan, the United States, and Great Britain, a pattern that to some degree remains in the early twenty-first century.

As China entered the twentieth century, its foreign trade was strongly associated with the coastal regions of the country and the Chang Jiang, and the role of foreigners with their special privileges was prominent. In part it can be argued that this was based on a mercantile pattern of trade and exchange that was established to benefit the various imperial powers that controlled the Treaty Ports. It was thus seen as both exploitative and humiliating for the Chinese. At the same time, this trade brought with it new ideas and innovations for doing business and also the beginning of new technical processes related to modern industry and production. In this sense, it assisted in China's initial steps toward the modernization and industrialization that began in the late nineteenth century and accelerated through the twentieth century.

TRADE IN CHINA AND ITS ROLE, 1949–PRESENT

Trade and especially foreign trade during the Maoist period was modest and restricted, based on the idea that a powerful socialist state should be self-reliant and not dependent on others. The principle was termed *autarky*, and it implied a strong sense of going it alone and not allowing or encouraging reliance on any other countries. Thus trade was used mainly to meet real scarcity in items that could not be produced at home. Moreover, in China local areas were supposed to be self-sufficient and were discouraged from looking outside for goods or services. Thus the principle of autarky was both a domestic and international policy. The result of this was to keep trade to a minimum, and China traded mainly with other Soviet-bloc states during the first two and a half decades of CCP control, although it maintained a considerable exchange with its colonial neighbor, the territory of Hong Kong.

In doing this, China rejected the notion of comparative advantage, with its associated outcome of regional specialization of production, among factors of production such as land, labor, capital, and technology. According to this idea, such production would allow different regions to produce the goods they could most efficiently produce and then to exchange such goods in trade; theoretically, this would benefit all producers. But after the economic reforms of 1978, China largely shifted its conceptual approach to accepting the idea that there are differences in comparative advantage that can be used to allow regional specialization of production, although a policy remains in effect that requires all regions to produce food-grain.

As early as 1972, China began to expand its trade with Western economies as its political relations improved with the United States and other countries such as Japan. Its trade began to grow from almost nothing in the mid-1970s, and China's whole concept of trade and its role in economic growth and development has shifted substantially since then. This is best seen in the rapid and almost astonishing growth of China's value of trade as a share of GDP. In the early years, it was as small as 4 percent of GDP, whereas by the early twenty-first century it had risen in value to more than 30 percent of GDP even as China's economy had grown rapidly (Lardy 2002; National Bureau of Statistics 2002). What is now clear is that China has studied the success of other East Asian nations that have used trade and especially exports to power their economic growth engines. The key model is Japan, but the examples of Taiwan and South Korea are also very compelling in demonstrating how export-driven strategies of trade, buttressed by industrial and economic growth policies, have driven rapid economic growth and development in the last three decades of the twentieth century.

VOLUME AND TRADE PARTNERS

China's foreign trade has grown extraordinarily rapidly in the last three decades. As Lardy (2002, 4) has stated, no other country has increased its role in the global economy so rapidly as has China in recent years. This is illustrated dramatically in table 7.5, which provides data on the growth in China's total trade from 1978 (US$20.6 billion) to 2003 when the total reached US$850.9 billion, an increase of more than fortyfold. Lardy further notes that China had increased its share of world trade to the point where it was the seventh-largest trading nation in the world in 2000. This is a remarkable achievement that affirms the claim made above that China has indeed elected to use an export-driven model of economic growth to propel its development as it enters the twenty-first century. Only in one of the last fifteen years has there been a deficit in

Table 7.5. China's Total Value of Imports and Exports, 1978–2003 (in Billions US$)

Year	Total Imports and Exports	Total Exports (FOB)	Total Imports (CIF)	Balance
1978	20.64	9.75	10.89	−1.14
1980	38.14	18.12	20.02	−1.90
1985	69.60	27.35	42.25	−14.90
1990	115.44	62.09	53.35	8.74
1991	135.63	71.84	63.79	8.05
1992	165.53	84.94	80.59	4.35
1993	195.70	91.74	103.96	−12.22
1994	236.62	121.01	115.61	5.40
1995	280.86	148.78	132.08	16.70
1996	289.88	151.05	138.83	12.22
1997	325.16	182.79	142.37	40.42
1998	323.95	183.71	140.24	43.47
1999	360.63	194.93	165.70	29.23
2000	474.29	249.20	225.09	24.11
2001	509.76	266.15	243.61	22.54
2002	620.77	325.59	295.17	30.43
2003	850.99	438.23	412.76	25.47

Source: National Bureau of Statistics 2004.

Table 7.6. China's Foreign Trade with Key Trading Partners, 2003 (US$)

	Exports	Imports	Total
Japan	59,422,600,000	74,150,800,000	133,573,400,000
United States	92,633,200,000	33,938,900,000	126,572,100,000
Hong Kong	76,288,600,000	11,119,100,000	87,407,770,000
South Korea	20,096,400,000	43,134,700,000	63,231,100,000
Taiwan	9,004,090,000	49,360,038,000	58,364,470,000
Germany	17,535,700,000	24,340,500,000	41,876,200,000
Singapore	8,868,500,000	10,483,800,000	19,352,300,000
United Kingdom	10,823,720,000	3,570,340,000	14,394,060,000

Source: National Bureau of Statistics 2004.

China's terms of trade, and in 2002 China had a surplus of US$30.4 billion. It is clear that trade offers enormous advantages for China. This trade engine in turn is based on China's recent success as a manufacturing center for many products, a matter to discuss when we examine the commodity composition of its trade.

This rapid growth in trade has led China to focus most of its activity and exchange on its immediate neighbors in East Asia as well as on other leading market economies such as those of the United States, Germany, and Britain. In 2003, China's leading trade partner was its regional neighbor Japan; the value of this trade was US$133 billion (see table 7.6), and China had a small deficit. The United States was China's second leading trading partner with a total of US$126 billion in trade. China, according to its trade figures, had a substantial surplus with the United States amounting to roughly US$60 billion, although the United States claimed the number was in fact a much larger amount.[2]

Another key trading partner is Hong Kong, with whom China has an enormously favorable balance or surplus amounting to more than US$65 billion, and much of this is reexports, that is, goods manufactured in China and sent out through Hong Kong for shipment to other final destinations, including the United States. Two other key regional trade partners are South Korea and Taiwan. In both cases, as seen in table 7.6, China has a substantial trade deficit, because China is buying the products that it needs at competitive prices from regional producers with low transport costs. China's trade deficit with Taiwan amounts to more than US$22 billion, and it may be that China is also pursuing political goals by making itself a critical buyer of goods from the Taiwan economy. The evolving trajectory and terms of the China-Taiwan trade is a topic for continuing study because it can provide clues into the emerging political as well as economic relationship between these two parts of China.

THE COMMODITY COMPOSITION OF CHINA'S FOREIGN TRADE

When we think of the composition of China's trade, it is useful to think of the *factor content* of the products China imports and exports, that is, the share of the value of the product that is related to the various factors of its production such as land, labor, capital, and technology. This is a conventional means of analyzing trade structure and can be done quantitatively in detailed trade studies. Although such an analysis exceeds the scope of our discussion, nevertheless it is a useful way to think about China's trade and its overall economic structure as we go about assessing the role of trade in China's development.

In 1980 half of China's exports derived from the primary sector, and only about 12 percent were manufactured goods. This would suggest that a strong share of what was then a relatively modest amount of exports was derived from land as a factor of production.

In 2001 only about 10 percent of China's exports derived from the primary sector, while 90 percent were produced in the secondary sector and were described as manufactured goods. What we can infer from this is that China has now shifted to a much greater use of its labor and capital as factors of production in the content of its exported goods. If we were to examine more specifically the nature of the various products among these manufactured and exported goods, we would discover that many of them have substantial labor content as a share of their total value, and thus we could conclude that China is making good use of one its greatest comparative advantages: low-cost labor. It is this approach both to manufacturing and to its related trade in a global trading system that has enhanced China's remarkable recent rise as a powerful competitive force among the world's industrial powers and that is causing considerable concern among many nations such as Mexico and among China's Southeast Asian neighbors, which also seek to share in the global market for low-cost textile goods, garments, footwear, sporting equipment, machinery, and other products with a significant labor content in their total value.

On the import side, the pattern is similar although the changes are not as striking. For example, in 1980 about 35 percent of China's imports were primary sector goods, including petroleum, and 65 percent were manufactured goods. In 2001, 81 percent of China's imports were manufactured goods, including a significant share of transportation equipment, and only about 19 percent came from the primary sector, again including petroleum. Thus China continues to need manufactured goods, but today these are more sophisticated and higher-end manufactures such as chemicals, plastics, vehicles, aircraft, and high-tech machinery. At the same time, the country also continues to import some foodstuffs and related primary sector goods, as well as petroleum, an import commodity that is increasing as China continues to struggle in its search for petroleum self-sufficiency while its consumption grows rapidly in step with its growing auto usage.

The China market continues to be both a dream and a frustration for businessmen and manufacturers. The idea of "oil for the lamps of China" remains a goal for commercial operators and entrepreneurs everywhere, but the reality is that the Chinese market has proven difficult to break into (Studwell 2002). Moreover, China's recent rise as a major manufacturing power has made this dream more unrealistic, for it is increasingly clear that few external producers of manufactured goods will be able to undersell China in its ability to produce a vast array of goods, including increasingly more sophisticated industrial and electronic products, at low cost. The next two or three decades are likely to see China enhance its position and power as a great manufacturing center and formidable trade competitor. China's recent entry into the WTO should help other countries gain official entry to its markets, but China's increasing competitiveness in the many products it manufactures will allow it to maintain a strong position as it meets the challenge of a more open domestic market for its vigorous foreign competitors such as Japan, the United States, Germany, and Britain. It now has the capacity to satisfy much of its domestic demand for goods and services, and it continues to develop its internal technical capacity and the quality of its workforce to meet the challenges of globalization.

Spatial outcomes related to China's rapidly growing economy will continue to yield new spatialities of production, consumption, and distribution. Continuing investment in transportation as well as in commercial and industrial infrastructure are proceeding at a frenetic pace in the coastal as well as the interior regions of the country. Hong Kong and Shanghai are two keys to the international commercial, manufacturing, and shipping marketplace, while Beijing, as China's capital, has a very strong international presence in banking, finance, and research and development. Meanwhile there are literally scores of other cities, both coastal and interior, that are also advancing their goals and roles in the marketplace and assessing their positions and their chance to be key future players as China extends its reach into the global economic system.

Notes

1. In discussing and analyzing the Chinese economy, it is especially wise to be cautious in the use of Chinese economic data. While Lardy (2002) complains about the quality and accuracy of economic data, perhaps reflecting a commonly held view among many economists and other social scientists, Holz (2003) has analyzed in depth some of these data and concluded that this perception is probably not accurate as a general proposition. Holz has concluded that there is probably not a great deal of deliberate falsification of Chinese economic data; at the same time he agrees that there may well be a substantial margin of error in much of the official Chinese statistical data.

2. Trade figures vary according to the source of the information. Each country typically seeks to report a maximum import quantity based on cost, insurance, and freight (CIF), while minimizing the value of its exports, to gain the maximum advantage in bilateral or multilateral trade discussions. Consequently, trade data may not be consistent among various sources.

References Cited

Cannon, Terry. 1990. Regions: Spatial inequality and regional policy. In *The Geography of Contemporary China*, ed. Terry Cannon and Alan Jenkins. London: Routledge, 28–60.

Cartier, Carolyn. 2001. *Globalizing South China*. Malden, Mass.: Blackwell.

Dicken, Peter. 2003. *Global Shift: Remaking the Global Economic Map in the 21st Century*. 4th ed. New York: Guilford.

Eckstein, Alexander. 1977. *China's Economic Revolution*. Cambridge: Cambridge University Press.

Fairbank, John K. 1992. *China: A New History*. Cambridge, Mass.: Belknap.

Fan, C. Cindy. 1995. Of belts and ladders: State policy and uneven regional development in post-Mao China. *Annals of the Association of American Geographers* 85 (3): 421–49.

———. 2005. Modeling interprovincial migration in China, 1985–2000. *Eurasian Geography and Economics* 46 (3): 165–84.

Han, Sun Sheng, and Clifton W. Pannell. 1999. The geography of privatization in China, 1978–1996. *Economic Geography* 72:272–96.

Holz, Carsten. 2003. Fast, clear, and accurate: How reliable are Chinese output and economic growth statistics? *China Quarterly* 173:122–63.

Lardy, Nicholas. 1998. *China's Unfinished Economic Revolution.* Washington, D.C.: Brookings Institution Press.

———. 2002. *Integrating China into the World Economy.* Washington, D.C.: Brookings Institution Press.

Li, Siming. 2000. China's changing spatial disparities: A review of empirical evidence. In *China's Regions, Polity, and Economy,* ed. Siming Li and Wing-shing Tang. Hong Kong: Chinese University Press, 155–86.

Liang, Zhang, Andrew J. Nathan, and Perry Link, eds. 2001. *The Tiananmen Papers.* New York: Public Affairs Press.

Lin, George C. S. 2000. State, capital, and space in China in an age of volatile globalization. *Environment and Planning A* 32:455–71.

Loughlin, Philip H., and Clifton W. Pannell. 2001. Growing economic links and regional development in the Central Asian Republics and Xinjiang, China. *Post Soviet Geography and Economics* 42:469–90.

Marton, Andrew. 2000. *China's Spatial Economic Development: Restless Landscapes in the Lower Yangzi Delta.* London: Routledge.

Murphey, Rhoads. 1974. The treaty ports and China's modernization. In *The Chinese City between Two Worlds,* ed. Mark Elvin and G. William Skinner. Stanford, Calif.: Stanford University Press, 17–72.

National Bureau of Statistics. 2002. *Zhongguo tongji nianjian 2002* [China statistical yearbook 2002]. Beijing: China Statistics Press.

———. 2004. *Zhongguo tongji nianjian 2004* [China statistical yearbook 2004]. Beijing: China Statistics Press.

Naughton, Barry. 1988. The third front. *China Quarterly* 155:381–86.

———. 1995. *Growing Out of the Plan.* Cambridge: Cambridge University Press.

Oi, Jean. 1995. The role of the local state in China's transitional economy. *China Quarterly* 144:1132–49.

Oshima, Harry. 1987. *Economic Growth in Monsoon Asia: A Comparative Survey.* Tokyo: Tokyo University Press.

Pannell, Clifton W. 1992. The role of great cities in China. In *Urbanizing China,* ed. Gregory E. Guldin. Westport, Conn.: Greenwood, 11–40.

———. 2002. China's continuing urban transition. *Environment and Planning A* 34:1571–89.

Pannell, Clifton W., and Laurence J. C. Ma. 1983. *China: The Geography of Development and Modernization.* London: Edward Arnold.

Premier Zhu. 2003. Government work report delivered at the first session of the Tenth National People's Congress. March 5. www.chinadaily.com.cn/highlights/nbc/news/319zhufull.htm.

Skinner, G. William, ed. 1977. *The City in Late Imperial China.* Stanford, Calif.: Stanford University Press.

Studwell, Joe. 2002. *The China Dream: The Quest for the Last Great Untapped Market on Earth.* New York: Atlantic Monthly Press.

Sun Yat-sen. 1953. *Fundamentals of National Reconstruction.* Taipei: Chinese Cultural Service.

Veeck, Gregory, ed. 1991. *The Uneven Landscape: Geographical Studies in Post-reform China.* Geoscience and Man Series, vol. 30. Baton Rouge: Geoscience Publications, Louisiana State University.

Wei, Yehua Dennis. 2000. *Regional Development in China.* London: Routledge.

Wu, Yuan-li. 1967. *The Spatial Economy of Communist China.* New York: Praeger.

Yeung, Henry Wai-chung, and George C. S. Lin. 2003. Theorizing economic geographies of Asia. *Economic Geography* 79:107–28.

CHAPTER 8

Agriculture: From Antiquity to Revolution to Reform

Early Farming Traditions

The origins of agriculture in China are lost in time, but most scholars favor multiple hearths of domestication dispersed throughout what became modern China. One was most certainly within the valleys of the Huang He (Yellow River) and its tributaries. Scholars usually locate another in South or Southwest China, including the areas now incorporated as Guangdong and Guangxi provinces. There are written records of rice (*Oryza sativa*) cultivation from as early as 5000 B.P., but production in southern China most likely predates this. Archaeological remains of seeds thought to be millet and rice found near Hangzhou in Zhejiang province have been radiocarbon dated to 8500 B.P. These deposits and other excavations of crop remains provide ample evidence that sedentary agriculture, as a way of life in China, could be at least 8,000 years old (Zhao 1994, 49; Sun 1988, 193).

Chinese agriculture is popularly associated with rice cultivation, but China's farmers have made many other vital contributions to the global food system. The list of Chinese domesticates or hypothesized domesticates is long and includes tea (*Camellia sinensis*), hemp for seed, fiber, and medicinal use (*Cannabis sativa*), several species of melon (*Cucumis*), foxtail millet (*Setaria italica*), proso millet (*Panicum miliaceum*), soybean (*Glycine max*), adzuki bean (*Vigna angularis*), several types of onions and chives (*Allium fistulosum* and *Allium tuberosum*), buckwheat (*Fagopyrum esculentum*), peaches (*Prunus persica*), apricots (*Prunus armeniaca*), and some types of oranges (*Citrus*) and kiwi fruit (*Actinidia*). Crops thought to have secondary hearths of domestication (initially domesticated elsewhere but altered through crop selection) in China include mustard rape (*Brassica juncea*), radish (*Raphanus sativus*), Chinese faba bean (*Vicia faba*), some types of apples (*Malus*) and pears (*Pyrus*), eggplant (*Solanum melongena*), and possibly ginger (*Zingiber officinale*) and turmeric (*Curcuma longa*; Smartt and Simmonds 1995). Early farmers worked not only with grain crops, but also with a broad range of dicots, herbaceous shrubs, and trees to produce a considerable array of useful foods and fibers. These crops were cultivated in a growing range of environments as Chinese territory expanded in all directions from its early dynastic origins within the Wei and Huang valleys.

China's farmers also developed or adapted many important agricultural technologies, some in use (virtually unchanged) to the present, such as gravitational and mechanical irrigation, wet-rice production practices, terracing and other land reclamation techniques, anaerobic composting, multiple cropping, and the extensive use of organic materials for improving and maintaining soil fertility. The first recorded use of insects as biological control mechanisms, in approximately A.D. 340, was the use of a type of ant to control mites and spider infestations on orange trees in Guangdong province (Needham 1981, 13). More than any other nation on earth, the Chinese have transformed the landscapes in which they live for the purposes of agricultural intensification by irrigating, manuring, terracing, draining, burning, and deforesting. An irrigation system located in Sichuan province called Dujiangyan, has operated continuously since 400 B.C., supplying water to over 500,000 ha of cropland—an area 1.25 times the size of the U.S. state of Rhode Island.

Legend has it that the sage-emperor Shen Nong transformed Chinese culture and society through the introduction of agriculture and herbal medicine sometime during the third millennium B.C. Another of these sage rulers, Emperor Yu (Yu the Great, 2197 B.C.), is credited with taming the disastrous floods of the Huang He, and inventing irrigation for wet-rice cultivation. As a result, Yu saved the Chinese people from widespread famine. Such apocryphal stories illustrate the salient role of agriculture in the origins and growth of Chinese civilization.

Agriculture, then, has a central place in China's history as well as its present. From ancient times it has been the nation's very economic foundation. A steady growth in population, combined with natural disasters and refugees from warfare, has constantly pushed China's farmers to expand and farm with greater intensity. As mentioned in chapter 2, much of China's lower-quality arable land, particularly in the northcentral and northwest portions of the nation, would not be farmed in a nation with less pressing needs. For China, however, land shortages have been an issue at least since the Tang dynasty (A.D. 618–907). Even regions with very limited rainfall or extreme slope were brought into cultivation as regional population pressures increased. Over the centuries, the cultivation of marginal land in China, without environmental safeguards, led to countless local ecological collapses that are an important, if overlooked, aspect of the tapestry of China's long history.

Large-scale deforestation, due to agricultural expansion and population growth (and a resultant demand for charcoal and construction materials), led to increased flooding and the siltation of rivers and streams from soil erosion. The American geographer George B. Cressey estimated that in the years from the Eastern Han dynasty (A.D. 25–220) to 1950, there were 1,621 major floods in China (1955, 93). Despite massive investment since the inception of the People's Republic of China (PRC), there have been hundreds of devastating floods since 1949. These crises, as well as other natural disasters common in China such as droughts, typhoons, and earthquakes, underscore how the fate of the Chinese people remains closely linked to that of their land. An early study of Chinese court records by the Student Agricultural Society of the University of Nanjing found that between 108 B.C. and A.D. 1911, there were 1,828 major recorded famines (Mallory 1926). Through China's long dynastic history, these famines resulted in political instability and even in toppled dynasties as the fire of rebellion sprang from the hot coals of starvation, hopelessness, and destitution. Even at present, China's leaders are rightly wary of any policy that could put the nation's ability to feed its people, rural and urban, at risk.

Modern Realities and Challenges

Understanding the relationship between a healthy agricultural sector and the history and progress of the Chinese people is vital for a clear picture of contemporary China. The ancient saying *Zhu yu feibao wu gu weibao* (The most precious things are neither pearls nor jade, but the five grains) underscores the importance of good harvests and food security. If China's agricultural sector cannot effectively meet the growing demands of its people, severe social, political, and economic problems with implications far beyond the agricultural will invariably develop (Y. P. Huang 1998, 166–70). Given the importance of food supply, it is natural that concerns regarding long-term food security in the face of China's still-growing population should attract the attention of scholars in China and beyond (Brown 1997; Y. P. Huang 1998; Kueh 1995). However, as will be discussed at length later in the chapter, the World Bank estimates that although China will definitely need to import grain in the coming decades—particularly wheat, soybeans, and livestock feed—its official goal of maintaining roughly 95 percent self-sufficiency for major food products through 2020 seems reasonable despite Lester Brown's 1995 pronouncement (Brown 1995, 30–31).

Moreover, despite ongoing structural shifts in the economy and a gradual decline in the share of the labor force in the sector, more than 324.87 million people remain employed in the Chinese agricultural sector (*China Agricultural Yearbook* 2004, 127). In addition, consumption of labor-intensive agricultural products in China's cities and exports to the rest of the world increased dramatically in the past decade. Increasingly in a post–World Trade Organization (WTO) era, China's farmers are linked economically to the global food system. In 2003, China exported US$23.7 billion in agricultural products with a growing portion coming from processed fruits, vegetables, essential oils (mint, sesame), and medicinal plants (*China Statistical Abstract* 2004, 160). The official government goal is to double these exports by 2008, reflecting the importance of the "global supermarket" to China's plans for its agricultural sector. The farm sector is of strategic importance not only because of national food security and exports, but also because it must continue to provide acceptable employment opportunities for a massive rural workforce still significantly larger than the population of the United States. If both food and employment are not provided, massive migration to the cities and social instability will be the inevitable result. The success, then, of the agricultural sector in continuing to meet these goals for China's people is a critical requirement for continued economic, political, and social stability in the next century.

China's Agricultural Sector

CROP OUTPUT LEADS THE WORLD

As noted previously, the list of crops initially domesticated in China is long. However at present—with a few exceptions—important agricultural products in China are the

Table 8.1. China's International Rank and Gross Production for Selected Agricultural Products, 2003

Product	Country Rank	Gross Production (1,000 metric tons)	Percentage of Sown Area Nationally*
Cereal grains	1	374,287	50.40
Meat of all types	1	69,329	n.a.
Cotton lint	1	4,860	3.35
Soybeans/other beans	4	21,275	9.83
Groundnuts	1	13,420	3.32
Rapeseed (oil and cake)	1	11,420	4.74
Sugar cane	3	90,235	0.92
Tea	2	768	not estimated
Fruit	1	145,174	not estimated

* Crops account for most sown area. Other major crops include tubers (6.56%), other oil crops such as sesame (0.49%), vegetables/melons (11.99%), sugar beets (0.26%), medicinal plants (0.53%), and tobacco (0.86%).
Sources: National Bureau of Statistics 1999; 2004, 472, 497, 1006.

same as those in the EU or the United States. Currently China is the world's largest producer of rice, wheat, meat, tobacco, cotton, fruit, and rapeseed (see table 8.1).

Through the centuries, China's farmers have proven very flexible. For example, they were quick in the past to adopt "foreign" crops such as peanuts, corn, and potatoes, and they are just as willing to produce new crops for export today. The New World crops of peanuts, corn, and potatoes introduced by the Portuguese in the mid-1500s are now some of the most important in China's vast agricultural complex. The adoption of crops such as corn and potatoes that could be grown on sloped land (unlike rice) permitted further intensification of labor and land inputs, but did not really change how crops were grown in China. Indeed, Lardy argues that in terms of China's agricultural technology, little changed from the fourteenth to the twentieth century (1983, 7–12). This criticism cannot be leveled at the present time—the past twenty years have seen more changes in the farm sector than in the previous two hundred. Currently China has one of the world's largest and most ambitious bioengineering research efforts, and its agricultural, aquacultural, and husbandry sectors are now among the world leaders in research and development (Huang, Rozelle, Pray, and Wang 2002; Xu and Bai 2002).

FARMING SYSTEMS AND MULTIPLE CROPPING

Most of the capital-intensive technological advances that have characterized Western agriculture since the Industrial Revolution were not adopted in China until quite recently. If these innovations are used as a technical "yardstick," then certainly China fell behind the West sometime early in the eighteenth century. Nonetheless, there were still important advances in China that permitted greater output—predicated on increasingly intensive use of land and labor. The most distinctive characteristic of Chinese agriculture vis-à-vis Western agriculture lies not in the particular crops that are grown, but in how these crops are produced. Until quite recently, crops were supplied with a remarkable diversity of organic nutrients that permitted the production of two or even three crops on the same land, year in and year out. These intensive systems had high and sustainable yields but also very high labor requirements. In the West, the high cost of labor—-and in major agricultural nations, a relative surplus of arable land—resulted in highly mechanized agricultural systems that are land extensive and capital intensive. In China, at least historically, the reverse was true. With its very high population density, and very limited arable land, China's agricultural systems tended to become ever more land and labor intensive. Through the centuries, China's farmers—seeking to minimize the capital used per unit of land and per unit of output—developed farming methods that were in accordance with available resources. Faced with very limited supplies of land but a surplus of labor, farmers and local government officials—beginning more than one thousand years ago during the Tang dynasty—began to experiment with more intensive land-use methods that eventually grew to hundreds of distinct *multiple cropping systems* dependent on large applications of organic manures, ash, pond mud, and crop residues (Wong and Guan 1998).

Multiple cropping involves growing more than one crop per year on a given unit of land. The crops can be sown either sequentially, simultaneously, or in a staggered fashion that allows for the most effective use of each field given the demands of the crops. There is evidence that multiple cropping systems were in use as early as the Eastern Han dynasty, but the most important early reference guide is the classic Chinese agronomic text *Qi Ming Yao Shu* (The Main Principles Favoring the People) compiled and promoted from the fourth to the sixth century. The early use of these complex systems not only reflected an understanding of the symbiotic relationships between different crops (which crop should follow another for best results), but on a more sophisticed level, indicated a knowledge of the radiation and moisture requirements of crops at different times during their growing stages. Figure 8.1 depicts some of the most popular multiple cropping systems in use in China at the present time.

For centuries, China's farmers were renowned for their careful collection and processing of organic materials for use on their fields. To some extent these traditions continue, but in more developed regions, the time and labor costs associated with these sound ecological practices have reduced their popularity. Throughout China, chemical fertilizers are now much more important than organic fertilizers, and evidence of overuse is easily observable in the eutrophication of lakes, canals, and rivers (see chapter 2). Further, chemical residues on grain, fruits, and vegetables are a major source of concern and anger among China's urban consumers, and demands for better food-safety regulations represent a very important challenge to agricultural planners at the present time.

AGRICULTURAL INNOVATIONS

Early dynastic-era innovations or land improvements such as canal building and irrigation also dramatically transformed China's rural landscape over the centuries. In prosperous times, local officials could petition the government for local land-improvement projects. This distinguishes China from most other nations in their respective classical eras. Once canals were built, more and more farmland could be irrigated and

JAN	FEB	MAR	APR	MAY	JUN	JUL	AUG	SEP	OCT	NOV	DEC

RICE / WHEAT, BARLEY

BROAD BEANS / RICE / RAPESEED, PEAS

WHEAT, BARLEY / EARLY RICE / LATE RICE /

CORN, MILLET / WHEAT, BARLEY

PEAS / SOYBEANS, SWEET POTATOES / WHEAT, BARLEY

BARLEY / COTTON / WHEAT

BROAD BEANS, GREEN MANURES / COTTON, CORN / RAPESEED, PEAS

PEACH, APPLE, APRICOT TREES / RAPESEED

WHEAT, BARLEY / SOYBEANS / CORN /

WHEAT / WATERMELON / LATE RICE / BARLEY

WHEAT / EARLY RICE / CRAYFISH / BARLEY

BARLEY / CORN / WHEAT

COTTON / WHEAT

PEANUTS, CORN / PEAS

Period in transplant bed

Figure 8.1. Common Multiple Cropping Systems in China

used for high-productivity rice production, which in turn increased imperial revenues (see photo 8.1). Usually canals were planned by local elites, permitted by government officials, and made possible through the use of local government tax revenues and corvée labor provided by local farmers, reflecting a symbiotic relationship between the farmers, the local gentry, and the state during the dynastic era. As at the present time, judicious government investment in agricultural infrastructure in the dynastic era was critical for China's food security.

Photo 8.1. The Grand Canal in Hangzhou, Zhejiang province, 1987. Photo by Gregory Veeck

China's Agricultural Regions

As befits a large country, China's environmental diversity is paralleled by a remarkable range of agricultural systems. On the largest scale, China can be divided into two main regions: a water-rich South relying heavily on rice production; and a water-poor North that produces the lion's share of China's wheat, barley, corn, and other coarse grains (see chapter 2 and map 8.1). In recent years however, these crop regions have blurred as changes in technology and consumer demand have resulted in changes in crop production. For example, the amount of area sown to rice in North China has increased rapidly because of the development of new short-season varieties of rice that can be grown as far north as the Russian border. This would be equivalent to growing rice in northern Canada, which is not where most people expect rice to be grown (see map 8.2). The cultivation of rice in China today also illustrates the effect of market reform and commercialization on China's farm systems. The amount of land sown to rice within traditional rice-growing areas in South and Southeast China has declined as farmers

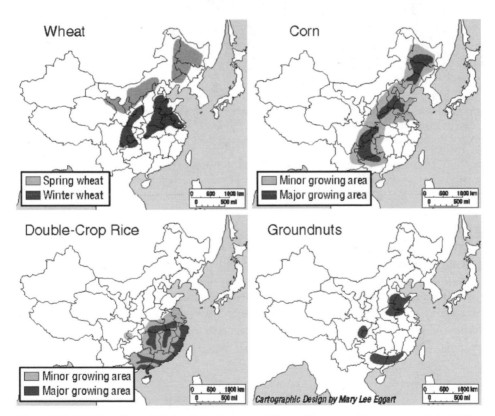

Map 8.1. Distribution of Selected Crops in China. **Source:** *China Agricultural Atlas* (Beijing: Cartographic Publishing House); United States Department of Agriculture Foreign Agriculture Service, 2005, www.fas.usda.gov. Cartographic design by Mary Lee Eggart.

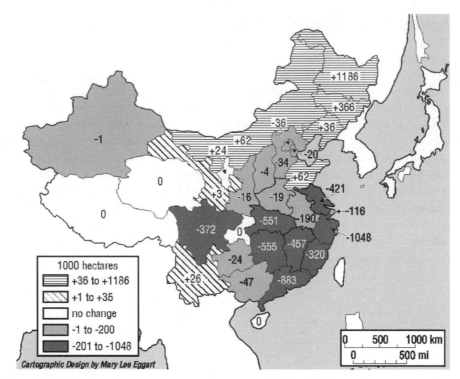

Map 8.2. Changes in Area Sown to Rice in China, 1985–2001. *Source: China Agricultural Yearbook* 1986, 163; National Bureau of Statistics 2002, 395. Cartographic design by Mary Lee Eggart.

have switched to more lucrative aquacultural products, fruit, vegetables, and specialty crops (mint, grass seed). In Northeast China, however, irrigated rice offers much greater returns than the traditional corn and spring wheat. So, despite potential water shortages and ecological damage in the future, rice production in the Northeast has exploded since 1985 in farmers' pursuit of comparative advantage. Farmers here, even paying more for water, can generate much more income from rice, especially because imports of corn and soybeans from the United States and other nations (a result of post-WTO economics) holds domestic prices for these crops down.

China's nine major terrestrial agricultural regions are depicted on map 8.3. It is interesting to note that the distinction made earlier between North and South China, along the axis of the Qinling Mountains, remains as a dividing line across several of the regions. The following sections will introduce these regions in greater detail.

The Northeast

Long called Manchuria in the West, this region (Dongbei) is composed of three provinces: Heilongjiang, Jilin, and Liaoning. The region is centered on the great Songliao, or Northeastern Plain, which is rimmed by mountains on the west (Greater Hinggan), north (Lesser Hinggan), and east (Changbai). The plain is generally low and rolling, and the northern reaches are swampy. In the 1950s the cultivation of this vast

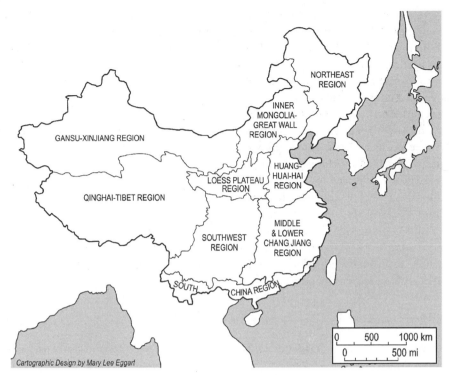

Map 8.3. Agricultural Regions of China. **Source:** Adapted from the *China Agricultural Atlas* and *Economic Atlas of China* (Beijing: Cartographic Publishing House). Cartographic design by Mary Lee Eggart.

expanse of relatively unpopulated land held great promise as a new base for agricultural production. Except for its southern flank, the Songliao Plain has only been farmed intensely for the past one hundred years. Cold weather and periodic droughts limit the crops that can be produced here but irrigation and special short-season varieties ameliorate these problems. The most important crops include spring wheat, corn, soybeans, potatoes, and sugar beets. As noted earlier, when water is available, specially bred short-season rice is an increasingly important crop.

"Han" China acquired the Northeast relatively recently. Consequently, population density is lower, per capita arable land area is greater, fields are larger, and mechanization has proceeded more smoothly. In Heilongjiang especially, large-scale farm equipment like that used in the United States is common. In fact, American firms such as John Deere and International Harvester have enjoyed strong sales here in the past two decades, reportedly due to superior service and the quick delivery of replacement parts. Many of the largest farms in the Northeast are the state farms that are still controlled and managed collectively by the central government, the provincial government, or the military. The Northeast, and especially the far northeastern region known as the Sanjiang Plain on the Russian border (Three Rivers Plain) is one of China's final agricultural frontiers. As discussed in chapter 2, the conversion of these northern wetlands to farmland, especially on the Sanjiang Plain, is controversial, and threatens a very important and diverse ecological region. In the long run, this land conversion is not ecologically sound. Given the area's limited rainfall (400 to 700 mm per year), critics argue that large-scale grain farming here will exhaust the groundwater within decades, groundwater that took tens of thousands of years to accumulate. The Sanjiang Plain also accounts for a large portion of the nesting grounds for the red-headed crane and many other migratory avian species that are threatened by continued agricultural expansion. The exploitation of this area has elicited considerable concern within the international community, particularly in Korea and Japan, nations that have special cultural associations with the cranes.

The lower portions of the Northeast Plain produce corn and are quite accessible from the port of Dalian in Liaoning province. Imports of corn and soybeans from a variety of nations including the United States, Brazil, Mexico, and Argentina have lowered domestic prices, forcing investment in other crops. There are not many possible options this far north, and many farmers in Jilin and Liaoning provinces are discouraged by post-WTO prices, even if urban consumers enjoy lower prices for grain, meat, tofu, and cooking oil. Other regions—with lower transportation and heating costs (for greenhouses)—that produce vegetables, fruits, plants, and flowers for export have benefited from increased global trade in these products, but the grain farmers of the Northeast have lost comparative advantage and their fate is most uncertain.

Nei Mongol and the Area Northwest of the Great Wall

Primarily composed of grasslands devoted to herding, the dry and windswept Nei Mongol Grassland region in recent years has seen a significant increase in field crop cultivation. In the eastern portion of the region, commercial forestry is now discouraged with extensive logging bans and other restrictions, while the western portion is the site of the most ambitious reforestation effort in China's history. In part, this reforestation is intended to create extensive windbreaks, which will help stabilize the grasslands and reduce the massive volume of windblown soil that rains down upon Beijing, Tianjin, and the other large cities of the North China Plain throughout the fall and winter months. It will also protect the last small areas of old-growth forest in North China.

In the recent past, particularly during the Great Leap Forward (1958–1960) and the Cultural Revolution, efforts were made to convert Inner Mongolian grasslands to field-crop production. The plowing up of grasslands in Inner Mongolia during the Cultural Revolution, especially during the Take Grain as the Key Link campaign, turned 391,000 ha of good pasture into desert and resulted in more than 748,000 ha being invaded by sand. Severe environmental damage resulted as the area affected by desertification increased dramatically. Only recently have more reasoned strategies been applied, with much of the land being returned to pasture or being managed with more sustainable practices. In the next century, husbandry in the region will probably increase to meet the growing demand for meat including beef, lamb, and mutton. Of course, the wool from this area as well as from the Far Northwest supplies a growing high-end textile industry increasingly dependent on exports to North America, Japan, and Europe.

The Huang-Huai-Hai Region (East China Plain)

This region is defined by the drainage basins of the Huang He (Yellow River), the Huai, the Hai, and their great deltas. Long one of China's most densely populated and productive agricultural regions, it is currently troubled by severe water conflicts and declining grain production. Traditionally, most land here was double cropped with winter crops of wheat, barley, and rape, and summer crops of corn, peanuts, soybeans, and cotton. Again as in the Northeast, post-WTO imports of corn, soybeans, and wheat have forced production shifts to less-traditional products whenever possible. Since the early 1990s, farmers here have converted to fruit, vegetables, and other specialty crops that offer higher returns. Much of China's investment in developing capital-intensive export agriculture is made in this region and other agricultural regions along the coasts. The region has also long been one of the most important for swine production, and recently its western edge has also become important for commercial sheep production.

The Loess Plateau

The Loess Plateau takes its name from *loess*, the German term for thick deposits of windblown soil originating thousands of miles away on the steppes of Central Asia. Loess is distributed throughout many areas of northern China, but the greatest concentrations are found in this portion of Northcentral China along the middle reaches of the Huang He. This area, the Loess Plateau, covers an area of about 300,000 km², and accounts for about 65 percent of all of the deposits of loess in China. In fact, the Loess Plateau is the largest continuous deposit of loess in the world. It is the yellow color of the loess, which has eroded into the rivers and streams of the region for thousands of years, that gives the Huang He its characteristic yellow color and name (see photo 8.2).

Initially the surface of the Loess Plateau was extremely flat, sometimes with a gradient of only 1° or 2°. The loess here forms an almost continuous overburden on

Photo 8.2. Crop terraces in the Loess Plateau in Shaanxi province, 1990. Photo by Gregory Veeck

the land with deposited loess ranging from 50 to 300 m in depth. Because of the slopes' unconsolidated nature, significant erosion can occur even on slopes with a 3° to 5° gradient when bare loessal soils are soaked with water.

There is a poignant lesson to be learned from the badlands of the Loess Plateau. In early historical times (Han dynasty, 206 B.C.–A.D. 220), the Loess Plateau was thickly forested. Then, much of the plateau was a very important agricultural region that provided grain, lumber, and livestock to an expanding Chinese Empire. Times have changed. Today, travelers visiting the region can ride in a jeep or truck for miles without seeing more than a few scattered trees or some small, widely dispersed shrubs, and even these are recent, stemming from various reforestation campaigns over the past fifty years. Visitors will mostly see a seemingly endless panorama of barren yellow hills, gullies, and ravines.

At the present time, erosion on the Loess Plateau is viewed as one of China's most significant environmental problems. It is estimated that an average of 1 cm of loess is lost from the surface of the entire plateau each year. Ninety percent of the sediment load (1.6 billion metric tons/year) of the Huang He is derived from the Loess Plateau, despite its accounting for only 40 percent of the total area of the drainage basin. Not only does this massive silt load dramatically affect river navigation, seasonal flood events, and urban and industrial water quality for the middle and lower portions of the Huang He, it also represents the loss of a precious soil resource that this impoverished portion of China can ill afford to lose. In part because of its severely degraded environment, the Loess Plateau has been one of China's poorest regions for centuries and remains so at the present time.

Due in part to the difficult terrain, there are few good roads, meaning some villages are isolated for much of the winter. This limits commercial links to the outside world. In turn, tax revenues are low, limiting health care and educational opportunities. The people of the isolated rural villages of the Loess Plateau face a harsh existence. There is an expression, *huichiku*, which means to be able to bear hardship (literally, to eat bitterness). It is indeed a harsh and bitter life the farmers of the Loess Plateau must endure. Almost one-third of China's poorest counties, based on per capita income and gross national product (GNP), are found in this region.

Since 1949, considerable efforts have been directed at stabilizing the cropland of the Loess Plateau, but far greater efforts are needed. The Develop the West program currently underway has targeted this region for central government investments in agricultural infrastructure and terrace construction to improve conditions and reduce poverty. As a result, the government has promoted fruit production, especially of apples, and the Loess Plateau has become a major fruit-producing region with a significant amount of product entering the international market as juice concentrate. In 2005, China controlled about 43 percent of the export market in apple-juice concentrate.

The Middle and Lower Reaches of the Chang Jiang

This region is truly the agricultural core of China. Centered on the Chang Jiang (Yangtze River) and its many tributaries and large lakes, most of this region is a low-lying, well-watered, alluvial plain. Double cropping of winter wheat (or winter barley), rape, and

Photo 8.3. Cactuses grow in greenhouses near Xishan, Jiangsu province. These farmers are in a cooperative that exports the cactus leaves to Mexico and to Hispanic consumers in Los Angeles, California (2001). Photo by Gregory Veeck

rice is most common, although nonirrigated areas are given over to cotton, corn, peanuts, and other dryland summer crops. Traditionally, the mean yields of all of these crops are the highest in China.

The coastal areas of Jiangsu and northern Zhejiang provinces are at the center of a commercial agricultural revolution that has developed in the past several decades. As in the Huang-Huai-Hai region, vegetable, fruit, flower, and plant production in the lower Chang Jiang Valley has skyrocketed. Often supported by township-village enterprise (TVE) processing plants for freezing, salting, preserving, and drying farm produce, the demand for these products by urban consumers and international markets has dramatically altered the farm economy in these areas. Vegetables, flowers, and fruits—often tied to export opportunities—are the crops of choice, except on larger-scale specialized grain farms where farmers are allowed to subcontract larger areas if they agree to produce only grain (see photo 8.3).

As industrial expansion occurs along the Chang Jiang from Shanghai to Wuhan, prime agricultural land is being lost. Further, water for irrigation is often polluted due to point-source emissions from factories. Zoning regulations are constantly being rewritten and upgraded in an effort to mitigate these problems. However, environmental problems continue to the present, in part because local agencies will not (or cannot) enforce the regulations. The harsh fact is that industry is more profitable than farming (even vegetables), and local officials are reluctant to slow rural industrial growth because this would threaten their status, lower tax revenues, or weaken local support.

The Southwest Region

The Southwest includes two main subregions: the Sichuan Basin and the significantly higher Yunnan-Guizhou Plateau. The former includes some of the best cropland in China; the latter possesses some of the worst. The Sichuan Basin has long been a vitally important granary for China, and its agricultural productivity in part accounts for the locations of the great cities of Chengdu and Chongqing. With the area's abundant water resources, irrigated rice is produced whenever terracing is possible, with high-yield corn and soybeans on the higher slopes. Too far inland to be influenced by imported grain, the region promises to continue to be China's most agriculturally diverse region. The Sichuan Basin also has one of the greatest concentrations of pigs in China, because corn and swine production are complementary production strategies.

Despite these ample water resources, however, the remaining portions of the region are mountainous and poor, with agriculture less developed than in all other parts of southern China. This is a result of the extremely rugged terrain and a very poor road system. Except for the Sichuan Basin, good quality soils are often only found in the narrow alluvial valleys that cut through the sharp mountains and limestone landforms. The terrace systems that are employed in the steep terrain give the region a distinct beauty. In fact, many visitors to China argue that the famous karst landscapes of the Yunnan-Guizhou Plateau constitute the most beautiful natural scenery in China (see chapter 2).

Recent efforts to stabilize slopes and reforest the region to establish a third forestry base have been complicated by this rugged terrain. There are few good roads, little rail transport, and few navigable rivers. While timber resources and the potential for the forestry industry are significant, particularly for the production of high-quality hardwoods used in the manufacture of furniture and household furnishings, transport problems and a lack of technical expertise have limited the growth of the industry. The Southwest is also a major citrus-producing region, but faces competition from other areas of South China and, ironically, from lower-cost imports from Southeast Asia. Again, with investments to improve transportation and expand terrace areas, this region could make much greater contributions to China's national food supplies. These developmental monies must come from the outside, however, as there is little that can be expected from local sources.

The South China Region

Although it comes as a surprise to many people, China's southern region is mostly composed of low mountains and hills (90 percent of the land area), with alluvial plains found along the coasts. The major basin is formed by the Xi Jiang (West River) and its tributaries, and the only large alluvial plain found in the entire region is found where the Xi Jiang and its distributary, the Zhu Jiang (Pearl River), empty into the sea. The Pearl River Delta has long been a famous agricultural region. Historically, most cropland here was double or triple cropped with a winter crop of wheat or rape followed by one or two crops of rice. Mulberry (for silkworms) and tea remain important nongrain crops. Very intensive land use is made possible not only by abundant water resources and a long growing season, but also by the fertile paddies created by organic fertilizer applications over many centuries. This intensive manuring resulted in the creation of rich anthropogenic soils where poor lateritic soils once dominated the natural landscape. The region is China's major source of cane sugar, citrus, aquacultural products, tropical fruits, and spices such as pepper. In a sense, post-reform changes in the Pearl River Delta agricultural system exemplify the contemporary problems associated with land conflicts in all of China's important agricultural areas (Wong and Guan 1998). Because it is adjacent to Hong Kong, public and private investors from China and abroad have flocked to the cities and towns of the delta to set up manufacturing plants with links to Hong Kong, Taiwan, and other nations. As these cities and their factories expand, an ever-increasing amount of arable land is being lost despite stringent land-use laws. As in the Chang Jiang Valley, conflicts over land use pit farmers and agricultural planners against more powerful local and regional supporters of urban and industrial growth. The productive land in the delta that led historically to its high concentration of commercial centers is now held hostage by the continued expansion of these centers in the modern era (Lo 1989). The Pearl River Delta, with some of China's most productive triple-cropped farmland—long famous for the production of rice, mulberry, tea, fruit, fish, crabs, and shrimp—is now the center of the most important new industrial region in Asia (Cartier 2001; Nickum 1995, 73–77).

The Gansu-Xinjiang Region

In absolute size, the massive region incorporating China's Far Northwest is second only to the great Qinghai-Tibetan Plateau. It is the driest region of China, with most of the region receiving less than 200 mm of rainfall per year. Only the Gansu Corridor on the southeast edge of the region can support rain-fed agriculture. Irrigated oasis agriculture has been important along the margins of this arid and semiarid region for several thousand years, and the region has played a central role in China's history, despite being so far from China's core. Its irrigation systems are fed by seasonal snowmelt from the east–west trending mountain chains that surround the basins. These are the oases (and qanats) that served as way stations for several of the ancient Silk Road routes (see chapter 2). The breakup of the Soviet Union in 1990 provided new opportunities for agricultural trade with the new Central Asian republics, but these links have yet to develop. In recent years, the oases have expanded rapidly, with a commensurate increase in grapes, melons, and other specialty crops. Some environmentalists argue that expansion has been too extensive, and express concern that the groundwater is being depleted quickly. Since 1990, deep-well irrigation systems have been continuously expanded, tapping the rich aquifers below the basins. When irrigation water is available, the cloud-free sky affords excellent radiation and the land—through human effort—is quite productive. Recently, irrigated cotton production and sugar beets have vied with grapes, Hami melons, dates, and other traditional oasis crops. This is China's newest cotton base, capitalizing on the long, hot days that are ideal for irrigated cotton. There is little doubt, however, that this expansion—without proper irrigation technology—threatens long-term groundwater resources. The potential here for future water shortages threatens a massive ecological collapse such as that which affected the Aral Sea region in Kazakstan. Another growing concern is salinization of cropland as irrigated areas are expanded.

Photo 8.4.   A Kazak manages his herd of goats in the foothills of the Tian Mountains in Xinjiang Autonomous Region, 2003. Photo by Gregory Veeck

Traditional herding activities continue in more remote or nonirrigated areas of the region, but there are growing herds of cattle competing with the more traditional herds of sheep, goats, horses, and camels. Recent efforts to modernize herding practices have been somewhat successful, and new drought-resistant perennial forage crops have altered the traditional migration patterns of the herders. Of course, population throughout the region is very sparse with the exception of the old oasis cities of Lanzhou, Ürümqi, Kashgar, Turpan, and Hami (see photo 8.4).

The Qinghai-Xizang Region

Much of this great plateau is over 4,500 m high, and the entire region is cold and dry most of the year. Nomadic herding of sheep, yaks, and horses remains important. In the valleys, cut by mostly seasonal rivers, spring wheat and barley is grown. Other important crops for subsistence farming include numerous varieties of potatoes and vegetables. In terms of farm extension work, efforts remain focused on improving local food supplies. It is reasonable to assume that the region will never fully meet local food needs.

Agriculture in Contemporary China

THE COMMUNE ERA

Any discussion of contemporary agriculture in China must begin with the commune system initiated by Mao Zedong in the early 1950s. This section will only summarize the aspects of the system most pertinent to the farm sector (see chapter 7 for a fuller discussion). At their peak, commune farms accounted for 90 percent of China's arable land. In 1973 there were approximately 50,000 communes in China. This number had decreased from around 74,000 in 1963, but the decrease resulted from an increase in the scale and size of the average commune (American Plant Studies Delegation 1975). Communes ranged in size from 25 to 130 km², and averaged fifteen thousand members. The commune system was not merely a theoretical experiment in social engineering. It was a fundamental aspect of Mao Zedong's vision of a strong and self-reliant rural China that would in turn serve as the foundation for the modernization of all of China. In this sense, it was remarkably different from the current system.

Although Mao Zedong's egalitarian vision of a cohesive, classless rural China organized under the commune system initially appealed to the peasants supporting the revolution in the late 1940s, their enthusiasm faded over time. Decades of hardship and deprivation, including the tragic Great Leap Forward, eroded most farmers' collective dreams of prosperity couched in equity. In the mid-1980s, one farmer from Haimen county in Jiangsu province summed up the commune era to me in this way: "Under Mao, we were equal—only equally poor."

In general, the commune era was one characterized by a limited diet, ration coupons, and shortages in both rural and urban China. Cooking oil, sugar, salt, cloth, grain, pork, soy sauce, eggs, liquor, and beer were but some of the staples included in a massive rationing system in which individual communes, cities, counties, and provinces all issued distinct coupons that could only be used within these jurisdictions. Fruits and off-season vegetables were seldom included in these systems because, frankly, before 1980 such products were so scarce that there was no reason to pretend that there was enough for everyone to have even a taste. Up until 1984, urban workers would have fruit only a few times a year, most often when their work units (*danwei*) would buy a truckload and then distribute bags of apples or pears at New Year's as a bonus. While there is still great room for improvement in rural areas at the present time, most scholars agree that conditions are dramatically better. Under the commune system, central planning, poor organization and transport, and the lack of a profit motive severely restricted the productive potential of the land.

The commune era was not merely a failure because of production and distribution issues. Most people in rural areas did not like living under the commune system. The amount of social control and intrusiveness of the *xiao ganbu*, or "little cadre," is frequently cited as one of the most annoying features of the collective farming system. No one had any privacy, and few persons wished to incur the wrath of local officials by suggesting alternative solutions to the increasingly pressing problems that built up over the twenty years of the commune era. Another frequent criticism was that high population and limited land created underemployment that was then exacerbated by bureaucratic bungling. Stories abound of how poor scheduling and organization reduced efficiency and production.

The remembrances of one farmer sums this up nicely. Over a beer in the late 1990s, this farmer recalled once in his youth when fifteen to twenty workers stood around a half-acre of paddy that they were supposed to weed, smoking different types of leaves for five or six hours to see which plants tasted the most like tobacco. They smoked leaves until they ran out of matches. The actual weeding took ten to fifteen minutes. On returning home eight hours later, they told the production team leader that they had finished the field. Nonetheless, the entire group was sent back to the same field the next day to complete the task. This time they had no matches. Shaking his head and laughing in disbelief, he told me that after a while when working on the commune, you stopped asking questions, you went where you were told to go, and you waited until you were told to come back. It was like a bad dream.

Still it must be recognized that there were important successes during the commune era, notably in farm mechanization, irrigation, organic agriculture practices, multiple cropping systems, and plant breeding programs. The famines of the war years (World War II and the civil war) were truly horrible, and older people can still vividly remember the servitude and hardship before 1949—particularly during the Japanese occupation and the civil war. The commune era was a lot better than life under the Japanese. More to the point, however, the successes of the commune system were too few, too far apart, and touched the lives of too few people too lightly. In short, nothing associated with the communes seemed to work very well, despite so many good intentions and an undeniable nobility of purpose.

THE RESPONSIBILITY SYSTEM (*BAOGAN DAOHU*) AND THE 1978 RURAL REFORMS

The Responsibility System introduced in December 1978 broke up the communes and returned land to the control of farmers through a series of contracts. This daring change introduced by Deng Xiaoping changed rural China in countless ways. Unlike urban workers, who may be very unhappy with the present system if they have been laid off, virtually all farmers in China would agree that conditions have improved in recent years. The reform era's most radical departure from the commune era was the reestablishment of the household as the basic unit of farm production. Under the Responsibility System, each farmer contracts a specific amount of land from the village or township authorities, typically for twenty or thirty years. Since all Chinese people, present and future, own China's land, farmers cannot own land. Now, however, farmers can subcontract land from other farmers and then negotiate the terms of these exchanges privately. At first, rent for contracted land was provided in kind and delivered to public grain and oil stores. Now rents can be paid in grain or cash, but there are also more taxes of more types levied on each farmer as well. This policy shift was also significant because China's leaders realized that there would be clear winners and losers, both in terms of regions and individuals, as the new policies expanded and took hold. After December of 1978, the mantra was "to each according to their ability." This was very different from Mao's vision that "each should receive according to their needs" (Du 1986, 11). Farmers responded well to the Responsibility System. Many other economic reforms followed, and farmers, now controlling their profits, worked harder to increase output on their plots by introducing modern crop varieties and technologies. Yet land ownership remains a complicated and controversial matter. Farmers are reluctant to make improvements on land they do not own—especially when it is often taken from them by local governments looking to expand residential areas or establish a new factory.

The Responsibility System reforms were not implemented immediately in all parts of China. Some provinces such as Sichuan and Jiangsu began reforms earlier, while poorer provinces such as Shaanxi, Gansu, and Ningxia Hui Autonomous Region came along later. By the mid-1980s, however, almost all of rural China was operating under the new system.

During the commune era, food production barely kept up with population increases and the increasing urbanism that increased off-farm demand for food. After the reforms of 1978, grain production skyrocketed from 304 million metric tons (Mt) in 1978 to a peak of 512 Mt in 1998, after which global market forces led to a decline to 430.7 Mt in 2003 as farmers shifted to other more profitable crops (see figure 8.2). Overall grain production has not declined as much as it might have due to significantly higher yields per unit area (see figure 8.3). This was a result of better field management, better varieties, greater inputs of farm chemicals including inorganic fertilizers (see figure 8.4), improved irrigation, and the extensive use of field plastic for moisture retention in the North (Rozelle, Veeck, and Huang 1997). Average grain yields rose from 2,783 kg/ha in 1979 to a record 4,953 kg/ha in 1998 only to decline slightly in recent years as low grain prices, forced down by imports, limited investment (National Bureau of Statistics 2000, 386).

Of course, there are problems with the current system that China's rural planners must correct. The constant redistribution of small plots under contract by farmers offers limited effective mechanization. Farm scale is also still too small to permit either economies of scale or the pecuniary advantages associated with bulk purchases of farm inputs or farm products. Although the actual amount of land available to each household under the *Baogan Daohu* system varies by location, a rule of thumb is that each household will have around 5 to 10 *mu* (.34 to .68 ha). Pollution problems (see chapter 2) have also increased, with the more intensive use of more types of farm chemicals and more fertilizer (see figure 8.4).

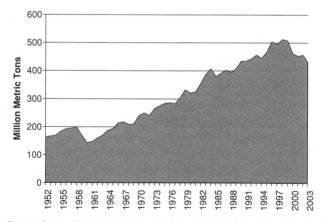

Figure 8.2. Gross Grain Production in China, 1952–2003. **Source:** National Bureau of Statistics 2004, 491; *Xin Zhongguo wushi nian tongji ziliao huibian* (Comprehensive statistical data and materials for fifty years of New China) (Beijing: China Statistics Press), 33.

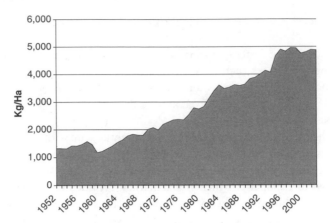

Figure 8.3. Mean Grain Yield in China, 1950–2003. **Source:** National Bureau of Statistics 2004, 490; Kueh 1995, 310–11.

Still, China's rural reforms are working (Fan and Nolan 1994). China's farmers are producing record amounts of food. A clear distinction must be made though between grain production and all of the other myriad farm products that are included in the sector. It is this distinction that has resulted in very different assessments of Chinese agricultural and food security by foreign and Chinese researchers and forecasters. Estimates for annual increases in grain production, the focus of most foreign research (Brown 1995; Smil 1993), range from 2.7 to 3.45 percent per year depending on the base year used to calculate the growth rate, while production of virtually all higher-value nongrain products such as fruit, vegetables, melon, livestock, and aquacultural products has grown at 9 percent per year or more (World Bank 1997, 8; see figures 8.5, 8.6, and 8.7). Chinese people have more food options, better quality food, and a more reliable supply than at any time in their history. There are more types of vegetables and fruits in a large urban market in China than in a typical supermarket in the United States or the EU in any season, thanks to the extensive use of greenhouses. China is now a price-setter

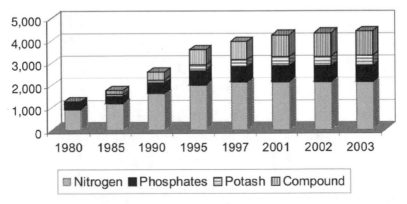

Figure 8.4. Inorganic Fertilizer Use in China (metric tons), 1980–2003. **Source:** National Bureau of Statistics 2004, 479.

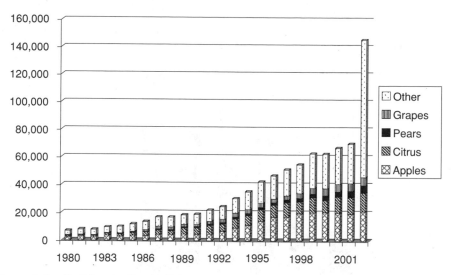

Figure 8.5. Fruit Production in China, 1978–2003 (1,000 metric tons). **Source:** National Bureau of Statistics 2004, 493.

in global markets for honey, apple-juice concentrate, frozen shrimp, crayfish, mint and other essential oils, condiments such as garlic and hot pepper sauces, frozen vegetables, and flowers (bulbs, orchids, even fresh flowers). While grain is the focus of Western concern, improving profits by moving to new products and markets is more important to China's farmers and rural planners.

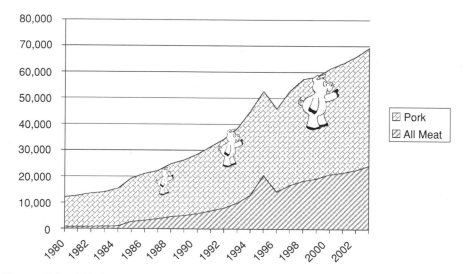

Figure 8.6. Meat Production in China, 1978–2003 (1,000 metric tons). **Source:** National Bureau of Statistics 2004, 406; *Xin Zhongguo wushi nian tongji ziliao huibian* (Comprehensive statistical data and materials for fifty years of New China) (Beijing: China Statistics Press), 34.

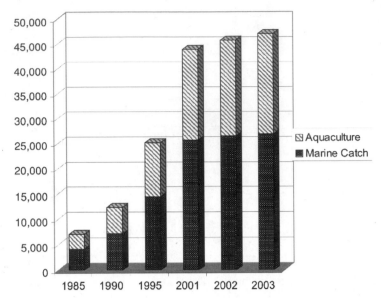

Figure 8.7. Fisheries and Aquacultural Production in China, Selected Years (1,000 metric tons). **Source:** National Bureau of Statistics 2004, 499.

The many benefits of a more diverse and sophisticated agricultural sector in China include (1) better jobs and pay as more products are processed locally in collectively owned TVEs; (2) greater tax revenues for local education and public works; (3) improved access to capital, technology, and business expertise stemming from joint ventures aiding local communities and improving local businesses; and (4) increasingly skilled labor, as locally produced farm inputs grow more sophisticated, which creates more opportunities for jobs beyond food processing.

For the individual farmer, there are dangers in shifting from grain to new crops. There is more risk, and less support from farm extension and relief agencies. Prices for nongrain crops fluctuate daily, and markets are more distant. Not only is transporting perishable vegetables, flowers, or fruit to market more expensive, but choosing the wrong market location, one that has a temporary surplus of the crop a farmer is selling, for example, drops the price dramatically. Given a transport system burdened by bottlenecks and cronyism, long-distance sales and transportation of fruits, vegetables, or flowers also has a potential for greater spoilage if a product ends up at the wrong market on the wrong day. Still, for many of China's farmers, the bottom line is that potentially higher profits justify the risks.

Farmers living near the east coast are more sophisticated than those in the rest of the country because of the coast's more diverse markets, including those for export crops and products. As a consequence, farmers living in proximity to large cities or within the coastal provinces have the highest rural incomes, while the more remote, less-commercialized, interior provinces report the lowest incomes (see map 8.4). In this sense, the inequity of space plays out in yet another way in the contemporary Chinese landscape with higher rural incomes in coastal areas.

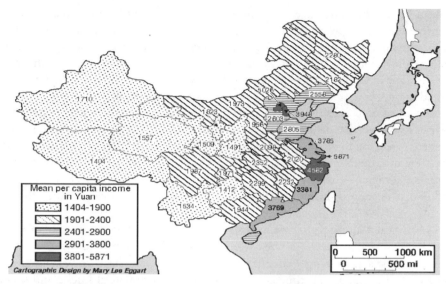

Map 8.4. Rural Per Capita Income in China, 2001. **Source:** National Bureau of Statistics 2002, 344. Cartographic design by Mary Lee Eggart.

FUTURE ISSUES

For China's farmers, the last twenty-five years has been a remarkable journey, transforming many of them from commune workers to entrepreneurs to price-setters in the global marketplace. China's farmers will continue to seek out production opportunities that incorporate exports to other countries. Exports stabilize domestic prices as well as opening up new niche opportunities for domestic producers and consumers. Trade disputes related to agricultural exports will increase, as other nations come under pressure to protect their own domestic fruit, flower, and vegetable producers. Perishables are more profitable, more risky, and so more contentious in every nation. Although the international grain trade is often fractious, the fights that are developing related to the growing trade in flowers and fresh and processed fruits and vegetables are sure to be worse.

Forest Resources and Production

Forests obviously serve several important roles in any nation, and China is no different. Commercial lumbering operations and tree crops are vital to the Chinese national economy, but so are forests with noncommercial importance. These include shelter-belt forests to slow wind erosion; upper watershed forests, which limit fluvial erosion rates and retain moisture in agricultural areas; and forests in ecologically diverse regions such as Hainan Island and the Southwest where many species of flora and fauna will be lost if greater investments are not made. Recent estimates of China's forested land as a proportion of total land area range between 12.7 percent and 16.55 percent. But presenting a clear, concise summary of existing forest resources is more difficult than it would first appear. In part this is true because so many forested areas in China are small and fragmented, and often represent land with multiple uses (Rozelle, Veeck, and Huang 1997). Efforts are underway to reverse deforestation, and to promote the development of commercial forest industries in new areas that are distinct from remaining old-growth forests.

As some indicator of the great impact that the centuries of human occupation have visited upon China, Zhao (1994, 41) estimates that in pre-agricultural times, as much as 40 percent of China's territory was forested. And even though efforts are underway to reverse the massive deforestation that has taken place, the centuries of abuse have exacted a great toll in many areas. Denuded landscapes in many regions, including the Loess Plateau, the Northeast, the Southwest, the South, and the middle-lower Chang Jiang, are common. Virtually all of the agricultural regions of China need reforestation, and efforts to address this problem have received considerable investment in the past decade (Smil 1984; Edmonds 1994).

Historically, Northeast China has had the country's most productive and extensive timber holdings. This area continues to be important for the forest industry, but tighter national control and stronger environmental protection laws have slowed old-growth logging in the region and stimulated the planting of commercial forests and shelter belts, particularly in eastern Inner Mongolia. Only as of 1993 had timber production from managed forests in the southern forest region (northern Guangdong, Guangxi, Fujian, and Jiangxi provinces) exceeded production in the Northeast—in part because of these regulations. Although wood quality in the Northeast is higher, southern China now produces 38 percent of wood cut, while the Northeast produces about 31 percent (United States Department of Agriculture 1995).

As China's planners work to shift the forest-products industry southward, competition from other land uses has become an obstacle in achieving this goal. Further, much of the forested land in the southern region, particularly in Jiangxi and Fujian, is covered by fast-growth durable species such as Masson's pine and cunninghamia, but market demand (and returns) for these woods are quite low. Commercial operations wishing to contract this land are deterred because the low market value of its cover will not finance reforestation. Still, with abundant rainfall and the virtual absence of old growth (except in some isolated mountain areas of Zhejiang and Fujian), physical and legal conditions for the establishment of new or replanted forests are better in southern China than elsewhere. The region also has the added advantage of proximity to markets and established transport systems that will keep total costs low.

Again, efforts have been underway for the last twenty years to establish a third commercial forestry region in the Southwest, primarily in Yunnan and Sichuan provinces. Many of China's most ecologically diverse and important forests are in this last region. High-quality hardwoods, bamboo, and other exotic species have been logged in these areas for centuries, often for the construction of temples and elite residences in the East. Until recently, little was done to reforest and to introduce appropriate commercial species into this remote region. With greater investment in transportation planned for the next decade, the area could become increasingly important. Already areas planted in tropical tree crops such as rubber, cocoa, coffee, and citrus have expanded dramatically in the reform era. Hopefully, a balance will be struck between the commercial uses of forestland and reforestation efforts for environmental and ecological purposes.

There are considerable opportunities for expansion of the Chinese forest-products industry, although new sources of investment capital and new production bases must be developed. There is virtually unlimited demand for paper and wood products in China's rapidly growing economy. Imports of wood and paper products of all types in 1999 totaled over US$13.3 billion (National Bureau of Statistics 2004, 717). China has a considerable amount of land that could be reforested to produce commercial products, but for the industry to be competitive with imports, the entire sector must be refinanced, reorganized, and modernized. Further, key production centers must be shifted south-ward to take advantage of longer growing seasons. At present, China's forest resources are inadequate, and modern management techniques are being introduced as quickly as financially possible. The promotion of a modern forest-products industry will require considerable government support, including significant capital investment, especially in the poorer peripheral areas where many of China's forests are located. Joint ventures can supply some needed expertise and capital, but much more money is needed than what is available from nongovernment sources. Support is needed not only for refor-estation and management programs, but also for research and development, processing, technical support, and the development of marketing and distribution systems. The first step, however, is to improve the amount and quality of forested areas. Chinese planners hope to meet a goal of 20 percent of total national area sown with forest cover. This general goal, unfortunately, coincides with tremendous pressures to develop land or convert it for urban or industrial purposes. While virtually all planners agree that reforestation should be a national priority, it will be difficult to achieve, because forest products cannot produce sufficient revenues to stimulate the industry.

Trends in Aquaculture

One of the most distinctive aspects of China's agricultural sector has been its long reliance on ponds, canals, and rice fields for the production of fish, turtles, fresh-water crabs, eels, shellfish, shrimp, and crayfish. China maintains one of the largest fishing fleets in the world, but its freshwater aquaculture has increased steadily in the reform era. Aquaculture's share of total production increased from 16.4 percent of 4.6 Mt of product when reforms began in 1978 to 40 percent of a staggering 47.05 Mt in 2003 (see figure 8.7). China's neighbors have repeatedly called for more careful stewardship of the oceans, and there is hope that much of the current ocean catch will be replaced with coastal and lake aquaculture. This incredible tenfold increase in total catch is dwarfed, though, by the proportional increase in aquaculture as a share of total production. This rapid increase in production can be credited to the increased incomes of many urban Chinese during the reform era, in conjunction with a rapidly expanding export market. Even as production has skyrocketed, demand and prices have remained strong because urban workers prefer fish and shellfish to most other sources of protein after years of scarcity. Further, the labor-intensive nature of the production of pond-raised fish, shrimp, crayfish, and eels gives China's farmers a comparative advantage over producers in the West. This in turn has justified the use of better, more sophisticated—and more expensive—production technologies that result in greater efficiency and fewer losses to disease. Aquacultural experts from China's agricultural science institutes and universities have played a critical role in these improvements, and China is now one of the world leaders in aquacultural breeding and production systems.

The Balance Sheet: Environmental and Economic Challenges in the Farm Sector

While it is important to realize that there remain pockets of poverty in many rural areas, particularly in North Central and Southwest China—places poorly integrated with the national economy or with limited opportunities due to harsh environmental conditions—the past two decades have generally been prosperous ones for many of China's farmers, especially those near cities or in the East. Certainly it is difficult to know what the future will bring. Domestic shortages resolved by importation of a limited amount of foreign grain will probably be common in the coming decade. However, the magnitude of the increases in production for virtually all nongrain commodities since 1978 is, for any nation at any time, simply remarkable. These increases in production clearly exceeded the expectations of Western experts writing in the late 1970s, but this is not to say that revitalization of the farm sector has come without costs.

There is evidence that the environmental problems associated with agriculture in China have been greater than anticipated. At the same time, as farm-related policies have grown decentralized, leaving the central government with less power to address these issues, there has arisen a greater need for oversight. In most cases, the extent of the environmental problems is not clear. In contrast to readily available data related to crop production, studies suggesting an increase of environmental problems, particularly in poorer regions, have only been available in the last five years. As in all nations, including the United States, data on erosion; soil salinization; lowered water-table levels; surface-water pollution by nitrates, phosphates, and other farm chemicals; and soil exhaustion in China are incomplete and often unsystematic. Still, Chinese researchers are among the first to recognize that many of the country's environmental problems have increased in severity, particularly since the reform era began (Lin, Cai, and Li 1996). In addition to more severe environmental degradation and an increased incidence of environmental disasters brought about by the use of more marginal land, China faces a range of other environmental challenges associated with its agricultural sector. Second only to the loss of fertile land is the excessive use of inorganic fertilizers, especially inorganic nitrogen fertilizers, which invariably lead to highly polluted field runoff and the subsequent pollution of all surface water in the affected areas. If more sustainable approaches to crop production are not developed, an ensuing loss or pollution of cropland will exacerbate food shortages and require that greater and greater amounts of capital be used for food imports. There is a growing market in China for organic produce because of consumer concerns about an excessive use of farm chemicals on grains, fruits, and vegetables. This is ironic given that for thousands of years, China's farmers were experts in organic agriculture.

To be sure, many significant problems loom, but many challenges have already been met with remarkable success. There are significant problems in China's agricultural sector, and these have intensified or at least become more apparent, but overall assessments of change in productivity within the agricultural sector and the rural economy over the past quarter century tend to be very positive, especially when compared to other portions of the developing world for the same years. China's rural reforms, including the many problems that have emerged, represent a wealth of experience in development strategy, at a time when most traditional approaches are drawing increasing criticism. To evaluate China's agriculture sector at the present time, a balanced view is required that weighs the country's growth in comprehensive food security and dietary improvement against concurrent increases in environmental problems, rural income inequity vis-à-vis urban incomes, and ongoing, prejudicial rural policies of many types that have frustrated and angered many of China's farmers, provoking dozens of "riots" every day somewhere in rural China.

References Cited

American Plant Studies Delegation. 1975. *Plant Studies in the People's Republic of China.* Washington, D.C.: National Academy of Sciences.

Brown, Lester. 1995. *Who Will Feed China? Wake-Up Call for a Small Planet.* Worldwatch Environmental Alert Series. London: W.W. Norton.

———. 1997. The future of growth. In *State of the World*, ed. L. Brown, C. Flavin, and H. French. New York: W.W. Norton, 12–14.

Cartier, C. 2001. *Globalizing South China.* New York: Blackwell.

China Agricultural Yearbook. 1986. [Zhongguo nongye nianjian]. Beijing: China Agriculture Publishing House.

———. 1999. [Zhongguo nongye nianjian]. Beijing: China Agriculture Publishing House.

———. 2000. [Zhongguo nongye nianjian]. Beijing: China Agriculture Publishing House.

———. 2001. [Zhongguo nongye nianjian]. Beijing: China Agriculture Publishing House.

———. 2002. [Zhongguo nongye nianjian]. Beijing: China Agriculture Publishing House.

———. 2004. [Zhongguo nongye nianjian]. Beijing: China Agriculture Publishing House.

China Statistical Abstract. 2004. Beijing: China Statistics Press.

Cressey, G. B. 1955. *Land of the 500 Million: A Geography of China.* New York: McGraw Hill.

Du, R. 1986. The policy of allowing some people to get better-off first and the ultimate goal of common prosperity. In *China Agricultural Yearbook.* English ed. Beijing: Agricultural Publishing House, 11–13.

Edmonds, Richard Louis. 1994. *Patterns of China's Lost Harmony: A Survey of the Country's Environmental Degradation and Protection.* London: Routledge.

Fan, Qimiao, and Peter Nolan. 1994. *China's Economic Reforms: The Costs and Benefits of Incrementalism.* New York: St. Martin's.

Huang, J. K., S. Rozelle, C. Pray, and Q. Wang. 2002. Plant biotechnology in China. *Science* 295, no. 55 (January 25): 774–77.

Huang, W. 1998. Lumbering halted to save endangered natural forests. *Beijing Review* 41 (51): 8–11.

Huang, Y. P. 1998. *Agricultural Reform in China: Getting Institutions Right.* Cambridge: Cambridge University Press.

Kueh, Y. Y. 1995. *Agricultural Instability in China, 1931–1991.* Oxford: Clarendon.

Lardy, N. R. 1983. *Agriculture in China's Modern Economic Development.* Cambridge: Cambridge University Press.

Lin, J. Y. F., F. Cai, and Z. Li. 1996. *The China Miracle: Development Strategy and Economic Reform.* Hong Kong: Chinese University Press.

Lo, C. P. 1989. Population change and urban development in the Pearl River Delta: Spatial policy implications. In *The Environment and Spatial Development in the Pearl River Delta.* Beijing: Academic Books and Periodicals Publishing House.

Mallory, Walter H. 1926. *China: Land of Famine.* New York: American Geographical Society.

National Bureau of Statistics. 1997. *Zhongguo tongji nianjian 1997* [China statistical yearbook 1997]. Beijing: China Statistics Press.

———. 1999. *Xin Zhongguo wushi nian tongji ziliao huibian* [Comprehensive statistical data and materials for fifty years of New China]. Beijing: China Statistics Press.

———. 2000. *Zhongguo tongji nianjian 2000* [China statistical yearbook 2000]. Beijing: China Statistics Press.

———. 2002. *Zhongguo tongji nianjian 2002* [China statistical yearbook 2002]. Beijing: China Statistics Press.

———. 2004. *Zhongguo tongji nianjian 2004* [China statistical yearbook 2004]. Beijing: China Statistics Press.

Needham, J. 1981. *Science in Traditional China: A Comparative Perspective.* Hong Kong: Chinese University Press.

Nickum, James E. 1995. *Dam Lies and Other Statistics: Taking the Measure of Irrigation in China, 1931–91.* Honolulu: East-West Center.

Rozelle, S., G. Veeck, and J. K. Huang. 1997. The impact of environmental degradation on grain production in China, 1975–1990. *Economic Geography* 73 (1): 44–66.

Smartt, J., and N. W. Simmonds. 1995. *Evolution of Crop Plants.* 2nd ed. Essex, U.K.: Longman Scientific and Technical.

Smil, Vaclav. 1984. *The Bad Earth: Environmental Degradation in China.* Armonk, N.Y.: M.E. Sharpe.

———. 1993. *China's Environmental Crisis: An Inquiry into the Limits of National Development.* Armonk, N.Y.: M.E. Sharpe.

Sun, J. Z. 1988. *The Economic Geography of China.* Hong Kong: Oxford University Press.

United States Department of Agriculture. 1995. *China's Forest Products Market.* Agricultural Trade Office of the Foreign Agricultural Service, January 3.

Wong, C. Y. A., and L. J. Guan. 1998. The application of remote sensing techniques to analyze the dike-pond resource sustainability in the Zhujiang Delta. *Zhongshan Daxue Xuebao* (October): 64–69.

World Bank. 1997. *At China's Table: Food Security Options.* Washington, D.C.: World Bank.

Xu, Z. H., and S. N. Bai. 2002. Impact of biotechnology on agriculture in China. *Trends in Plant Science* 7, no. 8 (August): 374–75.

Zhao, S. Q. 1994. *Geography of China: Environment Resources Population and Development.* New York: Wiley.

CHAPTER 9

Urban Development in Contemporary China

Youqin Huang

Known for its ancient metropolises, China has recently amazed the world with its rapid urban development as it enters the new millennium. Although China is still a predominately agrarian society with only 36 percent of its population living in cities in 2000, it has more people living in cities (456 million) than the total population of any other nation in the world except India (National Bureau of Statistics 2002). With millions of rural-to-urban migrants every year, China is also one of the most rapidly urbanizing regions in the world. This unprecedented urban development in China is transforming not only China's economy, urban landscape, and culture, but also the global economy with massive exports of products "Made in China."

Urban development in China has long been considered unique in balancing social equality and economic efficiency. Although socialist Chinese cities were formerly crowded and poorly serviced compared to cities in developed countries, they were virtually free of many of the urban problems that were widespread and seemed unavoidable in other developing nations, such as high crime and unemployment rates, and acute inequality (Whyte and Parish 1984). At the same time, China has achieved rapid industrialization and economic growth. Since 1978, economic reforms have injected new energy into Chinese cities, especially those in the coastal regions, which have contributed to the country's spectacular economic growth (see chapter 10). Many scholars and commentators have asked whether Chinese cities offer an alternative model for urban development in developing countries. In this chapter, we examine the dynamics of urban development in China, focusing on the post-1949 era. We will specifically consider the role of government policies and ideology, and how they affect the social and spatial structure of Chinese cities.

A Brief History of Chinese Urban Development before 1949

China has a long and elaborate history of urban development. Urban centers in China probably first appeared on the North China Plain during the Shang dynasty (1766–1122 B.C.), and a well-structured urban system—with a national capital, a number of regional centers and provincial capitals, and a network of county seats and commercial towns—was put in place that lasted for more than two thousand years (Skinner 1977; Ma 1971). There were about 3,220 cities and towns in China in the late eleventh century, and several cities had populations of more than 1 million (Steinhardt 1999; Ma 1971). About 6 to 10 percent of the Chinese population at the time lived in cities, but in absolute numbers, there were more city dwellers in China than anywhere else in the world before the mid-nineteenth century (Whyte and Parish 1984).

Traditional Chinese cities were mainly political and administrative centers with limited commercial functions (Skinner 1977; Ma 1971). The size of a city was often determined by its status in the administrative hierarchy, and this often corresponded to the rank of officials living in that city (Chang 1977; Sit 1995). However, during the Song dynasty (A.D. 960–1279), commerce grew significantly, especially in the port cities due to the expansion of maritime trade (Ma 1971). Later, a Chinese diaspora further contributed to the rapid growth of port cities because of their strong economic connections with Southeast Asian countries (Cartier 2001). In A.D. 1077 there were 170 large commercial centers in China, but as Ma (1971) has argued, in spite of the increasing importance of commerce in China, the rise and fall of its cities was still closely tied to political factors. For example, the site change of a capital usually led to a significant decline of the old capital city and a corresponding rise of the new (Steinhardt 1999). In addition, traditional Chinese cities served multiple functions associated with military, transportation, communication, religious, cultural, and intellectual activities (Mote 1977). Many Chinese cities prospered during the period of the tenth to the nineteenth century, and one foreign visitor reported that Nanjing in the late sixteenth century surpassed "all other cities in the world in beauty and grandeur" (Ricci 1953).

Despite China's long history of urban development and the existence of its many great metropolises, no single city dominated Chinese civilization as Rome dominated Roman history (Mote 1977). Chinese civilization did not see the city as superior to the countryside, thus there was no need to build one great city to express and embody an urban ideal. Despite their complex bureaucracy and urban sophistication, traditional Chinese cities had a rural component in both their physical and social organization, demonstrated by an urban architecture made up mainly of one- or two-story buildings in courtyard style that were rarely distinguishable from those in the countryside. An organic urban-rural continuum was achieved in China due to the freedom of social and geographic mobility between the two (Mote 1977).

Arguing from China's vast territory and diverse social and physical environment, Skinner (1977) suggests that there was not a single integrated national urban system in China but rather several self-contained regional systems defined by physiographic features such as river valleys and mountain ranges. Other scholars divided Chinese cities into coastal port cities and inland commercial and administrative centers. This dichotomous urban system was further strengthened in the middle of the nineteenth century when China was defeated by a newly industrialized Britain in the Opium Wars (Murphy 1970). As a result of this defeat, many of China's coastal and river cities (known as Treaty Ports) were forced to open up to foreign trade (see map 9.1). Hong Kong and Macau were the first foreign enclaves to be occupied by Britain and

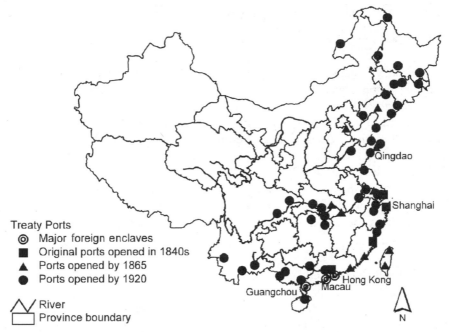

Map 9.1. Treaty Ports and Foreign Enclaves. *Source:* Edmonds 1990, fig. 3.3.

Portugal, respectively, and were only recently returned to China's sovereignty (in 1997 and 1999). Treaty Ports such as Shanghai, Nanjing, and Qingdao were also forced to concede special areas to different Western powers (e.g., the United States, Germany, Britain, and France), and in those areas, Western-style architecture dominated, and foreign rules and foreign ways of life prevailed (Whyte and Parish 1984). Because of their foreign trade, and as a result of regional resources shifting to the coast, these Treaty Ports began to grow disproportionately with respect to their former importance in the Chinese urban system. It should be noted here that despite a long history of urban development in China, large industrial cities did not appear in China until the early twentieth century when Russia and later Japan occupied China's northeastern region to extract mineral resources, mainly for their domestic economies. This rise of industrial cities in the Northeast added yet another layer to the urban system in China.

Although the growth of China's coastal cities during the nineteenth century can be attributed to foreign trade, many of the Chinese believe the Treaty Ports had a largely negative influence because of a resultant massive loss of wealth through unfair trade and the influx of opium, to which was added an increase in acute urban problems such as drug addiction, inequality, unemployment, and poverty (Hao 1986). These urban problems were further aggravated by the civil wars that followed (1927–1937, 1946–1949) and the Japanese invasion (1937–1945). As a result, when the Chinese Communist Party (CCP) came to power in 1949, it inherited an uneven urban system with widespread social problems. The CCP was determined during the following decades to build new Chinese cities that would be free of such problems.

Urban Development in the Socialist Era (1949–1977)

Since the establishment of a socialist government in 1949, urban development in China has veered sharply away from its ancient history, and industrialization—instead of administration and commerce—has become its driving force. Despite the country's rapid industrialization and economic growth, its socialist government controlled the growth of the cities, especially large cities, to avoid an "urban explosion" and related urban problems widespread in other developing countries. Having inherited an uneven urban system biased toward the coastal port cities, China's socialist government also aimed to create a spatially more balanced urban system. Using the socialist ideology of equality, the notion of "producer cities," and principles of socialist urban planning, socialist China achieved a unique path of urban development.

UNDER-URBANIZATION

Despite rapid urban growth in the 1950s, socialist China still had low levels of urbanization, with less than 20 percent of its population living in cities (see figure 9.1). At the same time, China had achieved rapid industrialization, with industrial output growing by twenty-one times during the period 1952–1982 (Lin 1998). This phenomenon of slow urban development accompanied by rapid industrialization has been called "under-urbanization," and is in sharp contrast to the "over-urbanization" common in most developing countries, where urbanization is much faster than what can usually be attained given specific levels of industrialization (Castells 1977). The Chinese government's strict control of rural-to-urban migration, its political campaigns with massive

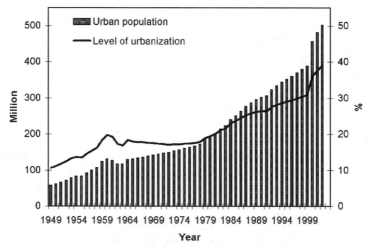

Figure 9.1. Urban Population and the Level of Urbanization in China. **Source:** National Bureau of Statistics (State Statistical Bureau) 1995, 2003.

deportation of urban residents, and a unique definition of urban population all contributed to under-urbanization in China.

In the 1950s, Chinese cities grew rapidly, with China's percentage of urban population increasing from 11.78 percent in 1951 to 19.75 percent in 1960 (see figure 9.1). In addition to a rapid, natural increase in urban population that resulted from postwar stability and an improvement in living conditions, the government was exerting very little control over rural-to-urban migration. China's economic development, by emphasizing industry, resulted in massive rural-to-urban migration in the 1950s (Kirkby 1985). Yet at the same time, one of the most important institutions in China—household registration (*hukou*)—was being set up, and it was fully implemented in the late 1950s to control rural-to-urban migration, among other functions (Chen and Seldon 1994). The *hukou* system divided the population into those with urban (nonagricultural) *hukou* and those with rural (agricultural) *hukou*. The division was mainly based on each individual's birthplace, and there were few ways for people to change their *hukou* status. Further, only people with urban *hukou* were entitled to welfare benefits such as state-supplied grains, free medical care, subsidized housing, guaranteed employment, and a pension. Thus the system defined an opportunity structure and social hierarchy within China, such that it has been called an "internal passport system" (K. W. Chan 1994). This system and a related food-rationing system imposed tight control over migration, especially rural-to-urban transfers. In addition, to get certificates of employment, potential migrants had to obtain permission from the local government at both their origin and their destination, which was often a difficult, lengthy, and bureaucratic process. At the same time, various coupons were required in the cities to obtain food, cloth, and other daily essentials, which made temporary migration very difficult, if not impossible. During the following two decades, the *hukou* system remained effective, and rural-to-urban migration was tightly controlled.

At the same time, the Chinese socialist government deported million of urbanites to the countryside, which resulted in stagnation and even reverses in urban development. The failure of the Great Leap Forward (1958–1960), coupled with bad weather, led to a significant decline in agricultural production and widespread famine. As it became increasingly difficult for China to support a large urban population, urban dwellers were deported to villages during 1961–1963, which resulted in a sharp decline in China's level of urbanization, from 19.75 percent in 1960 to 16.84 percent in 1963, a process called "de-urbanization" by some scholars. After a brief period of economic recovery, Mao Zedong then launched another radical campaign—the Cultural Revolution (1966–1976), in which urban youth, CCP cadres, and professionals were urged and often forced to move to the countryside to engage in manual labor. While there are no data on the actual number of urban-to-rural migrants, scholars estimate that it could have been as high as 49 million (Kirkby 1985). Despite this massive out-migration, the level of urbanization was maintained at around 17 percent because of a natural increase in urban population and a considerable in-flow of peasants to replenish the workforce.[1]

In addition, unique definitions of urban places and urban population contributed to the phenomenon of under-urbanization. Because of the *hukou* system and the government's implementation of "city-leading-counties" (*shi xia xian*),[2] it is a challenge to define urban population in China, as is suggested by the large body of literature on this issue (e.g., K. W. Chan 1988, 1994; Ma and Cui 1987; Zhang and Zhao 1998; Zhou and Ma 2003). The Chinese government has used four different definitions of urban population in its four censuses. There are two types of officially designated urban places in China: cities (*shi*) and towns (*zhen*). Both total population of cities and towns, and total population of cities and towns with urban *hukou*, were used to define urban population. Despite the fact that urban residents such as suburban farmers and rural migrants might have rural *hukou*, the latter definition (based on urban *hukou*) was more commonly used (K. W. Chan 1994). This definition was less problematic in the socialist era with its relatively small volume of temporary rural-to-urban migrants; yet in the reform era, it significantly underestimates urban population because of massive and ongoing rural-to-urban migration, and a more complex definition derived from actual occupation, residence, and *hukou* status has been recommended (Zhang and Zhao 1998).

SOCIALIST IDEOLOGY AND A BALANCED URBAN SYSTEM

Urban development in socialist China was heavily influenced by the socialist ideology of equality. With the exception of the rapid urban growth that was permitted during the initial postwar recovery period, the focus during most of the socialist era was on achieving controlled and balanced urban development. The official policy for urban development was to "strictly control the development of large cities, moderately develop medium-size cities, and vigorously promote the development of small cities and towns" (Kirkby 1985). To achieve such goals, various measures were used, including the allocation of state investment, the designation of new urban places, the strict control of migration into cities, and even the deportation of urbanites during various political campaigns. As a result, the number of small cities in China increased more rapidly than that of large cities, and the share in total population of small cities increased while that of large and medium-size cities declined (see table 9.1). There was also a significant containment of the growth of the very largest cities like Beijing, Shanghai, and Tianjin (Pannell 1981).

Because most of China's large cities are located in the coastal and northeastern regions (mainly as a result of foreign influence), a majority of state investment was channeled toward inland cities to achieve a regionally more balanced urban development.

Table 9.1. Number of Cities in China with a Nonagricultural Population greater than 50,000

City size	1953 N	1953 %	1979 N	1979 %	2000 N	2000 %
1 million+	9	5.49	15	4.55	40	6.26
500,000–999,999	16	9.76	28	8.48	53	8.29
50,000–499,999	139	84.76	287	86.97	546	85.45
Total	164	100.00	330	100.00	639	100.00

Source: Data for years 1953 and 1979 adapted from Kirkby 1985, table A5.9; data for year 2000 from National Bureau of Statistics 2001.

During the first Five-Year Plan (1953–1957), two-thirds of the nearly seven hundred large and medium-scale industrial projects established by the government were set up in inland cities (Cannon 1990). The hostile international political environment of the 1960s further encouraged the Chinese government to channel more than half of its state investment into inland mountainous areas, particularly in Sichuan province, a strategy that became known as the Third Front policy.[3] Although mainly used as a military strategy, the Third Front policy effectively promoted urban development in inland China. Thus a spatially more balanced urban system was created, despite the harsh physical environment of the interior and the country's historical bias toward its coastal regions (see map 9.2). In 2000, 295 (44.49 percent) cities were in the eastern region of China, 247 (37.25 percent) in the central region, and 121 (18.25 percent) in the western region.

The socialist ideology of equality had a profound impact on the spatial pattern of urban development in China. Although China's socialist government inherited an uneven urban system that was heavily biased toward the coastal port cities and industrial cities in the Northeast, it made substantial progress in developing a more balanced urban system.

SOCIALIST URBAN PLANNING AND URBAN SOCIOSPATIAL STRUCTURE

The internal structure of a city often reflects the cultural norms of its society and the ideology embedded in that society's urban-design and planning policies. Over the course of more than two thousand years, Chinese cities developed internal structures that were significantly different from those found in Western cities (Whyte and Parish 1984; Steinhardt 1999). Traditional Chinese cities often had a rectangular, symmetrical layout with an elaborate structure of city walls and gates symbolizing authority and security, providing protection, and representing Chinese cosmology (Chang 1977; Ma 1971; Wright 1977; Sit 1995; Steinhardt 1999; see figure 9.2). Most Chinese cities originally served as political and administrative centers, with government buildings and facilities dominating the city center, and commercial activities and ceremonial buildings relegated to the periphery (Skinner 1977). Today, remnants of traditional Chinese city planning are still visible in the inner cities of Beijing, Xi'an, and Nanjing.

Influenced by urban planning in the Soviet Union, the Chinese socialist planning system added another layer to the urban structure of Chinese cities, which as a result were characterized by three factors: (1) a focus on the symbolism of the city center, (2) an emphasis on industry, and (3) the desire for a cellular landscape based on work units (*danwei*). First, city centers were symbolically considered centers of cultural and political life. To glorify the socialist state, city centers were devoted to large, public squares for political gatherings, with wide boulevards and monumental public buildings (Sit 1995), in sharp contrast to the intensive development of commercial and business interests at the center of most Western cities. For example, at the center of Beijing, the largest public square in the world—Tiananmen Square—was constructed adjacent to the Forbidden City, the historical center of power. The square was surrounded by

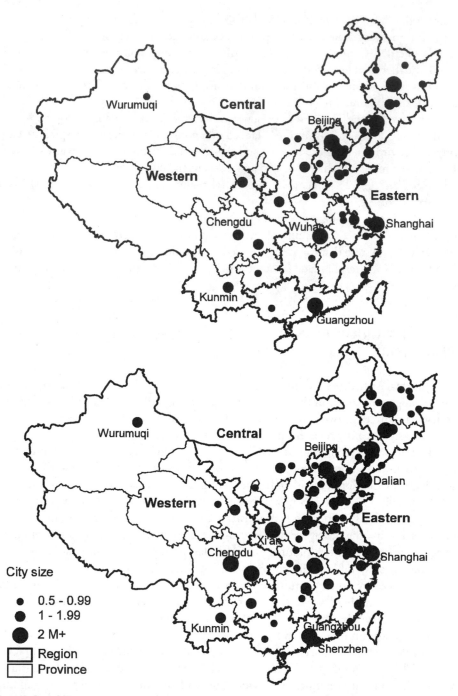

Map 9.2. Cities with Nonagricultural Populations greater than 500,000 in 1982 and 2000. **Source:** National Bureau of Statistics 2001.

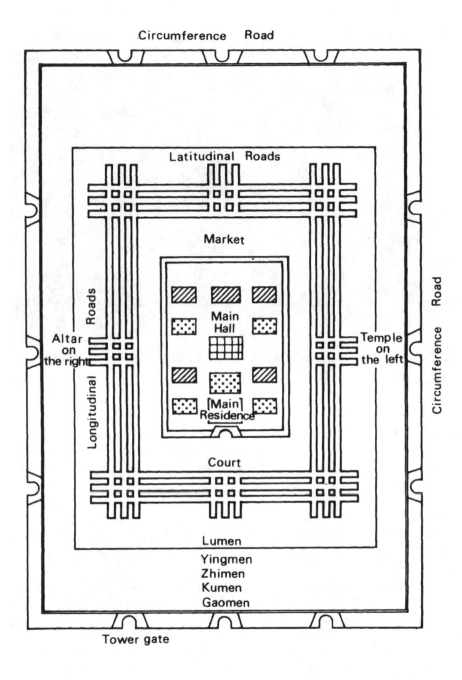

Circumference Road

Latitudinal Roads

Market

Roads

Main
Hall

Altar
on
the right

Temple
on
the left

Longitudinal

[Main]
Residence

Court

Lumen
Yingmen
Zhimen
Kumen
Gaomen

Circumference Road

Tower gate

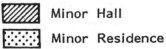 Minor Hall

Minor Residence

Figure 9.2. Typical Design of a Traditional Chinese City. *Source:* Sen-dou Chang, "The Morphology of Walled Capitals," in *The City in Late Imperial China*, ed. William Skinner (Stanford, Calif.: Stanford University Press, 1977).

Photo 9.1. Tiananmen Square in the heart of Beijing. Photo by Youqin Huang

monumental architectural structures devoted to political and cultural purposes, such as the Hall of the People, the Museum of History, and the Museum of Revolution, which were matched by the Memorial of the People's Hero at the center of the square (see photo 9.1). While the city center in Beijing is unique due to its capital status, many cities in China mimicked its design, with their public squares and government buildings located at city centers with wide boulevards radiating outward. Thus, the city centers of Chinese cities during this period often had the lowest intensity of land use, forming a doughnut-shape pattern of land use that is very different from the high-density development in Western urban centers.

Second, an emphasis on industry and the concept of the "producer city" were central to socialist planning (Ma 1976; Sit 1995). Nonindustrial cities like Shanghai were considered by the socialist government to be parasitic and to have been significantly debased by their colonial history. China's socialist government was determined to convert these "consumer cities" into "producer cities" by developing a large industrial sector. Even Beijing, the nation's cultural and political center, was no exception. Most state investment in Beijing went into industry, especially heavy industries such as steel mills, petrochemical plants, and power plants, which imposed tremendous pressure on local resources (especially water and electricity) and created severe environmental problems (Dong 1985). In 1981, Beijing became the second-largest industrial city in China. At the same time, only a very small proportion of state investment (1–3 percent of total urban fixed-asset investment, compared to 10 percent recommended by the UN) was for civic infrastructure. This emphasis on production resulted in a pattern of land use devoted mainly to industrial facilities, especially at the outer edge of cities, with much less for infrastructure, housing, services, and recreation. Not surprisingly, residential crowding and a lack of amenities and infrastructure were common complaints among residents of socialist Chinese cities (Whyte and Parish 1984).

Third, and related to this massive industrial development, self-contained work-unit compounds were constructed as the basic urban unit. In order to reduce traffic congestion and create "walking-scale" cities, work-unit compounds with public apartment buildings were built adjacent to employment centers, allowing employees from the same work unit to live together (Ma 1981). This was especially important in Chinese cities, where bicycles and buses were the main modes of transportation. In addition, basic social, subsistence, and recreational services, such as cafeterias, public bathhouses, grocery stores, small clinics, kindergartens, and small parks were provided in these compounds, all within walking distance (Ma 1981). In contrast to the specialized functional zones in traditional Chinese cities and most Western cities, a generalized, functional organization was achieved in socialist Chinese cities through these self-contained work-unit compounds, which provided employment, housing, and a range of other social services. Because of this close link between employment and housing, it was extremely difficult for a worker to move, even within a city. During the 1960s and 1970s, only 1 percent of urban households changed residence in one year, and the average length of residence in the same apartment was eighteen years—an extreme immobility compared to that of China in the past as well as that of other nations (Whyte and Parish 1984).

Corresponding to this cellular physical landscape was a relatively homogeneous society. Because housing was considered part of social welfare, it was provided by the state through work units, which usually built low-rise, standardized apartment buildings in the form of work-unit compounds. Apartments were then allocated among the work-unit employees, who paid only nominal rents. While there were some differences in housing consumption (Logan, Y. Bian, and F. Bian 1999), people working for the same work unit, including high-rank cadres and their subordinates in factories, or professors and their staff in universities, often lived in the same work-unit compound, if not the same building, and they shared similar housing conditions and amenities. Although most households suffered from poor housing conditions and severe crowding (Huang 2003), social stratification and residential segregation were minimalized in socialist Chinese cities. There were different social areas, but they were based mainly on land use, occupation, and population density, instead of on residents' socioeconomic status, as is the case in the West (Yeh and Wu 1995; Sit 2000). A relatively homogenous society was achieved through the massive provision of public housing in the form of work-unit compounds.

In sum, because of socialist planning that emphasized the symbolism of the central city, the concept of the "producer city," and the combining of residential and work space, urban structure in socialist Chinese cities demonstrated unique features such as low-density land use in the central city, generalized functional organization through work-unit compounds, a dominance of industry, use of uniform, low-rise housing developments, and societal homogeneity—all of which highlighted fundamental differences in urban structure among socialist Chinese cities, traditional Chinese cities, and Western cities.

Socialist ideology and socialist planning were clearly important, but we should recognize that urban development in socialist China was a complex process shaped by political, social, historical, and economic forces. For example, the constraints of limited resources and a hostile international environment were important to the socialist strategy of urban development. As Lin points out, "No single factor, whether ideological conviction or rational economic consideration is able to claim sole responsibility for the process of China's urbanization" (1998, 109). The socialist Chinese government, which desperately wanted to demonstrate its legitimacy and superiority, had to balance considerations of social and spatial equality against the need for economic efficiency in urban development, and this is never an easy task. The Chinese government often had to choose one or the other, or under different circumstances it sought compromises between the two (Lin 1998). Changes in the urban development strategy from the socialist era to the reform era—although they may appear to be radical—are in fact a continuation of this struggle for balance between equality and efficiency, with the focus lately shifting toward economic efficiency and urban growth.

Urban Development in the Reform Era (1978–Present)

After the more pragmatic Deng Xiaoping gained power in 1978, the Chinese government began to shift its focus from class struggle to economic development, from social and spatial equality to economic growth, and China has since experienced unprecedented urban growth and urban transformation. Cities have grown rapidly in both number and size, with 663 cities and an urban population of 456 million in 2000 (see figure 9.1). This is still low compared to other nations, but now 36 percent of China's total population is living in cities, a percentage that more than doubled during the period from 1978 to 2000. Chinese cities have also demonstrated higher degrees of urbanism with an increasingly cosmopolitan landscape, higher rates of mobility, rising consumerism, and increasing cultural and social diversity. This new pattern of urban development can only be attributed to changes in the Chinese government's philosophy of urban development and to the effects of economic reforms that have initiated institutional changes on many fronts. These changes include the integration of the urban economy with the world economy through the government's open door policy, liberation of the nonstate economy, a relaxation in migration control, and the privatization of the housing system.

GLOBALIZATION AND UNEVEN URBAN DEVELOPMENT

In 1978, the new Chinese leadership initiated an open door policy to utilize foreign investment and engage in international trade, a policy that has since brought profound changes to urban development in China. Through a strategy of gradualism, the open door policy was initially implemented in coastal cities before it was (recently) adopted nationwide. Four Special Economic Zones (SEZs) were established in 1979: Shenzhen,

Zhuhai, and Shantou in Guangdong province, and Xiamen in Fujian province—all within geographic proximity of Hong Kong and Taiwan (see map 9.3). With massive foreign investment from overseas Chinese and an influx of migrant labor engaging in newly established foreign or private enterprises, these SEZs met with immediate success and grew rapidly. In 1984 another fourteen coastal cities were opened up, and in 1985, Open Economic Regions around the SEZs or Coastal Open Cities were designated. Hainan Island and Pudong New District in Shanghai were added as the latest SEZs, in 1988 and 1990 respectively.

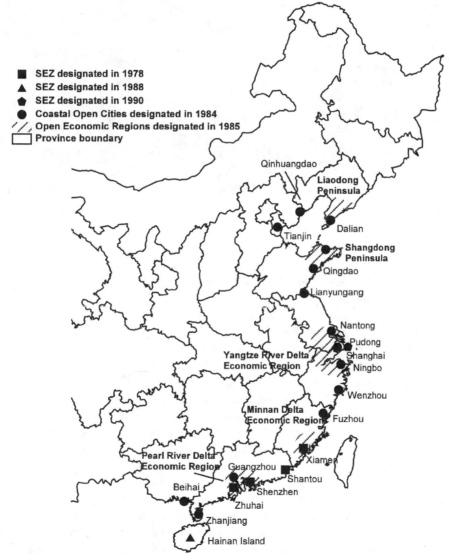

Map 9.3. The Gradual Open Door Policy Biased toward Coastal Cities. **Source:** Adapted from Phillips and Yeh 1990, fig. 9.4.

Photo 9.2. The urban landscape of Shenzhen. To the left of the river is Hong Kong. Photo by Youqin Huang

Because of this geographically biased open door policy and the better social and physical infrastructure in China's large cities, the majority of foreign investment has gone to large and medium-size cities in the eastern region. At the same time, the SEZs and Coastal Open Cities have benefited more from this globalization and have enjoyed higher economic growth rates than inland cities (Xie and Costa 1991; Fan 1992). For example, the urban population in Shenzhen and Zhuhai grew at 32 percent and 29 percent respectively during 1978–1984 (Xu and Li 1990). The industrial output in these two cities grew at 95 percent annually during the same period. Shenzhen, a once small village, has now been transformed into a modern, bustling city with a population of 1.4 million in 2002 (see photo 9.2). With three SEZs and two Coastal Open Cities, the Pearl River Delta region in Guangdong province has been one of the most rapidly urbanizing regions in China, with an urban population growing 7.70 percent annually during the period 1978–1986 (in contrast to 0.75 percent during 1957–1978; Xu and Li 1990). In addition to millions of workers migrating into the region from elsewhere, 60 percent of the delta's local rural population has given up farming and moved into nonagricultural sectors, many in manufacturing industries relocated from Hong Kong and Taiwan (R. Chan 1995). As a result, gross industrial output in the delta grew 16 percent annually during the period 1978–1986, much of it coming from a rapid expansion in Chinese products being exported to the global market (Xu and Li 1990).

Photo 9.3. Night skyline of the Pudong New District, Shanghai. Photo by Youqin Huang

The phenomenal transformation of Pudong New District from farmland in the 1980s to a financial district with a forest of skyscrapers (see photo 9.3) is another example of how Chinese cities are being transformed by the force of globalization. "Exo-urbanization" (Sit and Yang 1997) and "urbanization from outside" (Fan 1995) have been used to refer to this rapid urban development that has been induced mainly by foreign investment. The open door policy and globalization have changed the course of urban development in China, with the country's focus now shifting from spatial equality to economic efficiency, from inland to coastal cities, from small to large cities, and from self-reliance to internalization. An uneven urban development biased toward coastal large cities has been achieved.

"URBANIZATION FROM BELOW"

Towns and small cities in China served primarily as marketing and administrative centers throughout the nation's history, and remained stagnant until the early 1980s when they became centers of industrial production (Fei et al. 1986; Skinner 1977). In 1984 the State Council issued a landmark policy that allowed peasants to move to towns and small cities as long as they could provide themselves with food and shelter. Because of the millions of surplus rural laborers that had resulted from the Household

Responsibility System, this policy generated a massive rural-to-urban migration, with more than 5 million new urban residents added during the 1984–1988 period (Zhu and Gu 1991). Still banned from jobs in the state sector, most of these migrants in the early 1980s moved into rapidly expanding nonstate sectors such as services or privately or collectively owned industries, often called township-village enterprises (TVEs), that manufactured consumer goods from sneakers to electronics. These migrants provided a large pool of cheap labor for the nonstate sectors, and they were cheap because they were denied subsidized housing, medical care, pensions, and the other benefits that were enjoyed by employees in the state sector. Together with local governments' entrepreneurship, the nonstate sectors and especially the TVEs grew rapidly, contributing 72 percent of China's total industrial output in 1998. This influx of migrants and the phenomenal growth of nonstate economies have led to the rapid development of towns and small cities. To further promote the growth of small cities and towns, the government's criteria for designating towns were relaxed in 1984, which led to a surge in the number of designated towns, which went from 2,781 in 1983 to 6,211 in 1984, and to 9,121 in 1987. Between 1980 and 1994, 287 new cities were so designated (K. W. Chan 1994). This phenomena of indigenous urban development that is town- or small city-based and relies mainly on local initiatives and resources is referred to as "urbanization from below," and is in sharp contrast to "urbanization from above," that is, state-planned development based on large-scale industries in large cities (Ma and Fan 1994).

Towns and small cities are particularly vibrant in the Chinese coastal regions. For example, due to their proximity to large cities such as Shanghai, Changzhou, Wuxi, and Suzhou, many towns and small cities in the Chang Jiang (Yangtze River) Delta have benefited significantly from the economic, technological, and cultural spillover from these large urban centers (Tan 1993). In Zhejiang province, many towns and small cities have grown rapidly because of an influx of rural migrants who invested heavily not only in TVEs but also in housing and civic infrastructure. This has created so-called peasant cities like Longgang. Foreign investment in Guangdong province, mainly from overseas Chinese, has attracted millions of migrants from all over China and has transformed the province's towns and even villages into large cities. Dongguan, once a small town, now is one of the largest cities in China, with 5 million migrants among its 7 million residents. With a large number of vibrant small cities, towns, and industrialized villages, extended metropolitan regions or urbanized regions are taking shape in areas surrounding large cities in the Chang Jiang Delta and Pearl River Delta (Lin 1994; Zhou 2003).

Accompanying this phenomenal growth in towns and small cities are many problems such as pollution and loss of farmland (Tan 1993). Yet, urbanization from below has to some extent alleviated problems such as congestion and an overburdened infrastructure in large cities by channeling surplus rural labor into the towns and small cities. The urban development of these towns and small cities, however, emphasizes privatization and economic efficiency, an approach that is very different from the approach of urban development in the socialist era, which focused on equality; yet ironically, a smaller spatial inequality and phenomenal economic growth have been achieved, especially in the coastal regions.

MASSIVE RURAL-TO-URBAN MIGRATION AND A TWO-CLASS URBAN SOCIETY

In the socialist era, migration, especially rural-to-urban transfers, was tightly controlled through the *hukou* system. Since 1978, however, there has been an increasingly large volume of migrants, mostly rural-to-urban migrants, who have sought to take advantage of the new opportunities brought about by the reforms. Crowded transit centers, such as railway and bus stations and airports, provide the best testimony of the higher mobility in Chinese cities of the reform era. According to the 2000 Census, more than 30 percent of the Chinese population lived in a place different from their birthplace, and the estimated annual mobility rate was about 6 percent in the late 1990s—much higher than during the pre-reform era (which was, for example, 2–3 percent in 1977; see K. W. Chan 2001). Scholars have estimated there are 100–120 million in the so-called floating population—temporary migrants looking for jobs in Chinese cities (K. W. Chan 2001). Many factors contributed to this massive rural-to-urban migration, including rural reforms that released millions of surplus laborers from the land, the development of private sectors in cities, the reform of the *hukou* system, the phasing out of the rationing system, and the relaxation of migration controls.[4]

Rural-to-urban migrants unquestionably contribute to rapid urban development by providing their labor, skills, and talents and by filling employment and service gaps in cities. Yet these migrants are discriminated against by both existing institutions and permanent urban residents. The *hukou* system is under reform, and differences in economic opportunities and social benefits based on *hukou* status are shrinking (F. Wang 1997), but the discrimination against migrants has by no means disappeared. Based on *hukou* status, there are "permanent migrants" who are able to change their registration to their destination cities, and "temporary migrants" who are registered at places other than their destinations. The latter constitute the majority of migrants in Chinese cities (K. W. Chan 2001). Although permanent migrants enjoy employment opportunities and welfare benefits similar to those of urban residents, temporary migrants, who are mostly from the countryside, are not eligible for state employment and benefits in cities. They have to work in informal sectors and in temporary jobs—the so-called 3D jobs (demanding, dangerous, and dirty; K. W. Chan 2001)—and they often cluster in a few undesirable occupational niches such as in construction work (for men), and in sales and restaurant attendant positions (for women; Huang 2001). In addition, they are not allowed access to subsidized housing, which has dominated the housing stock in Chinese cities in recent decades. With underdeveloped private rental markets, most of these migrants have no option but to live in dormitories, trading markets, construction sites, hotels, and in peasants' houses, and they experience much worse housing conditions than local urban residents (Ma and Xiang 1998; Solinger 1995; F. Wu 2002). The emergence of dilapidated migrant enclaves in large cities is mainly a result of the limited housing options available to temporary migrants (see photo 9.4). Furthermore, the Chinese urban public generally have a negative attitude toward the migrants who have suddenly emerged in their cities, which is further perpetuated by negativity in the media. Migrants are often blamed for rising crime rates, overcrowding, overburdening of the transportation system, and even deterioration of the urban environment, such that

Photo 9.4. The largest migrant enclave in Beijing, Zhejiang Village. Photo by Youqin Huang

local municipal governments have periodically attempted to deport them and demolish their settlements (L. Zhang 2002). Persistent negative public discourse, together with a discriminatory institutional system, offers this floating population little chance to be assimilated into mainstream urban society, and a two-class urban society is emerging in China (Solinger 1995; K. W. Chan 1996).

HOUSING PRIVATIZATION AND URBAN SOCIOSPATIAL RESTRUCTURING

One of the most visible changes in Chinese cities is the appearance of new housing estates with different architectural styles and amenities, in sharp contrast to the previously uniform, utilitarian apartment buildings in work-unit compounds (see photo 9.5). As part of China's overall market transition, housing reform has contributed to a rapid development of private housing and to a profound transformation of the urban landscape and sociospatial structure. Urban households in China for the first time in decades enjoy various housing options and significantly improved housing conditions. Paradoxically, however, the Chinese are now also experiencing the effect of significant intra-urban inequality and residential segregation.

In the socialist era, housing was considered part of the social welfare benefits that the government should provide to its urban citizens. Through massive construction of public housing and the socialist transformation of existing private housing, the

Photo 9.5. New private housing in suburban Beijing. Photo by Youqin Huang

government successfully transformed a market-oriented housing system into a welfare-oriented system dominated by public rentals. As a result, less than 20 percent of all houses in China were privately owned in the 1980s.

Public housing was allocated according to a set of nonmonetary criteria such as marital status, job rank, seniority, and family size (Bian et al. 1997). Because rent was often less than 1 percent of household income, households enjoyed de facto ownership of their apartments (Tolley 1991). But while the public housing system improved housing conditions for the masses, there were also a number of problems, such as a severe housing shortage and poor housing quality, which were mainly a result of the low-rent policy (X. Q. Zhang 1998; Wang and Murie 1999).

After pilot experiments in several cities, nationwide urban housing reform was launched in 1988 to introduce market mechanisms into the housing system, and these reforms continue. First of all, while existing public housing now is being privatized through subsidized sales and rising rents, new private housing built by domestic and foreign developers is being added to the stock rapidly. Housing built by households themselves, and mainly for owner-occupancy, are also being encouraged, especially in small towns and cities (X. Q. Zhang 1998). Second, in contrast to the confiscation of private homes in the socialist era, homeownership is now being actively promoted through various methods. For example, public housing is being sold at a fraction of its market price to encourage sitting tenants to purchase their dwellings. "Affordable housing," that is, private housing with government-controlled prices, is only for sale to low-to-medium income households (State Council 1998). To further help Chinese households purchase homes, a mandatory long-term housing saving system—the Housing Provident Fund—has been set up, through which public employees contribute no less than 5 percent of their wages to their own accounts, which is then matched with the same amount from their work units. Recently, commercial housing loans have become another important source for financing home ownership. The Industrial and Commercial Bank of China, the largest commercial bank in China, had issued US$42.9 billion in home mortgages by the end of October 2002, and individual home loans increased by thirty-eight times during the period from 1997 to 2002 (*China News Digest* 2002).

Urban households, which in the relatively recent past had few housing choices other than waiting in long lines for subsidized rental housing, now can choose between public and private housing, and between rental and private home ownership. After several decades of suppression during the Maoist era and following recent promotion campaigns by the government, home ownership is clearly preferred by most Chinese. According to the 2000 Census, 72 percent of households in cities and 78 percent of households in towns owned their homes. While there are significant variations between cities, overall China's rate of home ownership is among the highest in the world, especially considering that its rate of home ownership was less than 20 percent in the 1980s and only 47 percent in 1996 (Huang and Clark 2002). Despite alarmingly high housing prices, especially in large cities like Beijing, most households are able to purchase their homes at relatively cheap prices because of persisting housing subsidies. For example, in 2000 more than 85 percent of home owners in Beijing paid less than 50,000 yuan (US$6,046) for their home, and 83 percent of renters paid less than 100 yuan per month (US$12), while the average annual wage income was 16,536 yuan (US$2,017; National Bureau of Statistics 2001).

Housing reforms have significantly improved housing consumption in Chinese cities. Per capita living space increased from 3.9 m^2 in 1978 to about 10 m^2 in 1998 (National Bureau of Statistics 1999). Yet compared to international standards, housing consumption in urban China is still low, and Chinese households still suffer from severe residential crowding. In 2000, each urban household had 2.27 bedrooms on average, while the average household size was 3.03 persons (National Bureau of Statistics 2002). More than 25 percent of urban households lived in dwellings with one or no bedroom. And in large cities like Shanghai, it is even more crowded, with more than 44 percent of households living in units with one or no bedroom. "A room of one's own" is still a dream for most households in Chinese cities (Huang 2003).

The ongoing housing reform has brought many benefits to urban households such as diverse housing options, better housing conditions, and higher occupational and residential mobility. Yet none of these come without trade-offs. Increasing social and spatial inequality is becoming a concern in China's previously rather homogeneous urban society (see photos 9.4 and 9.5). Instead of representing similar class backgrounds and living in similar work-unit compounds as was common in the socialist era, urban households are now sorted into different types of housing and neighborhoods. With the emergence of high-end gated communities and dilapidated migrant enclaves, China's relatively homogeneous urban society based on work-unit compounds is rapidly disappearing, and one with social separation and residential segregation is emerging. There is a real concern among scholars that this increasing residential segregation and housing inequality may lead to problems such as homelessness, slums, decayed urban areas, and social conflict.

NEW CITIES IN A NEW MILLENNIUM

Despite gradualism and a relatively short period of reforms, profound changes have taken place in Chinese cities. While there are still some vestiges of socialist urban planning, such as large public squares and uniform apartment buildings, Chinese cities are now beginning to display features of modern cities, including high-rise office buildings, suburban housing estates, large shopping centers, and specialized districts for entertainment and high-tech industries.

In contrast to a previously cellular urban structure based on work-unit compounds with comprehensive functions, specialization and differentiation are now being pursued in Chinese urban planning, and the results are evident in the spatial restructuring of land use and the transformation of urban landscapes. First of all, large housing estates, separate from employment centers, have been developed—mostly on the outskirts of cities—to accommodate households from different work units. But while people can now live in neighborhoods away from the watchful eyes of their colleagues, in general they have to commute longer and farther to work. This increasing separation between residential and work space, together with a surge in the use of private automobiles, has made traffic a daily concern in most Chinese cities, despite recent aggressive expansion and upgrading of the road and highway systems (see photo 9.6). Central cities are still preferred by most urban residents, but suburbanization is also taking place outside of many large cities as a result of improvements in transport between central cities and their suburbs, and there has been a massive development of new housing in these suburbs (Zhou and Ma 2000).

With ongoing urban land reform that allows land transactions and rent capitalization, large business and commercial centers that require intensive land use are being developed, often at city centers. Consequently, high-rise buildings and skyscrapers have mushroomed, which has significantly changed the skylines of many Chinese cities. Beijing, where the city center is a huge basin defined by Tiananmen Square and one-story Forbidden City, is building a new central business district on the east side of the city center where many high-rise office buildings, large hotels, and convention facilities are already located. Urban planners and decision makers in Beijing clearly envision a Western-style central business district comparable to those in Hong Kong, Paris, and New York. Further, with more than one hundred foreign banks and financial institutions, Pudong New District in Shanghai is becoming a financial district (see photo 9.3), and Shanghai is on the road to becoming an international financial center. In addition, different specialized districts—such as Zhongguancun High-Tech Zone in Beijing, the so-called Silicon Valley of China—foreign enclaves, and restoration districts are taking shape in large cities (Gaubatz 1995).

In obedience to an ideology of "production first, consumption later," the consideration of aesthetics was never a primary objective in Chinese socialist urban planning. Most buildings created according to this ideology were utilitarian and had similar

Photo 9.6.   Different transports jam a major street in Chongqing. Photo by Youqin Huang

designs, giving little personality to Chinese cities. Now all that has changed: municipal governments spend millions to beautify their streets, and every city in China is trying to build a unique urban landscape. The recently renovated pedestrian street Wang Fu Jing (Beijing's Fifth Avenue), is decorated with flowers, fountains, and Christmas lights (see photo 9.7). Xidan Culture Square in Beijing is characterized by postmodern statues dotting well-manicured lawns—in sharp contrast to the bare cement of Tiananmen Square—whereas the skyscrapers in Shanghai's Pudong New District are lit up each night, attracting millions of tourists. Similar makeover projects are taking place elsewhere. The recent decentralization of China's fiscal system has given local municipal governments unprecedented freedom in resource mobilization, which has enabled them to improve their urban infrastructures and environment (W. Wu 1999).

With increasing globalization, Chinese urban residents are also getting a taste of Western consumption and lifestyles. In addition to imported Western goods (from cars to cosmetics) and recreational activities (from surfing the Internet to golfing), they have also embraced the Western (particularly American) fast foods provided by major chains in their cities, chains such as KFC, Pizza Hut, McDonald's, and Starbucks. The first KFC outlet opened in Beijing in 1987. It is the largest KFC restaurant in the world, with five hundred seats in a three-story building, and it was an instant hit, setting the record for both single-day and annual sales in 1988 among the more than nine thousand KFC outlets worldwide (Yan 2000). In similar fashion, the first McDonald's in Beijing served more than forty thousand customers on its opening day April 23, 1992 (see photo 9.7). Within five years, thirty-five more McDonald's had been opened in Beijing;

Photo 9.7.   The Wang Fu Jing Shopping Center in Downtown Beijing. Photo by Youqin Huang

and thousands of similar establishments have opened in other Chinese cities. These fast-food establishments function more as social than as eating places in China because they provide the Chinese with an environment in which to experience a Western culture and lifestyle (Yan 2000).

In addition, Chinese cities, especially the large, coastal cities, are being transformed by international architectural firms and designers. Major landmark buildings in cities like Beijing, Shanghai, and Guangzhou are often designed by foreign architects—in contrast to the emphasis in the socialist era on self-reliance. For example, the tallest building in China and the fifth tallest in the world, Jinmao Tower in Pudong New District (see photo 9.3), was designed by Skidmore, Owings and Merrill, an American firm; while the pearl-shaped National Grand Theater in Beijing and bright Pudong International Airport in Shanghai were designed by French architect Paul Andreu. Major stadiums and the Olympic village being built in Beijing for the 2008 Olympic Games, the first magnetic levitation railway in Shanghai, Citic Plaza in Guangzhou, and even the city hall in Shenzhen were all designed by Western architects, who in this way are creating an international urban landscape in China.

But as Chinese cities such as these have become larger and more cosmopolitan, a whole set of new problems has emerged, including increasing social and spatial inequality, overcrowding, traffic jams, pollution, homelessness, and high crime and unemployment rates, despite the fact that the government has constantly attempted to avoid such social problems. Two decades ago, the Chinese government decided to shift its focus from social equality to economic efficiency, and today it is facing the dilemma of balancing these two again in its bustling cities.

Conclusion

As should not be surprising in a nation with the longest urban history in the world, urban development in China has followed a changing path, from a mature urban system before the middle of the nineteenth century to unbalanced urban development biased toward the Treaty Port cities during colonial times, then to strictly planned and controlled urban development in the socialist era, and now to a more market-driven urban development biased again toward the coastal cities. Despite constant shifts in ideology and changes in urban policies, especially since 1949, it is clear that the Chinese government has striven to achieve both sociospatial equality and economic efficiency in its urban development policies by emphasizing one aspect more than another as time and circumstance demand. While it is debatable whether the Chinese government has been successful in this regard, it is certain that China has avoided "urban explosion" and its associated urban problems, which have been widespread in many developing countries. Characterized by its under-urbanization, its changing path, its spatially and hierarchically balanced urban system, and a mixture of traditional, socialist, and modern urban landscapes, urban development in China is certainly unique. The classic theories of urban development based on European experience are inadequate to explain urban development in China, and country-specific perspectives, concepts, and theories need to be developed (Lin 1994; Fan 1999; Ma 2002). While the important roles of history, globalization, and local initiatives in China's urban development should be recognized, socialist institutions and urban policies embodying the government's ideology have been more important in shaping urban development in China, especially since 1949. Ma (2002) argues for a political economy perspective, one that emphasizes the role of the state as the ultimate decision maker, regulator, and participant in urban development in China. Despite a drastic shift in urban policies and different patterns of urban development, the central role of the state has not changed significantly. In the socialist era, the state developed the *hukou* system to control rural-to-urban migration and urban growth; used state investment to achieve a desired urban economy and a balanced urban system; applied its principle of spatial and administrative organization to reduce rural-urban inequality; and initiated political campaigns such as the Great Leap Forward, the Cultural Revolution, and the Third Front that had a direct and profound impact on urban development. In the reform era, despite globalization of production, the infusion of foreign capital, significant privatization, and decentralization of fiscal and political power to local places, the state (including local governments) continues to play a central role in urban development and urban transformation (Ma 2002). As we have suggested in this chapter, it was the state that designed gradual and spatially biased open door policies, encouraged the development of nonstate sectors, allowed rural-to-urban migration in a controlled fashion, and blueprinted the privatization of the housing system. Despite recent economic reforms, China is still politically a socialist nation with one dominate party, and the state still plays an important role in its urban development.

Notes

1. Because of the different welfare benefit entitlements owed to the urban and rural populations, it was considered a calculated political decision for the government to send part of its urban population to the countryside and at the same time to attract peasants to cities (Zhao 1981).

2. To promote integration between the countryside and cities and to guarantee a supply of food and vegetables to the cities, rural counties surrounding an existing large city were often incorporated into the city proper (Lo 1987). Population in these counties, predominately rural, was therefore sometimes included in the total population of cities and towns and thus became "urban" population, leading to an inflation in apparent urban populations.

3. The First Front was regarded as China's highly vulnerable coastal cities, and the Second Front was a vague intermediate zone between the First and Third fronts.

4. The food-rationing system was phased out in the 1990s, and temporary registration certificates were created to allow migrants to live in cities.

References Cited

Bian, Yanjie, et al. 1997. "Work units" and the commodification of housing: Observations on the transition to a market economy with Chinese characteristics. *Social Science in China* 18 (4): 28–35.

Cannon, Terry. 1990. Region, inequality, and spatial policy. In *The Geography of Contemporary China*, ed. Terry Cannon and Alan Jenkins. London: Routledge, 28–59.

Cartier, Carolyn. 2001. *Globalizing South China*. Malden, Mass.: Blackwell.

Castells, Manuel. 1977. *The Urban Question: A Marxist Approach*. Cambridge, Mass.: MIT Press.

Chan, Kam Wing. 1988. Rural-urban migration in China, 1950–1982: Estimates and analysis. *Urban Geography* 9 (1): 53–84.

———. 1994. *Cities with Invisible Walls: Reinterpreting Urbanization in Post-1949 China*. Hong Kong: Oxford University Press.

———. 1996. Post-Mao China: A two-class urban society in the making. *International Journal of Urban and Regional Research* 20 (1): 134–50.

———. 2001. Recent migration in China: Patterns, trends, and policies. *Asian Perspective* 25 (4): 127–55.

Chan, Roger C. K. 1995. Urban development strategy in an era of global competition: The case of Hong Kong and South China. In *Globalization and Regional Development in Southeast Asia and Pacific Rim*, ed. Gun Young Lee and Yong Woong Kim. Seoul: Korea Research Institute for Human Settlements, 202–27.

Chang, Sen-dou. 1977. The morphology of walled capital. In *The City in Late Imperial China*, ed. William Skinner. Stanford, Calif.: Stanford University Press, 75–101.

Chen, Tiejun, and Mark Seldon. 1994. The origins and social consequences of China's *hukou* system. *China Quarterly* 139:644–68.

Chen, Xiangming, and William L. Parish. 1996. Urbanization in China: Reassessing an evolving model. In *The Urban Transformation of the Developing World*, ed. Josef Gugler. London: Oxford University Press.

China News Digest. 2002. Home loan market booming in China. November 25.

Dong, Liming. 1985. Beijing: The development of a socialist capital. In *Chinese Cities: The Growth of the Metropolis since 1949*, ed. Victor F. S. Sit. Oxford: Oxford University Press.

Edmonds, Richard Louis. 1990. History: Historical perspectives on the current geography of China. In *The Geography of Contemporary China: The Impact of Deng Xiaoping's Decade*, ed. Terry Cannon and Alan Jenkins. London: Routledge, 61–78.

Fan, C. Cindy. 1992. Foreign trade and regional development in China. *Geographical Analysis* 24 (3): 240–56.

———. 1995. Developments from above, below, and outside: Spatial impacts of China's economic reforms in Jiangsu and Guangdong provinces. *Chinese Environment and Development* 6 (1 and 2): 85–116.

———. 1999. The vertical and horizontal expansions of China's city system. *Urban Geography* 20 (6): 493–515.

Fei, H.-T., et al. 1986. *Small Towns in China: Functions, Problems, and Prospects*. Beijing: New World Press.

Gaubatz, Piper Rae. 1995. Urban transformation in post-Mao China: Impacts of the reform era on China's urban form. In *Urban Spaces in Contemporary China: The Potential for Autonomy and Community in Post-Mao China*, ed. Deborah S. Davis et al. Washington, D.C.: Woodrow Wilson Center Press.

Hao, Yen-Ping. 1986. *The Commercial Revolution in Nineteenth-century China: The Rise of Sino-Western Mercantile Capitalism*. Berkeley: University of California Press.

Huang, Youqin. 2001. Gender, hukou, and the occupational attainment of female migrants in China (1985–1990). *Environment and Planning A* 33 (2): 257–79.

———. 2003. A room of one's own: Housing consumption and residential crowding in transitional urban China. *Environment and Planning A* 35 (4): 591–614.

Huang, Youqin, and William A. V. Clark. 2002. Housing tenure choice in transitional urban China: A multilevel analysis. *Urban Studies* 39 (1): 7–32.

Kirkby, Richard. 1985. *Urbanization in China: Town and Country in a Developing Economy, 1949–2000 A.D.* London: Croom Helm.

Li, Si-ming. 2000. The housing market and tenure decision in Chinese cities: A multivariate analysis of the case of Guangzhou. *Housing Studies* 15 (2): 213–36.

Lin, George C. S. 1994. Changing theoretical perspectives on urbanisation in Asian developing countries. *Third World Planning Review* 16 (1): 1–23.

———. 1998. China's industrialization with controlled urbanization: Anti-urbanism or urban-biased? *Issues and Studies* 34 (6): 98–116.

Lo, C. P. 1987. Socialist ideology and urban strategies in China. *Urban Geography* 8 (5): 440–58.

Logan, John, and Yanjie Bian. 1993. Inequalities in access to community resources in a Chinese city. *Social Forces* 72 (2): 555–76.

Logan, John, Yanjie Bian, and Fuqin Bian. 1999. Housing inequality in urban China in the 1990s. *International Journal of Urban and Regional Development* 23 (1): 7–25.

Ma, Laurence J. C. 1971. *Commercial Development and Urban Change in Sung China (960–1279)*. Ann Arbor: University of Michigan.

———. 1976. Anti-urbanism in China. *Proceedings of the Association of American Geographers* 8:114–18.

———. 1981. Introduction: The city in modern China. In *Urban Development in Modern China*, ed. Laurence J. C. Ma and Edward W. Hanten. Boulder, Colo.: Westview.

———. 2002. Urban transformation in China, 1949–2000: A review and research agenda. *Environment and Planning A* 34:1545–69.

Ma, Laurence J. C., and Biao Xiang. 1998. Native place, migration, and the emergence of peasant enclaves in Beijing. *China Quarterly* 155:546–81.

Ma, Laurence J. C., and Gonghao Cui. 1987. Administrative changes and urban population in China. *Annals of the Association of American Geographers* 77:373–95.

Ma, Laurence J. C., and Ming Fan. 1994. Urbanization from below: The growth of towns in Jiangsu, China. *Urban Studies* 31 (10): 1625–45.

Mote, Frederick W. 1977. The transformation of Nanking, 1350–1400. In *The City in Late Imperial China*, ed. William Skinner. Stanford, Calif.: Stanford University Press, 101–54.

Murphy, Rhodes. 1970. *The Treaty Ports and China's Modernization: What Went Wrong?* Ann Arbor: University of Michigan, Center for Chinese Studies.

National Bureau of Statistics (State Statistical Bureau). 1995. *Zhonguo chengshi tongji nianjian 1995* [Urban statistical yearbook of China 1995]. Beijing: China Statistics Press.

———. 1999. *Xin Zhongguo 50 nian tongji ziliao huibian* [A collection of statistical data on 50 years of New China]. Beijing: China Statistics Press.

———. 2001. *Zhonguo chengshi tongji nianjian 2001* [Urban statistical yearbook of China 2001]. Beijing: China Statistics Press.

———. 2002. *Zhongguo 2000 nian renkou puchan huizong* [Tabulations on the 2000 population census of China]. Beijing: China Statistics Press.

———. 2003. *Zhonguo chengshi tongji nianjian 2003* [Urban statistical yearbook of China 2003]. Beijing: China Statistics Press.

Pannell, Clifton W. 1981. Recent growth and change in China's urban system. In *Urban Development in Modern China*, ed. Laurence J. C. Ma and Edward W. Hanten. Boulder, Colo.: Westview.

Phillips, David R., and Anthony Gar-on Yeh. 1990. Foreign investment and trade: Impact on spatial structure of the economy. In *The Geography of Contemporary China: The Impact of Deng Xiaoping's Decade*, ed. Terry Cannon and Alan Jenkins. London: Routledge.

Ricci, Matteo. 1953. *China in the Sixteenth Century: The Journals of Matthew Ricci, 1583–1610.* Trans. Louis J. Gallagher. New York: Random House.

Shenzhen Statistical Bureau. 1990. *Shezhen Statistical Yearbook, 1990.* Beijing: China Statistics Press.

Sit, Victor F. S. 1995. *Beijing: The Nature and Planning of a Chinese Capital City.* New York: Wiley.

———. 2000. A window on Beijing: The social geography of urban housing in a period of transition, 1985–1990. *Third World Planning Review* 22 (3): 237–59.

Sit, Victor F. S., and C. Yang. 1997. Foreign-investment-induced exo-urbanization in the Pearl River Delta, China. *Urban Studies* 34: 647–77.

Skinner, G. W. 1977. Introduction: Urban development in imperial China. In *The City in Late Imperial China*, ed. William Skinner. Stanford, Calif.: Stanford University Press, 1–32.

Smith, David A. 1996. *Third World Cities in Global Perspective: The Political Economy of Uneven Urbanization.* Boulder, Colo.: Westview.

Solinger, Dorothy J. 1995. The floating population in the cities: Chances for assimilation? In *Urban Spaces in Contemporary China: The Potential for Autonomy and Community in Post-Mao China*, ed. Deborah S. Davis, Richard Kraus, Barry Naughton, and Elizabeth J. Perry. Washington, D.C.: Woodrow Wilson Center Press.

State Council. 1984. Guowuyuan guanyu nongmin jinru jizhen luohu wenti de tongzhi [Circular of the state council concerning the question of peasants entering towns for settlement]. *Guowuyuan gongbao* [*Bulletin of the state council*] 26:919–20.

———. 1998. Guowuyuan guanyu jingyibu shenhua chengzhen zhufang zhidu gaige jiakuai zhufang jianshe de tongzhi [A notification from the state council on further deepening the reform of urban housing system and accelerating housing construction]. State Council documentation no. 23.

Steinhardt, Nancy S. 1999. *Chinese Imperial City Planning.* Honolulu: University of Hawaii Press.

Tan, K. C. 1993. China's small town urbanization program: Criticism and adaptation. *GeoJournal* 29 (2): 155–62.

Tang, Wing-Shing. 1997. Urbanization in China: A review of its causal mechanisms and spatial relations. *Progress in Planning* 48 (1): 1–65.

Tolley, George S. 1991. Urban housing reform in China: An economic analysis. Washington, D.C.: World Bank/International Bank for Reconstruction and Development.

United Nations. 1999. *World Urbanization Prospects.* Washington, D.C.: United Nations Press.

Wang, Feng. 1997. The breakdown of a Great Wall: Recent changes in the household registration system of China. In *Floating Population and Migration in China: The Impact of Economic Reforms,* ed. Thomas Scharping. Hamburg: Institute of Asian Studies.

Wang, Ya Ping, and Alan Murie. 1999. *Housing Policy and Practice in China.* New York: St. Martin's.

Whyte, Martin King, and William L. Parish. 1984. Chinese urban structure. In *Urban Life In Contemporary China.* Chicago: University of Chicago Press.

Wright, Arthur F. 1977. The cosmology of the Chinese city. In *The City in Late Imperial China,* ed. William Skinner. Stanford, Calif.: Stanford University Press, 33–74.

Wu, Fulong. 1997. Urban restructuring in China's emerging market economy: Towards a framework for analysis. *International Journal of Urban and Regional Research* 21:640–63.

———. 2002. Sociospatial differentiation in urban China: Evidence from Shanghai's real estate market. *Environment and Planning A* 34:1591–1615.

Wu, Weiping. 1999. Reforming china's institutional environment for urban infrastructure provision. *Urban Studies* 36 (13): 2263–82.

———. 2002. Migrant housing in urban China: Choices and constraints. *Urban Affairs Review* 38 (1): 90–119.

Xie, Yichun, and Frank J. Costa. 1991. The impact of economic reforms on the urban economy of the People's Republic of China. *Professional Geographer* 43 (3): 318–35.

Xu, Xueqiang, and Si-ming Li. 1990. China's open door policy and urbanization in the Pearl River Delta region. *International Journal of Urban and Regional Research* 14 (1): 46–69.

Yan, Yunxiang. 2000. Of hamburger and social space. In *The Consumer Revolution in Urban China,* ed. Deborah S. Davis. Berkeley: University of California Press, 201–25.

Yeh, Anthony Gar-on, and Fulong Wu. 1995. Internal structure of Chinese cities in the midst of economic reform. *Urban Geography* 16 (6): 521–54.

Yeh, Anthony Gar-on, and Xueqiang Xu. 1997. Globalization and the urban system in China. In *Emerging World Cities in Pacific Asia,* ed. Fu-chen Lo and Yue-man Yeung. Tokyo: United Nations University Press.

Zhang, Li. 2002. Spatiality and urban citizenship in late Socialist China. *Public Culture* 14 (2): 311–34.

Zhang, Li, and Simon X. B. Zhao. 1998. Re-examining China's "urban" concept and the level of urbanization. *China Quarterly* 154:330–81.

Zhang, Xin Quan. 1998. *Privatisation: A Study of Housing Policy in Urban China.* New York: Nova Science.

Zhao, Lukun. 1981. Zai lun laodong jiuye wenti [A further discussion on the employment question]. *Renkou Yanjiu* [*Population Research*] (4): 18–24.

Zhou, Yixing. 2003. Gaige kaifang tiaojian xia de zhongguo chengshi jingji qu [Urban economic regions in China under reform]. *Dili Xuebao* [*Acta Geographica Sinca*] 58 (2): 271–84.

Zhou, Yixing, and Laurence J. C. Ma. 2000. Economic restructuring and suburbanization in China. *Urban Geography* 21(3): 205–36.

———. 2003. China's urbanization level: Reconstructing a baseline from the fifth population census. *China Quarterly* 173:176–96.

Zhu, Baoshu, and Guoqian Gu. 1991. Renkou qianyi fenxizhong de diyu koujing wenti [The spatial specification in the migration analysis]. *Renkou Yanjiu* [*Population Research*] 6:28–34.

CHAPTER 10

Reform and Challenge in China's Industrial Sector

The landmark economic reforms of December 1978 began in agriculture, but the industrial sector has been the great engine of China's economic growth for the last quarter century. China's major challenges—ensuring sustainable development, improving environmental protection, countering hyper-urbanization, controlling population growth, and maintaining stable foreign relations—all are influenced by the long-term health of its industrial sector. Reforms in the Chinese industrial sector range from closing unprofitable plants, improving product quality, cutting massive state subsidies to unsuccessful firms and factories, streamlining banking and export regulations, and promoting exports. As might be expected, winners and losers have emerged from the dramatic shakeup resulting from China's movement to a market economy. Stories of newly made millionaires vie for space in Chinese newspapers with articles on the sad plight of hundreds of thousands of laid-off, state-owned-factory workers. For young, college-educated, urban Chinese, this is the best of times for a career related to industry and manufacturing. On the other hand, for many of the folks working on the factory floor, the future is far less rosy because many firms have closed or are closing amid a reduction in subsidies and in the significantly more competitive environment of the post-reform era. This chapter documents the most important challenges facing China's industrial sector, and it includes an extended discussion of strategic industrial resources and the role that these resources play in the industrial sector. The chapter also provides a summary of the new industrial landscape that has evolved in China across space and time in the face of China's reform politics and policies.

Domestic and Global Implications of Chinese Industrialization

China's expanding role in international politics is closely related to the complex industrial issues that Chinese planners must address in the coming decades. Global trade in light manufactures originating from China, and the complex questions related to this trade, will constitute seminal economic and political debate for both workers and consumers throughout the world for at least the next fifty years (see chapter 7). China's entry into the World Trade Organization (WTO) and a twenty-year-long surge in manufactured goods at once provide considerable challenge and opportunity for other nations. The value of China's exports increased a staggering 44.9 times over the years from 1978 to 2003 (US$9.75 billion to US$438.2 billion). Over the same period, imports—especially in energy, ores, and industrial technology—also increased dramatically, from US$10.9 billion to US$412.8 billion. The majority of China's exports, 90.1 percent, are industrial manufactures. As fundamentals of comparative advantage and supply and demand have taken root in China's reformed, market-oriented economy, the export of labor-intensive Chinese manufactured goods has moved to the center of many current global trade issues. China's low-cost labor, as well as its controversial government subsidization of specific firms, industrial infrastructure, industrial research and development, and improved transport result in internationally competitive products with respect to both price and quality. Labor groups and governments of developed nations have reacted quickly to try to stem the flow of imports from China, but with little effect.

China's industrial products constitute more than household goods, shoes, clothing, toys, and novelty gifts. The country's entry into more sophisticated manufacturing sectors has been surprisingly swift. The production of more sophisticated products, particularly electronics and computer components, has brought Chinese firms into fierce competition with those of more industrialized nations—and much earlier than expected. China's diverse and balanced export strategy has firms of many different "ownership" types selling virtually any product you might imagine (see Made-in-China.com for some idea of this great range of goods). Chinese industrial planners have pinpointed for growth "four main high-technology targets: computers, information technology, pharmaceuticals, and new materials" (Walcott 2002, 352). Direct competition with North America, the EU, Japan, Korea, and Australia in these higher-end categories has set the stage for more complex international relations, and ensures that China will play a major role in the world's trading system and the global economy throughout our lifetimes.

In the past, if agriculture was the key link to China's well-being, there is no question that the promotion of sustainable growth in the industrial sector is now most important. Despite agriculture's successes (see chapter 8), the farm sector—even with processed exports—is simply not profitable enough to drive China's overall national development. Already, growth in the industrial sector, especially in the expansion of light industry into rural areas, has increased wages and living standards in many locations. Industrial growth has generated significant increases in tax revenues for reinvestment in public welfare, while siphoning off surplus labor from the farms. Increased returns to both labor and capital have profoundly influenced Chinese society. Most Chinese working steadily in industry now live better, earn more, and dream about better lives for themselves or their children. Higher wages and greater productivity allow for the expansion of the service sector and the growth of the tax base, which spreads the benefits of industrial growth far beyond the factory gate.

On the other hand, there are many daunting problems facing China's industrial sector that must be addressed, and quickly. Mandatory fiscal reform for state-owned enterprises (SOEs), predicated by decades of debt, has already created massive lay-offs concentrated in China's old, heavy-industry cities and regions. In traditional SOE cities, unemployment may be as high as 20–25 percent. The out-of-work—and retired workers who have lost their pensions as the state-industrial system has collapsed—feel frustrated and abandoned. Many now have given up on the formal sector, and work at or below the poverty line as street vendors or in the informal service sector. These unemployed or underemployed workers face constant uncertainty, never knowing in advance if they will be able to find enough work to feed their families. More than wages are at stake. Promised healthcare and retirement benefits disappear entirely or are paid out grudgingly and at inadequate levels as numerous state firms are shuttered. These problems have resulted in significant social unrest and grave concerns about the future. This instability is all the more difficult to handle by workers who expected cradle-to-grave employment under the old communist system. Further, there remains an important, coastal bias to industrial reorganization, and the benefits of this reorganization have fallen mostly to the citizens of the coasts, as later sections of this chapter will clearly indicate.

In addition to China's many pressing economic concerns, environmental problems due to its expanded industrial production have coincided with economic growth, especially beyond China's larger cities. The larger and more diversified industrial sector that has emerged in many rural areas throughout China has led to a proliferation of pollution problems (Economy 2004). Pollution of groundwater is common, and getting worse. Air pollution in China's major cities has never been as bad as it is now—and it is getting worse as more and more people buy automobiles—but now smaller cities are also reporting polluted air as well. Only in the late 1990s did citizens' groups start to demand a more rigorous and successful government response to industrial pollution. There are currently more than 2,000 environmental NGOs (nongovernmental agencies) demanding environmental protection at the present time, but this is a very difficult set of problems to address, and many citizens have grown frustrated by the lack of government support, especially at local levels. Environmental protection related to manufacturing is a critical issue, yet regulations are difficult to enforce for a variety of reasons. Leaders in rural and suburban areas, traditionally places with weak environmental monitoring systems and limited environmental protection staff, must address these problems with very limited resources. Shutting down polluting factories reduces employment and may be unpopular in the short term despite the fact that polluting factories may cause long-term health problems. Exactly how to restrict polluting firms, and deciding who will pay for the clean-up of current and past industrial sites, is controversial. Reconciling industrial growth and environmental protection is now widely recognized at the highest levels of Chinese government as a prerequisite for sustained economic expansion.

The Industrial Sector Defined

It will be useful from the outset to define what is meant by the industrial sector. *Industry* encompasses both finished manufactured products (e.g., computers, pharmaceuticals, telecommunications equipment, household goods, food products, and clothing) and primary products (e.g., energy, paving products, construction materials, industrial chemicals, iron or steel and other metals and ores used in manufacturing, and farming inputs). These latter materials have undergone as much of a boom in China as have the former. Higher incomes and revenues from industry and a rapidly expanding service sector have created greater internal demand for transport, housing, and public infrastructure. To China as a developing nation, the importance of these heavy industry products vis-à-vis all industrial output is greater since China's transport systems, including road, rail, and water routes, remain inadequate. The state must continue to provide, and promote, investment in these areas in order to ensure that Chinese products of all types move freely and inexpensively (and thereby remain competitive). Similarly, affordable housing and improvements to public infrastructure are always desperately needed in China, and demand for building materials, including concrete, glass, paint, wood, and construction-grade steel, appears almost insatiable.

Industrial Location as a National Development Debate

Industrial output has increased at an unprecedented rate—for any nation—since 1978 (see figure 10.1). But aggregate statistics, however impressive, reflect only a part of the story. There is an important spatial aspect related to this rejuvenation of the industrial sector. As in all times and places, rapid growth of the industrial sector has not benefited all places in equal measure, and industrial output has increased the most in the coastal provinces (see map 10.1). The higher wages and tax revenues associated with the growth of industrialization combine with other political and economic factors to create significant differences in quality of life and economies across China's provinces. Typically, places with the most industrial employment tend to have better overall standards of living. While there is some debate as to the extent of regional inequality in

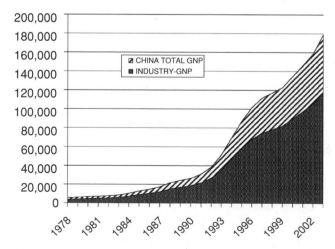

Figure 10.1. China's GNP and Share from Industry (100 million yuan in current value). **Source:** National Bureau of Statistics 2002, 409.

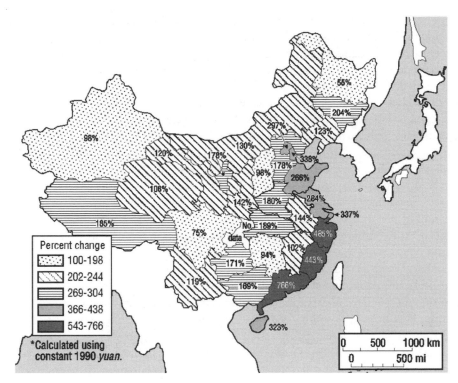

Map 10.1. Percentage Change in Industrial Output by Province, 1990–2001. **Source:** National Bureau of Statistics 1991, 397; 2002, 425. Cartographic design by Mary Lee Eggart.

China (depending on the measurement used), it is safe to argue that the Chinese coastal provinces, especially in the South and East, have advanced more than most interior regions (Fan 1995; Lin 2002; Shen 1999; Wei 1996).

This uneven distribution of wealth and development is partially attributable to the industrial desirability of some locations over others. Prior to the Industrial Revolution in Europe, high-density settlements in agrarian states tended to be found along coasts, or within alluvial lowlands and valleys, where food and agricultural commodity production was most reliable due to access to water, quality soils, and efficient transport. Coastal or riverine settlements dominated, and emerged as great cities (the core) controlling the interior (the periphery). In contrast to this general model (which also applies to China), modern industrial inputs such as ferrous and nonferrous ores and coal are found in greater concentrations in mountainous or plateau regions (the periphery) due to a range of geologic factors. In China, most of its strategic reserves of fossil fuels, minerals, and metals are found in the western and central portions of the country and in the Northeast, whereas the most rapid growth in manufacturing has occurred within historic industrial bases located largely in the eastern coastal region or along the great east–west thoroughfare of the Chang Jiang (Yangtze River). It is this east coast core, at once more powerful politically and economically, that sets the terms of China's trade and investment.

There are also historical factors to be considered in the genesis of China's contemporary industrial map. China's earliest manufacturing bases—driven in part by the decisions of early Western firms (textiles and other light manufactures) to locate in accessible coastal cities during the unequal treaties period (see chapters 3 and 9)—were virtually all located in the East. Starting in 1949, Mao Zedong tested a variety of approaches, including policy initiatives and directed investments, to promote the relocation of industry to interior regions. These strategies evolved in distinct historical periods, each with particular domestic goals, and tempered by equally different foreign policy concerns (see chapter 7). Still, despite these efforts, China's coastal areas today remain home to most of the nation's major manufacturing firms.

Mao Zedong interpreted China's uneven spatial economy circa 1949 as a legacy of coastal capitalist enclaves. Consequently, he introduced policies intended to develop the interior for economic and strategic political reasons. In retrospect, with a few exceptions, these efforts to promote parity through state investments in industry in the western and central portions of China were not very successful.

The current spatial distribution of China's industrial sector, then, reflects both historical and environmental factors, including resource location, regional availability of investment capital, technical expertise, and transportation infrastructure. More recently, reform-era policies have emphasized local decision making, agglomeration effects, and efforts to exploit the comparative advantages held by each region or province. In general, the industrial plant in the best location, having the best technology, the lowest transport costs, and the best product will be most likely to survive in contemporary China. Simply put, these recent, market-oriented reforms have benefited plants and companies located near the largest urban markets (both capital and consumer) with access to efficient ports, and in some interior cases, along superior transport arteries. Once again, this gives manufacturing bases in East China distinct advantages at the present time (Walcott 2002; Wei and Fan 2000; Yeung and Chu 2000).

As a consequence of ongoing problems with regional equity, a major development thrust of the first decade of the new millennium has been a national effort called the Develop the West program, which started in 2000 (Tian 2002). The program provides a variety of investments, incentives, and subsidies to motivate both domestic and international investors to invest heavily in industrial production and infrastructure in West and Central China. The beneficiaries will be China's six westernmost provinces—still home to 350 million people and covering 6.8 million km^2. This ambitious, government-driven program provides clear proof that the state will still play an active and vital role in China's economic development policies for decades to come—even if growth is more costly in certain regions. Market forces will mostly determine which firms survive, but the government will continue to manage regional development efforts to mitigate the impact of freewheeling market economics. The role of the state in ameliorating regional imbalances is currently the focus of much debate, and promises to be one of the central issues in China's domestic politics. China's future economic success may well be dictated as much by the success of government development efforts as by the economics of the marketplace. Western reports on China's economy tend to focus on the latter, treating government intervention as an evolutionary stage to be shed as soon as possible, but a more accurate appraisal would see China as moving toward the "state corporatism" practiced by Japan, South Korea, and Taiwan, where the government role in managing the industrial sector is both significant and enduring.

Background: Industry in Traditional China

China's industrial history is, in relative terms, rather short. Manufacturing in traditional China largely concentrated on the same products that had been produced for millennia. The technical transformations that revolutionized Europe's social, economic, and political relations in the 1700s did not occur in China. The reasons for this are complex. There was no shortage of technical understanding and competence, but inventions with potential industrial applications were not applied in China as they were in Europe and later in North America and Japan. Fundamental understanding of chemistry, physics, and metallurgy in classical China rivaled or exceeded that of Europe in the same period. This knowledge led to many commercial applications in Europe, but a domestic "industrial revolution" did not occur in China. Shortages of capital and strong central government control may partly explain these different trajectories. During the late dynastic era, most existing industries in China, such as silk manufacture, salt production, tea processing, and food processing (rice mills or oil-pressing plants), were owned by local elites but closely monitored and taxed by departments within the imperial court bureaucracy. Exports of the most lucrative products, such as silk, tea, and porcelain, were controlled by the court through licensed firms, often with lucrative relationships to government officials. This system of strict, if sporadic, control may have limited local initiative (Braudel 1986, 586). Lucian Pye (1972, 82) has argued for the limiting effect of arbitrary taxation and internal taxes and tariffs (*liken*) on capitalist-style industrial expansions. Wallerstein (1976) adds strict court regulation, a largely agrarian economy, and a highly stratified social system that limited the rise of a merchant class (in contrast to European guildhalls) to the mix.

Interestingly, local manufacturing in traditional China was also organized by guilds, but the role (and power) of the guilds did not change over time, as it did in Europe. Absentee landlords, evolving as a direct result of the imperial system in which influential families maintained costly residences both at home and in the capital, also may have limited local investment in proto-manufacturing activities. For these reasons, investments in modern industry were not made in China at the same time that such investments were expanding rapidly in Europe and the United States.

Local manufacturing of simple, labor-intensive products in all rural areas cannot be completely dismissed. While making a limited technical contribution to China's future industrial growth, countless small-scale local firms, operating in the face of constantly shifting taxation and control, forged a strong entrepreneurial spirit in Chinese character and culture. The support of such activities by leading local families in particular regions of China, such as Jiangsu, Zhejiang, or Fujian provinces, would later provide expertise in the reform era, when flexibility and daring in the marketplace would once again be rewarded.

In the period prior to 1949, rural manufacturing efforts in most areas of China often concentrated on the agro-processing of consumer products such as rice- and sorghum-based alcohol, soy, rough cloth, farm implements, fermented foodstuffs, and noodles. Partial processing reduced weight, lowered transport costs, and extended trade areas. Beyond these products, however, villages and small towns and their rural hinterlands had little or no industry, and most farm households were largely self-sufficient by necessity.

A major turning point came after the first Opium War (1839–1842) with the advent of a subsequent era known as the unequal treaties period. As foreign governments and businesses occupied coastal areas after the 1840s, output of manufactures such as textiles, tea, glass, and porcelain grew slightly, but profits were collected by foreign investors rather than reinvested to improve factories or production efficiency. As a consequence, the quality of manufactures and the way they were produced in China remained unchanged for much of the period. The dominant role of foreign powers in China's early industrial history was remarkable. After the first decade of the twentieth century, more than 80 percent of Chinese shipping, 30 percent of cotton-yarn spinning, 90 percent of the rail network, and 100 percent of iron production was under foreign control.

The greatest concentration of Chinese industries, including textiles, emerged within the Chang Jiang Valley and Jiangnan (southern Jiangsu and northern Zhejiang provinces). These regions, together with Shanghai, accounted for more than one-half of China's industrial output even as late as the 1930s (Brandt 1989, 76). Notably, the renowned prosperity of Jiangnan's agricultural economy provided capital that nurtured investments in the mechanization of traditional textile industries. At present, this region is among the most prosperous in all of China.

This eastern concentration of capital, technology, and low-cost transport represents an important legacy of the unequal treaties period in that the industrial base by 1949 was spatially concentrated in a few coastal cities, Jiangnan, and in ports on the Chang Jiang. In practical terms, all of these regions were first controlled by foreign capitalists, and then nominally by the Japanese until the end of World War II. In the 1930s, the cities of Shanghai, Tianjin, Qingdao, Hangzhou, Suzhou, Beijing, Nanjing, and Wuxi accounted for around 94 percent of the total industrial output of China.

A second industrial base was in the northeastern provinces, a legacy of Japanese occupation from 1905 to the end of World War II. Resource-poor Japan invested heavily here through the puppet state of Manchukuo, concentrating on ore extraction and ferrous metal production. The transport system of the Northeast (Manchuria), a legacy of Japanese occupation and exploitation, is more advanced than in most interior regions of China even at the present time. In summary, China's prerevolutionary industrial base was extremely small, technologically backward even for the time, and very spatially concentrated in the coastal regions. When the Japanese took control of eastern China after 1931, some industry did move into the interior—particularly into the Sichuan Basin—but such relocations were minor in scope. Before the two world wars, it is estimated that China had 3,890 factories, of which 1,290 were in Shanghai. Sichuan, home to Chongqing (Chongking), the wartime nationalist capital, had only 33 factories. By the end of 1941, there were 1,350 privately owned industrial plants of all sizes in Free China (areas not controlled by the Japanese)—mostly in Sichuan. This spatial concentration of industrial production and associated expertise, credited to foreign interests and advantageous export and import locations on the southern and eastern coasts, remains a critical component of contemporary discussions of China's industrial geography and resource use at the present time. Coastal concentrations of skilled labor, capital, managerial expertise, research universities, and foreign connections all helped ensure that many of China's factories would never stray too far from the coasts even in the Maoist era, and certainly not under the market-oriented policies of the present.

Stages of Industrial Development after 1949

During the last fifty-five years, China's leaders have followed several different approaches to industrial development. These approaches reflected changes in China's domestic political patterns and changing relations with foreign countries. Eight fairly distinct periods of industrial development between 1949 and the present can be identified. The mercurial changes in policy responsible for these periods have had many noticeable effects on the industrial landscape. Again, location plays an important role in the current situation. The fundamental imbalance between the location of most of China's strategic resources in the western and central portions of the nation and China's historic manufacturing bases in the Northeast and on the eastern seaboard should remain foremost in the minds of readers. Issues related to resource accessibility are familiar themes in the histories of many nations, particularly large nations such as Russia, Canada, Brazil, the United States, South Africa, and Australia. As we saw in chapter 1, China's leaders are faced with the dilemma of expanding industrial output while trying to promote regional equity and environmental protection at the same time.

REHABILITATION AND RECOVERY (1949–1952)

Immediately after the Chinese communist revolution (1949), virtually all factories still in operation after twenty years of Japanese occupation and civil war were nationalized, in keeping with the communist vision of the ideal state as manifested in the Soviet Union. While the efficacy of this policy is now commonly criticized, the Soviet Union, in retrospect, provided the only viable model in accordance with communist ideology. China was a largely agricultural and commercial society, torn asunder by decades of war and unrest, and its industrial base was small, concentrated, and poorly integrated with the national economy. China was faced with a possible U.S.-supported invasion by the Nationalists who were based on Taiwan, and it had only a tenuous grasp on its outer regions, where local warlords continued to have considerable influence. The state had to rapidly increase or initiate production of all strategic materials needed for the defense and the consolidation of the nation. Given these political realities, China's planners were logical in trying to rapidly expand domestic output by substituting labor for scarce capital and technology to meet immediate needs. Growth rather than efficiency was the critical impetus for many of the state's policies. Further, as Western diplomacy effectively sealed China off from the rest of the world, Mao Zedong quickly realized that China must be self-sufficient. By 1952, the capacity of China's industrial output had returned to prerevolutionary levels, and the nation was ready to undertake long-term programs to develop the economy.

THE FIRST FIVE-YEAR PLAN (1953–1957)

Following the Soviet model, and encouraged by Soviet advisors before its relations with the Soviet Union soured in the late 1950s, the Chinese central government took the dominant role in determining how China's industrial expansion was to proceed. Massive state investments in key industries such as metallurgy, oil and gas, mining, and transport quickly followed. The commune system used for agricultural production (see chapters 7 and 8) was quickly introduced in urban areas as well—for all types of factories. These urban communes still represent an important aspect of the morphology of Chinese cities. Large, state-owned factories were designed to be as self-reliant as possible. Workers lived on the factory grounds or in housing blocks nearby. Elementary schools and kindergartens were located on the grounds of each factory so young children could walk to school and visit with parents at lunch. Major factories all issued scrip (rather than cash) that could be exchanged at factory stores for necessities such as soap, toilet paper, and seasonings. Clinics owned and managed by each large factory provided routine health care. This utilization of space, played out in the local political arena in the absence of market forces, contributed to China's socialist urban landscape. As the factories expanded, space in the cities and suburbs became scarce, and boundary walls between work units (*danwei*), ubiquitous in China's cities even to the present, went up everywhere to delimit property boundaries and prevent incursions by other factories or *danwei* of other types. The historical evolution of the industrial *danwei* system, then, has greatly influenced the appearance and layout of Chinese cities up to the present time (see chapter 9).

The performance of the industrial sector increased during the first Five-Year Plan, partly as a dividend from peace. Existing plants were used more intensively, and new industrial projects were constructed when funds were available, with emphasis on the construction of heavy-industry infrastructure, including iron and steel mills, machine tool and die plants, construction material plants, and mining- or metallurgy-related processing plants. Over 80 percent of the nation's total industrial investment during this period went to heavy industries. In an effort to counter the effects of pre-1949 investment patterns, approximately 55 percent of total investment and approximately 75 percent of all monies invested in plant construction were allocated to inland areas. Consequently, many industrial centers in the interior grew rapidly, including Baotou, Wuhan, Lanzhou, Taiyuan, Xi'an, and Luoyang. This change in policy was based on Mao's belief that a much faster rate of economic growth could be achieved by complete public ownership of the economy, guided by highly centralized planning, and by encouraging the masses to work harder through spiritual incentives (that is, propaganda) rather than material incentives.

THE GREAT LEAP FORWARD (1958–1960)

Few goals of the Eighth Congress of the Chinese Communist Party, convened in September 1956, were as touted, or as radical, as the introduction of a national plan for super-accelerated industrialization. China's leadership estimated that three five-year plans would be needed to industrialize the nation. As a consequence of these plans, the disastrous Great Leap Forward was introduced in 1958 with the slogan "Twenty years in a day." In addition to the introduction of the commune system borrowed from agriculture, industrial growth was theoretically to be assured through the use of "backyard" furnaces for the production of pig iron, which then could be further processed in centralized mills or cold worked into farm implements and construction steel. The output from most of these operations turned out to be of very poor quality—often useless. The Great Leap was an unmitigated disaster, and all Chinese, urban and rural, grew frustrated in the face of extreme hardship and mass starvation in many areas. Estimates range up to 30 million deaths as a result of the program and the concurrent famines. The Great Leap placed a special emphasis on the development of local industries because this was in line with Mao's desire to upgrade the level of economic growth in rural areas and in the western provinces. A rural commune system, completed in 1958, provided the mechanism for administering rural industrialization.

RECOVERY AND READJUSTMENT (1961–1965)

Fundamental policy changes were made after the Great Leap in response to its tragic results. Agriculture, again described as "the foundation of the national economy," was assigned top priority for development. Industrial growth was based on systematic and more cautious planning, with a heavy emphasis given to those sectors that could support agricultural development. The entire economy recovered slowly but steadily, and consumer goods, especially those for peasant consumption, were produced in greater quantity to mollify frustration in the rural areas. This recovery was based mainly on the more effective use of existing facilities rather than on the construction of new projects.

By 1964 the economy had made sufficient progress to prompt Premier Zhou Enlai to announce at the Third National People's Congress that the economy had recovered and that it was time to modernize the nation based on the "Four Modernizations" of industry, agriculture, national defense, and science and technology. The expression "Four Modernizations," however, was never mentioned in the following decade because of various upheavals caused by the Cultural Revolution. Still, it is important to realize that the basic blueprint put forth in early Four Modernizations documents reappeared in 1975, and became national policy shortly after the death of Mao Zedong in 1976.

THE CULTURAL REVOLUTION (1966–1969)

China's economic development has always been closely linked to its domestic political events, which in hindsight, has caused clear problems. Economic decisions always have political contexts, but rapid-fire shifts in policy focus and investment certainly inhibited China's efficient industrialization.

The Cultural Revolution brought profound and often violent changes to Chinese society, which adversely affected the nation's industrial performance. The extent to which the Cultural Revolution disrupted the industrial economy, however, was not as great as one might have expected. Large-scale disruption of industrial enterprises, transportation networks, and raw-material supplies were confined primarily to isolated areas in the early phase of the movement, with the exception of a few major cities such as Beijing. Even by 1967, efforts were being made to prevent the fervently excited Red Guards from further damaging the economy. Still, the initiative of local cadres critical to further industrialization in the interior was stifled. Local officials were often scared into inactivity, and efforts to improve industrial output and efficiency were delayed. Further, the outbreaks of xenophobia that occurred during the Cultural Revolution gave rise to an almost complete self-imposed national isolation. Foreign trade stagnated, and the importing of foreign equipment was strongly discouraged, increasing the technology gap between China and the industrial nations of the world. Most Chinese colleges, research institutes, and universities were closed for at least some portion of the Cultural Revolution. This resulted in later shortages of industrial scientists and technicians and a lack of managerial expertise, which led to further inefficiencies and widespread losses at most manufacturing concerns.

REORIENTATION (1970–1976)

During this complex and poorly understood period, a precarious balance of power existed between pragmatists led by Zhou Enlai and radicals led by the now infamous (and later purged) Gang of Four, which included Mao's last wife. The former group ultimately gained the upper hand, but again time was lost. Ultimately, with the consent of an ailing Mao, Zhou Enlai engineered a more Western-friendly foreign policy. One important reason for this change was China's desire to obtain Western technology to accelerate economic development—especially industrial production. On the whole, national economic growth registered impressive gains during this period, and by 1974 the nation's industrial output had more than doubled from that of 1967. Growth in output for heavy industry fueled most of this domestic recovery. For the first time since 1949, credit was used in foreign trade to purchase advanced, if expensive, Western technology, with the goal of catching up to the developed countries. The living standard of the average Chinese person began to improve during this period, but not at the pace of the post-1978 period.

THE FOUR MODERNIZATIONS (1976–2000)

The goal of the Four Modernizations program was made quite clear. By the end of the century, China was to be at the forefront of the world's industrial nations in a number of areas. Per capita gross national product (GNP) was to reach US$1,000, largely based on industrial expansion. The return to Four Modernization policy is clearly an important benchmark in China's economic history, and heralded the adoption of many strategies that were later to be championed by the resilient Deng Xiaoping.

ONGOING REFORM IN THE INDUSTRIAL SECTOR (2001–Present)

The manufacture of products truly in demand keeps people working and spending their wages in a growing economy. A mere twenty-seven years ago, China had legendary inefficiencies in planning, production, and distribution, and it produced a very limited mix of products almost exclusively for the domestic market (Organization for Economic Co-operation and Development 2002). Gross output had gone up most years since 1949, but the quality of most products was inferior to those traded on international markets. In retrospect, scholars generally agree that reliance on state subsidies and centralized planning isolated factories and their management from the frustration of consumers and other downstream users of their products. The poor quality of manufactured goods in the early years of "new" China was initially accepted as yet another cost of true political and economic autonomy, but the times have changed. Currently, consumers are protected by government-sponsored complaint hotlines, product warranties, and even lemon laws that prosecute firms that produce shoddy goods.

In 2005, many dozens of high-quality, low-cost Chinese products are found in every American home. The United States is hardly unique in its consumption of Chinese goods, as thousands of Chinese products are now industry-leaders throughout the world. International trade has not only provided China with profits and higher wages, it has also required competitiveness, modern manufacturing technologies, sophisticated product marketing and advertising, up-to-date distribution systems, and modern managerial expertise. Most importantly, as China's consumers, particularly those in the cities, have grown more prosperous, domestic demand for manufactured goods of all types has also exploded, clearing the way for greater and greater levels of production (Veeck and Burns 2005).

The Importance of Economic Reform in the Industrial Sector

Increased production of higher-quality goods is but one aspect of China's reforms. The more important story concerns the new attitudes and perspectives of the Chinese economic planners charged with industrial restructuring, a restructuring that is as much about the changing "geography" of industrial growth and the ways it influences migration and regional equality as it is about increases in trade and productivity. Although there are many reasons for the dramatic changes to the economic landscape, two overriding policy agendas stand out: (1) allowing the continued decentralization of industrial planning—brought about by privatization and new forms of collective ownership—that lies at the core of China's industrial resurgence; and (2) continuing the ongoing efforts that have radically transformed the industrial sector along with rural society and culture by promoting (or permitting) the dispersal of industry into rural areas. Indeed, in a mere twenty-five years, China's entire industrial sector has been restructured and revitalized, rebuilt from the top down *and* bottom up as state policies have been initiated and adjusted in the face of the actions of countless millions of entrepreneurs throughout the cities and the countryside. Tariffs for domestic protection remain in many industries, but will be reduced and eventually removed due to WTO agreements.

Nothing represents the changes inherent in China's most recent "industrial revolution" as well as the declining importance of China's SOEs (see figure 10.2). Once the very hallmark of China's industrial sector, SOEs accounted for only 18.8 percent of total output in 2005, whereas in 1978, SOEs accounted for 77.6 percent of total output value. Currently, there are also many more types of enterprise ownership, including private firms (21.0 percent), share corporations (18.4 percent), and collective-ownership types such as township-village enterprises (TVEs; 16.8 percent). Private or share-holding firms, including foreign firms, that simply did not exist in 1978, accounted for 40 percent of output in 2004 (National Bureau of Statistics 2004, 513).

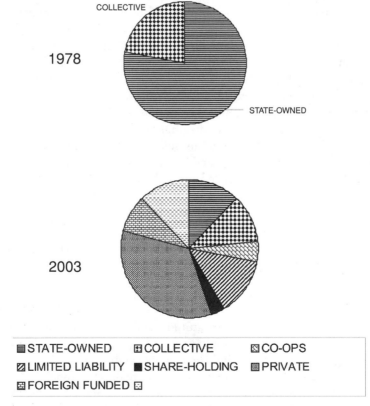

Figure 10.2.   Industrial Firms by Type of Ownership (percentage of all firms with sales over 5 million yuan). *Source:* National Bureau of Statistics 1980; 2003, 513.

Changes in ownership are part and parcel of the cost-cutting processes mandated by Beijing. The government has given clear notice that annual subsidies to money-losing factories will be phased out within a decade (or less). Management must either nurse their firms to profitability or expect their firms to be closed, with everyone losing their jobs. Even strategic industries such as steel, transport, and chemicals are increasingly being forced to deal with competitive market realities because the massive losses characteristic of many of the largest SOEs are no longer tolerated. Many "heavy industrial" SOEs have already been broken up or privatized, with many more on the auction block. Factories and firms are encouraged to consider public sources of capital through public stock offerings, employee purchase, the addition of foreign partners, or outright sale to new investors.

State Ownership of Strategic Resources and Its Implications

China's extractive industries, including mining and the energy sector, provide several excellent case studies of the effects of reform-era policies on SOEs, and offer a useful background on these critical resources. China is well-endowed with the mineral resources vital for economic development. Reserves of 148 kinds of minerals have been surveyed and assessed, and except for fossil fuels, China has sufficient domestic supplies of all strategic resources needed for continued industrial growth. But as mentioned earlier in the chapter, these resources are often in the wrong places vis-à-vis processing and manufacturing plants, and consumers.

Of the many cases that might be cited, the closely related iron, steel, and coking coal industries offer an interesting example of the locational mismatches confronting China's industrial planners. Coal of varying types and quality is distributed extensively throughout many regions of China, with the most important concentrations in the central and southwestern provinces or autonomous regions of Shanxi, Shaanxi, Inner Mongolia, and Guizhou (see map 10.2). Traditionally, Shanxi province, with the greatest deposits of coking and non-coking bituminous coal, has been the center of China's coal industry—so much so that it's known as the "coal province." In 1990, the date of the last comprehensive survey of coal resources, China's reserves were estimated to be 954.4 billion metric tons (Mt), with an annual output of 1.08 billion Mt, ranking it first in the world (*National Economic Atlas of China* 1994, 74). Demand for 2005 is estimated at 0.87 billion Mt. As pressure to reform SOEs mounted in the mid-1980s, planners had to decide which locations would qualify for loans to upgrade equipment and which mines would be closed. The scale of this restructuring process was truly daunting. Over sixty thousand small mines were scheduled for closing by 2006. Such decisions, combining central planning and market economics, are both economically and politically difficult. Many coal-mining areas are among China's poorest, and mining jobs—while dangerous—pay better than staying on the farm. For example, of China's total measured coal reserves, 62 percent are located in northern China, where income

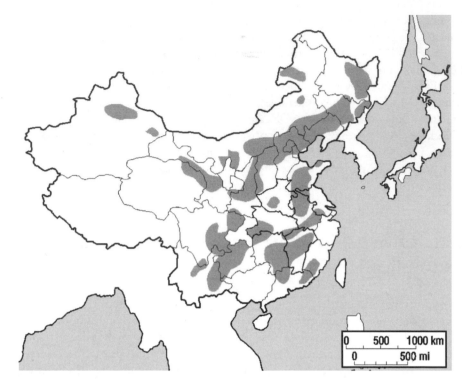

Map 10.2. Major Areas of Coal Production in China. **Source:** *National Economic Atlas of China 1994* (Hong Kong: Oxford University Press, 1994), 119–22. Cartographic design by Mary Lee Eggart.

amounts to less than 6 percent of national total (Sun 1988). Yet if market reform is to become a reality, inefficient mines of many types, including coal, must be closed.

The majority of the largest steel mills that depend on this coal are located in the East: in Liaoning (Northeast China), in the cities of the North China Plain provinces, and in the cities of Wuhan (Hubei) and Shanghai. In addition, however, there are still too many small, inefficient steel mills that must be consolidated (see map 10.3). Further, China's housing and transport booms are greatest in the eastern provinces, and as a consequence, there is a massive demand here for construction-grade steel. Unfortunately, about 95 percent of China's iron ore deposits are classified as low-grade ores, with an average iron content of 32 percent, and only 5 percent of reserves are classified as high-grade ores, with an iron content over 60 percent. The major ore-producing areas are found in Yunnan (Panxi area), Hubei (centered on Wufeng), Jiangsu-Anhui (Ningwu area), Hebei-Shanxi (Hanxing and Wutai areas), Hebei (Jidong areas), and Liaoning (Anben area; *National Economic Atlas of China* 1994, 15). Applying the most advanced technology, much of this ore could be processed profitably, but at present, a significant share of China's building boom relies on its growing steel imports. China's steel production ranked first in the world in 2005, the tenth year at this rank, but its production costs were higher than those of most other major international producers. Steel plate shipped from South Korea or Japan to Shanghai, Tianjin, or Dalian can be

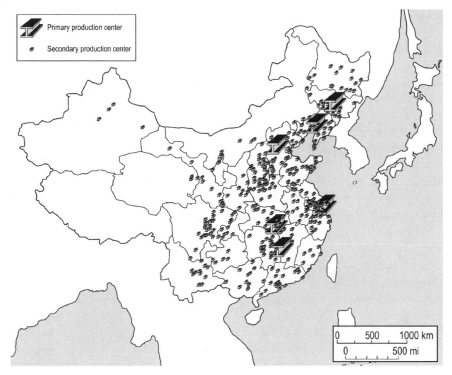

Map 10.3. Production of Pig Iron, Steel, Ferroalloy, and Rolled Steel in China. **Source:** After the *National Economic Atlas of China 1994* (Hong Kong: Oxford University Press, 1994). Cartographic design by Mary Lee Eggart.

significantly cheaper than the same product produced domestically upriver in Wuhan. At the same time, demand for scrap steel in China has doubled the world market price in the past three years, further illustrating China's insatiable demand.

The Energy Sector

The bane of every developing nation's industrial sector is a shortfall of available energy. Beyond the inconvenience of brownouts, temporary energy shortages can snarl transportation networks, close factories, and threaten health and human services. For China, anticipating and addressing energy supply issues, while working to produce cleaner energy, is a critical issue related to its continued economic growth. If China's industry is to expand, greater and greater amounts of energy will be required.

At present, China remains largely dependent on coal for its energy needs. Demand for crude oil, however, is growing rapidly with the expansion of the transportation network and a dramatic increase in automobile ownership. There are also health dividends to be considered in shifting from cheaper coal to other more expensive energy alternatives (which at least in the short term will mean more imports). For the rural

Chinese, respiratory diseases are the third leading cause of death (18.72 percent). In cities, respiratory disease is also ranked third, and accounts for 14.63 percent of all deaths (National Bureau of Statistics 2002, 782). Many of these deaths can be credited to the extremely polluted air in China's cities and to the use of high-sulfur soft coal in rural homes, which are tightly sealed during the winter.

Coal accounted for 70.3 percent of total energy production in 1978 and actually rose to 74.2 percent in 2003. Logically, coal production accounts for most of China's electric power generation, with hydropower making up a large portion of the remainder. Reflecting growing imports, coal accounted for 67.1 percent of China's total energy consumption in 2003. As noted above, coal is a very dirty source of energy. In 1997, total SO_2 emissions reached 21.59 million Mt, making China the world leader. China is also second only to the United States in emissions of greenhouse gases. With greater industrialization, these problems will only get worse.

Industry was responsible for 68.9 percent of China's total energy consumption in 2003, but this will soon change as more and more successful, urban Chinese purchase cars and build larger living spaces. This will not only increase overall energy consumption, it will also shift China's demand toward petroleum and gasoline—the energy resources in shortest supply. Improvements in energy efficiency have been made and will continue, but conservation will provide only a small fraction of future needs unless there are radical changes in basic industry and power-generating technologies. A study by the Rand Corporation estimates that China will be importing approximately 60 percent of its oil and 30 percent of its natural gas by 2020 (Downs 2000). Domestic production of oil and natural gas has risen, but it cannot meet demand that is expected to continue to increase for the next several decades. Total domestic energy production rose from 627 Mt of SCE (standard coal equivalent) in 1978 to 1,603 Mt in 2003, increasing just over two and one half times in twenty-four years.

Since 1996, China has been a net importer of crude oil, importing 19.9 Mt that year. Further, 53 percent of its imports came from the Middle East in 1996, but as much as 81 percent could come from the region in 2010. There are clear foreign policy issues that are linked to such dependence, and China has recently made overtures not only to Iran and Sudan, but also to Venezuela in an effort to broaden its energy supply base. The future is difficult to predict, but Gao (2000, 48) predicts China's imports will increase fivefold from 1996 to 2010. Based on statistical trend analysis, he expects imports in 2010 to range from a low of 90 Mt to a possible high of 103 Mt.

There are still many important unknowns regarding China's domestic oil reserves, and exploration is ongoing, with assistance from many multinational firms including Royal Dutch Shell, Exxon, Marathon, and British Petroleum. Joint ventures have played a dominant role in this exploration, especially in the Far Northwest and in the South China Sea fields. The presence of these firms reflects their belief in the growth potential of the China market and the government's desire to expand production as quickly as possible. Exploration within the South and East China seas has both economic and geopolitical overtones, however. Many other nations contest all or part of the Chinese claims in the South China Sea, particularly in the areas around the Spratley Islands. Fortunately, all recognize the need for a peaceful adjudication of these claims. Where

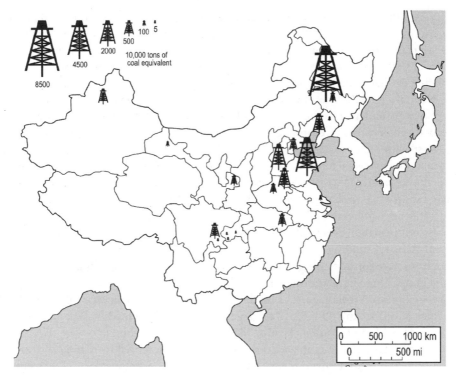

Map 10.4. Production of Crude Oil and Natural Gas in China. **Source:** After the *National Economic Atlas of China 1994* (Hong Kong: Oxford University Press, 1994). Cartographic design by Mary Lee Eggart.

and how China acquires its oil, whether domestically from contested offshore locations or from imports, will be a major foreign policy issue.

In 1975, about one-half of the nation's crude oil came from the Daqing field in Heilongjiang province (see map 10.4). The Shengli fields in Shandong province and the Dagang field in Hebei province combined to contribute another quarter of all production in 1975. Greater investments in exploration are planned through 2010 to better exploit offshore fields in the East China Sea as well. The great Daqing field in the Northeast remained China's largest oil field in 2005, but its share of total production has declined considerably as new fields are developed. Also, the cost of production in Daqing, where many wells require the use of high-pressure heated water to force the crude to the surface, has risen since the early 1990s, and production is in decline.

New fields are needed. Some of the most promising recent expansions include several major fields in Xinjiang Autonomous Region. It is expected that by 2008, crude oil output from Xinjiang will reach 50 Mt, equivalent to that currently produced by the Daqing field. Quite recently, there has been some concern that the Xinjiang fields may not be as extensive as once thought. This may explain China's recently signed long-term agreement with Kazakhstan to jointly develop a massive pipeline to transmit oil from the Caspian Sea region to refineries in China—a sort of geopolitical energy insurance policy. Another pipeline is planned to connect Russian fields to the Xinjiang refineries at a cost of more than US$2 billion. These projects will take many years to complete, and are really contingent on finding as-yet unidentified international financing. Still, such plans reflect China's emergence as a regional power capable of accessing sufficient financing to change these "pipedreams" into reality.

Natural gas in 2004 accounted for only 2.8 percent of China's energy consumption, but efforts are underway to increase this to 5.6 percent by 2010 and 9.8 percent in 2015, largely through increased domestic output. Natural gas production is largely located in the West with major fields in the Tarim and Junggar basins of Xinjiang, in Qinghai province, and in several major fields in Sichuan province. As with coal, major consumers are in the East, and again massive investments are required to transport the gas from these distant sources to the East. There is a new pipeline (the East–West Gas Transmission Project) from Sichuan to Hubei province nearing completion that should increase both supply and demand. Eventually this will link to another new pipeline from Xinjiang (Tarim Basin) if funding for the project can be procured. Offshore locations that are thought to have considerable gas reserves include the Donghai and Chunxiao gas fields in the East China Sea. Currently, the largest producing field is the Yacheng 13-1, with proven reserves of 3 trillion cu. ft., with the gas largely shipped to the cities of Guangdong province (Cordesman 1998, 52). The target market for these fields will be the cities of East China, including Beijing, Tianjin, Shanghai, and Hangzhou.

Hydroelectric power is an area that has both great potential for China and strong support in the central government. Hydropower today accounts for 7.7 percent of China's energy production and 7.4 percent of its consumption (National Bureau of Statistics 2004, 275). The notorious Three Gorges project, discussed in chapter 2, is just one of dozens of major hydroelectric projects that are being developed, and China leads the world in hydropower potential. Out of 680 gigawatts (GW) of explored resources, the Ministry of Electric Power estimates that 380 GW can be harnessed for the generation of electricity. There are genuine concerns, however, regarding the environmental impact of hydroelectric dams—in China and everywhere else in the world. Nonetheless, China has pursued a very ambitious program of dam construction for power generation, water management, and irrigation. In the past forty years, China has built twenty-six major hydropower plants, with another twenty currently under construction. While much has been made of the Three Gorges project, the Ertan hydroelectric power plant on the Yalong (a western tributary of the Chang Jiang), which generates 17,000 gigawatt hours (Gwh) annually, is currently Asia's largest. Ten more multipurpose dams are planned for the Yalong alone, illustrating the importance of hydropower in the coming years. Lower power costs will also prove a powerful incentive for industrial relocation or expansion, bringing industries to the southwestern provinces of Yunnan, Guangxi Autonomous Region, and Sichuan, where many of these dams are being built.

Wind power has received considerable attention, and there are currently 120,000 small, household wind turbines—mostly in remote areas. The largest wind farm in China was established in Shandong in 1986, and it has been upgraded to a capacity of 14 megawatts (MW) with the help of Danish development funds. Recently, extensive wind-turbine fields have been established in several locations in northcentral Xinjiang as well. The overall impact of wind power in China, as in most nations, is minor at the present time, but holds promise for the future.

Completing this census, we will note that China has significant uranium reserves, and has embarked on a very ambitious plan to expand its nuclear power production. Since 2000, China has brought eight new nuclear reactors online for a total of eleven, with several more in construction. Critical components for all these reactors were imported from France, Canada, and Russia. Chinese scientists are working to develop their own domestic expertise, however, and soon hope to produce major reactor components domestically to save on foreign exchange.

Further Reforms of the Manufacturing Sector

Often overlooked in discussions of China's industrial production are the banking and investment reforms that now ensure that China's entrepreneurs and potential investors have access to the capital they need for investment. Further, reform of the industrial sector has stimulated a new-found appreciation of managerial expertise and the educational opportunities required to generate this expertise, which is vital in the competitive environment forged by ongoing reform policies.

The transformation of China's industrial sector also reflects a quiet but steady changing of the guard at the managerial level. Times have changed, and it has proven difficult for long-term factory managers, who were often political appointments, to change with them. Whereas meeting state-established gross-production quotas was once the most important goal for factory managers, now improvements in efficiency, product quality, management, and marketing have become central concerns. Greater efficiency and meeting the bottom line are now keys to advancement and job security.

China's international success in exports has been outpaced by the growth of domestic markets that, in reality, are more critical to continued success, given the size of China's workforce. The overall growth of the industrial sector has generated higher wages, which have allowed for a massive expansion of the service sector, which in turn has spread the benefits of economic reform across Chinese society. Higher wages, for better or worse, make for a nation of consumers. The saturation rate for televisions, refrigerators, water purifiers, and other household durables in China's cities has reached 85–100 percent. This explosion in demand for consumer products, however, has also been matched by heavy-industry output that has provided the strategic materials needed for a rapidly developing national economy. Figure 10.3, although it offers just a snapshot of a few products, underscores just how fast China's industrial capacity has grown.

Industrial wages for TVEs and private firms are directly related to product demand and productivity per worker. Of course, given varying levels of economic development, wages vary considerably across provinces. In reality, the within-province variance in wages, urban versus rural, for some provinces is as great as province-to-province differences (see map 10.5). As discussed in chapter 8, farm incomes have risen in the past quarter century, but off-farm rural incomes (TVEs) and urban incomes have increased much more quickly due to the growth in industry and manufacturing.

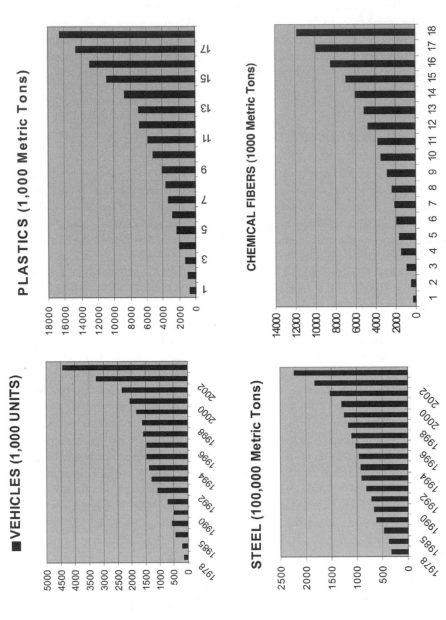

Figure 10.3. Changes in Output for Indicator Manufactures, Selected Years from 1978 to 2003. **Source:** National Bureau of Statistics 2003, 559–63.

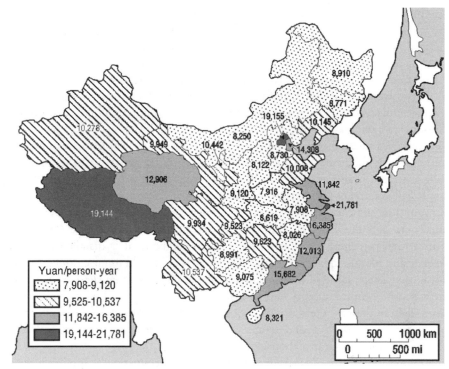

Map 10.5. Average Annual Wage for Staff and Workers by Province, 2001. ***Source:*** National Bureau of Statistics 2002, 145. Cartographic design by Mary Lee Eggart.

The role that high-tech and value-added products play in producing the patterns on map 10.5 should be acknowledged. High-tech plants are generally located in the coastal provinces. Further, most of the high-tech industrial parks established by provincial or municipal governments have been located in coastal cities, although there are exceptions with the large interior cities such as Xi'an (Walcott 2002).

Challenges to Continued Industrial Growth

China's industrial planners are faced with an abundance of challenges similar to those facing most capitalist nations. Still, the past matters, and China's industrial restructuring also deals with issues that are unique to China's historical situation, its domestic politics, and its rapid industrial transformation. Labor and population issues, environmental problems, and growing regional inequity are just a few of the more important concerns.

In an idealized version of China's national shift to market-style capitalism, the reform of SOEs could be achieved simply by letting the invisible hand of the marketplace "sort things out" as quickly as possible. From this perspective, reform would best be brought about by the quick sale of all state factories and industries to the highest bidders (the Russia model). Ideally, "cash-flush" investors would be waiting to rush into these "great deals." The new owners, "inspired" by the success of leading capitalists in America, Europe, or Japan, would then modernize their plants, their products, their organizations, and their workforce, and become competitive very quickly. Certainly, the pundits agree, there would be hard times for some people, but everything would work out in the end. Unfortunately, this is not what has happened in Russia or China!

The problem facing China's industrial planners is how to get from the present to the future without creating massive social unrest, fiscal chaos, unprecedented environmental pollution, and the loss of billions of dollars in "sunk capital" if fixed assets are not effectively used to engineer the transition. Some amount of labor unrest and protest occurs every day and in every major city in China. It is not covered by the Western press, but be assured it is always going on! With state subsidies cut to the bone, and plants being faced with either arriving at profitability or being shutdown, bloated workforces continue to be trimmed as firms fight for survival. The sword of market reform and China's entry into the WTO cuts both ways. Some firms, sold by the state, immediately lay off a high percentage of their workers as new equipment is installed to increase efficiency and product quality. Subsidized housing is often sold to raise capital for plant renovations. These are hard decisions made by good people, managers trying to find their way out of unprofitability and to ensure the profits that will keep their factories open and keep their workers working. Still, there is a simmering frustration among the Chinese unemployed or underemployed that is exacerbated by concurrently rising medical, education, insurance, housing, and food costs.

Looking for a job is a daunting experience in any country, but in China, few of these laid-off workers have the skills or education needed to quickly find new positions. There are many regulations that are supposed to protect these workers, but you cannot eat regulations, and enforcement is lax. Often local governments or closing factories do not have the resources to meet their financial obligations to these workers, let alone the funds to train them for other work. It is not unusual in any major city in China to see 200 to 300 laid-off workers standing around a park (or the same number in each of a dozen parks) and waiting for temporary work.

There is also evidence that the decline of the SOE system and the overall growth in the industrial sector may be exacerbating China's environmental problems. The growth of small private or collective firms may inadvertently promote the loss of arable land, increase point-source air and water pollution, and allow the under- or unregulated disposal of toxic industrial wastes and byproducts. Although SOEs are under increasing pressure to improve their environmental record, under-funded provincial and city environmental protection agencies are having a more difficult time monitoring conditions in the rapidly multiplying smaller factories. And while the environmental record of factories in urban China may not be very good, the urban offices of the Chinese State Environmental Protection Agency (SEPA) generally have staff and some influence. Rural and suburban areas, however, once largely without polluting industries, have fewer SEPA inspectors and far less influence with local governments.

The Huai River Basin, situated between the Chang Jiang and Huang He (Yellow River) basins, is an excellent case in point. Once quite poor due to isolation, poor soils, and endemic flooding, the region has recently become notorious for polluted groundwater and high cancer rates. With some of the lowest-cost labor in China and local governments that provided a favorable business environment, the region saw the movement of many firms into its area. Unfortunately, many of the factories that relocated into the region, including China's largest monosodium glutamate plant, have ignored SEPA regulations and poured industrial waste into the Huai (Economy 2004). Even with pressure from Beijing, many local officials aid the factories because higher wages and tax revenues mean more to them than even the immediate threat of groundwater pollution and the sickening of friends and relatives.

Conflicts associated with water and energy use and their pricing have also increased dramatically. As in all nations, industrial expansion has led to concurrent increases in the use (and misuse) of these resources. Pricing of water and its availability has become a hotly debated public issue because industrial expansion in major cities such as Shanghai and Beijing has created constant shortages. More than two hundred of China's major cities currently experience chronic water shortages, and the total water deficit for these cities alone has been estimated at 100 Mt per day (Smil 2000, 189). These are complex problems that may never be completely resolved, but they are now topics of discussion and are regularly reviewed by the media. China has come a long way in a short time in this regard.

Summary and Future Considerations

China's industrial expansion will continue into the foreseeable future with both positive and negative implications. On the plus side, for many of China's people, the transformation of China's industrial sector has systematically resulted in a higher standard of living. This is not only true in China's cities, but for many places in rural China as well. The "new China" anticipated with fierce dedication by Mao Zedong in 1949 now is a reality—and in large part this is due to new policies associated with the industrial sector.

Still, the market can be a harsh taskmaster, and many firms throughout China have gone bankrupt because of dated technology, poor management, high transport costs, or the production of obsolete products. Problems related to unemployment and underemployment must be addressed, and social services for the unemployed and underemployed must be both extended to rural areas and strengthened in the cities. Again and for complex reasons, there has been a tendency for firms in China's traditional manufacturing regions to fare better than firms elsewhere. The government's new Develop the West initiatives will help address regional equity issues, but will also mean government involvement at many levels in industrial decision making—an involvement that has not served China well in the past. Environmental degradation of air, land, and water resources will require better monitoring and enforcement of regulations—again involving the government. All of this government intervention will pit local manufacturing interests against government initiatives and may encourage corruption or continued lax enforcement. If these problems are not addressed, health issues and post hoc pollution-mitigation efforts will only negate the gains made through industrial expansion and sectoral economic growth. We must hope that China's leadership will recognize the cancerous effects of unsustainable policies as genuine threats to a sustainable society and a secure future.

References Cited

Brandt, Loren. 1989. *Commercialization and Agricultural Development: Central and Eastern China, 1870–1937*. Cambridge: Cambridge University Press.

Braudel, Fernand. 1986. *The Wheels of Commerce*. Vol. 2 of *Civilization and Capitalism, 15th–18th Century*. New York: Harper and Row.

Cordesman, Anthony H. 1998. *The Changing Geopolitics of Energy—Part VI: Regional Developments in East Asia, China, and India*. Washington, D.C.: Center for Strategic and International Studies.

Downs, Erica Strecker. 2000. *China's Quest for Energy Security*. Santa Monica, Calif.: Rand Corporation.

Economy, Elizabeth. 2004. *The River Runs Black*. Cornell, N.Y.: Cornell University Press.

Fan, C. Cindy. 1995. Of belts and ladders: State policy and uneven regional development in post-Mao China. *Annals of the Association of American Geographers* 85 (3): 421–49.

Gao Shixian. 2000. China. Chap. 2 in *Rethinking Energy Security in East Asia*, ed. Paul B. Stares. Washington, D.C.: Brookings Institute.

Lin, Shuanglin. 2002. China's infrastructure development. In *China's Economy into the New Century: Structural Issues and Problems*, ed. John Wong and Ding Lu. Singapore: Singapore University Press.

National Bureau of Statistics. 1980. *Zhongguo tongji nianjian 1980* [China statistical yearbook 1980]. Beijing: China Statistics Press.

———. 1991. *Zhongguo tongji nianjian 1991* [China statistical yearbook 1991]. Beijing: China Statistics Press.

———. 2002. *Zhongguo tongji nianjian 2002* [China statistical yearbook 2002]. Beijing: China Statistics Press.

———. 2003. *Zhongguo tongji nianjian 2003* [China statistical yearbook 2003]. Beijing: China Statistics Press.

———. 2004. *Zhongguo tongji nianjian 2004* [China statistical yearbook 2004]. Beijing: China Statistics Press.

National Economic Atlas of China. 1994. Bk. 2. Hong Kong: Oxford University Press.

Organization for Economic Co-operation and Development. 2002. *China in the World Economy: The Domestic Policy Challenges*. Paris: Organization for Economic Co-operation and Development.

Pye, Lucian W. 1972. *China: An Introduction*. Boston: Little, Brown.

Shen, Xiaoping. 1999. Spatial inequality of rural industrial development in China, 1989–1994. *Journal of Rural Studies* 15 (2): 179–99.

Smil, Vaclav. 2000. China's environment and natural resources. Chap. 14 in *The China Handbook: Prospects onto the 21st Century*, ed. Christopher Hudson. Chicago: Glenlake, 188–97.

Sun, Jingzhi. 1988. *The Economic Geography of China*. Hong Kong: Oxford University Press.

Tian, Xiaowen. 2002. China's drive to develop its Western Region: Why turn to this region now? Chap. 10 of *China's Economy into the New Century: Structural Issues and Problems*, ed. John Wong and Ding Lu. Singapore: Singapore University Press, 237–72.

Veeck, Ann, and Alvin C. Burns. 2005. Changing tastes: The adoption of new food choices in post-reform China. *Journal of Business Research* 58:644–52.

Walcott, Susan M. 2002. Chinese industrial and science parks: Bridging the gap. *Professional Geographer* 54 (3): 349–64.

Wallerstein, Emmanuel. 1976. *The Modern World Capitalist System: Capitalist Agriculture and the Origins of the European World-Economy in the Sixteenth Century.* New York: Academic Press.

Wei, Yehua. 1996. Fiscal systems and uneven regional development in China, 1978–1991. *Geoforum* 27 (3): 329–44.

Wei, Y. H., and C. C. Fan. 2000. Regional inequality in China: A case study of Jiangsu province. *Professional Geographer* 52 (3): 455–69.

Yeung, Y. M., and David K. Y. Chu. 2000. *Fujian: A Coastal Province in Transition and Transformation.* Hong Kong: Chinese University Press.

CHAPTER 11

Hong Kong before and after the Return

Christopher J. Smith

China's opening and economic reforms have brought great changes to the mainland, many of them positive. In preparing for its own modernization program, China was able to benefit significantly from the development trajectories of its offshore Chinese territories, Taiwan, Hong Kong, and Macau.[1] During the 1980s and 1990s both Taiwan and Hong Kong recorded economic growth rates that sometimes matched China's, but their spurt in growth began much earlier than it did on the mainland. What made the difference was the economic and political systems operating in Hong Kong and Taiwan, in comparison to the mainland. In the People's Republic of China (PRC) until the end of the 1970s, economic growth had been stifled by a command economy, and the living standards of Chinese mainlanders had fallen far below that of their overseas counterparts.

By the start of the new millennium, Deng Xiaoping's Four Modernizations program had enabled China to join Hong Kong and Taiwan as a major player in the global economy. By the early 1990s, it was apparent that de facto economic integration was occurring, especially between Hong Kong and China, a process that fuelled dreams (on China's part) and fears (elsewhere in the world) about a new economic superpower, often referred to as Greater China.[2] Trade and other economic interactions between Taiwan, Hong Kong, and the mainland increased significantly during the early reform years, and by the beginning of the 1990s their combined trade with the rest of the world was surpassed by that of only five other countries—the United States, Japan, Germany, France, and the United Kingdom. In 1997 when Hong Kong was returned to Chinese sovereignty, two-thirds of the triangle was completed formally, and China was aggressively seeking to ensure that the other third (Taiwan) would soon follow. But finding a workable solution to the Taiwan problem has turned out to be much more difficult than was the case for Hong Kong.

The core of the Greater China region lies along the so-called golden coastline of the mainland, in China's two southeastern provinces, Guangdong and Fujian. Because of the provinces' proximity and ethnic similarities, economic development in this region has been driven largely by direct investment from Hong Kong and Taiwan. Hong Kong has been the major financier, investor, supplier, and provider of technology to Guangdong province, and especially to Special Economic Zone (SEZ) cities Shenzhen and Zhuhai; and Taiwan can be seen in similar terms, particularly in its relationship to Fujian province and the Xiamen and Shantou SEZs. Before its return to China, Hong Kong was one of the dominant centers of trade and finance in East Asia. In addition to its traditional role as an entrepot for trade between China and the rest of the world, Hong Kong's unique combination of advantages helped to make it one of the world's most dynamic centers of light industry in the 1960s and 1970s. Its economic growth rates averaged above 8 percent per year for most of the three decades before the handover, boosting per capita income to levels higher than in almost all other parts of Asia. As we shall observe, however, Hong Kong began to witness an erosion of its traditional industrial competitiveness, largely because of rising labor costs. Hong Kong's response to this problem was geographically and ethnically unique: many local industrialists began to shift major parts of their production operations into Guangdong province—immediately adjacent to the mainland—where labor and land costs were significantly lower, and environmental constraints usually nonexistent or easy to bypass.

At roughly the same time, Hong Kong's traders were increasing their imports of Chinese-made goods, finishing and repackaging them in preparation for reexport. Many of the manufacturers who stayed in the territory began to upgrade their production processes to focus on higher-value products. All of this resulted in what amounts to a geographical division of labor, with Hong Kong still acting as the investment, commercial, and financial core of the South China region, and the coastal provinces of the mainland becoming an industrial periphery where most of the actual production occurred. This revitalized and restructured manufacturing economy, and Hong Kong's role as a reexporter, helped the former colony maintain its economic position within reach of the world's ten largest exporting countries. The development of the financial infrastructure needed to support Hong Kong's role as a global trader, as well as its unique geographical situation at the center of what was at the time the booming Asia Pacific region, established it as a center of international finance. In other words, as it had done in the past, Hong Kong was once again able to secure its reputation as a place to make and spend money.

A (Very) Brief History of Hong Kong

In the middle of the nineteenth century, what was considered a remote corner of the Qing dynasty was being used as a pawn in an international chess game between China and Britain. The territory in question, lying off the coast of Guangdong province, was more than 2,400 km from Beijing, which translated to a journey of at least two weeks, even by the fastest courier (Morris 1988). At that time this piece of land seemed, to the Chinese at least, to have no obvious geographical advantages: it had no settlements larger than small market hamlets, no resources of any apparent value to traders and industrialists, virtually no flat land to build on, a climate that was insufferably hot and humid for most of the year, and diseases that were endemic, including malaria, cholera, and typhoid.

Because of the area's apparent geographical disadvantages, most Chinese people, including the nation's leaders at the time, considered the area too peripheral to worry about, so scarcely a voice was raised in protest in 1842 when it was surrendered to the

British in a treaty that ended the first period of hostility between the two countries. During the next century and a half—in what is now a familiar story—this unprepossessing place would undergo a dramatic makeover, and would be transformed from its original state as a remote corner of the Chinese Empire to the place known around the world as Hong Kong. By the 1960s it had become an ultramodern metropolis: the busiest, richest, and liveliest of all Chinese cities at the time—a place in fact where most Chinese could only dream about living, and where foreign China scholars loved to return for rest and relaxation after a spell of fieldwork in the scarcity economy of the mainland. Today's Hong Kong, reunited with China, is actively involved in helping direct China's assimilation into the world economy: an appropriate role for a city that was shaped by the inclinations and aspirations of European, Chinese, and American enterprise, and one that has stood head and shoulders above all others as a concrete manifestation of global capitalism at its most successful.

In geographic terms, Hong Kong is a small island at the mouth of the Pearl River Delta in southern Guangdong province. As we have already noted, in 1842 part of what would later be called (by its new colonial owner at least) the Territory was ceded by the Chinese in perpetuity to the British, following China's defeat in the first Opium War (1839–1842). A 9 km^2 piece of the mainland (Kowloon; see photo 11.1) was added

Photo 11.1. Housing developments of different eras in Shamshuipo, Kowloon. Note that this area, which is on the flight path of the old Kai Tak airport, has seen the emergence of some high-rise apartment towers since the airport closed. Photo by Christopher J. Smith

to this in 1860—also in perpetuity—after another British victory; and a third, much larger area of the mainland, was added in 1898. This piece of land was referred to at the time (and is still today) as the New Territories. It was leased to Britain for ninety-nine years, reverting to China in 1997.[3]

In the second half of the nineteenth century, ninety-nine years probably seemed like an eternity to most of the negotiators, and few people on either side of the transaction were overly concerned about the precise wording of the treaties that handed the territory over to the British. Hong Kong–based merchants made use of the island's site and situation, and it gradually grew into a hugely successful port and financial center. The people of Hong Kong became well-known around the world for their industry, and for their legendary ability to make money. And as we began to see in the 1990s, once they were given the chance to try their hand at politics, even in the quasi-democratic arena of British colonialism, Hong Kong's people demonstrated that they could get interested in things other than making money. The image of political naïveté traditionally associated with Hong Kong—to the extent that it is anything more than a complete misconception—is hardly surprising in light of the fact that the British kept the vast majority of Hong Kong's citizens disenfranchised for more than a century. But as we shall see, in the new millennium the level and intensity of local political interest brought the people and politicians of Hong Kong into sharp conflict with the regime in Beijing.

It was as shrewd financial and commercial operators, however, that Hong Kong's people first earned respect around the world, rather than as savvy politicians or activists. During its 150 years as a British colony Hong Kong has, by almost all measures, been highly successful. Its life-expectancy statistics are better than Britain's, and its per capita gross domestic product (GDP) is catching up fast.[4]

Economic Development

In spite of Hong Kong's status as a British colony, its unique location meant that it operated for almost a century as an autonomous entrepot, servicing the trade between China and the rest of the world.[5] In 1890, 55 percent of China's imports passed through Hong Kong, and 37 percent of the colony's exports were bound for China. By 1940 these figures had increased slightly (Burns 1991; Davies 1990),[6] but the operation of this entrepot was seriously disrupted by the Japanese occupation of Hong Kong from 1942 to 1945, and by the Korean War in the early 1950s. As initially damaging as these external events were to Hong Kong's economy though, they eventually proved to be a blessing in disguise, because Hong Kong was forced to transform the base of its economy, shifting away from its traditional reliance on a trading role and more toward export-oriented manufacturing, for which it would become internationally acclaimed. Another fortuitous and unanticipated windfall for Hong Kong at about the same time was the relocation of a significant amount of industrial capital and enterprise from the mainland, especially from the cities of Guangzhou and Shanghai, following the communist takeover of the mainland in 1949. In addition, many mainlanders headed toward the "safe haven" that Hong Kong provided, which resulted in a massive increase in the colony's population, and became the basis for what the colony would become famous for in the following two decades: its supply of cheap labor, plus an enormous store of capital.[7]

For much of their history, Hong Kong's people have had to work furiously to overcome the territory's smallness and its virtual absence of natural resources. The development of a banking and insurance infrastructure supported Hong Kong's role as a transshipper of goods into and out of China, complemented by some small-scale industrial development, most of it relying on Chinese capital. Hong Kong developed its shipbuilding capacity during the early part of the twentieth century, and also became known globally for its textiles and food production. In the 1950s, after emerging successfully from the devastation of World War II and the chaos of the Japanese occupation, the colony began to reassert itself in the world of trade, and it quickly reached its prewar levels. At the same time, a policy of import substitution helped local businesses expand by encouraging production of the consumer goods needed to support a rapidly growing population.[8] During the next decades, Hong Kong's locational advantages, in addition to its supply of cheap labor provided by a constant flow of Chinese immigrants and its government's policies allowing free trade, worked to encourage the inflow of foreign capital and the further development of banking, financial, and shipping services.

The post-1949 diversification of Hong Kong's economy in the direction of export-oriented manufacturing was reinforced during the Korean War as a result of an economic embargo on trade with China. This trade embargo cut significantly into the entrepot function of Hong Kong. In 1952 for example, the value of exports to China was HK$1.6 billion, but this had fallen to HK$520 million by 1953, and to HK$136 million by 1956 (Ho 1992). As exports from China fell, local Hong Kong industries received a boost, especially in such areas as textiles, clothing, light metal goods, footwear, plastics, electronics, and optical instruments. Beginning in the 1970s however, Hong Kong's comparative advantage in the production of such goods was seriously challenged, especially by other economies in East Asia, some of which had wage levels that were significantly lower. The result was a gradual but perceptible shift in the direction of more sophisticated and higher-quality value-added production lines, but still with a clear emphasis on exports. The restructuring of Hong Kong's manufacturing base at this time was accelerated by the shift of some low-level production activities to factories on the mainland—particularly the production of such items as clothing, shoes, plastic toys, and luggage, which are now made almost exclusively in mainland factories. The net effect of this shift left practically no heavy industry in Hong Kong.

The magnitude of this transformation can also be noted in the changing structure of exports coming from Hong Kong. In 1960, clothing represented 29 percent of Hong Kong's export total, textiles 23 percent, electronics 2.5 percent, and precision instruments (watches and clocks) 0.7 percent. In 1988, the proportion of clothing was about the same (31 percent), but the textiles sector had fallen to only 7 percent, while electronic goods had increased to 22.4 percent, and precision instruments to 10 percent (Ho 1992, table 4.1, 76). In spite of this shift, Hong Kong's manufacturing sector—unlike Taiwan's—was still dominated, even in the early 1990s, by labor-intensive operations. In other words, the colony was not yet making any significant strides toward high-technology production methods. This was still the case by the start of the new millennium, and some researchers have suggested that this oversight or failure goes a long way toward explaining why the Hong Kong economy suffered such a serious downturn after the handover in 1997 (Castells 1999).

The growth of Hong Kong's export-oriented manufacturing was accompanied by a long period of rapid economic growth. During the 1960s, for example, GDP expanded by more than 10 percent each year, with the contribution of manufacturing to overall GDP increasing from 20 percent to more than 30 percent; and by 1971, 47 percent of Hong Kong's labor force was involved in manufacturing. Nearly a third of all manufacturing workers were in the textile business, popularizing the "Made in Hong Kong" label on clothing that became famous (or infamous) around the world. The driving force of the Hong Kong economy during the 1960s and 1970s was clearly the export sector, which grew at an average of 11.5 percent per year—twice the average rate of growth for the world as a whole. For the most part, the expansion of the economy generated a demand for labor that guaranteed nearly full employment and a healthy annual increase in wages. Inflation remained low (around 4 percent per year), and the economy benefited from healthy injections of direct foreign investment.

In addition to its manufacturing base, Hong Kong's growth was rapidly becoming dependent on the development of the service sector, especially in the areas of shipping, banking, insurance, and real estate. And at least before 1997, Hong Kong was also a major tourist attraction for visitors from all parts of the world, which contributed significantly to its local economy.[9] For the most part, Hong Kong was able to maintain a healthy balance of payments, and its currency remained relatively stable. These data, the consensus among most Hong Kong residents, and the opinions of outside observers all speak to what can only be described as a "success narrative": Hong Kong had achieved rapid and sustained economic growth with relative price stability, while at the same time realizing a substantial rise in real income and maintaining high levels of employment and a reasonable degree of income inequality (Ho 1992).[10] Hong Kong's economic performance from the 1960s through the 1980s had enabled it to catch up with some of the other global economic powers, particularly the United States and the United Kingdom. By 1988, for example, Hong Kong's per capita gross national product (GNP) was close to 70 percent of the United Kingdom's, and 50 percent of the United States'. In 1995 Hong Kong's per capita GNP (at US$22,990) was higher than the United Kingdom's, and 85 percent of the United States' (United Nations Development Program 1998, 125, 184).

Structural change in Hong Kong's economy continued throughout the 1970s and 1980s, with two major trends easily observable. One was an increasing focus on higher-value value-added goods (for example, garments and finished clothing increased their share in the economy relative to unfinished textile goods); the other was a marked shift toward the manufacture of electrical goods and appliances, such as watches and clocks. In the 1980s another important trend also became noticeable: a huge increase in the financial services sector, which had overtaken manufacturing as the largest employer category in Hong Kong's economy. The new jobs in this sector were mainly in what are generally referred to as *producer services*, including banking, investment facilities, insurance, real estate, and corporate services—all of which were providing the essential infrastructure for a growing number of foreign multinational companies located in the

Table 11.1a. Hong Kong: Persons Engaged in Selected Industry Sectors (in thousands)

Occupation	1982	1987	1991	% Growth 1982–1991
Manufacturing	847.2	867.9	565.1	−33.9%
Building and construction	82.1	72.5	59.5	−27.5%
Wholesale, retail, import/export, restaurants and hotels	517.7	657.4	914.8	+76.7%
Financing, insurance, real estate, business services	116.1	212.2	314.8	+230.7%

Source: Hong Kong Census and Statistics Department 1993.

Territory. By the early 1990s, manufacturing was contributing only 15 percent of Hong Kong's GDP, and employed only 33 percent of its workforce; in the decade from 1982 to 1991, the number of people employed in manufacturing in Hong Kong fell by almost 34 percent (see table 11.1a), and the contribution of manufacturing to overall GDP in Hong Kong during the same period fell by almost 27 percent (see table 11.1b). Not surprisingly, the contribution of the service sectors grew significantly through the 1980s.

By far the most impressive rate of growth within the last three decades was in Hong Kong's role as a world trader. In 1960, Hong Kong's exports were valued at US$0.69 billion, with Hong Kong ranked twenty-seventh in the world; but by 1985 its exports were valued at US$63.17 billion, making it the tenth-largest exporter in the world. In the 1950s and 1960s, a sharp increase in industrial production meant that the export of domestic-made goods began to outstrip the reexport of goods made elsewhere (mostly in China); and by 1970, domestic exports outranked reexports by more than 4 to 1. Throughout the 1980s, however, with the increasing economic integration of Hong Kong and South China, and the shift of many manufacturing plants to the mainland, the reexport business began to grow rapidly, much of it involving repackaging and improved presentation of goods originally made in China. By the end of the 1980s, reexports had moved ahead of domestic exports, and by the mid-1990s, about one-third of Hong Kong's exports consisted of reexports of goods produced in China, primarily by Hong Kong–based companies (Hong Kong Census and Statistics Department 1993).

The relative and absolute decline in the importance of manufacturing vis-à-vis services in the Hong Kong economy is the result of a combination of forces that were at work throughout the 1980s, one of which was the growth of protectionism around the

Table 11.1b. Hong Kong: Contribution of Economic Activities to GDP (%)

Occupation	1982	1987	1991	% Growth 1982–1991
Manufacturing	20.7	21.7	15.2	−26.60%
Building and construction	19.7	23.2	25.4	+33.00%
Wholesale, retail, import/export, restaurants and hotels	22.6	18.2	22.7	−0.14%
Financing, insurance, real estate, business services	7.3	4.7	5.6	−23.30%

Source: Hong Kong Census and Statistics Department 1993, tables 2.3, 2.4, 3.4, pp. 16, 26.

world (particularly in the United States), which made Hong Kong–produced garments and textile goods less competitive than they had been in the past. As noted already, one response to rising wage and land costs in Hong Kong was for manufacturers to shift an increasing proportion of their production activities to the mainland, especially Guangdong province, which is adjacent to Hong Kong. The growth of the financial and business sectors was in part a response to this growing trade with China throughout the 1980s, and a result of a sharp increase in foreign investment by Hong Kong capitalists on the mainland—in other words, the provision of these services was primarily a response to the growing demand for financial services to manage and coordinate trade and capital-flow activities.[11]

To investigate the forces underlying Hong Kong's emergence as an economic giant, it is useful to examine some comparisons between Hong Kong and the mainland (and, implicitly, between both of them and Taiwan). But first we should consider some of the important differences in the means of production in each society, with the key dimensions being the way *ownership* and *control* are exercised over the production of wealth. Ownership involves the question of who (or which institutions) have the power to appropriate and dispose of the income that accrues during the production process. In command economies such as those of the Soviet Union and Maoist China, ownership was largely a state prerogative; but in present-day China we now see the emergence of a combination of public and private ownership, while in Hong Kong almost all ownership is in the private domain. Control in this context refers to the power to make production and exchange decisions about what will be produced, as well as where, in what quantities, and at what price it will be sold. Again, control varies along a continuum from the extreme case of the old socialist command economies (which are now very few in number) to the other extreme of so-called free-trade economies like that of Hong Kong.

Hong Kong is often described as a laissez-faire economy in which the state neither owns nor controls the means of production (see table 11.2). It is generally assumed that in Hong Kong the state has adopted a deliberately low-key role in the economy, which serves the best interests of trade and industrial development. The contrast between Hong Kong and Taiwan along these lines is significant, because in Taiwan the state has clearly played a much more active role, particularly in financial and trade matters. It is important to point out here, however, that the Hong Kong business elite have performed some of the same functions as the state in Taiwan. For example, local banks

Table 11.2. A Classification of the Different Roles Played by the State in Economic Development

		State ownership of the means of production	
	Yes	**1** Command Economy China 1949–Present	**2** State Capitalism Taiwan post-1950
State control over the means of production	No	**3** Market Socialism China 1978–1995	**4** Laissez-faire Capitalism Hong Kong

that have grown into global giants have effectively guided investment strategies and helped to steer the colony toward rapid economic growth. Throughout the period of major economic growth, the government, led by a small cadre of British-trained civil servants, was able either to coopt its critics, or to accommodate them through policy changes.

Traditional explanations for Hong Kong's success as an exporter of industrial goods, and more recently as a center for global and regional financial services, focus on three factors: the lack of interference by the state in the conduct of industry and commerce (the laissez-faire dimension); the important role of a dynamic, indigenous business elite; and a long period of relative political stability (Burns 1991). The role of the state in Hong Kong's development is a controversial issue and has been subject to different interpretations. Under British rule, some members of the colony's elite took exception to the term *laissez-faire*, preferring such linguistic contortions as *positive non-interventionism* to describe the situation in which the government invested significant resources toward the development of Hong Kong's physical and human-capital infrastructure, but basically stayed out of the business of economic decision making. The role of the state at this time should not be underestimated, however, in the sense that state investment contributed significantly to improving the efficiency of the economy, which continued to make Hong Kong an attractive place for foreign investors. In a 1990 report, Davies interpreted *non-interventionism* to mean that

> anyone with enough money to invest in a small factory could do business freely with minimum encumbrance: low taxes, free trade, good communications, weak trade unions, minimal or no training costs, and no risk of confiscation. Hong Kong has been a free port since it was founded. . . . Manufacturers have benefited from duty-free raw materials. . . . Free trade has also boosted re-exports and tourism, since the colony is widely regarded as a huge duty-free shop. (1990, 5–6)

Even in the mid-1990s, Hong Kong's low taxes, both for individuals and corporations, were the envy of the world, and there continues to be no capital gains tax, while inheritances are taxed at an extremely low rate (Davies 1990, 6).

Whatever term is used to describe its economy, Hong Kong has become known as a place where, in economic issues at least, "anything goes," and it is relatively easy and cheap to start up a business.[12] The *Economist*, for example, ranked Hong Kong as first in the world in its Economic Freedom Index for 1997, an index that grades countries on the extent to which their governments' policies restrict or interfere with economic activities (see *World in Figures* 1997). The indicators used to make up this index include trade policy, taxation rates, monetary policy, the banking system, foreign investment rules and regulations, property rights, the proportion of economic output consumed by the government, regulation policy, size of the black market, and the extent of wage and price controls. Each country is then assigned a score ranging from 1 (the most free) to 5 (the least free). In 1997, Hong Kong scored 1.25, Singapore 1.30, and Bahrain 1.70, while the United States ranked seventh, with a score of 1.90, and the United Kingdom scored 1.95. At the bottom end of the Freedom Index were Ghana with 3.25 and Algeria with 3.25. Since then several other measures of global competitiveness have emerged, and Hong Kong consistently performs well on these indicators, though it showed some amount of instability during the tumultuous years after 1997.

Davies (1990) predicted that Hong Kong's business climate for the period 1997–2002 would deteriorate, primarily as a result of what he referred to as an "anticipated deterioration in the operating environment associated with the handover," in addition to "fallout" from the regional (East and Southeast Asian) economic crisis. Davies also predicted that Hong Kong would no longer be perceived as the best place in the world to do business, and there is some evidence to support such a conclusion, although the Cato Institute reported in 2004 that Hong Kong still had the highest degree of economic freedom in the world.[13] In spite of this, the consensus of opinion is that Hong Kong's relative decline is the result of a combination of factors, in addition to the externality effects of the regional economic downturn. The real damage, according to some commentators, has resulted from a perception, globally, that Hong Kong has become much more politicized than it was in the past. One prominent Western banker, for example, was quoted as saying,

> There is a feeling that Hong Kong has lost something. We all know that Singapore has a much more politicized environment than Hong Kong, but it has always been that way. There is a fear that this could be the beginning of an ongoing erosion and that things are going to get worse not better, whereas in Singapore at least you know things are going to stay the same. (*South China Morning Post* 1999)

It is important to point out that despite its image of uninterrupted economic growth, Hong Kong's economic rise has in fact been punctuated by some periods of crisis and recession: there was a banking crisis in 1965, for example, and a series of riots and disturbances among dissatisfied (predominantly working-class) groups in 1966 and 1967. In response, the government set up new consultative institutions, with local citizens and workers appointed to advisory boards and committees. At roughly the same time, the Hong Kong government embarked on an ambitious and comprehensive program of social-welfare service delivery: a huge public housing program was launched, compulsory education was initiated, and steps toward expanded welfare and health service provisions were taken. Hong Kong's impressive New Town redevelopment schemes were also introduced at this time, mainly as a way to decentralize housing and industrial development toward the New Territories and away from the crowded urban core areas of Hong Kong Island and Kowloon. These actions were complemented by significant infrastructural developments, including the building of highways, a subway system, a light rail system, and comprehensive port developments (see Burns 1991, 135–36).

Among economists, the majority view is that the role of the government in Hong Kong throughout this period (pre-1997) was kept to a minimum, and primarily involved the operation of the legal and police systems—which helped to make Hong Kong a relatively safe place to invest and live in—and the supervision of land management. It is also evident that throughout the pre-handover period, the government acted in a relatively authoritarian fashion, with political power highly centralized in the colonial civil service. The net effect of this was that when the handover occurred in 1997 and Hong Kongers were faced with the immediate prospect of being ruled by an authoritarian regime, many of them reported that they did not expect to see much difference, because they had never in fact really experienced true representation in the political realm. Members of the business elite, wanting to expand their influence over policy (and their own interests), had always been able to get themselves appointed to the parliamentary bodies, but in the 1980s Hong Kong could still be characterized as a place with a low level of political activism, and was far from being a truly representative democracy.

Another key advantage for economic development in the pre-handover era was Hong Kong's access to a large and organizationally weak labor force. The owners of capital could always find people able and willing to work long hours, in relatively poor conditions, for wages that were low by first-world standards—all without the threat of serious trade union interference. The general consensus of opinion is that the weakness of the Hong Kong workforce stemmed primarily from the colony's proximity to China, where a vast and never-ending supply of workers was available. With new workers entering the colony every day as illegal immigrants from the mainland, existing workers were no doubt aware of their expendability. In addition, the majority of Hong Kong's manufacturing—or what was left of it at this time—was organized in small- and medium-size factories, in which trade union activity was limited. What unions did exist tended to be small in scale, and their activities had been sharply circumscribed by government legislation.

One factor often mentioned in explanations of the strength of Hong Kong's manufacturing-based economy has been the cultural predisposition of a society dominated by Confucian traditions. It is (or was until recently) relatively common to hear arguments about the advantages of the Confucian value system for economic development. It is assumed that Confucianism somehow justifies the existing hierarchy in Hong Kong society, either in the political realm, the family, or the workplace. The net effect of this is the assumption that workers will come to accept or believe that those in positions of authority will act with compassion toward them, and that they, in return, should accept their lowly positions, work hard to maintain the status quo, and never question the apparent inequities of the system. The Confucian emphasis on respect and loyalty to one's superiors is translated into an acceptance of conformity, and a resignation toward a centralized, meritocratic bureaucracy, which is allowed to operate in a fairly authoritarian fashion. All of this contributes to what some local scholars and journalists have referred to as a "culture of submissiveness" in Hong Kong.

The Confucian system is also assumed to result in a particular type of industrial system that is organized in a communal or family-like manner, with a strong emphasis on team spirit, mutual respect, and loyalty—all of which translate into a strong work ethic and a sense that labor is in itself a source of satisfaction, and not just because of the material benefits it brings. Along these or similar lines, the advantages of the Confucian value system for industrial development have been stressed by numerous observers as a way of attempting to account for the economic "miracles" witnessed in Hong Kong and the other newly industrialized economies (NIEs) of Asia throughout the 1980s and the early 1990s. Although there is an ongoing debate on this issue, some academic writers and journalists have concluded that societies with strongly Confucianist traditions have had a marked edge in the global economy during recent decades. As has been noted:

> The Confucian value system encourages hard work, diligence and a rever-ential attitude toward education, given that such traits are widely perceived to be the most acceptable means of career-progression in a hierarchical sys-tem. This in turn implies that Confucianism encourages rapid human capital formation. (Chowdhury and Islam 1993, 33)

Although the Confucian model has some appeal as a way of accounting for East Asian economic miracles, in reality it raises more questions than it answers, which was apparent especially after some of these so-called miracle economies, including Hong Kong's, plummeted in the late 1990s. It is simply not true, for example, that *all* of the East Asian NIEs have the family-oriented organization assumed to be dominant in their economies. The model does not explain why economic success came only in the 1960s, when the societies in question had been Confucian-dominated for centuries; and there is also then the problem of explaining how economic success occurs in non-Confucian developing societies. On balance, it is sufficient to suggest that Confucianism is, at most, a contributing factor, and one that plays a part in Hong Kong's economic growth, though a number of other more causally dominant factors are also at work (Pye 1988, 86–92).

An additional caveat is in order here, concerning the amount of state control or supervision that has been exercised in Hong Kong over the years and the extent to which the relative absence of such control can account for the colony's rapid rise as an economic power. There is no doubt that the Hong Kong government has remained in the background, particularly in comparison to mainland China (and even Taiwan). Hong Kong is a free port. There are no exchange controls, no protection of industry, and few restrictions on private property; its taxes are low, and there are virtually no state-owned enterprises. Hong Kong largely sidestepped the heavily state-supported import-substitution phase adopted in Taiwan and other NIEs, so it was never necessary for its government to intervene by erecting trade barriers to protect local industries, or to make direct investment decisions for high-priority industries. An official statement released by the Hong Kong government in 1973 provides what might come as close as possible to a definition of the term *laissez-faire* by suggesting that

> Hong Kong is probably the only territory still completely faithful to liberal economic policies of free enterprise and free trade.... Economic planning is not a function of the government.... The government's role remains one of providing a suitable framework within which commerce and industry can function efficiently and effectively with a minimum of interference. (quoted in Burns 1991, 132)

In spite of such pronouncements, the pre-1997 Hong Kong government actually played a significant role in directing and influencing the success of the colony's economy.[14] One largely hidden role was in the subsidies the government provided to workers in the form of relatively low-cost food staples, particularly rice, fish, meat, and vegetables, as well as the provision of subsidized public housing for a large proportion of the population. This form of government intervention contributed to Hong Kong's economic success in two important ways. First, by intervening in the supply and distribution of basic foodstuffs and by subsidizing housing costs, the government kept inflation to a minimum, helped stabilize the local currency, attracted foreign investors, and boosted (what had been) a lucrative tourist trade. Second, by subsidizing the major expenditures (food and housing) of working-class households, the Hong Kong government kept real wages relatively low, and this helped make Hong Kong's exports competitive in global markets (Schiffer 1991, 182–88).

The Hong Kong colonial government also played a significant role in the provision of infrastructure, especially transportation and port facilities, and in helping create and maintain human capital, particularly in the areas of education, health care, and social services. All of this had an indirect effect, but it is thought to have contributed to Hong Kong's overall economic competitiveness by providing a healthy, well-educated, and decently housed population. Not surprisingly, expenditures on physical capital (infrastructure) and "social wages" increased significantly from the 1950s through the 1970s as a proportion of the government's total expenditures; and as a result, government spending represented a growing share of Hong Kong's GDP throughout the period, from less than 3 percent in 1950 to more than 10 percent in the mid-1970s. The government has also traditionally intervened directly in the market for land, which puts it at or close to the center of economic operations. Among the prime candidates for new development—by the mid-1990s at least—was Lantau Island, perhaps most famous for being the location of the world's largest seated Buddha. Much to the chagrin of many environmentalists in Hong Kong, it was Lantau Island that was selected to be the site of the largest set of infrastructure developments ever conceived for Hong Kong, including the building of a new airport at Chep Lap Kok, which opened for business in July 1998. Accompanying the new airport was a battery of new highways, railways, bridges, and tunnels needed to connect Lantau with Kowloon and Hong Kong Island.

The colonial Hong Kong government was also responsible for the supply of housing—which is mainly in the form of apartment blocks—and the relocation of industry. The government exerted considerable effort on several occasions to stabilize the financial sector, which helped to ensure Hong Kong's continuing attractiveness to foreign investors. At times this required the government to step in to rescue failing banks, stabilize the Hong Kong dollar, and keep interest rates low. The government has traditionally played an active role in monetary matters, and through its contin-ued "watch-dog" and supervisory activities, it has created a fiscal environment (of low taxes) conducive enough to attract both domestic and foreign investment. Further, the government continues to control the supply of land directly by being the owner of it, and indirectly through land reclamation and by establishing land-use stipulations and zoning requirements. When all of these behind-the-scenes contributions are considered, it seems appropriate to question the use of the term *laissez-faire* to characterize the role of the government in Hong Kong. As Schiffer (1991) concludes in fact, Hong Kong should no longer be championed as the quintessential example of free-wheeling market economics. "When one takes all of . . . [this] . . . into account, perhaps it is . . . time to revise our views of this last bastion of unfettered capitalism (195)."[15]

AN ASIDE: THE OTHER SIDE OF THE SUCCESS NARRATIVE?

To temper the triumphal story of economic integration between Hong Kong and China, it is important to remember that a dangerous precedent was being set by the huge transfer of manufacturing jobs from Hong Kong to the mainland, a transfer involving the export of "dirty" and heavily polluting industries. Although this may have been a boon for Hong Kong's immediate pollution problems, it was (and still is) extremely damaging to China; and many scholars are now coming to believe that there are also knock-on effects in Hong Kong. The prevailing winds blow into the former colony from the north, and this is thought to be one of the primary factors in the sharp decline in Hong Kong's air quality during the last decade. On many days throughout the year, Hong Kong finds itself shrouded in pollution, making many of its glass skyscrapers barely visible and prompting authorities to warn people to stay inside (see photo 11.2).[16]

Although variations in weather patterns are at least partly to blame, many locals are pointing fingers across the border, at the smoke-belching factories in China's neighboring Guangdong province. In 2002 Hong Kong's air pollution reached a record level on August 28 when the community of Tung Chung, close to the new international airport at Chep Lap Kok, recorded an air pollution index reading of 185 (on a scale where anything over 100 is considered dangerously high). The government issued warnings to people with heart or breathing problems to avoid physical strain, and told them not to

Photo 11.2. Hong Kong's new skyline, and the International Financial Center shrouded in pollution. Photo by Christopher J. Smith

go to places with heavy traffic. The concentrations of ozone and of factory and vehicle emissions that accumulate on the hot, still days of the Hong Kong summers have forced the Hong Kong government to begin developing a plan to deal with this problem, as part of what it describes as its effort to turn Hong Kong into a world-class city. Environmental officials have been pushing owners of high-emission diesel vehicles in Hong Kong to use cleaner fuels, such as liquefied petroleum gas; to date, the vast majority of Hong Kong's eighteen thousand taxis have made the switch.

In April 2002, Guangdong and Hong Kong environmental officials reached an accord, pledging to reduce emissions of pollutants such as sulfur dioxide and nitrogen oxide from power plants and factories by 2010, although specific actions were not immediately implemented.[17] The most serious offenders in Guangdong are thought to be sixty or more cement factories in the Pearl River Delta (almost every community in the delta had several such factories until quite recently). Also of particular concern to Hong Kong environmentalists are the production processes (again in mainland China) involved in making printed circuit boards for computers, which use as a cleaning solvent significant amounts of ozone-depleting chlorofluorocarbons (CFCs). There has also been a significant growth in the manufacture of Styrofoam and plastic products, which are used in China to make disposable lunch boxes and now water bottles, and which are literally being made by the billion every week for China's hungry and thirsty workers.

On the days when it can be seen, Hong Kong's dazzling skyline reminds us that the territory has been on the cutting edge of modern (and postmodern) architecture during the last three decades. The modernist impulse has also left its imprint on other parts of Hong Kong. In the early 1970s, for example, the government announced a blueprint for the development of a series of new towns in the New Territories. To date eight have been built, located approximately 20–30 km from downtown Hong Kong, and a ninth is now fully operating on Lantau Island, at Tung Chung, adjacent to the new airport. The town planners, borrowing some of their ideas from a model implemented in Britain in earlier decades, envisioned the New Towns as self-contained residential, manufacturing, and commercial centers. The towns were intended to provide decent and inexpensive housing for Hong Kong's crowded population; to alleviate the pressures of high-density living, particularly in Hong Kong Island and Kowloon; and to provide ample space for industrial development in open-field sites, which would allow a switch from the traditional high-rise factories in the crowded residential areas of Kowloon and the central district of Hong Kong Island.

In actual fact, the government's ambitious program of housing provision began earlier than this, in the mid-1950s, after a disastrous fire left fifty-three thousand people (mostly poorly housed Kowloon residents and squatters) essentially homeless. A newly established housing authority launched a huge rebuilding program, and by 1964 more than 240 new tower blocks had been built, providing small, subsidized apartments for some eighty-four thousand families. In subsequent developments, more substantial housing blocks were built, both in Kowloon, on Hong Kong Island, and in the New Territories, and by 1992, 45 percent of Hong Kong's population was reported to be living in subsidized public housing (Kelly 1986, 76–95).[18] As was also true in the British case, the original idea for Hong Kong's New Towns was to create relatively small communities with adjacent industrial zones, and thereby to reduce the overall amount of commuting. Beginning in the early 1970s there was a vast amount of new construction in the New Territories as the New Towns began to take shape. Within a decade, modern apartment towers had sprung up from what had once been rice fields or the sea, and thousands of families were able to move out of the crowded inner-city areas and into reasonably priced apartments. The population of Hong Kong Island itself remained relatively stable, at about 22–23 percent of the total population, with a small amount of absolute growth through the 1980s and into the early 1990s. By contrast, the population of Kowloon shrank considerably as old, dilapidated housing areas—including the infamous Walled City, now replaced by a new park—were torn down. The proportion of Hong Kong's population living in Kowloon fell from more than 55 percent in 1971 to 34 percent in 1992, and correspondingly, the New Territories experienced massive growth, from 17 percent to almost 44 percent of the total.

The New Town planning program may have successfully shifted the population away from the crowded core areas of Hong Kong, but it has had much less success in attracting jobs to the New Territories, which has thwarted its goal of self-sufficiency.[19] Although a subway line (MTR) was built to connect some of the closer parts of the New Territories, and surface rail lines (KCR) pass through the area en route to the mainland border at Shenzhen, the lack of mass transit links into all parts of Kowloon, Hong Kong Island, and the New Territories means that in the absence of local employment opportunities, many of the inhabitants in the more distant New Towns have a torturous commute into work on a daily basis. One of the reasons for the program's failure to expand the employment base of the New Towns has been an overall decline of manufacturing in Hong Kong relative to the growth of its service-based economy. Most new jobs have been in the financial and business-service realm, or in the tourism and consumption-service sectors, and the majority of these have of necessity remained in Hong Kong's traditional business districts, rather than moving out to the New Towns. In the period from 1990 to 1994, for example, there was a 20 percent growth in the number of people employed in the finance and insurance sectors, and it is estimated that two-thirds of the local Hong Kong workforce works in only 10 percent of the territory's total area (Do Rosario 1995, 60). The most dramatic cause of the problem, however, has been the relocation of hundreds of Hong Kong factories to mainland China, as a result of the increased ease of setting up business there, particularly in the SEZs and Open Cities of the Pearl River Delta. It has been estimated that 500,000 blue-collar jobs have been shifted into Guangdong province alone, jobs that might otherwise have been located in the New Towns. This phenomenon was not anticipated by the colonial government in the 1970s, when the original plans for Hong Kong's New Towns were announced.

In response to the problems faced by the 2.5 million people now living in the New Territories, ambitious new infrastructure plans were announced in the mid-1990s, including a plan for a new railway line connecting New Towns in the western part of the New Territories (Yuen Long, Tuen Mun, and Tin Shui Wai) to southern Kowloon, and the extension of a new subway line to Tseung Kwan O, in the southeastern part of the New Territories. These plans will add to the vast infrastructural developments that have already transformed Hong Kong in association with the building of the new international airport on Lantau Island.

Giving-up and Regaining Hong Kong

As the 1997 handover approached, many Hong Kongers became increasingly sensitive to events occurring on the mainland. It can be argued, however, that throughout the 1990s, the actual process of economic integration with China was gaining strength, so that when the actual event occurred, it was little more than a formality. As Hong Kong's influence on the mainland continued to grow, it became increasingly evident that China was unlikely to do anything to sabotage or slow down economic growth after 1997. As more and more private capital entered China from the colony, the local Chinese economies, especially in Guangdong and Fujian, were increasingly becoming disconnected from the Plan and thrust more than ever into the vortex of both regional and global economies. With each passing year, Hong Kong and South China became ever-more interlocked and interdependent, to such an extent that some observers characterized 1997 as a "sideshow."[20]

Before the handover, it was estimated that some US$20 billion had been invested each way. It was widely rumored at the time—although never substantiated—that Hong Kong entrepreneurs then employed more than 3 million workers in China, and that over one-third of the colony's currency was in common use on the mainland.[21] Guangdong township-village enterprises (TVEs) were investing in some of the choicest properties in Hong Kong's central financial district; and Hong Kong businessmen were regular investors in even the remotest rural areas of the mainland: opening restaurants and theme parks, building bridges, and sometimes even restructuring entire cities into small forests of skyscrapers to be leased as office space, hotels, and apartments. In other words, the handover was merely the legal imprimatur on what was rapidly becoming a fait accompli, and in South China the emergence of a huge, integrated economic region—the Pearl River Delta—was an established fact. None of this should obscure the fact, however, that there were some very pressing concerns, both political and economic in nature, related to the period immediately after the handover. Before focusing on such concerns, however, we should consider, if only briefly, the circumstances under which the transfer of Hong Kong to mainland sovereignty came about, and review why (and how) the transfer was negotiated.

After 1949, the new Chinese government insisted that Hong Kong (and the New Territories) had been "stolen" by British "imperialists" during the nineteenth century. Instead of demanding decolonization immediately, however, which might have meant sovereignty and freedom for Hong Kong, the PRC tolerated the status quo until the early 1980s. At that time, the British government began to negotiate with China to reach a settlement, bearing in mind that the expiration date for its New Territories lease was rapidly approaching. It was recognized that Hong Kong Island and the Kowloon peninsula depended heavily on the New Territories for food, and also as a location for their surplus population and industry, so a resolution of the lease issue was of the utmost importance.

After protracted negotiations, an agreement was reached in 1984 stipulating that China would regain sovereignty over Hong Kong in 1997, with the British continuing to be responsible for the administration of the colony until then. The full story of the negotiations leading to the Joint Declaration has been told many times, but one of the better accounts is laid out by Robert Cottrell in his 1993 book *The End of Hong Kong: The Secret Diplomacy of Imperial Retreat*. It is clear from Cottrell's account that among all of the British colonies, Hong Kong was in a unique position, in the sense that the British did not agree to grant Hong Kong its independence, but arranged for the territory to be returned to another country. The consequence of this arrangement was that, unlike other British colonies around the world, there was no gradual struggle in Hong Kong for independence, which meant that no strong leaders or political movements emerged with independence as their major platform. Some historians argued at the time that the British were never overly concerned about the fate of Hong Kong, finding it to be more of an annoyance and an embarrassment than anything else. Welsh (1996) reports, for example, that during World War II some of the top brass in the Foreign Office considered Hong Kong a "thorn in the side" of Britain, and secretly wanted to see it returned to China as soon as possible.

There is also a consensus that Hong Kong was not one of the issues that captured the imagination of then British prime minister Margaret Thatcher; although publicly she may have expressed concern about the future of Hong Kong, she was not really willing to push the issue of democratization with the Chinese during the negotiations. Perhaps this is another example of Thatcher's now-famous opportunism. She realized that in the early 1980s, Britain, with its own unemployment and economic problems, would not welcome and could not stomach the prospect of up to 6 million Chinese from Hong Kong lobbying for their right to enter Britain as a way to avoid becoming citizens of a communist nation. Consequently Thatcher, according to Cottrell (1993), began to push for Hong Kong's convergence with the mainland. It was not until Thatcher's successor, John Major, appointed his political ally and personal friend Christopher Patten to be the (last) governor of Hong Kong in 1992, that Britain made Hong Kong a priority, realizing that in addition to being an extremely valuable property, it was also the site of Britain's ideological struggle with the Chinese Communist Party (CCP) about whether, and how quickly, to push for democracy.

On the other side of the equation, China had decided not to push to have Hong Kong returned immediately after the 1949 revolution in part because it suited them to have the colony remain as a trading center linking them to the outside world. It is also frequently suggested that China's decision not to push on the Hong Kong issue was based on a decision among its leadership to focus on the Taiwan issue. Taiwan, and its potential reunification with the mainland, was always considered a much greater prize, in political terms, than Hong Kong, but there is no doubt that by the late 1970s, Hong Kong was seen by Deng Xiaoping as a key component in China's drive toward modernization. In other words, China needed Hong Kong, which was seen as a crucial player in China's program of economic reform and opening up. Interestingly though, in the first years of the millennium and certainly by 2004, it had become clear that Hong Kong needed China as much, if not more than China needed Hong Kong, at least in economic terms.

It is important to note that the negotiations leading to the 1984 Joint Declaration on Hong Kong were initiated by the British, who were keen to protect their own business and commercial interests. China, it has been suggested, was willing to be moderate in the negotiations to demonstrate to the outside world that it was sincere in its claim that any reunification with Taiwan could be achieved peacefully (Segal 1993, 31–51). The Chinese agreed that they would establish a special administrative region (SAR) that would have "a high degree of autonomy," except in the areas of foreign affairs and defense. The declaration specified that the laws currently in force in Hong Kong at the time of the handover would remain *unchanged*, and that the economic system would *not be altered for at least fifty years* (Cottrell 1993, 206). This is what has become widely known as the "one country, two systems" principle, and as we shall see, it was to become a major issue of dispute among Hong Kong residents and observers around the world.

The PRC identified its basic policies toward Hong Kong in the Joint Declaration, which provided the blueprint for a mini-constitution for the former colony—a document that became known locally as the Basic Law—and for the new Hong Kong SAR (HKSAR). What was most worrying to Hong Kong residents before the handover, and also to the British, were provisions in the Basic Law that prohibited treason, sedition, subversion, and what was euphemistically referred to by the Chinese as "the theft of state secrets" (this is the now-famous Article 23). Another provision of the Basic Law that caused concern was one that would allow China, rather than the government of Hong Kong, to declare a state of emergency in the event of any threat to local security (Article 18). Although the Joint Declaration guaranteed autonomy to the new HKSAR, many people were afraid that the Chinese government would renege on such promises if a real emergency arose.

It was obvious long before the handover date that Hong Kong's decolonization was always going to follow a unique trajectory because, as Segal pointed out, "there was . . . no precedent for returning close to 6 million people to the rule of those from whom most of them had fled" (1993, 52). China had promised Hong Kong that the "one country, two systems" principle would be resolutely followed; but in the aftermath of the Tiananmen Square massacre in 1989, many people in Hong Kong were anxious, distressed, and uncertain about what the future held in store for them.[22] Those who were wealthy enough, and had the right connections, set out to establish permanent residency and (later) citizenship in other countries for themselves and for their children. Many of them hoped it would not prove necessary to emigrate, but even if they did, they were optimistic that it would soon be possible to return to Hong Kong. At the end of the 1980s, it was widely believed that communist rule in China could not last for much longer, in light of what had already happened in the Soviet Union and Eastern Europe. After 1989, however, more Hong Kongers than ever before began to express their fears by "voting with their feet," emigrating at the rate of over sixty thousand each year, mainly to the United States, Canada, and Australia.[23]

In 1992 a former chair of the British Conservative Party, Christopher Patten, arrived in Hong Kong, thereby signaling an about-face in British policy toward its soon-to-be ex-colony, and this would bring Britain and China into a direct conflict that would last until the very eve of the transfer. Wasting no time at all, Patten set out to broaden the democratic base of Hong Kong by expanding the franchise for elections to the Legislative Council, lowering the voting age, and replacing corporate with individual voting. In his words,

> The best guarantee of Hong Kong's prosperity for as far ahead as any of us can see or envisage is to protect our way of life. . . . An integral part of this way of life . . . is the participation of individual citizens in the conduct of Hong Kong's affairs. (Sum 1995)

Governor Patten attempted to introduce into Hong Kong's political system such concepts as accountability and direct representation, to make sure that by 1997 a significant amount of democratization would already be in place. He was operating on two major assumptions: one, that after 1997 there would be relatively few opportunities for such changes to occur; and two, that the process of building democracy would be irreversible by the time the Chinese took over. He was essentially trying to implant a parliamentary style of government, and was putting the British in the role of moral protector of the Hong Kong people, which would allow him to preside over a British "exit in glory" from Hong Kong. During the transition the people of the colony would be protected, but Patten was also hoping they would become more assertive by demanding and exercising their political rights.

In Patten's view, the PRC would play the role of the opposition party in this saga, constraining or holding up the democratization process. The Chinese government, in response to Patten's proposals, consistently reiterated the themes that had been voiced in Deng Xiaoping's "one country, two systems" concept as early as 1982. It argued that Patten's proposals violated the provisions and the spirit of the Joint Declaration, and ignored the principle of convergence with the Basic Law of the HKSAR. From 1984 until Patten's appearance in 1992, the British government had not overly emphasized the issue of increasing the level of democracy in Hong Kong, preferring instead to encourage a slow but definite move toward democratization, while allowing a smooth transition to Chinese rule in 1997.

Arguably however, the events of 1989 had demonstrated to the British—and to many other governments around the world—that China might not be trustworthy and might quickly change its mind about Hong Kong, in spite of the spirit and the wording of the Joint Declaration. The Chinese were also worried by what had happened in 1989, and wanted to slow down the pace of democratization in Hong Kong (as well as at home).[24] By introducing proposals for changes in the 1994 and 1995 elections, Patten's actions (according to the PRC) constituted a "unilateral termination" of ongoing negotiations because, by the PRC's reckoning, decisions about election issues in Hong Kong were to be negotiated between the two governments (Britain and China), and not mandated by the British alone. What followed was a bitter war of words between the two sides. Ma Yuzhen, China's ambassador to Britain, was certainly not holding anything back in 1994 when he is reported to have said, "In the absence of an agreement between China and Britain, China will definitely disband and reestablish Hong Kong's three-tier councils . . . on July 1st 1997. Politically, China will resume the exercise of sovereignty over Hong Kong" (*Hong Kong Sunday Morning Post* 1994; see also Mirsky 1994, 16).

The Chinese threat, which had been obvious to many at home and abroad since the mid-1980s, was renewed in the early 1990s, when the British were warned in no uncertain terms that they needed to back down on the issue of democratization. From the Chinese perspective, not doing so would be interpreted as deliberate hostility and a direct challenge to China's sovereignty. The Chinese threatened to break all contracts pertaining to British business that continued after 1997, and to delay the starting date for construction of the huge new airport on Lantau Island. Contrary to Patten's wishes, the delays meant that the new airport would not open until after the British left, thereby thwarting any plans he had of making his personal exit with glory from the new airport he had personally engineered. As Mirsky noted just three years before the handover, "Under no circumstances . . . will Beijing permit the airport's opening day to be early enough for the hated Patten to cut the ribbon" (1994, 20).

At this point even some British observers felt that Patten was overstepping his powers. Sir Percy Craddock, who had been ambassador to China and was the chief negotiator for the Joint Declaration in the 1980s, felt that Patten's actions represented a real threat to the Chinese, and that they, in turn, might take out their resentment on the people of Hong Kong. As Craddock observed, "Heroics are fine when you face the consequences yourself. But heroics at someone else's expense, particularly someone to whom you stand in a position of trust, is another matter" (quoted in Mirsky 1994, 16).

In its continued response to Patten's proposals, China also made an appeal to nationalism, which involved repeating a litany of the colonial expansionism of the British who, it argued, had persistently plundered China and Hong Kong throughout the nineteenth century. Party propagandists argued that the PRC needed to act decisively to wipe out the shame of the past and to unify the Chinese by remapping Hong Kong as an integral part of China. It is important to observe that this type of top-down nationalism was quite different from many of the grassroots nationalistic movements occurring in other colonized entities around the world, where issues of self-determination and democratization were always close to the surface. As far as Beijing was concerned, Hong Kong had always been, and would remain, an integral part of China, and Beijing anticipated that the former colony would serve as China's portal for its ongoing program of modernization. It was hoped that Hong Kong would lead the way toward the creation of a Greater China that would eventually include Taiwan as well.

To move toward this goal, the Chinese government began to solicit support from among the richest and most influential members of Hong Kong society. Members of the business and professional elites were coopted by being asked to serve as Hong Kong advisors to the Chinese government. They were invited to Beijing, wined and dined extensively, and presented with certificates attesting to their patriotism as Chinese citizens. Other groups, such as the Hong Kong Federation of Trade Unions and the Democratic Alliance for the Betterment of Hong Kong, as well as the Liberal Party, were also coopted by the Chinese. In this way the Beijing government was able to establish what amounted to a multiclass bloc of support within Hong Kong that functioned more-or-less openly as a quasi-government alliance of groups acting as an alternative to the Legislative Council—which the Chinese considered to be a tool of the British colonial administration. Some very important figures in Hong Kong were willing to accept appointments to such Beijing-controlled advisory groups because it allowed them to be flexible: on the surface they could appear to support China, but at the same time they could wait, opportunistically, to see how the wind would blow after 1997. It was reported that many of them already had their citizenship certificates and permanent residency papers secured in other countries, in the event of a radical decline in Hong Kong's situation.

In the appointment of the advisory groups, the New China News Agency (Xinhua) played a major role, effectively operating in Hong Kong as the unofficial embassy for the PRC. Two of the leaders of the Hong Kong Democratic Party, Martin Lee and Szeto Wah, remained unpersuaded, and continued to oppose Beijing. In the elections of 1994 and 1995 the Democrats did well, with voters for the first time having an opportunity to elect, either directly or indirectly, all sixty members of the Legislative Council. In the March 1995 elections, Mr. Szeto, a strong Patten supporter, soundly defeated Elsie Wu (known locally as "Beijing Elsie"; see Sum 1995).[25]

The struggle for dominance in Hong Kong stacked the British and the Chinese up against each other, with each government attempting to identify its allies within the Hong Kong population. Facing the Beijing advisory groups was an equally multiclass set of Patten and democratization supporters, which included many government civil servants, democracy-minded capitalists, and a range of newly formed middle- and working-class groups representing such diverse interest groups as academics, social workers, liberal traders and merchants, and factory workers, as well as the loosely knit members of the Liberal Democratic Party, and a variety of independent leftward-leaning individuals.[26]

On the eve of the handover, Hong Kong was sharply divided into two opposing blocs, both of which were seeking to promote their own version of Hong Kong's future. On one side was a collection of groups wanting to keep open the discourse on further democratization, which set them in direct opposition to the PRC; the other side was attempting to hold together an opposition bloc by appealing to its members' sense of Chinese nationalism. The outcome of the struggle depended largely on the balance of forces between and within the alliances that had emerged on either side of the issue. This balance was mediated by continuing rounds of negotiations between the "conscious agents" (representatives of the British and Chinese governments) in the early to mid-1990s (Sum 1995). The complexity of the debate resulted in a multiplicity of meanings that "in the short term . . . enable[d] . . . individuals/groups to form new allies and, in the long term, may [have] significantly change[d] the political opportunity structure" (95).[27]

For China, it was evident that Governor Patten represented a walking nightmare, someone who stirred up ethnic Chinese sentiments on the streets of a city that was supposed to pass peacefully back to its rightful owners. It was not clear to outside observers what Patten's (and the British government's) actual goals were throughout this process. Some have suggested that Britain merely wanted to be seen as doing the right thing by favoring increased democratization at the eleventh hour in Hong Kong. Others believe there was a genuine belief that greater freedoms and guarantees did need to be built into Hong Kong politics before 1997. Judging from Patten's public statements, it appears that Patten believed that it was immoral for the British to "grovel" before the Chinese, as many world governments (including his own) had done in the past.

The Hong Kong SAR in the New Millennium

Any attempt to evaluate what has happened in Hong Kong in the years that have elapsed since the handover is fraught with obvious difficulties. Things have always changed very rapidly in Hong Kong, so an evaluation that may be accurate at the time of writing will probably be well off the mark by the time it is published. In addition, evaluations by their very nature are highly subjective; our view about what is happening today in Hong Kong and what might happen in the future is shaped very much by those whose arguments we happen to find the most persuasive. In terms of politics, at one end of the spectrum we can expect to find the Democratic Party of Hong Kong (Martin Lee and his supporters), which argues that China has not been keeping its promises with respect to the "one country, two systems" principle. This evaluation is probably very different from what we would hear from a representative of the pro-Beijing government in Hong Kong, at the other extreme. Meanwhile in Beijing, on the same end of the spectrum, if we ask how Hong Kong has progressed since the handover, what we are likely to hear in reply is a triumphant narrative that sounds much like government propaganda. Joshua Chi-Kong Law, for example, a young man who was formerly private secretary to the Beijing-appointed Hong Kong chief executive, Tung Chee-hwa, and who was appointed director-general of trade in August 1999, sees the current uncertainties more as opportunities for Hong Kong than as economic threats. On the topic of China's accession to the World Trade Organization (WTO), for example, which was seen by many as a potential problem for Hong Kong's continued economic leadership in the region, Mr. Law paints a glowing picture of the future. As the mainland market further liberalizes, he argues, enormous business opportunities will continue to emerge for Hong Kong. The territory's close proximity to and good knowledge and experience of mainland markets, he believes, will make all the difference in the immediate future, and will allow Hong Kong to play an even greater role as the gateway and middleman for the Chinese market, besides allowing it to participate directly in the economic development of the mainland. In his view,

> As we enter the new millennium, the HKSAR Government will continue to invest in the infrastructure to match the needs of the information age and the knowledge-based economy. Our mission is to provide an excellent environment here in Hong Kong for business to thrive and to take full advantage of the new challenges and opportunities ahead. (Law 2002)

Between these two extremes, it is possible to identify a number of overlapping categories of concern among Hong Kong citizens in the new millennium. Among the most important of these are the following four, which shed some light on what has been happening in Hong Kong since the handover in 1997:

- How do Hong Kongers think about themselves and their role in the world, now that they are no longer part of the British empire?
- Will Hong Kong be as wealthy in the future as it has been in the past, and more specifically, how will the economic impact of the post-handover period be felt by the ordinary people of Hong Kong?
- What happened when China tried to introduce legislation on the controversial Article 23 issue?
- Can the "one country, two systems" principle be made to work adequately?

HONG KONG IDENTITIES: HOW DO HONG KONGERS THINK OF THEMSELVES?

Once again we should introduce this issue by considering views that might be found at either end of a continuum. At one end we would expect to find a nostalgic sense of the past—perhaps an acute sense of loss as a result of the handover—and a belief that the situation is deteriorating. At the other extreme we could expect to find opinions like those of Mr. Law above, who feels that Hong Kong is doing splendidly as one of China's newest SARs. Starting with the first point of view—that of those mourning for the past—we could expect to hear at least some minor complaints about the loss of the colony. Usually this is heard very infrequently today, except perhaps at a meeting of the Hong Kong Royal Geographical Society—a group that is decidedly more British than anything one might come across in Britain itself! Something of this sort was apparent in the musings of British travel-writer extraordinaire Jan Morris, for example, when she wrote in the version of her Hong Kong book that was reissued for the handover event:

> To have created upon this improbable terrain, among an alien people, so far from home, a society not only stable, educated, prosperous and free, not only self-governed by the imperialists' own high principles, but also standing as a model and an inspiration to its mother China—that might be a last justification for the idea of imperialism itself. And even if that fulfillment were to survive only a generation, to be destroyed by yet another new brutalism, at least it would add a sad majesty to the aesthetic of Empire—a memorial to what might have been, as the shutters close upon the once exuberant colony. (quoted in Y.-L. R. Wong 2002, 141–42)

Few people in Hong Kong today would echo such blatantly imperialist sentiments, but it is plausible that some of them might feel a little confused or conflicted between their sense of themselves as being culturally Chinese, and their resistance to and rejection of the political system of the mainland. As Renita Wong has suggested in fact, some young, middle-class Hong Kongers might be in the uniquely privileged position of being able to construct themselves as free subjects, which in part stems from the Western-oriented way of life that the British brought to the Hong Kong in which these young Hong

Kongers grew up (Y.-L. R. Wong 2002). Some of them might, in other words, think of themselves as being located—ideologically—somewhere halfway between the colonized and the colonizing.

To test her hypothesis, Wong conducted in-depth interviews with a number of young Hong Kong citizens who were actively engaged in what she refers to as "development" projects in mainland China, programs focusing on such activities as educational campaigns, efforts to improve conditions and possibilities for China's women, and poverty eradication programs. As she had anticipated, most of those interviewed had long thought of themselves as culturally Chinese, but at the same time they appeared to be strongly opposed to the political system operating on the mainland. As Wong observes:

> China was imagined as their cultural "roots" which they desired to "go back" to—in both time and space. What the imaginary cultural roots, and hence China, represent are culture, history and landscape. Such a romantic imaginary of China, however, could not be sustained when some informants later in their post–high school years began to reach out for actual contemporary China. Being in touch with the realities of contemporary China, many of these individual Hong Kongers began to experience and construct China as the "inside"—a space of oppression and confined vision. The image of Hong Kong, on the other hand, was further affirmed as free. Between their identification with and alienation from China, individual informants experienced ambivalence in their colonial and national identities. (Y.-L. R. Wong 2002, 147)

The differences between Hong Kong and the mainland, and the perceived advantages of being born in Hong Kong, were obvious to these young people. One of them, who was actually born on the mainland, told Wong that for her, Hong Kong meant freedom. If she had stayed in China, she realized that she would probably have been married by then, with children (one or two, depending on where she lived), and that, hopefully, she would have a state job. This was clearly not a thought that appealed to her imagination; in fact, in her words,

> You know roughly what your fate will be inside the mainland. . . . But if you come out to Hong Kong, I think there are many more opportunities. I understand why people want to go to the States, or to Hong Kong. You'll have a very very different identity. . . . I think I was the only girl who finished university in my village. . . . If I was . . . [still] . . . inside the mainland, I would not have had these kinds of opportunities. (Y.-L. R. Wong 2002, 150)

From her discussions with a number of such young people, Wong concluded that the opportunity to go to China to be involved in development work created a "discursive space" for individual Hong Kongers when they traveled to mainland China (Y.-K. Wong 2002, 152). What emerged in fact amounted to a "liberalizing mission" on their side, giving them the opportunity to help with and speed up the opening up of China to the outside world. According to Wong, this represents a colonial discourse of "Hong-Kong-as-liberty," in which Hong Kong residents think of themselves as the liberal modern Chinese, whose mission it is to "free up" their ancestral country.

In spite of their individual differences in the realm of political orientation and preferred strategies for development, Wong's informants almost universally identified "human-capacity building" as the key to China's development, which involved solving the illiteracy problem of mainland China, and also creating civic space for the empowerment of grassroots population groups. Wong suggests that these two formulations of China's development problem are premised specifically on the Western ideology of liberalism—an idea that they were able to nurture in the relative freedom of colonial Hong Kong (Y.-L. R. Wong 2002).

HARD TIMES IN HONG KONG?

Putting aside these essentially positive views of Hong Kong—a Hong Kong that, according to Wong's research, can be seen as standing for something (in its past) that has certain beneficial effects (Y.-L. R. Wong 2002)—one of the most pressing concerns in recent years has been in the economic realm: specifically, the fear that Hong Kong's uncertain status after 1997 would amplify the problems inherent in the region as a result of the Asian economic crisis. Again, this topic is largely time-dependent because economic trends seem to rise and fall in rapid cycles, but over the course of the last nine years it has become clear that Hong Kong's economy has been more up and down than most people—locals and internationals—would have preferred. The general view is that these oscillations are due at least in part to the serious economic challenges Hong Kong faced immediately after the handover.

A precipitous drop in property prices in late 1997, for example, burst the economic bubble, and together with the emerging economic crisis in Asia, resulted in deflation, increasing unemployment, and a budget deficit in 1998. Hong Kong's real GDP fell by more than 5 percent in 1998, though it would bounce back again in 1999 and especially 2000, and then remain static in 2001 (see table 11.3). Nominal investment

Table 11.3. Hong Kong's Domestic Economy, 1999–2003

	1999	2000	2001	2002	2003
GDP at constant (2000) market prices (HK$ million)	1,169,474	1,288,338	1,294,306	1,318,743	1,361,036
Real GDP growth (%)	3.0	10.2	0.5	1.9	3.2
GDP per capita at current market prices (US$)	23,177	24,365	24,070	23,800	23,312
Inflation (%)	−4.0	−3.8	−1.6	−3.0	−2.6
Unemployment (%)	6.2	4.9	5.1	7.3	7.9
Foreign exchange (US$ billion)	96.26	107.6	111.2	111.9	118.4
Population growth (%)	2.5	0.9	0.9	0.9	0.2
Hang Seng Index (1964 = 100)	16,962	15,095	11,397	9,321	12,576

Sources: "Annual Report 2002—Annex and Tables," Hong Kong Monetary Authority; "Hong Kong Statistics—Frequently Asked Statistics," HKSAR Census and Statistics Department, 2004; "Hong Kong Statistics—Hong Kong in Figures," HKSAR Census and Statistics Department, 2004.

fell by 13.9 percent in 1998 and 17.4 percent in 1999; and it was not until 1999 that some measure of recovery occurred. It is clear, in other words, that it has been difficult to predict Hong Kong's economic trends, which is in itself a major cause for concern, in an economy that has been so strong for so many years.[28]

There is no doubt that Hong Kong experienced steady economic growth before 1997, even though the (then) colony's average growth was slower throughout the 1990s than the average for the other NIEs, especially Singapore (although all but Taiwan appeared to lose ground in 1998).[29] Growth at these rates implies that people's livelihoods were improving; and this is especially true if we look at the social indicators of development used by the UN in the calculation of its *Human Development Report* (e.g., life expectancy, infant mortality, and per capita availability of doctors and nurses).

The slowdowns and Hong Kong's negative turn in economic fortunes after 1997 suggest, however, that for many of Hong Kong's residents, the post-handover period has not been a prosperous time. This observation needs to be viewed in light of a neoliberal trend occurring at the same time, with the HKSAR government attempting to reduce the financial burden of social welfare provision. In announcing his economic plans in mid-2000, Hong Kong's chief executive Tung Chee-hwa made it clear that he would be looking for a healthy contribution from the voluntary services sector, in part to take the sting out of the declining role of the state in financing welfare services.

The most visibly evident impact of the handover uncertainties, though, has been in terms of rising rates of unemployment and wage cuts. In response to the new circumstances, many small businesses closed down or downsized considerably in the years after the handover, and the unemployment rate has reflected this, with unemployment increasing from 2.2 percent in 1997 to 6.2 percent in 1999, then growing again to 7.3 percent by 2002, and appearing to increase beyond that level in 2003 (see table 11.4). As bad as these statistics look, the actual situation may be even worse, because although many people have been able to get new jobs, in most cases they have faced cuts in both salaries and benefits. As Mok and Lau (2002) show in fact, the real index of pay per person across all industry sectors was 123.9 percent in 1992. This had fallen to 98.2 percent by 1996, and increased again in 1998 to 105.7 percent; 112.5 percent in 2000; 114.6 percent in 2001; and 118.0 percent by 2002. In other words, Hong Kong appears to have been showing a steady increase in real wage levels in recent years, but is still not back to the level of the early 1990s.[30]

One of the most telling outcomes of all of this was a steady increase in income inequality in Hong Kong all through the 1990s (K. W. Li 2001). Although there are no data available for the period after 1996, it is commonly believed that the trend has continued into the new millennium (Mok and Lau 2002);[31] and some local scholars have suggested that one reason for this is that people with information-technology skills who are laid off may be able to find new jobs that pay reasonably well, while those in less-skilled categories may not, especially those in the traditional manufacturing sector. This suggests that Hong Kong's fundamental economic restructuring has put those people who relied on the traditional sectors of the economy at a particular disadvantage.

During the last few years, the local Hong Kong newspapers have been carrying stories about workers who have been laid off from the industrial sector and who have been forced to take part-time jobs, for example at fast-food establishments, to try to

Table 11.4. Hong Kong: Statistics on Labor Force, Unemployment, and Underemployment

| Period | Labor force | | Unemployed (in 1,000's) | Unemployment rate (not seasonally adjusted) (%) | Underemployed (in 1,000's) | Underemployment rate (%) |
	Size (in 1,000's)	Percentage change over the same period in the preceding year (%)				
1997	3,234.8	2.3	71.2	2.2	37.1	1.1
1998	3,276.1	1.3	154.1	4.7	81.8	2.5
1999	3,319.6	1.3	207.5	6.2	96.9	2.9
2000	3,374.2	1.6	166.9	4.9	93.5	2.8
2001	3,427.1	1.6	174.8	5.1	85.5	2.5
2002	3,487.9	1.8	255.5	7.3	105.5	3.0

Source: Hong Kong Department of Statistics. http://kafuwong.econ.hku.hk/teaching/econ1003/2003F/labourstat.pdf.

make ends meet (*Ming Pao Daily*, January 21, 2000). Mok and Lau (2002) also show that between 1996 and 1999, the only income group in Hong Kong to experience real growth in income was the top quintile (114), with all other groups showing decreases that were proportionately greater the further down the pay scale.

FREEDOM OF SPEECH IN HONG KONG?

The issue that most observers predicted would be a problem after the handover, namely, the precise definition of what was involved in Article 23 of the Basic Law, did indeed rear its ugly head, although admittedly not until 2002, which was much later than most people had predicted. Article 23 requires that Hong Kong pass laws "to prohibit treason, secession, sedition, subversion against the Central People's Government [China], or theft of state secrets," and to prevent foreign political organizations from conducting political activities in the region, or from establishing ties with organizations within Hong Kong. The residents of Hong Kong realize that China's national security laws are extreme and are frequently used to suppress opposition. If the same system were to be put in place in Hong Kong, it is argued, there would be a real risk of damaging the freedom and the high degree of autonomy that Hong Kongers have come to expect (and that they thought were guaranteed by the "one country, two systems" principle laid out in the 1984 settlement). The only saving grace is in the words actually written into the Basic Law, which stipulate that Hong Kong "shall enact on its own" the laws that it needs, although some observers have suggested that the leaders in Beijing were probably relying on the traditionally submissive nature of Hong Kong's people to allow them to force this legislation through.

It was also feared that the new laws—drafts of which were promulgated from Beijing in 2002—would give additional powers to the police, allowing them to enter any suspicious premises, and to search and seize whatever and whenever they think it is appropriate, all without a warrant. A Hong Kong–based organization could, under the new laws, be banned if it is proved to be affiliated with a group that had been outlawed on the mainland, or one that had been classed as illegal because it was considered a danger to national security, which is the case for organizations such as Falun Gong. Members of the press in Hong Kong were understandably very worried about a further stipulation of the new laws, and wondered what exactly it was that would constitute the "unlawful disclosure of information concerning international relations and relations between the PRC and the SAR." In an evaluation of the new legislation, for example, Brown (2002) notes that

> many provisions in the new "consultation" paper have raised alarm among persons who care about preserving human rights and civil liberties in the SAR. The pending implementation of laws to comply with Article 23 is a very emotionally charged issue in Hong Kong, particularly because the article was deliberately added to the draft of the Basic Law immediately following the killing of students and other protestors in Beijing . . . in 1989. (122)

The PRC, working through its puppet government in Hong Kong, has continually pressured the media to censor itself, with some degree of success; but the drafting of the new laws suggested that Beijing had decided to take the extra step to make certain of press submissiveness in the future. In fact, as noted above, the Basic Law did not actually define these offenses, but suggested that the new HKSAR government should itself draft the needed legislation (Clifford and Engardio 2002), but as some critics have pointed out, the government could have chosen simply to modify its existing laws, which would have left civil liberties intact. Instead, Chief Executive Tung Chee-hwa chose to consult Beijing, and in collaboration they came up with measures that some Hong Kongers referred to at the time as "the last nail in the coffin" of their political freedom.

A draft of the legislation was presented in September 2002 for a three-month period of consultation, and after a slow start, objections were submitted in a variety of formats. When the community had digested what was being proposed, opposition rapidly gathered force, and at the end of the three-month consultation period, hundreds (probably thousands) of news reports, critiques, and analyses had been published in the local media. Numerous public forums had been held, including academic seminars organized by the legal community; and a preliminary list of more than four hundred items of comment and analysis had been prepared.

A protest march held on December 15, 2002, recorded a turnout of about 600,000 (to be matched the following Sunday by a rally in support of the government, with a recorded turnout of 40,000). Some 240 submissions were made directly to the Legislative Council. Chambers of commerce around the world, foreign governments, the House of Commons in the United Kingdom, and even the European parliament debated the issue, and a large U.S. congressional delegation visiting the Legislative Council publicly discussed Article 23 and its ramifications for free speech in Hong Kong. The English Bar and the International Bar Association also submitted their collective views, as well as human rights groups and numerous nongovernmental organizations (NGOs), including journalist associations, the Catholic Church, and an association of university librarians. Signature campaigns were mounted in Hong Kong and overseas, and by the cutoff date a total of 100,909 submissions had been received, of which 3,812 were from overseas; and 369,612 signatures had been collected, of which 29,099 were from overseas. The last time a consultation exercise in Hong Kong had this level of response was in 1987 on the introduction of direct elections to the Legislative Council, when over 134,000 submissions were received by the government.[32]

The Tung administration hoped to enact the new legislation by June 2003, and assuming the legislation was successfully implemented, the consequences would have been felt immediately. For example, "unauthorized and damaging disclosure of protected information" would have been a criminal offense; and the authorities would have been able to ban any sort of activities they considered to be contrary to "the interests of national security or public safety or public order." Critics feared that with the new measures, the curtailment of speech and political activity would be almost the same in Hong Kong as it was in China; some even suggested it would be worse. Such talk was disturbing to the residents of Hong Kong, because it was well-known that journalists in China are routinely removed from their posts, and sometimes even jailed for publishing what are officially described as "state secrets," even if these so-called secrets are nothing more serious than previously unreleased economic data.[33] Foreign business organizations also expressed concern, because the free flow of information had traditionally been one of Hong Kong's major attractions.

What was particularly worrying to many local people was that Hong Kong's leaders appeared to be closing their ears to complaints about the new measures, although some press releases during the early summer months of 2003 suggested that the version of the Article 23 bill that was to be finally presented to the legislature might be more lenient than the consultation paper distributed for public commentary. Officials also assured the public that their worst fears were unwarranted. "Clamping down on press freedom is the last thing we want," said Solicitor-General Robert Allcock. The fear, however, as Clifford and Engardio (2002) stated at the time, was that well-meaning public servants come and go, whereas the institutionalization of the new laws would put justice into the hands of statutes and the courts, thereby overriding the discretion of whoever is in power at the time. What Hong Kong needed, they suggested, was the establishment of clear laws that met international standards for freedom of information and association, but that also complied with Article 23. What most journalists argued in turn was that little change was actually needed, because, as Clifford and Engardio noted, "Five years after the handover, Hong Kong remains remarkably stable despite a feisty press and opposition parties. Leaders in both Hong Kong and Beijing must realize an open society is one guarantee of the city's continued prosperity" (2).

In what was perhaps one of the most significant moments in Hong Kong's recent history, in the face of public opposition to the introduction of the Article 23 laws, the HKSAR government decided to withdraw the proposal in September 2003 after massive public demonstrations (one of which involved over 500,000 people in a July gathering in Victoria Park). Most of the bill's critics were relieved when they heard of the surprise decision, but assumed that the bill had been withdrawn mainly for political reasons—related to the parliamentary elections to come in the following year—and that the government might try to introduce even more draconian legislation at a future date. Another possible explanation for the withdrawal might have been a decision by the government to retreat on this issue until the economic situation in Hong Kong had stabilized. Around the world, the decision was heralded as a decisive moment in the resistance to oppressive moves from Beijing, temporarily uniting voices from both sides of the overseas political spectrum. As one conservative U.S. politician reported,

> In July, the citizens of Hong Kong shocked their would-be masters in Beijing.... It is a great day for not only Hong Kong but free people everywhere that the PRC has yielded to this overwhelming demonstration of democratic aspirations. With the full support of this Congress, the people of Hong Kong are holding steadfast, recognizing that their island of freedom must remain a beacon of hope throughout China.[34]

ONE COUNTRY, TWO SYSTEMS?

The last item to be considered in this review of Hong Konger's concerns in the post-1997 period is clearly related to the Article 23 issue, but is more directly political, involving the extent to which the "one country, two systems" principle is being adhered to. Again, opinions are sharply divided on this issue, depending on who is talking, but there was enough concern by the year 2003 to ring some bells of warning. The Chinese authorities have heaped one tribute after another on Hong Kong's successes in the period after 1997 and the performance of Tung Chee-hwa as the chief executive. Vice-premier Qian Qichen, for example, the highest PRC official responsible for the HKSAR, said in 2002 that the Tung administration had chalked up "a very great achievement in implementing 'one country, two systems' "; and the official Xinhua news agency noted that during the past five years, Hong Kong's people running Hong Kong "had won the respect of the world" (Lam 2002). Some local journalists, however, have been trying to show the other side of this picture, and one of these is Willy Wo-Lap Lam, formerly the bureau chief responsible for China for the *South China Morning Post*.

For newspaper editors and journalists working regularly in China, there is a certain amount of risk attached to being too openly critical of the current regime and its policies; and since the 1997 handover, there have been fears—and a great deal of debate—about Beijing's increasing interference with media freedoms in Hong Kong. Around the time of the handover, the *South China Morning Post* was generally considered to be a relatively liberal newspaper, in the Western understanding of that term (see note 26). It appeared to have enough editorial independence to be mildly critical of the regime in Beijing, and did not seem to avoid reporting on events and running editorials that might be considered politically sensitive by the state leaders. In reality, it is always extremely difficult to assess the political leanings of a specific newspaper, and in the absence of any reliable data, it is difficult to judge the extent to which the *South China Morning Post* might now be maintaining a significant trend in the other political direction.

Judging from what little can be scraped together, however, there have been some very worrying indications. Many *South China Morning Post* readers in Hong Kong now openly criticize the paper for excessive cozying up to the Chinese government, especially after the paper was bought by Robert Kuok Hock Nien, a Malaysian businessman who is reported to have close ties to Beijing. Of particular concern was Willy Wo-Lap Lam's resignation in November 2000, which was interpreted in some quarters as a prime example of Beijing's "tightening the screws."[35] On the broader issue of media freedom in Hong Kong, additional concern was voiced after PRC president Jiang Zemin's furious outburst in Beijing in November 2000, which was filmed and replayed in Hong Kong (but not on the mainland). In this outburst, Jiang lambasted the Hong Kong press for being far too eager to criticize the regime, and "too naive" in their questioning (of him) about the methods to be used to elect (select) a new chief executive for the HKSAR.[36]

Lam suggests that there are several clear indications that Beijing has tended to favor the "one country" side of the principle, rather than the emphasis on the "two systems." Much of the problem, according to Lam, stems from the accountability or ministerial system that Chief Executive Tung Chee-hwa introduced to centralize power in his hands—and to further marginalize the *Democrats*, a generic term for all elected politicians who are in favor of a faster pace for establishing democracy. Under the ministerial system, which was a product of close consultation between Tung Chee-hwa's office and Beijing, the chief executive is empowered to appoint fourteen policy secretaries who report to him and serve at his pleasure. Until this development, the secretaries were mostly drawn from the ranks of civil servants, and were supposed to be politically neutral. The new system is interpreted (by Lam at least) as evidence of Beijing's distrust of senior civil servants, most of whom came through the ranks under British rule. This was indirectly confirmed by Vice-premier Qian Qichen, who told a Hong Kong television station that because Tung Chee-hwa was obliged in mid-1997 to retain former governor Chris Patten's senior staff, he insisted on running what amounted to a "one man show" during much of his first term. Qian Qichen added that Beijing had confidence that Tung would be able to do better in his second term, because under the accountability system he would be in a position to appoint his own people.

In a roundabout way, the vice-premier was repeating the familiar charge that certain top civil servants, perhaps out of residual loyalty to the British, were reluctant to work with Tung Chee-hwa—or Beijing. Tung Chee-hwa's new team, announced in the summer of 2003, included a coterie of "like-minded businessmen" and "pro-Beijing" individuals. This trend was even more obvious in the full Executive Council, or cabinet, whose membership was expanded from twelve to twenty. Apart from the fourteen secretaries, Tung Chee-hwa appointed five cabinet members who enjoyed Beijing's full trust. Prominent among these were two leaders of influential political parties: Tsang Yok-sing, the chairman of the pro-Beijing Democratic Alliance for the Betterment of Hong Kong; and James Tien, who headed the pro-government business-oriented Liberal Party. Since the two parties now controlled at least eighteen votes in the Legislative Council—less than half of whose sixty members are popularly elected—Tung Chee-hwa was guaranteed control over the legislature. The vice-chairman of the Hong Kong Democratic Party, Yeung Sum, said the Democrats were not intimidated by these changes because, he indicated, "Our image as the opposition party will become more clear-cut." Willy Lam, however, thought the new development would make it even easier for Tung Chee-hwa—and Beijing—to sideline pro-democracy politicians. In his interviews with the Hong Kong media, Vice-premier Qian Qichen tried to dampen expectations about a faster pace for the establishment of democracy in Hong Kong. He pointed out that "to promote democracy in Hong Kong, one cannot have Hong Kong emulating the systems of other regions." Qian Qichen's statement was seen as highlighting the undesirability of the HKSAR holding Western-style polls to pick Legislative Council members or the chief executive any time in the near future.

During the past two years (2004 through the first half of 2005), the most significant political developments in Hong Kong have been a self-initiated decision made by the Standing Committee of the National People's Congress in Beijing to preempt local debate on electoral reform and rule out universal suffrage in the 2007 Hong Kong chief executive and 2008 Legislative Council elections;[37] a Legislative Council election in September 2004 that was generally ruled to have been free and fair, but that saw the pro-democracy forces unable to record any significant gains in the number of seats they controlled; and the resignation of Chief Executive Mr. Tung Chee-hwa in March 2005. Chief Secretary Donald Tsang was selected to be the successor to Mr. Tung Chee-hwa.

Conclusion

Travelers to Hong Kong post-1997 come back with mixed stories. Some are convinced that nothing of significance has changed, although far more people are now allowed to vote than at any time in the past. Others, especially those who have spent any time speaking to Hong Kong residents, tell stories of much leaner times in Hong Kong. In the early years of the new millennium, the economic growth rate was way down, unemployment was rising, and the demand for consumer goods—in this, the mecca of consumption—was falling. Workers in the service industries, including retail and tourism, were noticing a sharp drop in their trade, and many residents had to look for second jobs to help pay their bills. Some observers think this was simply a transitional phase—and there is some evidence suggesting that a major economic growth spurt began in 2004—but others are more concerned for the long term. The super-rich of Hong Kong—who, judging by the number of luxury cars and apartments for sale, are a large and growing sector—are not very concerned, of course, because in all probability they took care of themselves and their family members long ago by stashing capital elsewhere and securing residential status abroad. The most likely losers in any oncoming failure of democracy will be the people who are unable to leave, those with nobody to arrange visas for them to allow them to live in the new suburban Chinatowns of Australia, New Zealand, Canada, and the United States.

Frequent visitors to Hong Kong, and many of its local residents, are reporting signs of the screws being tightened, ever so gradually, as each year passes. Conservative columnist Bruce Herschensohn, a regular visitor to Hong Kong, believes these gradual signs of tightening are now starting to amount to something that is much more sinister. As he notes,

> The skyline remains spectacular, the hotels are luxurious, the streets are crowded, and the shopping centers are chaotic. But on handover night, political cracks appeared in Hong Kong's foundation; in the intervening years, those cracks have gotten bigger. On that hot and rainy evening . . . 4,800 soldiers from the People's Liberation Army drove into Hong Kong with 21 antiriot vehicles. If nothing else, it was a signal. (2002, 1)

As Herschensohn points out, what was not part of the ceremony that night in 1997 was any mention of the enormous changes being made in the laws that governed Hong Kong. He lists some of these, by contrasting what he saw in 2002 with what was the case on June 30, 1997:

- Hong Kong's Bill of Rights was in full force; but on July 1st important provisions were thrown out.
- Hong Kong Legislative Council members were in office for terms scheduled to last until the 1998 elections; but on July 1st they were replaced with a "provisional legislature," its members approved by Beijing.
- The people of Hong Kong could say whatever they wanted; but on July 1st it was illegal to advocate the independence of Tibet, Taiwan, or Hong Kong.

- Anyone planning a public demonstration needed only to notify police so that traffic could be stopped; but on July 1st anyone hoping to organize an event with more than 50 participants—or 30 people in a procession—had to receive a "no objection" notice from the police seven days in advance (this could be denied for reasons that would not be identified until a later time).
- The incident in Tiananmen Square in 1989 was referred to as the "Tiananmen Square massacre"; but on July 1st it was henceforth referred to as the "June 4 incident."

To the people in Hong Kong who had hoped China would keep the promises implicit in the "one country, two systems" principle, these were ominous signs for the future. Even more worrying to some Hong Kongers, especially those in the business community, were fears that the economic crisis hitting Asia at about the same time would further compound their miseries.

Herschenschon also notes that in the trips he has taken to Hong Kong since 1997, he has found that the uniqueness of the place appears to be diminishing, pointing to a clear danger that Hong Kong—which has always been a thoroughly unique place—is fast becoming "just another Chinese city." This transformation is not likely to happen immediately, however, in part because Beijing has offered its "one country, two systems" arrangement to Taiwan, and does not want its domination over Hong Kong to be too obvious until it actually has jurisdiction over Taiwan. If and when that day comes, as Herschenschon notes, "the 'one country-two systems' promise will be nothing more than a phrase that will be quickly erased from Hong Kong's history books." Maybe the traveler's addiction to Hong Kong comes from memory more than it does from current experiences. As he observes, "I still have that longing to see it, walk its streets in the daylight and at night, and take the Star Ferry back and forth from Kowloon to Hong Kong Island just one more time, pretending that nothing has changed."

Notes

1. Taiwan is covered in chapter 13 of this book. Macau, a former Portuguese colony, was returned to China in 1999, two years after Hong Kong. Readers are directed to chapter 12 for further information about Macau, and also to Jonathan Porter's excellent book *Macao, the Imaginary City: Culture and Society, 1557 to the Present* (1996).

2. The emergence of a Greater China region was being discussed in many contexts in the early 1990s; see for example, Jones, King, and Klein (1992); Overholt (1993); and Schell (1994).

3. The history of Hong Kong has been told many times, but one book that stands out as among the best and most readable is Frank Welsh's *A Borrowed Place: The History of Hong Kong* (1996); there is also Jan Morris's more descriptive and personal account, *Hong Kong: Epilogue to an Empire* (1988).

4. To provide a North American analogy, Hong Kong has been compared to Puerto Rico, which became an American colony in the same year the New Territories was ceded to Britain. On most of the traditional quality of life indicators, however, Hong Kong is rated significantly higher than Puerto Rico (Welsh 1996): infant mortality is much lower, and life expectancy is much higher in Hong Kong; crime is significantly lower; literacy is almost universal; and the quality of public transportation is second to none (Mirsky 1994; Terrill 1991).

5. An entrepot port city is one whose primary urban functions focus on collection and distribution, and especially the handling of imported and exported goods as an international cargo hub. Other cities with a role similar to Hong Kong's are Rotterdam and Singapore, in the sense that all of them play crucial roles in global markets, not just as trading cities, but also as commercial hubs serving a wide range of surrounding cities, regions, and countries.

6. Of particular relevance here are two chapters of the Davies report: "The Industrial Revolution: From the 1950s to the 1970s" (Davies 1990, chap. 2), and "The Hong Kong Economy since 1984" (1990, chap. 3). The tone of the report, which is highly pessimistic, is a result of its publication immediately after the Tiananmen Square incident in 1989.

7. As Chowdhury and Islam (1993, see chap. 2, 28–41) observe, Hong Kong's population increased from 600,000 in 1945 to 1,600,000 in 1948, largely as a result of in-migration from China. But in 1949 alone some 330,000 immigrants arrived from the mainland, at a rate of 10,000 or more each week. See also Burns (1991).

8. It should be noted here that in comparison to Taiwan, Hong Kong's import substitution phase was much smaller and less significant, because its domestic market was too small to support this trend for long; see Ho (1992), and also Burns (1991).

9. The sharp drop-off in tourism after 1997 has been very worrying to Hong Kong's people and its business elite. It is assumed that the growth in tourism during the late 1980s and early 1990s was based, at least in part, on many tourists' desires to visit Hong Kong for "one last time" before it reverted to Chinese rule—and that phase has clearly peaked. Tourism statistics circulated by the Hong Kong government indicate that incoming tourists to Hong Kong increased from 2.6 million in 1982 to 8 million in 1992, and although average length of stay was relatively short (2–3 days), per capita spending by tourists increased during this period (this was especially the case for Japanese and Taiwanese tourists). Hong Kong's largest airline, Cathay Pacific, has begun to advertise very heavily, especially on the Internet, to try to turn this tourism downward trend around, even going as far as offering cheap package deals for tourists who want to use Hong Kong as a base for visiting other countries in Asia.

10. See also Li and Lo (1993) for a more detailed discussion of the development of Hong Kong's economy during this period. Some of the statistics quoted here are taken from Schiffer (1991).

11. See especially Hong Kong Census and Statistics Department (1993, chap. 2, 12–20). The trade statistics are provided by Ho (1992, table 1.1, 11). The statistics on the changing balance between domestic exports and reexports come from Davies (1990, 15–16).

12. To some extent this is still true today, as the World Bank's *Doing Business Database* indicates. The database provides objective measures of business regulations and their enforcement in 145 economies around the world. The measures employed assess the regulatory costs of doing business and can be used to analyze specific regulations that enhance or constrain investment, productivity, and growth. One of the measures, referred to as "the challenges of launching a business," uses the following criteria: the procedures required to establish a business, the associated time and costs involved, and the minimum capital requirement. In its report, the database indicates that Hong Kong entrepreneurs can expect to go through five steps to launch a business over eleven days on average, at a cost equal to 3.4 percent of gross national income (GNI) per capita, compared with a regional average of 100.5 percent of GNI and an Organization for Economic Co-operation and Development (OECD) average of 44.1 percent of GNI. In addition, there is no minimum deposit requirement to obtain a business registration number in Hong Kong. In other words, it is still much quicker, easier, and cheaper to start a business in Hong Kong than in most other places in the region, or in OECD countries. Other indicators in the database include the ease of hiring and firing workers, registering property, getting credit, protecting investors, enforcing contracts, and closing a business. For further

details, see the database website, http://rru.worldbank.org/DoingBusiness/ (accessed March 1, 2006).

13. In 2004 the Cato Institute published its *Economic Freedom of the World* index, which measures the degree to which the policies and institutions of different countries are supportive of economic freedom. The cornerstones of economic freedom are considered to be measurable by such indicators as personal choice, voluntary exchange, freedom to compete, and security of privately owned property. Thirty-eight components and subcomponents are used to construct a summary index and to measure the degree of economic freedom along five dimensions: (1) the relative size of government, (2) the legal structure and protection of property rights, (3) access to "sound" money, (4) facilities for international exchange, and (5) regulation of the economy; see, www.cato.org/pubs/efw/ (accessed March 1, 2006). Hong Kong has the highest rating for economic freedom on this scale, scoring 8.7 of 10, closely followed by Singapore at 8.6, with New Zealand, Switzerland, the United Kingdom, and the United States tied for third with ratings of 8.2. Among the other top ten nations are Australia, Canada, Ireland, and Luxembourg. Other large economies and their rankings are Germany, 22; Japan and Italy, 36; France, 44; Mexico, 58; India, 68; Brazil, 74; China, 90; and Russia, 114.

14. This argument is made very convincingly by Castells (1999), who concludes that Hong Kong is as "developmentalist" a state as the other NIEs, although in a different way.

15. A similar argument has also been made by Burns (1991) who subtitles his chapter on Hong Kong "Diminishing Laissez-Faire" to account for the subtle growth of government interventions. For similar accounts, see also Castells, Goh, and Kwok (1991); and also Cuthbert (1991). The role of the state in the maintenance of a labor force and state intervention in the provision of wage subsidies, particularly for the semiconductor industry in Hong Kong, is discussed by Henderson (1989).

16. One is tempted to say that the effects on air quality in Hong Kong are clearly visible, allowing for the fact that on many days very little at all is clearly visible, as indicated in a series of headline articles in the *South China Morning Post* in October 2004, and in a series of photographs showing the decreasing visibility from one side of the much-vaunted Hong Kong harbor to the other.

17. Guangdong officials, not surprisingly, have denied that Hong Kong's air-quality problems are mainly caused by pollution blowing in from the north, claiming there is no hard scientific evidence to support such a claim.

18. The New Towns program is also discussed by Castells, Goh, and Kwok (1991), and by Henderson (1989).

19. The planning concepts lying behind the Hong Kong New Towns is discussed in detail by Bristow (1984), but a more recent account is provided in a volume edited by Phillips and Yeh (1987).

20. I attribute this opinion to Ronald Skeldon, formerly Professor of Geography at Hong Kong University (personal communication, 1995).

21. It is important to point out that although these statistics are often quoted in newspapers and by local politicians (and even some academics), it is impossible to verify them, mainly because China does not appear to keep—or publish—statistics about ownership of all businesses.

22. The "one country, two systems" principle was introduced in reference to Taiwan in 1978, and was applied to Hong Kong in 1982. The basic idea was that China was to continue to practice socialism, and that Hong Kong would be allowed to retain its capitalist institutions for at least fifty years after 1997. See Sum (1995, 96).

23. The issue of out-migration from Hong Kong at this time is dealt with in Skeldon (1994); see especially "Setting the Scene," pt. 1, 3–20, and "Migration from Hong Kong: Current Trends and Future Agendas," chap. 18, 325–32.

24. This is suggested in an article written in the officially approved news magazine, *Beijing Review,* in its January 3–9 issue in 1994, 17 (quoted in Sum 1995, 73).

25. For a more detailed discussion of these issues, see *Economist* (1995), and a story reprinted in *China News Daily* (1995).

26. The term *leftward* here is used in the Western sense, rather than in the sense of the term on the mainland, where it would indicate support for the Maoist line and not for the *rightist* views of someone like Deng Xiaoping. In Hong Kong the term *leftist* identifies someone with politically liberal views, in this case, someone who would be in support of further democratization, and who would call for direct election (rather than appointment by Beijing) of the Hong Kong SAR's chief executive. The most illustrious, outspoken, and certainly the best-known of these leftists is known locally as "Long Hair." He wears jeans and a Che Guevara t-shirt, and he refuses to cooperate with the chief executive, Mr. Tung Chee-hwa. Against all odds, Long Hair was elected to the Legislative Council in the 2004 elections.

27. For a discussion of the confrontation between these two blocs, see *Far Eastern Economic Review* (1994).

28. Some data sets (see table 11.3, for example) show that Hong Kong's economy grew by more than 10 percent in 2000. But the global economic slowdown of 2001 hit Hong Kong very hard, along with most other countries in the region, and real GDP growth in 2001 was only 0.5 percent. There was then something of a recovery after that, with real GDP growth in 2002 reaching 1.9 percent.

29. The steady economic growth rate in Hong Kong pre-1997 helped to earn it the label, "the world's only industrial colony" (Mok and Lau 2002, 111). More significantly, Hong Kong's per capita (GDP) increased from HK$106,401 in 1991 to HK $120,540 in 1994; to HK$196,565 in 2000; but then fell to HK$194,969 in 2001, and again to HK$189,656 in 2002 (see www.info.gov.hk/censtatd/eng/hkstat/fas/nat_account/gnp/gnp1_index.html).

30. Data from the Hong Kong Census department shows that the biggest losses in the actual value of wages over this period were in the manufacturing sector, which fell from 124.5 in 1992 to below 92.4 in 1998, following with a climb again by the early 2000s to 115.8 in 2002. Workers' wages in the wholesale and retail trades followed basically similar patterns during this period.

31. The *World Development Index for 2002,* a World Bank publication, reports that Hong Kong's Gini coefficient, a traditional measure of income inequality, stood at 52.2, which placed it as the seventeenth most "unequal" country in the world, on a par with such places as Zambia, El Salvador, and Papua New Guinea (a Gini coefficient of 0 indicates perfect equality and 100 indicates absolute inequality). The poorest 20 percent of the population in Hong Kong had just 4.4 percent of the total national income, compared to the top or richest 20 percent of the population, who received 57.1 percent of the national income. The United States, as a comparison, had a Gini coefficient of 40.8 in 2002, with the poorest 20 percent of its population receiving 5.2 percent of total income, and the richest 20 percent receiving 46.4 percent; www.infoplease.com/ipa/A0908770.html (accessed March 1, 2006).

32. For more details, see chinalaw.law.yale.edu/Yale percent20speech.pdf (accessed March 1, 2006).

33. As a case in point, in 2004 a Chinese-American reporter for the *New York Times* wrote in advance of the actual announcement a story about the impending resignation of Jiang Jemin from all of his existing state positions. The result was that the reporter was arrested and jailed.

34. This is excerpted from a September 5, 2003, press release from U.S. Representative Christopher Cox, chair of the House Policy Committee; see cox.house.gov/html/release.cfm?id=690 (accessed March 1, 2006).

35. The Lam affair was covered widely by the Hong Kong media. Lam, according to statements released by the *South China Morning Post*, resigned after a restructuring of the paper's China Division. He claims, however, that he was never consulted about the proposed change, and in a prepared statement said the management's move was "unreasonable and disturbing." An *iMail* story reported that in a June 29, 2000, letter to the *Hong Kong Post*, the paper's owner accused Lam of "exaggeration and fabrication" after he (Lam) had suggested in a column that a group of Hong Kong tycoons—including Mr. Kuok—were told by Beijing to be more supportive of Chief Executive Tung Chee-hwa. Kuok's denial of this charge was supported by the other tycoons who attended the meeting, but Lam stood by his story.

36. Although many of them may be entirely scurrilous, reports posted on a Hong Kong–based website called *NOT the South China Morning Post* (www.ntscmp.com) suggest that not all is well at the *South China Morning Post*. Among the stories causing concern was one about the hiring of an editor from the official English-language newspaper of the regime in Beijing, the *China Daily*. Another story reported evidence that some *South China Morning Post* staff members had had their columns seriously censored or edited, and that others had been fired or forced to resign, presumably for being too critical of Beijing. Others reported the elimination of popular features for being too pointedly anti-Beijing, features including the popular World of Lily Wong cartoons, which lampooned many of the top leaders in Beijing (including the so-called Butcher of Beijing, Li Peng). Similar information appeared on another local online forum in 2000, *Hong Kong IceRed* (www.icered.com), where some local readers characterized the *South China Morning Post* as being humiliatingly pro-Beijing and far too lenient and uncritical of both China and the current chief executive of the SAR, Tung Chee-hwa.

37. The Standing Committee argued that its decision was based on the apparent lack of consensus on this issue in Hong Kong, and on Hong Kong's relatively short history of exercising democracy. The HKSAR government, not surprisingly, expressed its support for the decision, claiming that Beijing was trying to protect Hong Kong's stability and prosperity for the future. Most pro-democracy supporters criticized the National People's Congress and the Hong Kong government, suggesting that their response worked to undercut the "one country, two systems" principle and the notion that one day there could be Hong Kongers ruling Hong Kong. The issue featured largely in Legislative Council debates throughout 2004, and a demonstration organized in protest saw an estimated 300,000 people gathering in Victoria Park on July 1, 2004.

References Cited

Bristow, R. 1984. *Land Use Planning in Hong Kong: History, Policies, and Procedures.* Hong Kong: Oxford University Press.

Brown, D. A. 2002. "One country, two systems": The Hong Kong experience, 1997–2002. *American Asian Review* 20, no. 4 (winter): 83–138.

Burns, J. P. 1991. Hong Kong: Diminishing laissez-faire. In *Mini-Dragons: Fragile Economies in the Pacific*, ed. S. M. Goldstein. Boulder, Colo.: Westview, 104–43.

Castells, M. 1999. *End of Millennium.* Vol. 3 of *The Information Age: Economy, Society, Culture.* Oxford: Blackwell.

Castells, M., L. Goh, and R. H. Kwok. 1991. *The Shek Kip Mei Syndrome: Economic Development and Public Housing in Hong Kong and Singapore.* London: Pion.

China News Daily. 1995. Patten seems to lose ground as China stalemate drags on. (online).

Chowdhury, A., and I. Islam. 1993. *The Newly Industrializing Economies of East Asia*. London: Routledge.

Clear Harmony. 2003. An interview with Barrister Margaret Ng. February 23. http://clearharmony.net/articles/200302/10511.html (accessed March 1, 2006).

Clifford, M. L., and P. Engardio. 2002. Commentary: Is the sun setting on Hong Kong's freedom? *Business Week*, November 18, 2002. www.businessweek.com/magazine/content/02_46/b3808082.htm.

Cottrell, Robert. 1993. *The End of Hong Kong: The Secret Diplomacy of Imperial Retreat*. London: John Murray.

Cuthbert, A. R. 1991. A fistful of dollars: Legitimation, production, and debate in Hong Kong. *International Journal of Urban and Regional Research* 15, no. 2 (June): 234–47.

Davies, Ken. 1990. *Hong Kong to 1994: A Question of Confidence*. Special report no. 2022. London: Economist Intelligence Unit.

Do Rosario, L. 1995. New towns, old problems. *Far Eastern Economic Review* (June 15): 60.

Economist. 1995. China's magic tool for Hong Kong. March 18, 35–36.

Far Eastern Economic Review. 1994. Asia 1994 yearbook: Hong Kong. Politics/Social Affairs, 123–26.

Henderson, J. 1989. The political economy of technological transformation in Hong Kong. In *Pacific Rim Cities in the World Economy: Comparative Urban and Community Research*, ed. M. P. Smith. Vol. 2. New Brunswick, N.J.: Transaction Publishers, 102–55.

Herschensohn, Bruce. 2002. The political landscape changed completely for Hong Kong on July 1, 1997, and tremors have been going through the local community ever since. *WorldandI.com*, July 2002. www.worldandi.com/newhome/ (accessed March 1, 2006).

Ho, Y. P. 1992. *Trade, Industrial Restructuring, and Development in Hong Kong*. Honolulu: University of Hawaii Press.

Hong Kong Census and Statistics Department. 1993. *Hong Kong Social and Economic Trends, 1982–1993*. Hong Kong: Hong Kong Census and Statistics Department.

Hong Kong Sunday Morning Post. 1994. February 13.

Jones, R., R. King, and M. Klein, eds. 1992. *The Chinese Economic Area: Economic Integration without a Free Trade Agreement*. Paris: Organization for Economic Co-operation and Development.

Kelly, I. 1986. Hong Kong: A Political-Geographic Analysis. Honolulu: University of Hawaii Press.

Lam, W. W. L. 2002. Gloomy forecast for Hong Kong democracy. *CNN.com/World*, June 26, 2002. http://edition.cnn.com/2002/WORLD/asiapcf/east/06/25/Hongkong.woes/index.html.

Law, J. 2002. Hong Kong's economy is on the up-and-up. *tdctrade.com*, March 1, 2005. www.tdctrade.com/shippers/vol23_1/vol23_1_ind11.htm.

Li, K. W. 2001. The political economy of pre- and post-1997 Hong Kong. *Asian Affairs* 28 (2): 67–79.

Li, W., and K. W. K. Lo. 1993. Trade and industry. In *The Other Hong Kong Report*. Hong Kong: Chinese University Press, 109–26.

Mirsky, J. 1994. The battle for Hong Kong. *New York Review of Books*, April 7, 16–20.

Mok, K. H., and M. Lau. 2002. Changing government role for socio-economic development in Hong Kong in the twenty-first century. *Policy Studies* 23, no. 2 (June): 107–24.

Morris, Jan. 1988. *Hong Kong: Epilogue to an Empire*. New York: Random House.

Ng, M. 2003. In the shadow of the anti-subversion legislation. Lecture given at Workshop on Chinese Legal Reform, Yale Law School. http://kids.law.yale.edu/chinalaw/Yale%20speech.pdf (accessed March 1, 2006).

———. 2003. *Hong Kong at the Crossroads: The Future of Democracy and Freedom.* New York: Simon and Schuster.

Overholt, W. H. 1993. *The Rise of China: How Economic Reform is Creating a New Superpower.* New York: W.W. Norton.

Phillips, D. R., and A. G. O. Yeh. 1987. *New Towns in East and Southeast Asia.* Hong Kong: Oxford University Press.

Porter, Jonathan. 1996. *Macao, the Imaginary City: Culture and Society, 1557 to the Present.* Boulder, Colo.: Westview.

Pye, L. 1988. The new Asian capitalism: A political portrait. In *In Search of an East Asia Development Model,* ed. P. L. Berger and H. M. Hsiao. New Brunswick, N.J.: Transaction Publishers.

Schell, O. 1994. *Mandate of Heaven: A New Generation of Entrepreneurs, Dissidents, Bohemians, and Technocrats Lays Claim to China's Future.* New York: Simon and Schuster.

Schiffer, J. R. 1991. State policy and economic growth: A note on the Hong Kong model. *International Journal of Urban and Regional Research* 15, no. 2 (June): 180–196.

Segal, G. 1993. *The Fate of Hong Kong.* New York: St. Martin's.

Skeldon, R., ed. 1994. *Reluctant Exiles? Migration from Hong Kong and the New Overseas Chinese.* Hong Kong: Hong Kong University Press.

South China Morning Post. 1999. February 1. www.scmp.com/special/hkfuture/index.asp7 .html (accessed March 1, 2006).

Sum, N. L. 1995. More than a "war of words": Political reform period in Hong Kong. *Economy and Society* 24, no. 1 (February): 67–100.

Terrill, R. 1991. Hong Kong: Countdown to 1997. *National Geographic,* February, 101–39.

United Nations Development Program (UNDP). 1998. *Human Development Report.* New York: Oxford University Press.

Welsh, F. 1996. *A Borrowed Place: The History of Hong Kong.* Hong Kong: Kodansha International.

Wong, M. 2002. Record smog shrouds Hong Kong's dramatic skyline; Chinese factories blamed. Associated Press Online. September 11.

Wong, Stephanie. 2002. September 11, 2002. www.sfgate.com/cgi-bin/article.cgi?f=/news/ archive/2002/09/11/financial0727EDT0023.DTL (accessed March 1, 2006).

Wong, Yuk-Lin Renita. 2002. Going "back" and "staying out": Articulating the postcolonial Hong Kong subjects in the development of China. *Journal of Contemporary China* 11å (30): 141–59.

World in Figures. 1997. London: Economist Press.

CHAPTER 12

Macao (Macau)

AN EXPLORATION IN CULTURAL AND HISTORICAL GEOGRAPHY

The origins of the place known for the last 450 years as Macao, or *Ao Men* in Chinese *putonghua*, began in the somewhat isolated, out-of-the-way coastal margins of the Pearl River Delta near the exit into the estuary of one of the major distributary channels of the large Xi Jiang (West River) at what is believed to have been a tiny fishing village (see map 12.1). The impetus for the growth and change of this place came about through contact and interaction between Europeans, in this case the Portuguese, and the Chinese. The Portuguese were seeking to extend their influence from South and Southeast Asia, where they had established major trading and religious colonies at Goa on India's west coast and Malacca on the west coast of the Malay peninsula facing the Strait of Malacca. Their motivation was commercial, to profit from trade in various commodities and with various partners, as well as cultural, for they wished to spread the Gospel and gain converts to Christianity.

Cheng (1999) has asserted the two goals were complementary for the Portuguese, who sought to capture some of the trade monopoly that Arab traders had established in the Indian Ocean and nearby areas, and to counter the spread of Islam by spreading the Gospel and converting locals to Christianity. The Portuguese also were competing vigorously with other European powers, such as the Dutch, who were seeking to extend their own commercial interests along the seaward margins of Asia.

By contrast the Chinese, who had in the fourteenth century sent out a major fleet into the Indian Ocean, had redirected their interests into the interior of their empire, as the Ming dynasty sought to reestablish Chinese dominion over its imperial holdings and to revitalize the idea of Chinese hegemony in those interior regions where tributary relations were essential to maintaining Chinese sway over the far-flung and disparate interior regions of the empire. Thus, its leaders sought to minimize contacts with and the effects of the presence of foreign intruders who in their view had little to offer a celestial empire, and they insisted on maintaining only the most tenuous of links with places far removed and isolated from mainstream China. In this way, the Chinese signaled their disinterest in and disdain for the foreigners and their intrusive ways.

The Portuguese first arrived in this area in the early sixteenth century, perhaps as early as 1503. According to Charles Boxer (1948), the first Portuguese to visit China was a man named Jorge Alvarez, who in 1514 left a stone memorial or *padrao* on an island named Tamao near what is today Macao; and the first Portuguese ships to visit China's great southern port city of Canton arrived at the head of the Zhu Jiang (Pearl

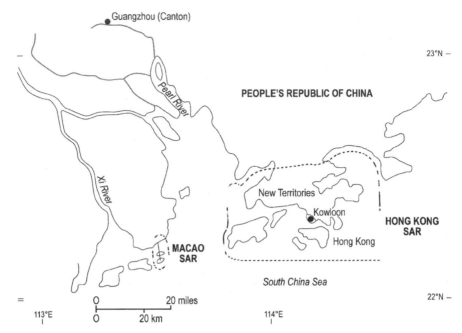

Map 12.1. Macao, Hong Kong, and the Pearl River Estuary

River) in 1517. The Portuguese eagerly sought a place to establish a trading post, but the Chinese, despite varying Portuguese efforts at different locations along the coast, would not allow them a permanent foothold. But in 1554, the Chinese finally allowed a temporary trading post on the island of Sanchuan about fifty miles southwest of Macao. This arrangement did not suit the Portuguese, however, and after further squabbling and negotiation, according to most historians and essayists, in 1557 the Chinese allowed the Portuguese to form a settlement on what had formerly been an island but had become attached to the mainland by a narrow neck of land, and this became Macao (Boxer 1984). Having been settled by the Portuguese in 1557, Macao was the first and oldest outpost of European influence in East Asia, and on December 20, 1999, it became the last such colony in Asia upon its return to China as a special administrative region (SAR) of the People's Republic of China (PRC), following the model of the earlier return of Hong Kong to the Chinese motherland in 1997.

Location and Environmental Setting

Physically, Macao is a tiny peninsula (7–8 km²) jutting off the tip of the southwestern flank of the Pearl River estuary on the southeastern coast of China at the point where several distributaries of the Xi Jiang empty into the South China Sea. The territory also claims two small islands (Coloane and Taipa) just south of the peninsula, to which

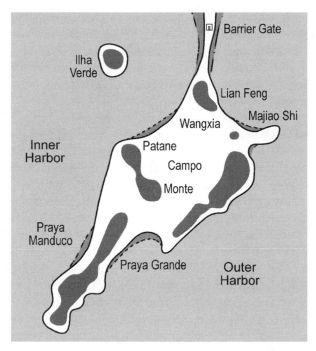

Map 12.2. Historical Map of the Macao Peninsula. **Source:** Modified from Porter 1996.

Macao today is linked by two bridges. Macao may be viewed as one leg or foot on the west or left side of a regional triangle of which Canton (Guangzhou) would be the apex at the north, and Hong Kong, across the Pearl River estuary, would be the right leg or foot on the east side (see maps 12.1 and 12.2).

All three cities lie just within the northern margins of the tropics, although their location on the edge of the huge Eurasian landmass brings cooler weather during the winter months; frost is rare. The climate regime is monsoonal with precipitation mainly during the warm summer months. About 2,000 mm of rain falls per year on average, some of it associated with the annual arrival of typhoons, the great low-pressure tropical storms of Asia's Pacific coast. The growing season is year-round.

The surface terrain and landforms suggested by the descriptive name Pearl River Delta offer a key to the nature of the region's landscape, and indeed are the reason for the early settlement and development of this region. This is one of China's major deltaic plains, an area of low-lying, alluvial floodplains characterized in ecological terms by high energy transfers in the natural systems and a considerable degree of biodiversity that has rendered the area very attractive for human settlement and exploitation of its natural environment and its rich and constantly renewing resources. The deltaic plain, however, is broken by low but rugged uplands, and mountains composed of granite and other igneous and metamorphic rock structures and material. The adjacent coastline is highly indented with numerous islands and coves, a fact that provides safe and convenient harbors and offers great opportunities for fishing, shipping, smuggling, and, formerly, piracy. It is therefore not surprising that South China and the Pearl River estuary became the center for early sailing, shipping, and commerce in China, and indeed was one of the oldest centers of China's contact with the outside world, maintaining a history of trade and shipping that dates back more than one thousand years.

Rise of Macao

Macao's origin and importance link it to the age of European exploration and the extension of the Europeans' desire to trade and to spread the Gospel, a desire that drove the advance of that exploration to East Asia. It was the farthest permanent extension of Portuguese power and influence, and it was the final point in the Portuguese-Asian empire that once extended from Goa on the Indian subcontinent to Malacca on the Strait of Malacca and finally to the China coast, though efforts were made to penetrate Japan, efforts that were in fact largely orchestrated from and based in Macao. Macao's story begins in the mid-sixteenth century with the arrival of Portuguese ships seeking to trade with China via Canton and the Pearl River region. These foreigners sought a permanent and commodious post to enhance their commercial efforts, yet the Chinese did not want them as permanent guests. Finally, an adequate if not convenient location was allowed them by the Chinese, as noted above, in an effort to keep the foreigners at arm's length and in a place as far and as isolated as possible from the larger city of Canton and the more civilized parts of the Middle Kingdom. This small, rocky peninsula had only a tiny fishing village. The peninsula was connected to the mainland by a sandbar that eventually formed a narrow isthmus and on which was erected in 1573 a barrier gate to separate the foreigners from the Middle Kingdom (Boxer 1948; Porter 1996; Cheng 1999).

A visit to Macao should always begin with a stop by the China Barrier Gate, where the visitor will have the opportunity to contemplate Macao's current situation as well as reflect on the last 450 years of European and Chinese relations. At the gate the visitor can view a series of mosaics that depict the growth and spatial development of Macao, from its earliest encounters with the West to the present. The visitor may also look through the gate and across to the bustling neighboring city of Zhuhai, a special economic zone (SEZ) that has grown explosively in the last twenty years. Perhaps most striking for the visitor will be the steady stream of pedestrians crossing the narrow isthmus as they move between the SAR of Macao and the PRC, just as they have done for almost 450 years.

In 1582 the Chinese agreed to allow the Portuguese to remain here based on an annual rental payment of five hundred taels of silver, the then valued currency in Ming China. This is an interesting point, as noted by Cheng (1999), who argues persuasively that Macao then was different from virtually all other colonies in Asia because its presence was tolerated and allowed by the Chinese rather than forced on them. Therefore it was not, *stricto sensu*, a colony. Rather, it was simply a site occupied by the Portuguese, and one where legal questions of sovereignty were not raised because the Chinese always assumed that it was their territory and that the Portuguese were in fact staying there at their sufferance. After the rise of Hong Kong in the mid-nineteenth century, Macao was formally ceded to Portugal as a permanent colony with a transfer of sovereignty in 1887 (Cheng 1999, 22–28). This lasted until 1979 when, by mutual agreement, Macao and the PRC described Macao as "Chinese territory under Portuguese administration," a status implying there would be a subsequent return to China, which came to pass in December 1999.

Macao's history and development trajectory as a Portuguese territory in Asia was one of ebbs and flows, linked principally to its role as a center of shipping and commerce for the Europe-China trade, and secondly to its varying role in spreading the Gospel, both Roman Catholic as well as Protestant. Initially, the settlement grew slowly owing to Chinese neglect and almost disapproval, whereby it remained largely isolated and simply a small garrison that periodically witnessed increased activity when trading was allowed at the neighboring city of Canton upriver. In these early days the settlement was occupied not only by Portuguese but by others brought by the Portuguese from Malacca, Goa, and even distant Africa. Thus the cultural makeup of the settlement reflected Portuguese activity and the taking of women from other Portuguese colonies for the Portuguese who had not brought wives. Churches were also constructed. Religion and the effort to spread Roman Catholicism in East Asia and on the Macao Portuguese beachhead were very important to the mission of early Portuguese maritime and colonial activity as seen in the travels and proselytizing efforts of Fr. Ignatius Loyola and his associates in the Society of Jesus (the Jesuits), and others such as Fr. Francis Xavier and Matteo Ricci (Cheng 1999).

The territory prospered and grew in the seventeenth century through its remarkable ability to serve as an intermediary in the China-Japan trade (Boxer 1984). Because these two East Asian countries were at odds over the rapacious conduct of Japanese pirates, Macao took full advantage of the willingness of the Japanese to permit Portuguese mariners and traders access to Nagasaki, at least until 1640, and in doing so were able to exchange precious products such as Chinese silk for Japanese silver. Profits from this trade provided the wealth that Macao used to improve its infrastructure and construct more and better fortifications and more churches, some of which survive and may be seen today. When the Japanese finally excluded the Portuguese owing to the heavy proselytizing of the Jesuit missionaries, the Macanese continued their silk and precious commodity trade with Manila, wherein the exchanged products were transshipped to the New World. This trade too was eventually declared illegal, but the Macao traders managed through various artifices to maintain some trade, even in the face of hostile or dangerous environments.

EIGHTEENTH- AND NINETEENTH-CENTURY MACAO

Continuing with the conceptual framework of the past geographies of Macao, we know that the China trade was the foundation and key to Macao's prosperity and indeed its very survival. This involved not just the Portuguese but also at various times the Japanese, Dutch, French, British, and even the Americans. All of these groups competed at times and at other times cooperated out of mutual interest owing to a lack of colonial bases out of which these various powers could operate.

The China trade continued erratically into the eighteenth and early nineteenth century, based on the exclusive nature of the Chinese *cohong* system of trade, which was monopolized by and operated out of Canton through an exclusive guild of local traders. Macao had its problems, however, because ships were getting larger and its harbor was increasingly subject to silting from the adjacent Xi Jiang and Zhu Jiang, a problem that ultimately came to be a limiting factor in its ability to compete effectively as a trading port. In 1839 the first of the Opium Wars broke out, and was settled several years later by the Treaty of Nanking that ceded Hong Kong to the British. This event was momentous for Macao because the British, with their superior fleet and aggressive merchants, occupied a much larger and deeper harbor (in Hong Kong) that was also well-protected from the devastating annual typhoons. Buttressed by their own colonial control mechanism, the British largely captured the trade and commerce of the Pearl River Delta, and Hong Kong took over the key function of the European-controlled gateway to China. This new presence led swiftly to the stagnation and decline of Macao's commerce, and the port soon became a moribund backwater.

One way to reconstruct the geography of early- and mid-nineteenth-century Macao is through a consideration and study of the visual images of the portrait and landscape painter George Chinnery. Chinnery was a successful English portraitist who painted in British India. He opted to move to the Portuguese territory of Macao and painted there, in what Guillen-Nunez (1997) describes as self-imposed exile, from 1825 until 1852, the year of his death. According to Guillen-Nunez,

> [Chinnery] the artist was captivated by the city's old colonial buildings, squares, and streets, as well as by its lively Chinese population and its culture. The city was by then already divided into the so-called Christian city, or the intramural Portuguese quarters, and the Chinese city, partly outside those walls. Equally important, residents of the Christian city included a small but powerful British and American community, providing the painter with a group of potential patrons. (35)

Chinnery painted the local scene—the landscapes, the structures, the boats, the people, and their activities. Through these sketches and paintings, Chinnery the artist revealed the *genre de vie*, the way of life of Macao's people in the mid-nineteenth century and provided a remarkable visual documentary of the local geography of Macao at that time. An examination of some of his paintings brings key themes into focus. Macao was, on the one hand, a commercial port city of fortresses and churches. These are the important structures seen in photos 12.1 and 12.2, and symbolize the Portuguese colonial influence in Macao despite the absence of true Portuguese legal sovereignty. Chinnery's views of the forts, the front of a Catholic church, and of the Praia Grande will all be recognizable to the contemporary resident of or visitor to Macao who knows or studies the city, although the specifics of these scenes have been much transformed in contemporary Macao. These are the tangible expressions and the reality of a foreign presence on Chinese soil in early- and mid-nineteenth-century Macao.

Photo 12.1.   Praia Grande Bom Parto Fort, Chinnery watercolor

Paralleling this reality is the Chinese presence as seen in the still-standing and famous A Ma Temple on the Inner Harbor side of the peninsula, the Chinese shophouses, and the Chinese street scenes with their vendors, sidewalk eateries, workers, and haulers, all depicting the vibrancy of urban street life for the Chinese since time immemorial. In

Photo 12.2.   View of Monastery of St. Francis, Chinnery watercolor

Photo 12.3. Macao Dwellings with St. Joseph Church behind, Chinnery watercolor

one especially striking image, we see Chinese shophouses and street scenes juxtaposed to a Portuguese colonial edifice, a church that reminds us of the challenging duality of nineteenth-century life (especially for the local people) in a bicultural Asian colonial city (see photo 12.3). What emerges as the past geography of mid-nineteenth-century Macao is a city that has a European aspect in its physical appearance but is almost always characterized by the presence of the local Chinese, who are easily and frequently identified in Chinnery's sketches and paintings by their distinctive headgear and hats. The physical, administrative presence in much of Macao was European and Portuguese; the human reality was local Chinese, omnipresent and always visible. This then was the geography of mid-nineteenth-century Macao.

SHIFTING FORTUNES, THE "COOLIE TRADE," AND MACAO'S DECLINE

To counter the decline in trade owing to the growing power of Hong Kong, Macao turned to another, darker aspect of commerce: trade in human beings. Thus began Macao's role in the infamous "coolie trade," the impressing and shipping of contract laborers from the Pearl River Delta to the New World (Porter 1996; Cheng 1999). For Macao, this began around 1846 as trade in human laborers was beginning to be heavily resisted and criticized in other parts of China, such as Amoy. Laborers were recruited from among the poorest Chinese farmers, who were typically duped by agents from nearby cities who then received a commission for each contract laborer, or "coolie," delivered to a way station, or barracoon. These laborers were then sent to waiting ships for transport under unspeakably harsh conditions to places such as Cuba or South America; often they did not survive the journey (Porter 1996). This trade was barely better than slavery, and few places in China wanted to be associated with it. Macao, searching for commercial prosperity and already having a reputation for prostitution and other illicit activities, served as a willing participant in this trade, and it continued for more than twenty years to act as a main point for collection and dispatch of "coolies" headed to the New World. Between 1846 and 1873, Macao accounted for 44 percent of the more than 320,000 contract laborers who were sent out of Chinese ports. There were huge profits to be made in this business, and the Macao traders were indeed guilty of encouraging this nefarious trade in human cargo. Gradually this human trade became untenable, however, as it was increasingly recognized as grossly exploitative and morally repugnant (Porter 1996; Cheng 1999).

Once this trade declined, Macao's role as a major port diminished rapidly, and it had to turn to other commercial activities to provide an economic base. Its decline continued, owing to the growth and dynamism of neighboring Hong Kong, except for a brief hiatus during the Second World War when it received European and Chinese refugees fleeing Japanese invaders. Macao's economic survival and future prosperity needed a new activity and function, and this gradually evolved into its role as a petty manufacturer and gambling and tourist center, Macao being in all these functions subordinate to and dependent on its association with Hong Kong. French geographer Jules Sion described Macao in 1928 in this way: "*Mais c'est aujourd'hui une fade envasée, une ville morte, remplie de couvents, comme au temps de Camoens. Quel contraste avec Hong Kong!*" "But today it is a harbor silted up, a dead city, full of convents just as in the time of Camoes [the Portuguese poet]. What a contrast with Hong Kong!" (Sion 1928, 137).

People and Society

Macao has always offered a fascinating meeting and mixing of Asian, European, and African peoples—a clear reflection of its colonial heritage. In its early days there were few women, and the European colonizers who brought women from South and Southeast Asia often took them as wives, quickly creating a Creole or mestizo society. Later, Chinese women entered the cultural mix and eventually European women as well. In the process of this intermarriage and mixing, a Macanese Creole group was created, defined as those of European and Asian or sometimes African ancestry. This group differed from what was seen as a typical resident of Macao. These people created their own Creole or pidgin language, again a mix of Portuguese with various different languages including local Chinese, Cantonese, and Fukienese. And they remain in Macao today, a small cadre of Macanese somewhat unsure of their own status in a world of changing political allegiances, but somehow clinging to a past that has all but disappeared in the rapidly growing and modernizing Chinese city of Macao (Porter 1996; Cheng 1999).

In 1830 Macao was reported to have a population of 12,500, and the Chinese population had already exceeded the number of all other residents. By 1851 when Macao was a leading port for the "coolie trade," the city's total population had increased to 26,900 (Porter 1996). During the nineteenth and early twentieth centuries, Macao's population grew, especially as more Chinese migrants moved in to take advantage of the better job opportunities. Gradually the social makeup of the city became more Chinese, and Chinese vernacular architecture began to characterize much of the land use and internal structure of the city aside from the fortresses, churches, convents, public buildings, and residential dwellings of the colonial elites.

World War II brought a surge in population as Europeans and Chinese, fearful of the invading Japanese, sought refuge in the neutral city. Many remained here throughout the war, captives in the sense that it was difficult for them to travel, but free from fear of incarceration at the hands of the Japanese military. At this time the city swelled to more than 250,000 but then began to decline after the war with the revival of Hong Kong as a center of British commerce and society.

In the ensuing decades, Macao's social development and population growth in part reflected developments in Hong Kong, but especially in the last twenty-five years, they have proceeded in parallel with events and developments in China associated with the economic reforms of 1978. These reforms were followed by the opening up of China in the 1980s and the establishment of the SEZs, one of which was the city of Zhuhai. This has galvanized the economy of the territory, and it has also provided the impetus for rapid population growth.

In 1970 the Macao population was 249,000, and this actually declined slightly to 242,000 in 1981. Within a decade though it had climbed to 356,000, an increase that mirrored the remarkably rapid development of Zhuhai and an enormous push to expand infrastructure and build high-rise structures as housing units in Macao. The latest census figures (2001) estimated the population of Macao at 434,000, with a birth rate of .75 percent, a death rate of .31 percent, and a rate of natural increase of .44 percent. The total fertility rate had declined to 0.8, however, well below the replacement level, which tells us that much of Macao's recent growth had in fact been driven by migration. Of this total population, Cheng (1999) has estimated that 7,000–10,000 may be identified as belonging to the Macanese Creole group, although this population is difficult to count with precision.

As the new millennium opens, it is clear that Macao has become a Chinese city in culture and society as it is drawn increasingly into the greater Chinese economy and polity. As in many cities along China's Pacific coast, there are numerous migrants who live in the city as temporary sojourners. Although it is difficult to know their exact number, estimates place these temporary workers at perhaps 100,000–200,000, a quantity that may push the true population of the territory to a figure over 600,000. These migrants are important for they provide labor services in construction, factory work, and low-end service activities (including the sex trade), jobs that locals may in fact avoid or be unwilling to do. Zhuhai next door has a far larger number of these temporary workers though, as do so many of the cities and towns in the Pearl River Delta. The economy of this region of China, with its very strong links to the global economy, simply could not operate or offer competitive products and services without the labor input of these migrants.

With its recently completed international airport, Macao is positioned to expand its tourist trade and seeks to become less dependent on the flow of tourists from Hong Kong. Yet gambling and the related "recreational sin" activities of prostitution and so forth do not come without a serious downside, because criminals and gangs are attracted to such activities. In the case of Macao, the city has long tolerated the presence of local Triad gangs, a kind of Chinese mafia that has grown out of traditional Chinese secret societies. These gangs commit serious crimes, including shootings in the casinos and kidnappings. Now that China has taken control of Macao formally, however, the authorities may insist on stricter control of crime, and such activities may become less frequent. Because lawlessness is a threat to Macao's important tourist trade, it is vital for the long-term prosperity of the territory to curb violent crime and improve the reputation of Macao.

Conclusion

As the Portuguese prepared to conclude their 450 years of occupancy, they attempted to ensure there would be a lasting remembrance of their stay. This attempt became increasingly controversial, because even the vestiges of colonial control were much resented by local Macanese, and those memorials that depicted Portuguese occupiers in perceived acts of violence or subjugation were removed (Cheng 1999). Yet there are some remaining structures that identify clearly the Portuguese presence, and the colonial imprint in places can still be seen clearly. The remaining fortresses, often on high and prominent locations, as well as the churches and the well-known tourist attraction of the facade of St. Paul's cathedral, are good examples. The Leal Senado (Loyal Senate) building and an imposing square with its attractive Western-style buildings offer a modern example of a city center that provides human scale and pleasant surroundings for pedestrians. Yet the bulk of the city is rapidly becoming modern, a prosperous and vibrant setting with four-story shophouses in the older center, while many peripheral sites witness a rapid replacement of the older, lower buildings with high-rise apartment houses (owing to the high cost of urban land and the need for high-density living). In this way, Macao is replicating its neighbor Zhuhai. And along the outer harbor are the large tourist hotels and casinos, which too are part of Macao's present and future.

At the beginning of the twenty-first century, Macao's geography is a fascinating mix of old and new, and by any and all accounts, it has been and remains an extraordinary place. It was the first European colonial beachhead and trading post in East Asia and indeed the last, and it offers the historian a somewhat checkered history of trading, proselytizing, gambling, and prostitution, with some fighting, fishing, and manufacturing thrown in, as well as commerce in human beings, as seen in its nineteenth-century "coolie trade." The territory has waxed and waned just as the tides ebb and flow on its shores. After thirty years of stagnation following World War II, it is once again prosperous and growing, although its nearby competitors are nipping at its heels, and in some ways it is already overshadowed by its larger neighbor, the SEZ of Zhuhai. The look of Macao and its European heritage is quickly being swept aside because its construction boom doesn't have the time, interest, or financial incentive to maintain the architectural heritage of colonial Portuguese Macao. As we watch the current remarkable and dynamic transformation of Macao, we ask ourselves what will distinguish this place in the future from any number of other South China coastal cities? Will it be its Portuguese colonial and commercial legacy, preserved in part perhaps for its tourist value or for some other symbolic value, or will it be its distinctive niche as a gambling and recreational city for East and Southeast Asia?

References Cited

Berlie, J. A., ed. 1999. *Macao, 2000.* Oxford: Oxford University Press.

Boxer, Charles R. 1948. *Fidalgos in the Far East, 1550–1770: Fact and Fancy in the History of Macau.* The Hague: M. Nijhoff.

———, ed. and trans. 1984. *Seventeenth Century Macau in Contemporary Documents and Illustrations.* Hong Kong: Heinemann Educational.

Cheng, Christina Miu Bing. 1999. *Macau: A Cultural Janus.* Hong Kong: Hong Kong University Press.

Edmonds, Richard L. 1989. *Macau.* Oxford: Clio.

Guillen-Nunez, Cesar. 1984. *Macau.* Hong Kong: Oxford University Press.

———. 1997. Introduction. In *Georges Chinnery: Images of Nineteenth-century Macao.* Macao: Macao Territorial Commission for the Commemoration of Portuguese Discoveries, 35–41.

National Bureau of Statistics. 2002. *Zhongguo tongji nianjian 2002* [China statistical yearbook 2002]. Beijing: Chinese Statistics Press, 887–907.

Porter, Jonathan. 1996. *Macau, the Imaginary City: Culture and Society, 1557–Present.* Boulder, Colo.: Westview.

Sauer, Carl Ortwin. 1963. *Land and Life: A Selection from the Writings of Carl Ortwin Sauer,* ed. John Leighly. Berkeley: University of California Press.

Sion, Jules. 1928. Asie des moussons. In *Geographie Universelle,* ed. Paul Vidal de la Blache and L. Gallois. Vol. 9. Paris: Libraire Armand Colin, 137.

Sit, V. F. S., R. D. Cremer, and S. L. Wong. 1991. *Entrepreneurs and Enterprises in Macau: A Study of Industrial Development.* Hong Kong: Hong Kong University Press.

CHAPTER 13

Taiwan

An Enduring East Asian "Economic Miracle"

By any standard, contemporary Taiwan (formally the Republic of China on Taiwan, or ROC) represents one of the few genuine economic miracles of the modern era. There are many lessons to be learned from Taiwan's experience and from the resilient people who have contributed to this dynamic success story. Success is all the more remarkable for the small, resource-poor island considering its tumultuous past century. The island was colonized by Japan for fifty years, occupied by the Chinese Nationalist Army, and drawn into the cold war by American containment strategies. Currently Taiwan faces the constant threat of invasion by the People's Republic of China (PRC). Paradoxically, Taiwan is currently the largest investor in the PRC, with more than sixty thousand Taiwan-registered companies operating on the mainland in 2004. The relationship between the PRC and Taiwan is extremely complicated—and while the two are technically still at war, the gradual resolution of their conflict will be central to peace and stability throughout the entire region.

Taiwan's position in the international community is quite curious. In the first decade of the new millennium, Taiwan is as isolated politically as it is integrated economically. The communist government of the PRC will not allow concurrent recognition of the PRC and Taiwan. As a consequence, only a handful of small nations have formal diplomatic ties with Taiwan, and Taiwan lacks a seat in the UN. Taiwan's international status remains unclear, but its economic progress in the past fifty years has been nothing short of spectacular. By any standard, Taiwan is a vital player in the global economy. A 2005 survey by the *Economist* ranks Taiwan's economy as the twentieth largest in the world (2005, 5). Further, participatory democracy has come of age in the past decade, with hotly contested multiparty elections held at all levels—from the presidency to all cities, townships, and towns.

Recent closely contested elections reflect a citizenry considerably divided on Taiwan's path for the next few decades. Voting patterns indicate clear splits between those who favor some process of unification with the mainland, those hoping to live with the status quo, and those who prefer independence; unfortunately, the latter is an option unacceptable to the PRC.

Under the cloud of this political uncertainty, Taiwan continues to prosper, offering many contrasts and much internal diversity. A modern global economy, it is matched by the many enduring influences of its traditional Chinese culture. Sophisticated international cities such as Taipei and Kaohsiung (Gaoxiong) are some of East Asia's largest, and coexist with tribal settlements seeking greater autonomy and a return to traditional economies. Like many places in East Asia, Taiwan's booming cities vie for resources with stagnating smaller towns and aging rural populations. Regional tensions pitting the traditionally wealthy northern part of the island with the emerging central and southern portions are also politically important.

Unlike the economies of much of East and Southeast Asia, the Taiwanese economy has continued to grow for much of the past decade. In 2005 the small island reported a GDP of over US$500 billion, and the third-largest holding of foreign exchange reserves in the world (US$239 billion as of November 2004). Taiwan's living standards are also among the highest in Asia, with a surprisingly equitable distribution of wealth. Certainly there are very rich and very poor people in Taiwan, but the great majority of its people have shared in Taiwan's economic prosperity and consider themselves middle class. Located 160 km off the coast of Southeast China (see map 13.1) but originally settled by sojourners from Australasia, Taiwan is now densely populated by the descendants of Chinese migrants. Out of a 2004 population of just over 24 million, more than 84 percent claim Taiwanese ancestry, and 14 percent claim more recent mainland roots. Indigenous peoples and foreigners constitute the final 2 percent. Given the island's relative size, Taiwan might be expected to be cohesive and homogeneous, and in many

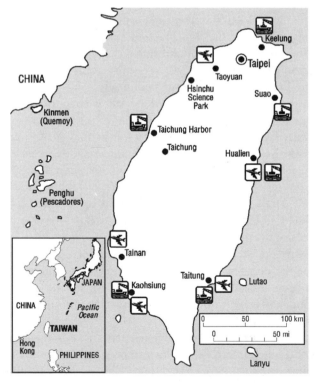

Map 13.1. Location Map of Taiwan. **Source:** Electronic Atlas of Taiwan, http://sites .inka.de/sites/kajetan/index.htm. Cartographic design by Mary Lee Eggart.

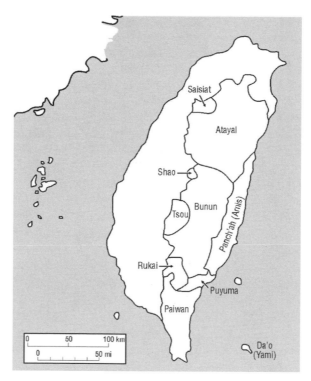

Map 13.2. Taiwan's Indigenous People. **Source:** Chen 1999. Cartographic design by Mary Lee Eggart.

ways it is a small and accessible place. Yet its accessible location and its past century of conflict have made Taiwan an unusual and highly distinctive place within the Chinese cultural realm. The island's role as a refuge for Chinese Nationalists (Kuomintang or KMT; also Guomindang or GMD) following communist ascendancy on the mainland in 1949 represented only the last of many diverse waves of migration by myriad ethnic groups from Australasia and southern and eastern China. These migrations over the millennia have created a diverse cultural mosaic among the current population that sometimes splits along ethnic lines during elections. At the present time, the island to some extent represents a microcosm of mainland China with major populations of ethnic Taiwanese and Hakka, ten groups of indigenous peoples (Atayal, Saisiyat, Tsou, Shao, Paiwan, Rukai, Puyuma, Ami (Panch'ah), Yami, Bunun; see map 13.2), and large numbers of Chinese from Fujian and Guangdong provinces.

Initially one might be surprised by so much diversity and so many contrasts, for the island is only the size of the U.S. states of Maryland and Delaware combined. However, while the island is small, there is also a considerable degree of environmental diversity, which is reflected in population densities ranging from below 100 persons/km^2 in the mountainous eastern county of Hualien to over 9,000 persons/km^2 in Taipei (see map 13.3).

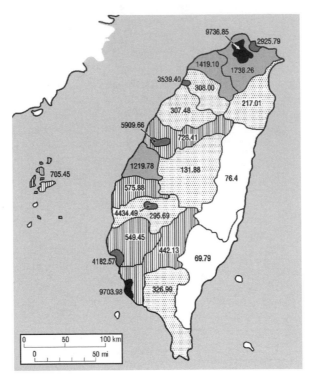

Map 13.3. Taiwan Population Density by County, 2000. **Source:** www.gio.gov.tw/ Taiwan-website/5-gp/yearbook/chpt021.html; http://sites.inka.de/sites/kajetan/Html/ Density/Preview.htm. Cartographic design by Mary Lee Eggart.

Taiwan and its future is linked to China by geography, culture, history, economy, and most importantly, politics. Contemporary political and economic relations between China and Taiwan indicate that Taiwan's destiny will remain closely tied to that of Greater China. Additionally, the long-standing security relationship between Taiwan and the United States also assures that the ultimate resolution of the relationship between Taiwan and the mainland will be one of the decisive foreign policy issues in America's near future. As much as many in the United States would wish that the Taiwan Problem could be solved without U.S. participation, this is not realistic. The United States is linked to Taiwan in too many ways. Politics, cultural origins, and increasingly linked economies aside, a sharp distinction remains between the life of the average person living in Taiwan and a person living in the PRC. The complex ties between Taiwan and Japan and the United States play a significant role in these differences.

Historical Background

COUNTERINTUITIVE ORIGINS

Archaeologists have found evidence of human settlement in Taiwan that dates back 12,000 to 15,000 years. Distinctive artifacts indicate a variety of Australasian cultures settled in the southern and eastern portions of the island. Other settlers came from the Asian mainland and apparently settled at slightly later dates along the northern and western coasts (Stainton 1999). Chinese from the southern provinces of Fujian and Guangdong have migrated to Taiwan and the adjacent Pescadores Islands (a handful of small islands within the Taiwan Strait separating Taiwan from the mainland) for many centuries, although only in the last three and a half centuries have their numbers been significant enough to justify the incorporation of Taiwan as a part of the Chinese polity. Historical records indicate that Chinese migrated to the Pescadores as early as the ninth century.

In those ancient times, the resources on these islands were shared and sometimes contested by three groups: Chinese immigrants, Japanese pirates, and Taiwanese natives from a variety of indigenous culture groups. Probably the first settlers of Chinese origin to establish permanent habitation on Taiwan arrived in the thirteenth century seeking refuge from invading Mongols. During that century, the first imperial administrative office was established on the windswept Pescadores. Despite these early administrative claims, rampant piracy forced the closing of the local administrative office in 1388 and resulted in waning Chinese influence for two centuries. It was not until 1558 that the Chinese reestablished an administrative presence in the Pescadores and assumed control over Taiwan as well.

Substantial permanent Chinese settlements emerged on the island of Taiwan in the late sixteenth or early seventeenth century. From 1620 on, Chinese entrepreneurs visited Taiwan regularly and promoted settlement on the southwest coast. Trade in camphor, deer antlers, and tea linked indigenous peoples in the interior to these growing Chinese commercial settlements. Conflicts between the Chinese and the indigenous people were common as agricultural expansions—supported by Chinese troops—forced a number of these groups of indigenous peoples into the interior mountains. Complicating this settlement history during the seventeenth century were periods of coastal occupation by two European colonial powers. Taiwan has been in fact occupied and colonized by three foreign powers in its long history: the Dutch (1624–1662), the Spanish (1626–1642), and the Japanese (1895–1945). The Dutch controlled significant portions of Taiwan from 1624 to 1662, but settlement was focused on a few major coastal settlements along the southwest periphery. Later they occupied the port city of Keelung (Jilong) after expelling the Spanish from the northeast coast. In many ways, the Europeans treated Taiwan as a stopping point on the way to other places, taking on meat, water, and fruit. Few inroads were made beyond the coasts. Though significant today in terms of contemporary politics, the interior uplands of the island were then inhabited almost exclusively by largely autonomous indigenous groups. Even under Japanese administration that began in December of 1895, the mountain dwellers were recognized as semiautonomous. Some of Taiwan's indigenous peoples who did live along the southern coasts were relocated to interior reservations once the Japanese instituted "modern" pacification strategies copied from America in the early 1900s.

Internal politics and the overthrow of the Ming dynasty by the Manchus in 1644 resulted in far-reaching changes in Taiwan. The island became a refuge for Ming loyalists under Cheng Cheng-Kung (Koxinga), who was able to cast out the Dutch colonials (Copper 1999). Cheng also promoted extensive immigration of Chinese exiles to Taiwan. Cheng's rule established a Chinese majority on Taiwan that has never been threatened. Records indicate that toward the end of Cheng Cheng-Kung's rule, nearly 100,000 Chinese had settled on the island with the major concentration in the Southwest.

THE BEGINNINGS OF MODERNIZATION

The Ming loyalists held out for two decades, but in 1683 the island was incorporated into the Manchu empire (Qing dynasty). For two centuries thereafter, Taiwan remained a prefecture of Fujian province and a frontier of Chinese settlement. The island occupied a strategic Pacific location, but China's inward orientation of that period gave the island little commercial importance, and in truth, it received scant attention. By the late nineteenth century, however, an increasing threat of maritime invasion by Europeans and the Japanese illustrated Taiwan's special importance and its military vulnerability to the Manchu imperial court. Consequently in 1888, the Manchu emperor established Taiwan as a separate Chinese province and upgraded its administrative position to keep pace with the island's growing commercial and strategic significance.

The Sino-Japanese War (1894–1895) again radically altered Taiwan's history. The Chinese quickly lost the war, and this surprising outcome exposed China's many strategic weaknesses—pitting a modern Japanese army and navy against antiquated Qing ships and coastal defenses. The terms of the Treaty of Shimonoseki, which settled the conflict, relegated all Chinese living in Taiwan to the status of Japanese colonial subjects. A short-lived uprising by the island residents was met with brutal force by the new Japanese government. Taiwan loyalists were quickly and violently subdued. By the end of the year, resistance had been crushed, and Taiwan would remain a Japanese colony for the next fifty years. Under colonial status and control, the potential benefits of indigenous political and economic reform were lost. Japan's efforts to more efficiently administrate the island and its promotion of export agriculture have implications to the present.

THE JAPANESE PERIOD: ECONOMIC GROWTH AND POLITICAL STAGNATION

The Japanese colonial occupation was a harsh time for Taiwan's people. The Taiwanese, like colonial peoples everywhere, were disenfranchised politically and given second-class status, which largely excluded them from the educational and administrative opportunities available to the city-dwelling Japanese. Residents were forced to adopt Japanese names, to learn and use the Japanese language, and were conscripted into the Japanese military, all in the name of cultural assimilation. Over time, many of the island's young men were shipped to mines and factories throughout the far-flung Japanese Empire as the demands of World War II escalated and labor shortages increased.

Although it is controversial, some scholars still maintain that the colonial period was somewhat beneficial for Taiwan. There is considerable evidence that Japanese efforts to promote agricultural modernization and commercial development were successful in setting the stage for later gains achieved in the post–World War II period. Examples of this are most dramatic in two sectors: capital improvements and agriculture. Capital improvements in Taiwanese infrastructure completed during the Japanese colonial period included the construction of a north–south railway and highways that constituted a modern and integrated transportation system by the mid-1920s. With the exception of a few coastal areas, mainland China would wait more than forty years for similar infrastructure. Closely linked with these transportation projects was the construction of modern deep-water ports at the northern (Keelung) and southern (Kaohsiung) ends of the island, and the construction of related cargo-handling facilities (see map 13.1).

Fundamental alterations to the agricultural system were equally important. After the Japanese introduction of scientific agriculture, Taiwan generated more rice and sugar for export to Japan because of its improved land and irrigation systems, new crop varieties, and land reform. Greater efficiency also freed labor for factories. Advances in agronomy, marketing, and the distribution of commodities led to rapid increases in production and the commercialization of the agricultural system. Colonial Japanese administrators also introduced new techniques in medicine and public health that resulted in a rapid decline in the island's death rate. Without a concurrent decline in birth rates, the net effect was to produce a rapidly growing population. The underpinnings, then, for a modern economy were laid down during the fifty years of Japanese colonial rule, but at considerable psychological and economic cost to the native Taiwanese population.

RESTORATION TO CHINA: 1945

Following the Japanese defeat in World War II, Taiwan was restored to Chinese control as part of the Potsdam Agreement, the blueprint for the new postwar order among the Allies. Oddly enough, relations between the Taiwanese and the mainland KMT Chinese administrators and troops that came to liberate them from the Japanese were tense from the outset. Corruption was rampant, and the native Taiwanese remained second-class citizens, just as before. On February 28, 1947, a spontaneous revolt broke out, initiated by the cruel murder by customs police of a Taiwanese woman selling contraband cigarettes. For ten days the Taiwanese rioted, seizing control of many government buildings in many cities and towns in protest of the heavy-handed rule of the KMT. Secretly, KMT governor Chen Yi cabled for troops from the mainland to subdue the rioters. Two divisions were sent, arriving on March 9, and occupying Taipei. In the end, from 10,000 to 50,000 Taiwanese were killed (depending on conflicting estimates). Each year to the present, these martyrs are commemorated on what is now known simply as "2-28," for the date of the first murder. The fact that this event is still memorialized fifty years later exemplifies the powerful animosities and mistrust that remain between some Taiwanese and mainlanders even to the present.

After 1949 and the victory of the Communists on the mainland, the KMT government, and more than 1.2 million refugees and soldiers, retreated to Taiwan and established an exile government in Taipei as the Republic of China on Taiwan. The costs of integrating this great influx of people and soldiers into an inflation-riddled economy were significant. Expectations of Taiwanese elites for self-autonomy, after the defeat of Japan, had been high, and after 2-28 the Taiwanese had both hated and feared the KMT army. The arrival of the often unruly and undisciplined KMT troops led to many armed conflicts and frequent rioting. Many Taiwanese leaders were killed or jailed.

Taipei and its surrounding regions absorbed most of the mainland refugees. The concentration of power and investment in the city at this time created its dominant status. To the present, Taipei and its suburbs represent Taiwan's largest concentration of people, with 2.8 million persons in 2004. Perhaps more significantly, preferential industrial and infrastructural investments within the Taipei-Keelung Metropolitan Region, which began in the 1950s, soon made northern Taiwan the wealthiest and fastest-growing region in Taiwan, with a population of more than 6.31 million residents. This dense concentration of linked cities and suburbs currently accounts for 42.9 percent of Taiwan's urban population, and is one of the most densely populated areas in the world.

In recent years, international politics have favored the PRC over Taiwan. In 1971, Taiwan was expelled from the UN as the legitimate government of China. In 1979, the United States officially recognized the PRC and it no longer recognizes Taiwan, although a close, unofficial relationship was established that continues to the present. These pragmatic decisions, based largely on trade opportunities and the realization that the PRC is an emerging global power, have left Taiwan largely isolated and with few official friends and allies. Over the past several decades, Taiwan's leaders have tread lightly—recognizing the delicate line that must be followed. As we've noted, there are considerable divisions among the population about what comes next. Based on a survey conducted in late 1994, there is evidence that approximately 10 percent of voters in Taiwan would prefer to quickly force the issue of independence (*Economist* 2005, 5). Still, many more voters would like independence or greater autonomy from the mainland. The Democratic Progressive Party (DPP) surprised many by winning not only the presidential elections in 2000 and 2004, but also many other positions. The evolution of multiple political parties notwithstanding, the KMT government that fled the mainland and established military rule on Taiwan for four decades still remains Taiwan's most powerful, and will play a central role in the eventual resolution of this conflict.

Taiwan's Physical Environment

Like most of the islands that rim the eastern flank of the Eurasian landmass, Taiwan is mountainous. Lying 160 km east of the Chinese province of Fujian across the shallow Taiwan Strait, the egg-shaped island resembles a giant block tilted up on its eastward margin to form a sharp dip into the Pacific. A series of north–south trending ridges form the interior of the island (the Central Mountains) and slope more gently westward blending into a series of flanking basins and plains (see map 13.4). These plains are widest in the Southwest and taper off toward the North. About two-thirds of the island is composed of rugged uplands, and numerous peaks crest above 3,000 m. The cross-island highway is popular among hikers and the scenery in the mountains is some of East Asia's best.

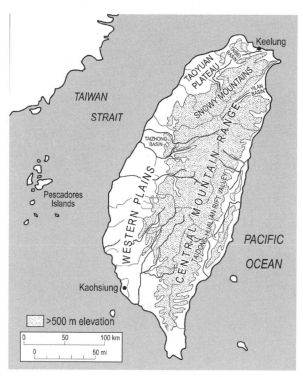

Map 13.4.   Topographic Map of Taiwan. **Source:** Pannell and Ma 1983, 265. Cartographic design by Mary Lee Eggart.

CLIMATIC PATTERNS AND IMPLICATIONS

Taiwan's location on the Tropic of Cancer and the high elevations of its main mountain range result in a distinctive climate that played an important role in its history. Taiwan lies on the northeast margin of the tropics and is heavily influenced by East Asian monsoon patterns. In general, weather is influenced by northeasterly winds during the winter and southwesterly winds during the summer months. In both cases, these winds are marine-influenced and bring considerable precipitation. Many locations report 2,560 mm or more of rainfall annually (see map 13.5). The northern tip of the island receives much of its rain in the winter. By contrast, the western and southern parts of the island, lying in the winter orographic shadow, have a comparatively dry and pleasant autumn and winter, and experience significant precipitation in the spring and summer when it is needed for intensive rice cultivation. Frost and snow occur only at the higher elevations in the center of the island.

Characteristic late-summer and autumn typhoons annually sweep across Taiwan. These great tropical storms, originating east of the Philippines, bring enough rainfall to generate a secondary seasonal peak of precipitation. Unfortunately, the intensity of the accompanying winds and rain wreak considerable damage. Development has intensified

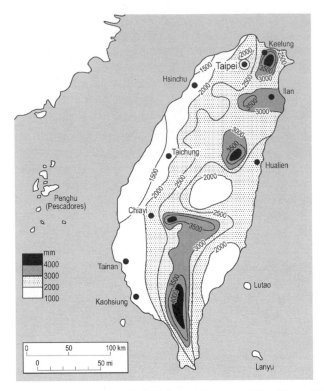

Map 13.5.   Average Annual Rainfall of Taiwan. ***Source:*** After Hsieh 1964; Electronic Atlas of Taiwan, http://sites.inka.de/sites/kajetan/index.htm. Cartographic design by Mary Lee Eggart.

both the economic losses and the physical effects of these storms as deforestation, urban sprawl, and uncontrolled construction of luxury hillside housing increase the financial losses associated with these storms.

HYDROLOGY AND RESOURCES

Most of the island's rivers are short and swift flowing. None is more than 105 km in length, and all are useless for navigation except by shallow-draft vessels. Still, many of these streams possess considerable hydropower potential. Hundreds of dams, beginning with Chinese efforts during the Qing dynasty, have been constructed to harness this energy and water. Most projects are multipurpose and are generally tied into water storage, irrigation systems, and flood control. The river and channel management systems are vital to the agricultural plains and basins of western Taiwan. Further, the resulting reservoirs are now critical to the supply of drinking water to Taiwan's major cities.

Taiwan is poorly endowed with strategic minerals—again making the economy's remarkable growth all the more amazing. Aside from limited deposits of coal, copper, sulfur, and gold, all of which have been mined heavily since Japanese colonial times and are largely exhausted, only very modest quantities of petroleum (oil and gas) and salt exist for commercial exploitation. The extent of offshore petroleum resources remains uncertain, but preliminary surveys suggest promise for the Taiwan Strait and East China Sea (see chapter 10). Of course, these are both areas that Taiwan and the PRC jointly claim, and exploitation in the current decade—even joint exploration—does not seem realistic.

HUMAN ADJUSTMENTS AND MODIFICATIONS OF THE ENVIRONMENT

Taiwan entered the Chinese polity relatively late, but as in so many other parts of the Middle Kingdom, the imprint of Chinese activities is everywhere. Most of the low-lying, level areas have long been cultivated, with preference given to rice when irrigation was available. Since the turn of the century, and especially since World War II, a rapidly growing population and increased per capita domestic consumption have necessitated the protection of land resources on the island and coastal land reclamation. Many sunset industries (those industries past their prime or declining) have moved to mainland China, and the people of Taiwan have gotten an environmental dividend from the departure of polluting industries such as metal plating and auto-parts production.

Taiwan is small (35,960 km^2). The island is incredibly crowded—more so even than Japan, with an average population density of almost seven hundred persons per square kilometer. Cities, home to 69 percent of the population are even more crowed (see map 13.3). Over the centuries, Taiwan's people, with their distinctive cultural systems, managed their meager resources well—at least until the relatively recent drive to industrialization. Economic growth, especially from 1950 to 1980, then came at the cost of localized environmental pollution of air and water. Further, the impact of crowding has also been great. Much arable land has been paved over by urban sprawl and lost forever. Foul air from factories and automobile exhaust remains a great problem in all of Taiwan's large cities. Water quality in Taipei and other major cities is also poor by any standard. Some streams and farmland are heavily polluted with industrial effluents. Regular flooding, including spillover from inadequate drainage systems in many low-lying areas of the largest cities, sends polluted water into residential areas. The loss of wetlands mirrors that of most nations as encroachment along the coasts, where reclaimed land accounts for a significant portion of new construction, is most extreme. Further, past deforestation by large state-connected mining and forestry concerns, and the construction of elite residential housing on slopes, has led to landslides and the premature siltation of many small and medium-size reservoirs. Regulations related to environmental protection are now very stringent, but enforcement has been irregular and often has political overtones. In response to these problems, environmental groups brought these issues to the general public with success in the 1990s, and Taiwan is now aggressively addressing environmental concerns. In 1974, only 0.2 percent of Taiwan's land was incorporated in nature preserves, but by 2000, this had increased to 12.6 percent.

Modern Life

Urban Taiwan, in particular, is very cosmopolitan. There are few major international retail or commercial firms not represented in Taipei, Kaohsiung, Taichung, or Tainan. In turn, Taiwan's major corporations are some of the world's largest—with far-flung holdings in North America and Europe as well as an increasingly important presence in China and Southeast Asia (Callick 2003). Recently Taiwan has developed vibrant film, music, and fashion industries whose stars play to audiences throughout the Pacific Rim and are treated very much as they are in the West. Mass consumption is increasingly the norm, although the savings rate remains higher than in North America or Europe. Social issues such as a generation gap, widening disparities between rich and poor, urban-rural conflicts, and the splintering of the political system by special interests are as great as in any other postindustrial state. To some extent, Taiwan's global culture vies with its local culture, and the island's people live in two worlds. Life in Taiwan is fast paced; the pressure to succeed is great. Competition begins even in elementary schools as students are faced with weeklong, island-wide examinations that will determine their academic future.

Although most citizens maintain that Taiwan's society and culture, above all, are Chinese in origin and character, unique features still make Taiwan a separate, identifiable segment of China's sphere of influence. A significant portion of younger Taiwanese, for example, prefer to see themselves as Taiwanese, rather than Chinese. A poll conducted in 2005 indicates a remarkable shift in Taiwanese self-perceptions over the past twelve years. The percentage of the population that identified themselves as Taiwanese rose from 17 percent to 41 percent. In the same decade, those who identified themselves as Chinese dropped from 26 percent to 6 percent (*Economist* 2005, 5). To an outsider, this may seem like splitting hairs, but for many, this is representative of Taiwan's feelings about unification. But there are justifications for both independence and unification. Taiwan was a relatively recent addition to China. Prior to this century it was a crude frontier, receiving often impoverished Chinese immigrants, largely from Fujian and Guangdong provinces in Southeast China. A number of different dialect groups were involved, bringing the island diverse religious customs and practices. After 1949 a new group of Chinese, largely from North and Central China, began arriving, and they too brought their distinct dialects, habits, and traditions. Further, influences from Japanese and American culture over the past fifty years have also been profound. This distinct past, quite unlike that of mainland China or Hong Kong ensures that Taiwan embodies a unique version of Chinese culture.

THE CHALLENGE OF SOCIAL RELATIONS AMONG TAIWAN'S ETHNIC GROUPS

Among the many identifiable ethnic and social groups on Taiwan, two groups are probably most significant, the Taiwanese and the mainlanders, with place of family origin (*laojia*) rather than place of birth the controlling distinction. Mainlanders, although coming from every province of China, are often treated by the Taiwanese as a single political group. While not homogeneous by any stretch of the imagination, once on Taiwan, they are all seen as mainlanders because they were involved with the KMT. These mainlanders typically speak Mandarin Chinese. This group, composing roughly 14 percent of the population, continues to be more or less distinct, although intermarriage has softened the distinctions. During the long martial-law period, mainlanders came to dominate Taiwan's military, security, and police apparatuses, and also until quite recently controlled the national government assembly and bureaucracy.

To assume that Taiwan's remaining population is a cohesive, homogeneous group in opposition to the mainland dominance of the island is also incorrect. In addition to the so-called native Taiwanese, as of 1997 there were officially 389,000 self-identified indigenous people living in Taiwan. As noted earlier in the chapter, these indigenous people were originally relocated to poor and isolated mountain areas and to reservations established by the Japanese. Increasingly, these aboriginal Taiwanese today seek work and advancement in Taiwan's major cities. An emerging indigenous rights movement, following similar movements in many nations in the 1980s and 1990s, has bloomed following the lifting of martial law and subsequent political reforms. The three largest of these groups are the Ami (Panch'ah), the Paiwan, and the Atayal. The politics of the indigenous people's rights movement are complex and tied closely to green issues, student issues, and the political reform movement (Chen 1999).

MODERNITY AND MOBILITY

Taiwan's population is concentrated predominantly in the alluvial plains and basins of the northern and western parts of the island. The most densely populated sections are the western and northern coastal areas that were settled by the Chinese over five hundred years ago. As a consequence of this concentration of wealth and later political power, major transportation networks emerged to service these important agricultural areas. As the economy changed, Taiwan's major cities also evolved within this originally agricultural hinterland. Recent infrastructural improvements have opened up more of the interior, but it still remains relatively isolated (see map 13.6).

Within the densely populated western portions of the island, major cities are dotted at intervals from Keelung, Taoyuan, and Taipei in the North to Taichung, Tainan, and Kaohsiung in the South. The largest concentrations of people are still found in the Taipei Basin in northern Taiwan and in the large plains in the Southwest that contain Tainan and Kaohsiung. Recent migration has been primarily rural to urban in nature, with people moving to the largest cities of the Taipei-Keelung Metropolitan Region, and the important industrial port city of Kaohsiung.

It is a paradox that despite extremely high population density, Taiwan is facing genuine labor shortages that are currently being met with a variety of guest-worker policies that admit workers from Southeast Asia and the Philippines, and with a wholesale exodus of manufacturing operations of many types to overseas factories (outsourcing). Of course, temporary status is unpopular with the guest-workers, who wish for more security in their lives. Regardless of the outcome, the arrival of low-income workers from other countries and "illegals" from mainland China poses new challenges to the

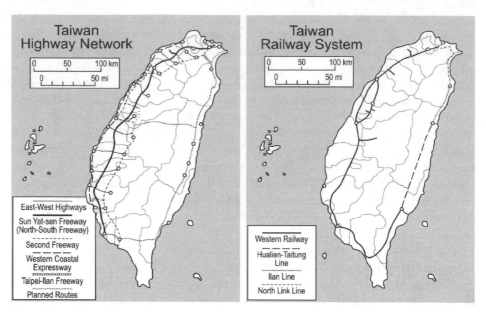

Map 13.6. Taiwan's Highway Network and Railway System. **Source:** Pannell and Ma 1983; Electronic Atlas of Taiwan, http://sites.inka.de/sites/kajetan/index.htm.

social fabric of Taiwan. The lives of these workers are most dreary and lonely; there is not yet a place for these people in Taiwanese society.

RELIGION AND RELIGIOUS PRACTICES

Few aspects of culture reflect the juxtaposition of Taiwan and the mainland as clearly as religion. Religious freedom is a constitutionally guaranteed right in Taiwan. As of 1997, just over 54 percent of the population, or 11.8 million persons, were self-reporting religious believers. In addition to traditional Confucian, Buddhist, Taoist, and folk temples, a full complement of Christian churches and mosques is found in all major cities. Religion for most of the inhabitants of Taiwan is similar to traditional Chinese religion, and is a blend of assorted beliefs and customs that allow for the worship of ancestors and locally important deities. In addition, as specific occasions demand, Buddhist, Taoist, or Confucian ceremonies may take place and supplement the more commonplace forms of worship.

Chinese religion and religious practices as they exist today in Taiwan are fundamentally different from Western religion—a fact often side-stepped for a variety of reasons in discussions of the topic. First, religious beliefs in Taiwan involve a number of different deities, many of which may be local in character. Westerners frequently do not understand that the exclusive monotheistic nature of Judaism, Christianity, and Islam is alien to the traditionally polytheistic Chinese approach. Second, Chinese religious participation is sporadic and depends more on annual occurrences tied in usually to the lunar calendar or to some crisis or benchmark in the life of the individual. Thus, a person having difficulty of some sort may seek relief through a religious soothsayer or shaman; alternately the person may go to a temple and seek guidance through traditional methods of divination, such as casting divination blocks or sticks; or if that doesn't work, they may pray to Jesus. Reflecting a fusion of Christian activism and Asian religion, in recent years Buddhist organizations in Taiwan have become socially aware, engaging in programs for youth, education, and social welfare (Copper 1999).

CHANGING SOCIAL CONDITIONS

The primary unit of social organization in Taiwan, as in China, traditionally has been the extended family—where three or even four generations live together. In the face of Taiwan's economic development, it is only natural that there have been major changes in traditional social relations, especially in the past few decades. Housing in the cities is expensive and space is limited. In addition, long school days, evening "cram schools" to aid in college entrance examinations, and increasingly popular preschools reduce the need for grandparents to help with children. These changes are more obvious in urban areas, which increasingly dominate Taiwan society. In contrast to the past, most families in urban areas now exist as nuclear units composed of parents and children.

Rural society, however, is also changing with equal or greater speed. Modern mass media extends everywhere in Taiwan, and the images of modernity are ubiquitous. Cable television provides access to stations from Japan, Hong Kong, and the West. The draw of modern city life is strong, pulling rural workers to seasonally migrate to factories and construction work in the cities. The potential for greater economic and educational opportunities in the neighboring cities and towns has drained off many rural workers, especially the young. Many farm families send children to better-equipped urban schools to increase their chances for advancement in the highly competitive educational system. Once you have lived in the city, however, it is difficult to go back to the often hard and uncertain life on the farm. During planting and harvest seasons, labor shortages are now common in many rural areas, and foreign labor (Thai and Filipino), once confined to the factory, is now common in farm areas as well.

Agriculture

Agricultural production in Taiwan was long the foundation of its stable and prosperous economic system, and steady gains in agriculture dating back to the Japanese occupation provided the means to feed a rapidly growing population and to finance ongoing development projects. Indeed, Taiwanese agriculture offers many lessons to other nations and is a model of productivity under conditions of extreme crowding and limited resources. Under the Japanese, more than 90 percent of the workforce was engaged in agriculture. In the years from 1953 to 1960, the agricultural sector accounted for an average of 28.5 percent of GNP. By 1995, this share had fallen to only 3.6 percent of GNP, and had declined to just over half of that again by 2004 (Howe 1998, 129; Statistical Abstract of National Income 2004, table 6). Times have changed, and farmers face hardship as they are forced to respond to changing domestic and international market conditions evolving in the shadow of recent World Trade Organization (WTO) agreements. Grain production has declined, but the value of output of the agricultural sector has never been higher due to significant increases in vegetables, fruit, cut flowers and plants, and betel nut. In this respect, the agricultural sector is more productive than ever before because its specialty crops—required by an increasingly affluent society, or for export— earn much more cash per unit area than rice. But Taiwan's very real security issues, including the threat of a naval embargo, still require management of foodstuffs. This means some form of subsidy must be provided vis-à-vis opportunity costs for labor and in recognition of the continued importance of the rural vote. Under government sponsorship and the direction of the Taiwan Agricultural Research Institute (TARI), Taiwan's agricultural research program has emerged at the millennium as one of the most creative and sophisticated in the world. Techniques of rice and fruit cultivation, vegetable propagation, biotechnology research, aquaculture, and animal husbandry developed by TARI have been studied and diffused throughout the world. Changes in Taiwan's agricultural sector reflect changes in the greater economy and Taiwan's vital engagement of the global economy.

The Commercial and Industrial Sectors

Paralleling the radical changes in the agricultural economy over the last half century has been a series of equally far-reaching changes in the nature of commerce and industry in Taiwan. Although set in motion six decades ago, the most spectacular changes in industrialization and commerce are very recent; most have occurred in the past two decades with Taiwan becoming a dominant player in information technology (IT) components. Prior to the 1980s, Taiwan's history of industrialization closely mirrored that of other successful nations. Success in IT, however, makes contemporary Taiwan distinct even when compared to the nations of Europe. This success in IT has earned Taiwan the name Silicon Island, but increasingly, IT investments are made by Taiwanese firms operating in mainland China. China is now the world's largest exporter of IT hardware, but 60 percent of these exports are made in China by Taiwanese companies. Acer, Taiwan's largest IT firm, is the world's fifth-largest producer of personal computers. And in 2004, Taiwan ranked first in the production of twelve different IT product categories including notebook PCs, monitors, motherboards, scanners, keyboards, and computer mice.

Copper (1999) argues that there are seven factors that should be given credit for Taiwan's industrial success: (1) the expansion of industrial employment, (2) increases in labor productivity, (3) U.S. economic assistance, (4) privatization, (5) a high rate of local savings and foreign investment, (6) a solid economic infrastructure, including transportation and port facilities, and (7) excellent planning by both the government and the business community (133).

Taiwan's success story actually developed over the past fifty years. Progress in industrialization under the Japanese was limited and predictably associated with extractive industries (e.g., smelting) and the processing of agricultural commodities and forest products, but infrastructural improvements were critical to later success. During the 1950s through the 1970s, however, industrial production exploded, with aggressive state-initiated investment policies made within a select number of targeted industries. Initially, the production of labor-intensive goods was dominant, under a strategy of import substitution. The government quickly adjusted this strategy, though, and shifted to a strategy of export promotion. Domestic production for import substitution developed only just before (ten years) export-oriented manufactures. In reality, Taiwan's success must be credited to a balanced policy of import substitution and export-oriented development, despite the fact that these policies are frequently mutually exclusive in textbooks. Economic planners understood that a small island peopled by consumers with limited purchasing power could hardly sustain a major industrial development policy. Foreign trade is essential for Taiwan. State-directed manufacturing efforts were combined with high levels of capital reinvestment targeting the production of those labor-intensive exports that could quickly return the investment.

Massive state investments were also made in education in anticipation of the need for a highly skilled workforce. High levels of reinvestment and a balanced distribution of large and small firms that can react quickly to changes in the marketplace remain important characteristics of Taiwan's overall development strategy. The textile industry provides a useful example. In 1980 there were two hundred cotton and wool mills on the island, and natural-fiber textiles and clothing were major export categories. In the late 1980s, rising labor and input costs put Taiwan at a disadvantage for the processing of natural fibers. With state support, the industry reinvented itself through the production of synthetic fibers. By 2000, Taiwan ranked third in the world in the production of man-made fibers, producing 4 million metric tons of cloth, 80 percent of which was polyester. More recently, again in response to rising labor costs, even the synthetic fiber industry has begun to move offshore, with the mainland and Southeast Asia as favored destinations. Taiwanese firms provide capital, technology, managerial expertise, and marketing, while benefiting from lower plant and labor costs. Obviously there are significant political overtones and environmental implications in the relocation of sunset industries from Taiwan to China and countries in Southeast Asia. In 2005, there were 300,000 Taiwanese factory owners, managers, and their families living in the Shanghai Metropolitan Region, and upwards of 1.2 million Taiwanese living in China.

Somewhat unique to Taiwan among the world's major industrial nations, however, is the reliance of its major firms on outsourcing production to smaller subcontractors. The relationship between the large firms that invest in research and development, and the medium and small firms that actually produce the product is interesting. In 2003, 85 percent of Taiwan's IT output was actually manufactured by medium and small firms that were linked to larger firms by short-term contracts or that had been spun off from these firms. The importance of several hundred thousand small and medium firms to Taiwan's economy continues to be a distinct feature of its manufacturing history. Still, the industrial giants that are known as *chaebol* in Korea and *keiretsu* in Japan are not without parallel in Taiwan. Evergreen is currently the second-largest container-shipping firm in the world, and Acer controls a major share of the EU computer market. Taiwan Semiconductor Manufacturing and United Microelectronics are hardly household names, but these two Taiwanese companies account for around 70 percent of the world's foundry production of silicon chips, a foundry being a semiconductor manufacturer that produces chips for other manufacturers (*Economist* 2005, 10). Other large Taiwanese firms with strong government connections (e.g., Koo's Group, Formosa Plastics Group, and Shinkong Group) are multinational, with plants, commercial offices, and distribution systems throughout Europe and North America.

The changes inherent in the post-WTO global economy are easily observable in Taiwan. At the beginning of the new millennium, the share of the economy and of the workforce controlled by industry and manufacturing in Taiwan is declining, just as agriculture declined in the 1970s. Taiwan's experience is important, possibly foretelling coastal China's evolution, but also reflecting the future of most developed industrial nations as well. Further, Taiwan's transition to a post-Fordist (nonmanufacturing) economy reflects the powerful impact of globalization on even a strong domestic economy. Capital-intensive manufacturing and recent growth in the service sector have replaced labor-intensive industries. In 1986, industrial production still accounted for more than 50 percent of Taiwan's GDP. By 2004, it had declined to approximately 30 percent of GDP. As the share of employment devoted to agriculture and manufacturing declines, services including insurance, banking, education, tourism, and government employment will increase in importance. As was the case for agriculture in the past, these shifts in employment and economy will again have far-reaching effects on the fabric of Taiwanese society in the future.

Taiwan's commercial and financial institutions grew in equal measure with the industries that initially supported the island's economic modernization through export trade and manufacturing. Now, even as domestic manufacturing declines in importance, the banks remain and have created new international roles, linked less to fluctuations in Taiwan's economy than to those of the global economy. There are 471 financial institutions in Taiwan, with the largest still controlled by the government. Bank reform, stimulated by WTO agreements, is currently a priority, and more than a dozen government-linked banks have been privatized in recent years. Foreign international banks are represented in Taiwan, but the scope of financial services for these banks remains restricted by government regulation, amid fears of increases in capital and competitive interest rates that might threaten less-efficient domestic institutions. Still, Taiwan has come a long way in a short time. An increasingly more open and sophisticated financial sector has facilitated the exchange and transfer of money required by offshore manufacturing and rapidly growing foreign trade.

Political Geography and the Challenges of the Future

Taiwan's political history has always been tumultuous. This is a simple fact, but one that demands that we again quickly review the role of absolute location in political histories. Taiwan has always been contested space. It was first settled by tribal people of proto-Malay origin, but then eventually colonized by Chinese farmers with superior force—seeking alluvial land and escape from crowded conditions in Fujian and

Guangdong. The indigenous peoples were pushed to the interior, resulting in conflicts among these peoples as well as a growing Chinese hegemony along the coasts. A half century of European colonial control—again projecting superior force—followed in the early seventeenth century. This was succeeded by the restoration of the island to Chinese control when Koxinga defeated the Dutch. In 1888 during the Qing dynasty, the imperial court became convinced of Taiwan's strategic value and upgraded the status of the island, only to lose it to Japan's growing empire. Fifty years of Japanese colonial rule began in 1895. In 1945, Taiwan was returned to the Chinese. Regulations promulgated by the KMT, but with clear Japanese roots, created rigidly hierarchical internal political units and subunits that continue to the present. This high level of centralized control must be credited for the efficient use of development capital when Taiwan's economy expanded rapidly in the 1970s and 1980s.

As Taiwan's economic growth has increased, its people have demanded greater political freedom and local representation. Recently, independent investigations associated with these growing demands for local autonomy, a more politically involved public, and an increasingly vigilant press have uncovered serious abuses in the past and at the present time that have challenged voters' faith in the central government. Still, the political reforms beginning in the mid-1990s would probably not have been realized without the prosperity fostered by the state corporatism characteristic of the KMT era. As Taiwan's multiparty political system matures, it is difficult for us to anticipate how domestic politics will influence the country's international diplomacy, but to be sure this is a factor that did not exist until the late 1990s.

TAIWAN'S POLITICAL FUTURE

In 1972 President Nixon journeyed to China, and representatives of the United States government signed the now famous Shanghai Communiqué. U.S. and Chinese communist positions toward Taiwan are enumerated in this document, and these positions suggest something about the future status of the island. In brief, the PRC affirmed that Taiwan is Chinese territory and will be returned to the fold in the future. It is a matter of domestic politics, according to the Chinese, and the United States has no legitimate basis for involvement. The PRC thus allowed no possibility of the interpretation of a "two-China" policy or an independent Taiwan. The United States for its part acknowledged that Taiwan is Chinese, reaffirmed its interest in a peaceful settlement of the Taiwan question, and agreed to phase out its military support through the sale of defensive weaponry and information-gathering technology as conditions permitted. Since the signing of that communiqué, the United States has officially recognized the PRC and dropped its recognition of Taiwan. But the United States continues to have close relations with Taiwan through a formula for nongovernmental relations and a law (the Taiwan Relations Act) that established two semiofficial organizations, the American Institute in Taiwan, and Taiwan's Coordination Council for North American Affairs in the United States. These two organizations, staffed by diplomatic personnel either retired or temporarily on leave from government agencies, have worked effectively since 1979 to promote continued economic, academic, scientific, and cultural exchanges in a pragmatic but unofficial manner. At the same time, the United States has terminated its bilateral defense treaty with Taiwan and withdrawn official diplomatic recognition of Taiwan in favor of recognition of the PRC (U.S. Department of State 1980).

ALTERNATIVES FOR CHANGE AND THE FUTURE

There is little Taiwan can do to affect the politics of other countries. Further, it is unlikely that either the government, as presently constituted, or the collective will of the people would support political reintegration with mainland China at this time without very significant guarantees for long-term autonomy. Finally, Taiwan is strong and rich enough to defend itself against any kind of attack except full-scale military assault. Moreover, even if the communist government could mount the amphibious force necessary to invade the island, such a solution would be prohibitively destructive for the invaders, for Taiwan, and the coastal province of Fujian. With seventy thousand Taiwan-funded firms operating in the mainland, and up to 1,200,000 Taiwanese business people and their families living there, war would have devastating effects for all (Callick 2003; *Economist* 2005). Thus, a military solution to the question, at least in the short term, would appear to come at too great a cost.

The alternatives are complex and politically charged on the domestic front as well as in the international arena. Given the mainland's explicit rejection of an independent state, a formally separate Taiwanese state is also unlikely in the short run. And domestically, many Taiwanese would oppose efforts to declare the unilateral independence that would result in the creation of an independent nation. Still, Taiwan is de facto an independent nation. From an American point of view, one can affirm the "Chineseness" of Taiwan, as did the U.S. State Department in the Shanghai Communiqué, while maintaining that the problem be resolved peacefully. The American position appears to be a wait-and-watch posture in which the United States plays a passive role by allowing Chinese of different political outlooks to decide and resolve their own political destinies (U.S. Department of State 1980).

Unilateral unification also seems problematic, even if force could be used. Domestic problems in the PRC must also be considered. Tensions manifest as core or periphery conflicts challenging the national government suggest that the current political system in the PRC still has problems of control and governance. A fractious Taiwan would be difficult to control. Democracy has taken fifty years to emerge in Taiwan, and few would be willing to return to the fold without sound and credible guarantees for the long-term maintenance of this system.

Conclusion

Taiwan remains a place of great promise and horizons, as well as a place of pressing uncertainties and problems. The people of Taiwan in many ways have made their good fortune and have used the island's meager resources to their advantage. Its location along the southeastern flank of the Chinese mainland is highly accessible and lies across the main shipping and air lanes connecting East Asia with Europe, South and Southeast Asia, and North America. The ambitions of Taiwan's people, and the odd role Taiwan played in the cold war, coupled with this location, have propelled Taiwan into the global economy. Such a location and economic situation have led to the rapid population growth and economic development of the island in recent decades. Today, Taiwan has one of the highest standards of living in Asia. Yet these rosy economic conditions cannot shield it from the troubled political situation, a difficulty that may yet destroy the progress of the recent past if reason and patience do not prevail.

References Cited

Callick, Rowan. 2003. Taiwanese exodus to the motherland. *Australian Financial Review*, January 17, new section, 1.

Chen, Yi-fong. 1999. Economic, social, and political geography of the indigenous people's movement in Taiwan. PhD diss., Department of Geography and Anthropology, Louisiana State University, Baton Rouge.

Copper, John F. 1999. *Taiwan: Nation-State or Province*. Boulder, Colo.: Westview.

Economist. 2005. Dancing with the enemy: A survey of Taiwan. January 15, special nation report.

Howe, Christopher. 1998. The Taiwan economy: The transition to maturity and the political economy of its changing international status. In *Contemporary Taiwan*, ed. David Shambaugh. Oxford: Clarendon.

Hsieh, Chiao-min. 1964. *Taiwan-Ila Formosa: A Geography in Perspective*. Washington, D.C.: Butterworths.

Pannell, Clifton W., and Laurence J. C. Ma. 1983. *China: The Geography of Development and Modernization*. New York: Halsted Press.

Stainton, Michael. 1999. The politics of Taiwan's aboriginal origins. Chap. 2 of *Taiwan: A New History*, ed. Murry A. Rubinstein. Armonk, N.Y.: M.E. Sharpe.

Statistical Abstract of National Income. 2004. Republic of China. eng.stat.gov.tw/mp.asp?mp=5 (accessed March 1, 2006).

U.S. Department of State. 1980. *Review of Relations with Taiwan*. Current policy no. 190 (June 11, 1980). Washington, D.C.: Bureau of Public Affairs.

Index

About the Authors

Youqin Huang is assistant professor in the Department of Geography and Planning and research associate at the Center for Social and Demographic Analysis at the State University of New York, Albany. She teaches courses related to population, China, and statistical and spatial methods. Her research has mainly focused on two areas: one is housing behavior, residential mobility, neighborhood change, and urban structure; and the other is migration and urbanization, in both China and the United States.

Clifton Pannell is professor of geography and associate dean of arts and sciences emeritus at the University of Georgia. His China research focuses on economic, population, and urban geography, and he currently serves as an editor of *Eurasian Geography and Economics*.

Christopher J. Smith is jointly appointed as professor in the Department of Geography and Planning and the Department of East Asian Studies at the University at Albany, SUNY. Smith is an urban geographer whose research has been focused on East Asia, especially China. His recent work has been concerned with the social and cultural consequences of China's transition away from socialism.

Gregory Veeck is professor of geography at Western Michigan University, teaching undergraduate and graduate courses related to research methods, environmental studies, Asia, and China. His topical research interests include agriculture and rural economic and environmental issues in China, East Asia, and the United States.